Foreword

I joined the National Association of Teachers of Singing (NATS) in June 1983, having discovered its existence from some excellent books about singing emanating from the United States. *Singing, the Mechanism and Technic,* by William Vennard, was compelling reading! NATS bulletins delivered four times a year were an added incentive. NATS was celebrating is 40th anniversary at their Convention in New Orleans (December 27–30, 1984) at the Marriott Hotel. I went to New Orleans and came away convinced that here was much to be gained from such a gathering and from belonging to an association that could organise such an event.

In July 1987, I attended the First International Congress of Voice Teachers in Strasbourg. It was sponsored by (NATS) and the Great Britain Association of Teachers of Singing. I recall that there were 600 in attendance. My imagination found it hard to cope with that number of singing teachers in one place!

Edward Baird, President of NATS, chaired the last session at Strasbourg. He urged more countries to form national associations. There was enthusiasm at the public microphone — I remember the Swiss contingent saying they had gone to lunch unattached and left as an association. As the only the resident Australian present, there was not much I could do!

This was resolved soon after I arrived home, with an invitation from the famous Australian tenor, Ronald Dowd, who had recently returned to live in this country. “Would I join the staff of the first Summer School for Singers at Bathurst from 9 to 16 January, 1988?” To complement this event, there was a plan to invite teachers to observe activities in the school for a couple of days and to hold a formation meeting for a National Association of Teachers of Singing. We had a meeting, took the hat around, and so it all began.

Now I am happily writing this foreword, which I understand to be the first book to be published by ANATS. We are about to be 23 years old, and I congratulate those who have organised and authored this publication, as well as the many people who have supported ANATS since its inception. I hope there will be many more milestones to follow. Can I suggest one? How about a publication of our history for our 25th anniversary?

Enjoy the conference, and the book!

Janet Delpratt AM, DUniv
Professor of Voice
Queensland Conservatorium Griffith University
National President of ANATS 1997–2003

Janet Delpratt has been associated with the Queensland Conservatorium at Griffith University since it opened in 1957, first as a student and then as a staff member. She was Chairman of the Vocal Department for 18 years and still teaches there. In 1998, she received a Personal Chair for excellence in teaching, the first such appointment in an Australian University. Janet has performed with most of the principal orchestras in Australia and has taken part in many concerts and recitals. From 1988 to 1998, she was a member of the voice staff of the Bathurst Summer School of Singers founded by the famous Australian tenor, Ronald Dowd. Here, she helped establish the Australian National Association of Teachers of Singing, ANATS, of which she was National President from 1997 to 2003. Janet has given master classes in New Zealand, Japan, Hong Kong and Australia and in 1994 was one of the seven teachers chosen from around the world to teach at the Third International Congress of Voice Teachers in Auckland. Professor Delpratt was honoured in the 2009 Queen's Birthday Honours List with the award of AM for her services to music and the teaching of singing.

Perspectives on Teaching Singing

Australian Vocal Pedagogues Sing Their Stories

Edited by Dr Scott Harrison

www.
AUSTRALIANACADEMICPRESS
.com.au

First published in 2010
Australian Academic Press
32 Jeays Street
Bowen Hills Qld 4006
Australia
www.australianacademicpress.com.au

National Library of Australia Cataloguing-in-Publication entry

Title:	Perspectives on teaching singing: Australian vocal pedagogues sing their stories / edited by Scott Harrison.
Edition:	1st ed.
ISBN:	9781921513732 (pbk.)
	9781921513749 (ebook: pdf)
Subjects:	Singing--Instruction and study--Australia Music--Study and teaching--Australia.
Other Authors/ Contributors:	Harrison, Scott D. (Scott David), 1962-
Dewey Number:	783.007094

Cover illustration by ©istockphoto.com/DSGpro.
Cover designed by Maria Biaggini.

Contents

Acknowledgments

I would like to acknowledge the support of this volume by Griffith University and the Australian National Association of Teachers of Singing. I would also like to thank the many researchers who anonymously reviewed contributions: your feedback is greatly appreciated. To the contributors, thank you for accepting the invitation to be part of this project: your enthusiasm for the task has been overwhelming.

Queensland Conservatorium Research Centre, Griffith University (Director: Professor Huib Schippers) has supported this publication.

My personal thanks go to the research assistant on this project, Wendy Hargreaves: your eagle eye for detail and willingness to put family, studies and other matters on hold is greatly appreciated. Finally to Jessica O'Bryan: thank-you for all you do to support me.

Scott D. Harrison
Editor

Disclaimer

The views expressed in this volume are not necessarily the views of the editor (with the exception of Chapter 1), the Australian National Association of Teaching of Singing or Griffith University.

Chapter
1

The State of Play: Voice Teaching in Australia in the 21st Century

Scott D. Harrison

This chapter seeks to provide some background as to the nature of singing teaching for Australian society in the 21st century, and give a framework for the chapters to follow. The primary purpose of the volume is to provide a snapshot of current research and practice in singing teaching across the country. This is the first time such a diverse array of contributions has been collected and published. The contributions are by no means exhaustive. Rather, they aim to represent practitioners from varied contexts, genres, locations and backgrounds. This chapter begins and ends with a rationale for the teaching of singing. Using two groupings, singing in schools and singing in studios, recent trends are explored, and these are interwoven with brief introductions to the chapters later in the volume. Towards the end of the chapter, a brief explanation of the themes to be explored in the volume provides both a stocktake of current trends and a perspective of the territory for future research and practice.

Why Teach Singing?

As teachers of singing, we hardly need to justify the importance of singing to ourselves. We are sometimes placed in the position of advocating for singing to the broader community — parents, educational authorities, government agencies and others. At the beginning of a volume such as this, perhaps a rationale for our craft is warranted. In *Singing as Communication*, Welch (2005, p. 254) noted that:

- Singing can be a form of group identification.
- Singing can be a transformation activity culturally.
- Regular singing activities can communicate a sense of pattern, order and systematic contrast to the working day and week.
- Singing can be used as an agent in the communication of social change.

Involvement in singing has the capacity to cross socioeconomic status, geographical location, age, level of training, physical capacity and psychological state. As the peak body for singing teaching in this country, the Australian National Association of Teachers of Singing (ANATS) has a responsibility to promote vocal education and research in all genres and at all levels, both for the enrichment of the general public and for the professional development, advancement and interest of both singers and teachers (See ANATS constitution at www.anats.org.au). This volume aims to assist ANATS and other members of the singing teaching community in achieving this goal. Callaghan begins her chapter (Chapter 2) with the revelation that teaching of singing in Australia has not always been regarded as a profession. Using Schulman's concepts of content, pedagogical knowledge and pedagogical-content knowledge, she describes ways in which professionalisation can occur for all members of the profession.

ANATS members (and the singing teaching community at large) fall into three broad categories: school-based teachers of singing (choral/individual), tertiary-based educators and private studio music teachers. For the purposes of this introductory chapter, this will be collapsed into two groupings: the teaching of singing in schools and teaching in the tertiary/private studio. This is not to deny that there is some overlap in these categories; some of institutional matters raised apply equally in school and tertiary settings, and not all tertiary environments incorporate studio-based one-to-one teaching (though the Bologna declaration [see Tuning, 2004] embraces individual tuition as a core requirement for tertiary music teaching). The reader will discern, however, that the contributions from across the country dictate the organisation of the volume and hence, this chapter.

Singing in Schools

Data generated from ANATS members for a Music Council of Australia project (Harrison et al., 2008) indicate that many members are engaged in school-based activities, with responsibility for choral conducting, individual tuition and, in a small number of cases, classroom music teaching. Writing in 2005 about collaborative approaches to vocal education (The CAVE project), Harrison called for the "recognition of the different but equally valid contributions of studio teaching, the small group model, vocal class, primary and/or secondary music classes and choirs in the process of vocal education". This notion finds support in the work of Apfelstadt, Robinson and Taylor (2003), who suggested "a desire to promote healthy singing, to develop vocal musicianship and to maintain the integrity of the voice while doing justice to various musical styles" can be achieved through varied modes of delivery (p. 25). In Harrison et al. (2008), ANATS members commented on the strength of vocal programs in schools:

> [Singing] brings the school community together in a shared and positive activity ... helps young people gain confidence in expressing themselves and broadens their musical horizons.
>
> The School music program is diverse and exciting for the kids and this makes the teaching environment stimulating and interesting.

Many school curriculum documents divide the content into variations of musicology/analysis, composition and performance. Young (2009) located performance in the centre of the curriculum noting, "Within the area of performance, the voice is the key to developing the musical skills of students" (p. 64). Singing is also recognised for the way in which it contributes to other aspects of schooling. Commenting on their work at Melbourne High School, Bayliss, Lierse, and Ludowyke, (2009) noted that at exam time, students affirmed that singing "was bliss". It not only provided a catharsis from mounting tension, but also a powerful sense of camaraderie and renewal of shared purpose. In this particular context, there is evidence dating back over 100 years, with a student mentioning the role of singing in the school magazine of 1907 thus:

> Our singing lessons are such that they rank amongst the most pleasant of all. They are at the same time invigorating and tranquillising. A "tuneful tonic" without which our work would, at times, tend to the monotonous. (*Vox Humana*, 1907)

However, the role of singing in schools at the turn of last century is somewhat at odds with current practice. In terms of sheer numbers, Chasling (2003, pp. 25–26) reported that in 1897 a choir of 5000 was formed for the Jubilee celebration of Queen Victoria. Chasling also noted that a choir of 10,000 performed for the inauguration of the Commonwealth of Australia in 1901. The 1901 choir, according to Chasling "sang moderately difficult repertoire with changes of tempo, dynamics and metre. Three and four part singing was common, as was singing at sight". This comment would appear to be at variance with a recent headline in a national newspaper that claimed, "Australians can't sing ... they chant, they don't chime" (Megalogenis, 2004). Does this mean that the quality of singing has declined in recent years?

Pascoe et al. (2005) noted in the National Review of School Music Education that

> While some schools, particularly primary schools, introduce and support ensemble singing and singing in choirs, there is relatively little vocal music in secondary schools apart from specialised music schools.

The literature supports such a statement, with one respondent in Harrison's (2006) study commenting that

> Singing and the quality of singing varies enormously from school to school ... the determining factor is often the skill of the music teacher (if indeed there is a specialist teacher in the school) and that teacher's determination to make singing happen in the school.

The status of singing in schools was also brought to the attention of the singing community by Chapman (2006), who referred to singing in western cultures as

> an elitist activity — for the talented rather than the community. The tragic loss of school-based singing during the past three decades has served to distance children from this vocal heritage. (p. 1)

Where singing is part of school culture, it frequently falls below instrumental music in terms of a "pecking order" of music activities. Adler and Harrison (2004) developed a hierarchy of musical activities based on gendered attributes in schools in Canada and the United States. The hierarchy could be represented for the Australian setting and removing the gender bias as shown in Figure 1.1.

This would appear to concur with findings from 2006 that indicated

> In general, vocal ensembles and vocal training are considered second or third string to instrumental ensembles and training. In certain schools, singing is not even considered to be an instrument to study and is not treated with the same respect as other instruments. The students are expected to learn a "serious" instrument (non-vocal) and keep singing just for the choirs (Harrison, 2006)

ANATS members noted that one reason for this could be lack of training on vocal production and vocal health in teacher training (Harrison, 2008). This concurs with the findings of Vaughan (1998), who cites teachers' poor knowledge of, and inability to deal with, the vocal health issues associated with adolescence. In this volume, Willis discusses this issue in some detail in Chapter 9, and Ancell provides some practical ideas based on his extensive experience working with the male changing voice in Chapter 10. In Chapter 19, Hughes and Callaghan pursue the role of singing in schools in more

```
┌─────────────────────────────────────────────────────────┐
│  ● Jazz / Big Band                                         │
│  ● Concert Band                                            │
│  ● Orchestra                                               │
│  Instrumental   ● Individual Instrumental Lesson           │
└─────────────────────────────────────────────────────────┘

┌─────────────────────────────────────────────────────────┐
│  ● Music Theatre                                           │
│  ● Jazz / Show Choir                                       │
│  ● Choir                                                   │
│  Vocal   ● Individual Singing Lesson                       │
└─────────────────────────────────────────────────────────┘
```

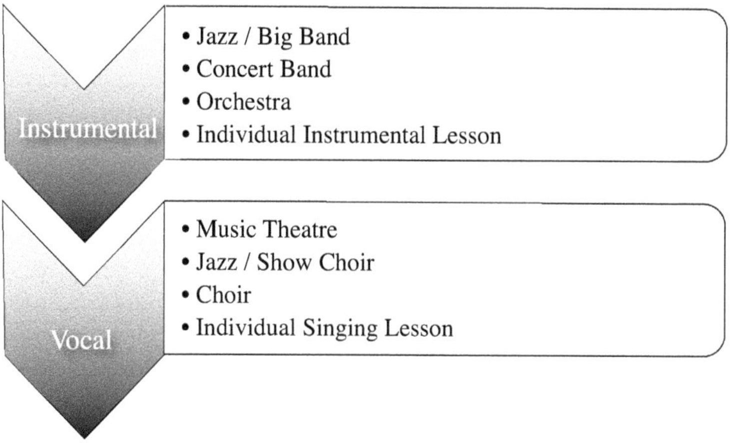

FIGURE 1.1

Hierarchy of School Musical Activity

detail. The development of vocal pedagogy courses in tertiary institutions has also assisted in alleviating this situation.

Tertiary and Private Studio Teaching

The teaching of singing at the tertiary level and in the private setting has generally followed the time-honoured traditions of the master-teacher/pupil relationship. One of the challenges in this field is the lack of research into teaching and learning practices related to this dyad. In conservatories and universities, The Reflective Conservatorie Conferences (2006, 2009) and Nactmus National Conference (2007) have sought to address this paucity of knowledge. As a result, there is a growing body of research that investigates alternative models of tertiary teaching (Lancaster, 2007; Daniel, 2003; Lebler, 2007; Latukefu, 2009; Bennett & Hannan, 2008; Gaunt, 2010; Mills, 2004; Burt-Perkins, 2008).

Less is known about the private studio, despite the fact that the studio music teacher "has played a pivotal role in the training of instrumentalists and voice students in Australia for over a century" (Lierse, 2008). Lierse goes on to note that the private studio, as a cottage industry, is unregulated and the quality of work is variable. In 2008, ANATS members indentified one of their main difficulties as being the sense of isolation brought about by teaching alone. While studio teachers welcome the opportunity to address individual needs in students and the flexibility of working hours, this independence has the disadvantage of a lack of collegial support and social interaction. Like their school-based colleagues, studio-based teachers have expressed a lack of recognition of the educational validity of music and voice teaching, and a lack of recognition of the training and expertise of music teachers. Later in this book, the contributions of Callaghan (Chapter 2), and Hughes and Callaghan (Chapter 19) seek to address this, through professionalisation of the singing teaching community and advocacy, respectively.

Many private teachers come to singing teaching when their performance careers are in decline, whereas others successfully maintain dual careers as performer–teachers. Tertiary institutions often engage professional practitioners to help bridge the gap between the educational experience and the demands of the profession itself. Schindler (2009) has investigated this concept from the perspective of her own experiences, and in this volume (Chapter 3) she presents the experiences of other performer–teachers in Australian tertiary settings. Similarly, O'Bryan's chapter (Chapter 4) examines this further through the eyes of iconic Australian classical singers of the recent past. Cowley also opens the door to her studio through an action-research approach. In Knowledge, Skill and Art in Studio Teaching: A Reflection on Practice (Chapter 8), she provides a cycle of learning and teaching in the voice studio of the 21st century. Using reflective practice, Cowley reflects on major interactions between voice science and vocal pedagogy. Similarly, Collyer (Chapter 6) discusses the challenges in keeping up with scientific developments affecting vocal pedagogy, calling for professional bodies (such as ANATS) to address the content and delivery of professional development to its members. As a teacher of classical singing and a lecturer in vocal pedagogy, Nisbet (Chapter 7) asks the questions, "What do I need to know or do to be the best singing teacher I can be? How can I help my students be the best singers they can be?" As she pointed out, these questions are not exclusive to the tertiary setting or to classical singing; these issues are at the core of this volume and our profession at large.

The Australian environment presents unique challenges to the teacher of classical voice. Singers and teachers of singing are either located in high concentration in capital cities, or working in geographical isolation in remote and regional settings. Though close to Australia's largest city, teachers of singing in Newcastle describe the challenges inherent in regional centres in McMahon's contribution (Chapter 5). Aside from these geographically based challenges, the specific requirements of Australian repertoire present their own demands. Using reflecting journalling as a lens, and drawing on her vast experience of this genre, Aggett further unpacks some of the gems of classical Australian vocal repertoire in Chapter 12.

LoVetri (2002, 2008) has called for the need for pedagogy centring on non-classical styles; particularly in relation to registration, genre and timbre. Several chapters in this volume seek to address this domain. In Chapter 14, Bartlett pursues this notion and challenges the one-size-fits-all concept. The chapter offers a connection between classical and non-classical performance and pedagogy, contrasting elements of technique and vocal production of each genre. Similarly, in Chapter 11, Bourne, Garnier and Kenny seek to address the lack of scientific literature in relation to styles other than classical and operatic singing. Developing Wilson's (2003) review of the literature surrounding music theatre pedagogy, Bourne et al. report on the findings from a survey of experienced music theatre pedagogues from Australia, the United Kingdom, the United States and Asia, focusing specifically on the teaching of registration. Wilson's chapter (Chapter 18) also focuses on aspects of music theatre pedagogy, and describes the particular challenges found in teaching cabaret. She calls for dedicated undergraduate and postgraduate courses designed to train singing teachers in the specifics of music theatre and cabaret.

Hughes (Chapter 15) also incorporates the role of reflection, informative feedback and reflexivity as a means of addressing the complexity of vocal artistry in popular culture music (PCM). The use of this term opens up discussions about the teaching of non-classical styles, often referred to as Contemporary Commercial Music (CCM). In Robinson's contribution (Chapter 17), the pedagogy for contemporary worship singers is investigated. Like students of cabaret and music theatre, the contemporary worship singer is, as Dawson (2005) noted "exposed to classical pedagogy, which does not equip them for [singing in] their church environments" (p. 3). Using the results from a recent national survey, Robinson highlights for the first time the specific pedagogical needs of this unique, burgeoning member of the singing community. Still in the non-classical domain, Hargreaves (Chapter 16) examines the teaching of jazz improvisation to singers. This is an area that is often overlooked, because the specific needs of singers in the jazz environment are subsumed into the training of instrumentalists. Six key learning areas are put forward to assist teachers in working through this issue with their students.

This diverse array of contributions across a variety of settings is seemingly disconnected. However, on analysis, it is possible to discern a number of trends revealed throughout the volume.

Themes, Trends and Perspectives

A number of broad themes can be extracted from the writings in the following pages. Acknowledgement of these trends is evidence of the state of play in singing pedagogy in this country, and provides a platform for future research. The themes identified throughout the volume include the nature of singing as an embodied instrument, the changes in language use in vocal pedagogy, the interdisciplinary nature of 21st-century voice teaching, the role of technology and the distinctive nature of Australian vocal pedagogy.

As singing teachers, we are acutely aware of the issues associated with working on an instrument housed completely within the body. Historically, pedagogy relied on the use of the senses. This was followed by a concentration on voice science (which continues to this day). The chapters in this volume represent a balance of science-based components in teaching, and the holistic approach that recognizes the role of "self". The contributions using journalling, singing as self-discovery and biography feature this theme quite strongly.

Related to the balance of sensory and scientific approaches, there has been an observable change in the use of language in singing pedagogy. Where pedagogues of the past and present used predominantly Italian terms (*passaggio, appoggio, bel canto* and so on), voice science has given teachers an opportunity to refer to anatomical terms and descriptors that accurately reveal the process of singing. Readers beware! There is a bewildering array of acronyms sprinkled throughout the volume — TA-CT, P.A., CCM, PCM! Despite the advances of recent years, singing pedagogues and researchers still struggle to find the most appropriate language to describe registers, particularly questions such as, "How many registers?" "How do we define register change?" and "What labels do we give them?" A number of chapters within this collection deal with these issues in remarkable clarity. The other area still finding its feet in relation to terminology is the non-classical area. As mentioned earlier, this field can rightfully claim the need for new approaches to pedagogy that consider the burgeoning demands of the sector. The call for pedagogy of this nature has been impeded, to some extent, by a lack of suitable terminology with which to describe the needs of these singers.

Technological advances dating back several centuries have been documented in relation to the teaching of singing. The accessibility of tools for physiological measurements has transformed voice science and resultantly, vocal pedagogy. The capacity for real-time feedback, the domestication of recording devices and the proliferation of recorded works have all made substantial contributions to the ways in which singing classrooms and studios operate. These notions are all apparent in a number of contributions in the volume.

A fourth theme evident in the volume is the nature of collaboration. From the data presented in this collection, the days of one master-teacher who dominates the pedagogical exchange appear to be numbered. Today, voice teachers rely on interdisciplinary collaboration to ensure the best possible results for their students. Furthermore, some chapters point to the singing lesson as an example of co-constructed knowledge, where the student perspectives provide valuable feedback for the teacher about their teaching and performing.

The final theme apparent in the volume is the distinctive nature of Australian vocal pedagogy. Further to the earlier comments about the unique challenges presented by Australian geography, there are also indications that Australia leads the way in many aspects of singing teaching. Some authors have chosen this volume to disseminate current research that has an Australian basis, but also provides perspectives that are replicable in other settings. For example, the principles of teaching in regional Australia, working with the contemporary worship singer, or singing an Australian art song may well have resonance for teachers of singing in other contexts. Australian society is distinctive, but if the reader substitutes an English, American or other environment into each of these settings, the role of the singing teacher may be quite similar.

Conclusion

This chapter began with Graham Welch's (2005) comments on the role of singing in society at large. Although this research was published in the United Kingdom, it still has relevance in Australia today. Looking further back, it is perhaps unsurprising to find that William Byrd set down the following reasons "to perswade every one to learne to sing" in England almost 500 years ago. In the preface to Psalmes, Sonnets & Songs (1588) he writes:[1]

- It is a knowledge easely taught and quickly learned, where there is a good Master and an apt Scoller.
- The exercise of singing is delightfull to Nature and good to preserve the health of Man.
- It doth strengthen all parts of the brest, and doth open the pipes.
- It is a singular good remedie for stammering in the speech.
- It is the best meanes to procure a perfect pronunciation, and to make a good Orator.
- It is the onely way to know where Nature hath bestowed the benefit of a good voyce; which guift is so rare as there is not one among a thousand that hath it; and in many that excellent guift is lost because they want Art to express Nature.
- There is not any Musicke of Instruments whatsoever comparable to that which is made of the voyces of men, where the voyces are good and the same well sorted and ordered.

- The better the voyce is, the meter it is to honour and serve God therewith; and the voyce of man is chiefely to be employed to that ende.

Or, to put in the words of an esteemed Australian pedagogue: "We are, after all, walking musical instruments and singing is part of our birthright" (Chapman, 2006, p. 1).

Endnote

1 This presents Byrd's words verbatim. In modern parlance, we would naturally use more inclusive language — and different spelling!

Acknowledgment

The author would like to acknowledge the assistance of Wendy Hargreaves in extracting the themes from the volume for analysis in this chapter.

References

ANATS Constitution. Retrieved April 4, 2010, from http://www.anats.org.au/

Apfelstadt, H., Robinson, L., & Taylor, M. (2003). Building bridges among choral conductors, voice teachers and students. *Choral Journal, 44*(2), 25–33.

Adler A., & Harrison, S. (2004). Swinging back the gender pendulum: Addressing boys' needs in music education research and practice. In L. Bartel (Ed.), *Research to practice: A biennial series: Questioning the music education paradigm* (pp. 270–289). Toronto, Canada: Canadian Music Educators Association.

Bayliss, C., Lierse, A., & Ludowyke, J. (2009). Singing through life at Melbourne High School. In S. Harrison (Ed.), *Male voices: Stories of boys learning through making music* (pp. 135–155). Melbourne, Australia: ACER.

Bennett, D., & Hannan, M. (2008). *Inside, outside, downside up: Conservatoire training and musician's work.* Perth, Australia: Black Swan.

Burt-Perkins, R. (2008). Students at a UK conservatoire of music: Working towards a diverse employment portfolio. In D. Bennett & M. Hannan (Eds.), *Inside, outside, downside up: conservatoire training and musician's work* (pp. 49–60). Perth, Australia: Black Swan.

Chapman, J. (2006.) *Singing and teaching singing: A holistic approach to classical voice.* Oxford, UK: Plural Publishing.

Chasling, M. (2003). The choir of 10,000 in artistic practice as research. *Proceedings of the XXVth Annual Conference, Australian Association for Research in Music Education* (pp. 25, 26), Melbourne, Australia.

Daniel, R. (2003, April). *Innovations in piano pedagogy: A small-group model for the tertiary level.* Paper presented at Research in Music Education Conference, Exeter, UK.

Dawson, A. (2005). *Voice training and church singers: The state of vocal health of church singers of contemporary commercial styles in charismatic evangelical churches*

(Unpublished dissertation), Queensland Conservatorium, Griffith University, Brisbane, Australia.

Gaunt, H. (2010). One-to-one tuition in a conservatoire: The perceptions of instrumental and vocal students. *Psychology of Music, 38*, 178–208.

Harrison, S. (2005). The CAVE project: Collaborative approaches to vocal education. *Australian Voice, 2005*(11).

Harrison, S.D. (2006, October) *Where are we going? Directions for vocal tuition in schools.* Paper presented at ANATS National Conference, Canberra, Australia.

Harrison, S.D., Cowley, R., Connell, K., & Southcott, I. (2008). The role of singing in the broader music education landscape. *Music Council of Australia Knowledge Base.* Retrieved February 28, 2010 from http://mcakb.wordpress.com/support-activities/music-education-other/

Lancaster, H. (2007, July). *Music from another room: Real-time delivery of instrumental teaching.* Paper presented at the NACTMUS National Conference, Queensland Conservatorium of Music, Brisbane, Australia.

Latukefu, L. (2009) Peer learning and reflection: Strategies developed by vocal student in a transforming tertiary setting. *International Journal of Music Education, 27*(2), 124–137.

Lebler, D. (2007). Student-as-master? Reflections on a learning innovation in popular music pedagogy. *International Journal of Music Education. 25*(3), 205–221.

Lierse, A. (2007). Studio music teaching in Australia. *Music Council of Australia Knowledge Base.* Retrieved February 21, 2008 from http://mcakb.wordpress.com/support-activities/music-education-other/

LoVetri, J. (2008). Contemporary commercial music. *Journal of Voice, 22*(3), 260–262.

LoVetri, J. (2002). Contemporary commercial music: More than one way to use the vocal tract. *Journal of Singing, 58*(3), 249–252.

Megalogenis, M. (2004, July 7). Anthems are useless in a nation of tone deaf chanters. *The Australian*, p. 11.

Mills, J. (2004). Working in music: The conservatoire professor. *British Journal of Music Education, 21*(2), 179–198.

Pascoe, R., Leong, S., MacCallum, J., Mackinlay, E., Marsh, K., & Smith, B. (2005). *National review of school music education: Augmenting the diminished.* Canberra, Australia: Australian Government.

Schindler, M. (2009). "Where was I when I needed me?" The Role of Storytelling in Vocal Pedagogy. In B. Bartleet & C. Ellis (Eds.), *Music autoethnographies: Making autoethnography sing/making music personal* (pp. 181–196). Brisbane, Australia: Australian Academic Press.

Tuning Project. (2004). 'Tuning education structures in Europe'. An educational evaluation framework for the Lisbon Strategy and the Bologna Declaration Process. Retrieved October 27, 2009 from http://tuning.unideusto.org/tuningeu

Vaughan, L.T. (1998). The missing males: Factors which contribute to low participation of adolescent boys singing in secondary school (Unpublished Masters thesis). Sydney Conservatorium of Music, University of Sydney, Australia.

Vox Humana (1907). Anonymous student. *Our school magazine*. Melbourne, Australia. Melbourne High School.

Welch, G.F. (2005). Singing as communication. In D. Miell, R. MacDonald & D. Hargreaves (Eds.), *Musical communication* (pp. 239–259). New York: Oxford University Press.

Wilson, P. (2003). Sinful modern music: Science and the contemporary commercial singer. *Australian Voice, 9*, 12–16.

Young, A. (2009). The singing classroom: Singing in classroom music and its potential to transform school culture. In S. Harrison (Ed.), *Male voices: Stories of boys learning through making music* (pp. 62–78). Melbourne, Australia: ACER.

▪ ▪ ▪ ▪ ▪ ▪ ▪ ▪ ▪

Chapter 2

Singing Teaching as a Profession

Jean Callaghan

This chapter discusses professionalism in the teaching of singing, applying the model of expert teaching proposed by Shulman (1987), which requires the teacher to have three types of knowledge: content knowledge, pedagogical knowledge and pedagogical-content knowledge. Applied to the teaching of singing, this means that teachers need a knowledge of the singing voice, a knowledge of teaching and how these two kinds of knowledge come together in the service of different singers.

Singing teachers have always been concerned with voice, music and language, and how to convey to students a knowledge of these elements in a way that allows them to be learnt as an embodied, holistic performance skill. The majority of teachers are, or have been, singers, so they bring to their teaching their own empirical knowledge of singing and, in a broader sense, performing. However, in dealing with students at different levels and with different learning styles, this craft knowledge can now be complemented by a wide range of knowledge accumulated through experimental and qualitative research in many disciplines.

We now have access to material from voice science on the anatomy, physiology and acoustics of voice that answers many of the questions singing teachers have had on such matters as breath management, resonance and registers. We have research on music and language, on acting and movement — what they have in common, how they differ and how they are best taught. There is research on neurology, cognition, psychomotor learning, and theories on different learning styles and the teaching that best supports them. Knowledge of these different disciplines and how they come together in singing performance are the professional expertise of the singing teacher in contemporary society in the 21st century.

Introduction

In Australia, teaching singing has not always been regarded as a professional endeavour. However, with a long tradition of classical singing dating back to the 19th century, singing teaching has gradually developed as a profession, with the formation of the Australian National Association of Teachers of Singing in 1988, the inauguration in 1995 of the scholarly journal *Australian Voice*, and since then, the growth of tertiary pedagogy courses, thus suggesting that it is now so regarded. Definitions of what constitutes a profession tend to change over time, because professions operate in social settings, and these have changing values and expectations. Sociologists agree that for an occupation to be regarded as a profession, practitioners need to meet several criteria. The most commonly cited criteria are:

- possession of a specialised body of knowledge and skills acquired during a prolonged period of education and training;
- making decisions for the client on the basis of general principles, theories or standards;
- having a service orientation, which implies an absence of self-interest and applying diagnostic skill and competent application of knowledge to the special needs of the client; and
- regulation by a professional body (Schein, 1972, pp. 8–9).

The specialised body of knowledge and skills required by a teacher of singing in contemporary society in the 21st century comprises a long list and covers a wide range. Experience and analytical skills are then required in forming general principles, theories and standards, and applying them to clients' needs.

Shulman (1987) identified three types of knowledge necessary for expert teaching:

- Content knowledge — knowledge of the subject matter to be taught.
- Pedagogical knowledge — knowledge of how to teach.
- Pedagogical-content knowledge — teaching expertise particular to the content.

It is these three types of knowledge that provide the basis for the discussion in this chapter. The chapter provides an overview of the cross-disciplinary influences that in the 21st century inform our knowledge of what singing is, what best practice in teaching is and how to bring these together in the service of the singer. It is important to note that we now have access to material from voice science on the anatomy, physiology and acoustics of voice that supplies much of the content knowledge of singing voice relating to breath management, phonation, resonance, registration and vocal health.

We have research on neurology, cognition, psychomotor learning, and theories on different learning styles and the teaching that best supports them, providing much of the pedagogical knowledge. We have research on music and language, and on physical skills training that supplements the music performance pedagogical-content knowledge that goes back to the early 17th century. For teachers in the 21st century, knowledge of these different disciplines and how they come together in singing performance constitute the specialised body of knowledge of the profession. This chapter begins with a description of the physical bases of voice production; what we know about the vocal instrument and how it works.

The Content Knowledge of Singing

Nowadays, singing teachers need to have excellent content knowledge. In the past 40 years or so, a great deal of scientific material has been published on various aspects of vocal physiology and acoustics. This evidence appears in the publications of many different disciplines — physiology, medicine, speech pathology, acoustics and linguistics, as well as singing and voice science — and until recently, had not reached the majority of singing teachers. However, teachers can now refer to publications that bring this material together specifically for their field; for example, Callaghan (2000); Thurman & Welch (2000); Chapman (2006); Nair (2007); Dayme (2009).

The Vocal Instrument

Specifically, singing teachers can benefit from a knowledge of what comprises the vocal instrument and how that instrument functions. Regarded as a musical instrument, the voice consists of the respiratory apparatus as an actuator producing breath energy, the larynx as vibrator and the vocal tract as resonator. These body parts need to be aligned in a posture that maximises their coordinated working, directed by the brain in producing the requisite pitch, loudness, duration and timbre, and responding to higher-level demands in relation to musical phrasing and articulation of text.

The Energy Supply (Breath)

Efficient breath management is vital for control of pitch and duration, and to some degree of timbre and loudness. The breathing mechanism involves the diaphragm, lungs, rib cage, and thoracic and abdominal muscles. For singing, efficient inspiration means taking in the required amount of air quickly and without unnecessary muscular tension in the articulatory structures. The controlled expiration for efficient singing requires coordinated working of the muscles of the ribcage and abdomen to provide the subglottal pressure appropriate for the required pitch and intensity of sound and for the length of phrase (Callaghan, Hughes, & Power, 2009). Because singing makes heavier demands than speech, breathing needs to be much more energetic and expansive.

The Basic Sound (Phonation)

The basic vocal sound (the voice source spectrum) is produced by the vocal folds of the larynx. The larynx is a cartilaginous structure at the top of the trachea, with joints held by ligaments and operated by small muscles. Its primary function is as a valve that closes to prevent foreign matter entering the airway or to help sustain pressure in heavy lifting, childbirth, urination or defecation. The vocal folds consist of muscles covered by mucous membrane, the space between them called the glottis. The vocal folds open and close and vibrate in response to both muscular and aerodynamic factors (Callaghan et al., 2009, p. 43). Their vibration produces phonation, the frequency of the vibrations being the pitch of the vocal sound, expressed as frequency or Hertz (e.g., A4 equals 440 Hz).

The interrelation of subglottal pressure and vocal fold resistance affects airflow at the glottis. The onset of phonation may be breathy, balanced ("simultaneous") or glottal (pressed, hard), with the type of onset important for both musical aesthetics and vocal efficiency. Neither breathy nor pressed phonation is efficient. Although breathy or glottal onsets may sometimes be used, balanced onset most easily achieves the efficiency of flow phonation.

Fundamental frequency (pitch) may be controlled by changing lung pressure, contracting the cricothyroid (CT) muscles or by contracting the thyroarytenoid (TA) muscles to change the length, stiffness and effective vibrating mass of the vocal folds. These mechanisms may be interdependent. Pitch may also be affected by vertical larynx position and laryngeal tilt, achieved by extrinsic laryngeal muscular activity.

Vibrato is a regular frequency and intensity modulation of the voice, which probably comes from a physiological tremor in the laryngeal muscles (Titze, 1994). Many vocal tract structures, such as the jaw, velum, tongue and pharyngeal walls, may rhythmically pulse in synchrony with the vibrato. Consistent vibrato is an expected element of classical vocal tone; it is used in different ways in other genres and styles. Normal vibrato features pitch modulation of approximately one semitone and a rate of 5.5–6.5 Hz (Callaghan, 2000). In order for vibrato not to interfere with the melody, its extent needs to decrease for rapid pitch changes.

The Resonator (Vocal Acoustics)

The cavities above the larynx — the pharynx and the interconnected mouth and nasal cavities — comprise the vocal tract, with the air in the vocal tract acting as a resonator. The acoustics of the vocal instrument are largely reliant on the configuration of the vocal tract, causing some sounds of the complex

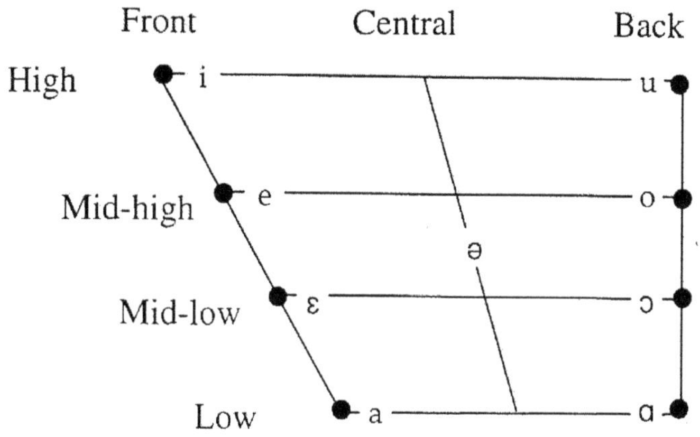

FIGURE 2.1

Vowel quadrilateral.

voice source to be damped, and others enhanced and producing the particular timbre of the voice. Changes in the configuration of the vocal tract are achieved by movements of the articulators — the lips, the tongue, the jaw, the velum or soft palate and the pharynx — with these articulators also involved in word articulation. Vocal tone and word articulation are thus interdependent (Callaghan et al., 2009, p. 43).

Vowel production involves lip and tongue shape, jaw opening and soft palate position. Linguistic vowel classification refers to the oral cavity position of the main body of the tongue in the oral cavity — high-low and front-back — and to the degree of lip rounding or spreading. In the traditional vowel quadrilateral, /i/ is at the high front corner (the tongue is high anterior in the mouth), /u/ at the high back corner (the tongue is high posterior in the mouth) and /ɑ/ at the low back corner (the tongue is low posterior in the mouth). Other vowels, such as the neutral /ə/, are classified as central. Vowels may also be classified as "closed" (the tongue near the palate) or "open" (the tongue low, at the bottom of the mouth), which may also be related to jaw opening.

The tongue position in effect produces two acoustic resonating chambers, with each chamber amplifying acoustic energy near its resonances and reducing energy at frequencies far from the resonance. Those frequencies that are amplified produce resonance peaks, called formants. The fundamental frequency (musical pitch) is labelled F0, and the formants are F1, F2, F3 and so on from lowest to highest. The first formant is particularly affected by jaw position and the second formant by tongue shape. It is the relationship between F1 and F2 that defines a vowel.

Vocal intensity can be significantly increased by tuning formants close to voice source harmonics. A louder sound can be produced by lowering the jaw and moving the lips forward and inward at the corners, but in operatic style high in the female range, this strategy causes formant frequency differences between vowels to gradually disappear as the fundamental frequency increases, resulting in words being difficult to distinguish. For music theatre and commercial styles, it is more usual to sing with a higher larynx and use clear consonantal transitions to make words more intelligible.

The singer's formant is what provides the exciting ringing quality of the professional classical singing voice. This quality is essential for singers to be heard clearly over large orchestras, electronic instruments or background noise. Sundberg (1991) identified the singer's formant as a cluster of high spectrum peaks appearing near 3000 Hz (approximately F#7) in all vowels. The acoustic effect may be reinforced by the fact that the ear is highly sensitive to frequencies around 3000 Hz.

Current research indicates that production of the singer's formant cluster is dependent on a long closed phase in the vocal fold vibratory cycle, narrowing the vocal tract immediately above the larynx, a wide pharynx and articulatory adjustments, which maximize resonance coupling between the two main cavities. It may also involve aryepiglottic constriction and ventricular fold narrowing. Most research on the singer's formant has assumed a "classical" timbre. This contrasts with the sound used in belting, which has strong harmonic overtones as high as 10,000 Hz (McCoy, 2004).

Registration

For centuries, singing teachers have been concerned with the changes in vocal quality that occur as the singer moves through the range; what causes them and how they should be dealt with in order to produce the vocal quality aesthetically appropriate for the music being sung. Each pitch range of similar vocal quality is called a register, defined by the 19th-century singer/teacher/researcher Manuel Garcia as "a series of consecutive homogeneous sounds produced by one mechanism, differing essentially from another series of sounds equally homogeneous produced by another mechanism" (Garcia, 1894/1982, p. 8). However, much confusion has arisen from the fact that registration relates to a complex of factors concerned with pitch and timbre, and until the late 20th century it was unclear what the mechanisms involved were. This has given rise to what Timberlake in 1990 called "terminological turmoil".

Since the work of Vennard (1967) and Hollien (1974, 1984), it has been acknowledged that registers are essentially laryngeal events, occurring at predictable frequencies in different voice types. When in phonation the glottis closes against breath pressure, there is a complex balance of the tensions of the laryngeal muscles. Their action affects the degree of vocal fold adduction and the force of that adduction. The main agonist–antagonist function of the TA and CT muscles is to change fundamental frequency through lengthening/shortening, thinning/thickening and tightening/relaxing the folds. Because these changes alter the complex voice source, they also produce changes in voice quality. These changes are what we label "registers".

There are two main categories of register: those where the action of the TA muscles is dominant and those where the action of the CT muscles is dominant. The TA muscles are largely thickeners/shorteners of the vocal folds, the CT thinners/lengtheners. This affects the manner in which the vocal folds oscillate, including the ratio of time the glottis is closed versus open (closed quotient) and the thickness of the folds. However, because pitch and resonance changes are also involved, within those two main categories there are subdivisions.

Those registers dominated by TA production occur at lower pitches, and are characterised by a relatively high closed quotient, greater vocal fold mass per unit of length and, generally, strong acoustic energy in high harmonics. TA-dominant registers are: pulse (fry); chest in men (heavy mechanism, modal); operatic head voice in men; and chest voice and belting in women (McCoy, 2004, p. 65). In pulse, the CT muscles completely release, with vocal fold length determined solely by the action of the TA muscles. In this register, there is increased energy in the lower partials. In the other registers, both TA and CT muscles simultaneously contract, but TA action is dominant.

Those registers dominated by CT production occur at higher pitches and are characterised by a relatively lower closed quotient, vocal fold oscillation almost exclusively along the medial margins of the vocal folds, and less acoustic energy in high harmonics. CT-dominant registers are: middle and head (light mechanism) in women, male falsetto and female flageolet (flute, whistle). In falsetto and flageolet, the TA muscles completely release, with vocal fold length determined solely by CT action. In the other registers, both CT and TA muscles simultaneously contract, but CT action is dominant.

Because register change is regulated mainly by the ratio of TA and CT activities, if the ratio is changed abruptly, the register change is also abrupt and clearly heard. If the change is also associated with a discontinuity of vocal fold vibrations, a "break" results. If the ratio is changed gradually, the register change is also gradual and less perceptible.

For teachers, knowledge of the principles of vocal registration, coupled with an analytical musical ear, is vital in guiding students to achieve the sound appropriate to the aesthetics of the genre and style. In some instances, singers may judge an abrupt change in timbre to serve aesthetic demands, as in yodelling, or sometimes in the large leaps used by composers for emotional effect. In many other instances, a blended tone is required and singers need to achieve register change through a dynamic balance of breath pressure and flow, and resonance adjustments.

Resonance adjustments can be achieved by vowel modification and jaw opening. Modification to an adjacent vowel (from back vowels to more central, from front vowels to more central, from closed vowels to more open) is used at register changes as pitch rises, in order to achieve a close alignment of source harmonics with vocal tract resonances. The teacher's analytical ear, coupled with a knowledge of vowel production and vowel modification, will guide the singer in making the adjustments needed to achieve this alignment of harmonics with resonances. While subtle adjustments occur in skilled singers throughout the entire range, precise adjustments are particularly critical at register changes.

Titze (1994) demonstrated that all researchers had found the major register transition occurring between D4 (294 Hz) and G4 (392 Hz), spanning six voice categories. This major register transition represents the primo passaggio for females and secondo passaggio for males. Miller (1986), while not ruling out individual variation, did suggest D4 (294 Hz) as the passaggio for bass, E-flat4 for sopranos and dramatic baritones, E4 for mezzo-sopranos and dramatic tenors, and G4 for lyric tenors, spinto tenors and contraltos. While it may not be possible to state with certainty the pitch at which a register shift will occur in a given voice, the general pattern across voice types is clear; the major shift occurs lowest in the bass and highest in tenor and contralto. For teachers, this information is key to determining voice type, which rests not only on the singer's range and comfortable tessitura, but also on the pitch of register changes.

Overall Control of the Instrument

The musical instrument that is the voice is the whole person — body parts responding in particular coordinations to express thoughts and emotions, verbal meanings and musical meanings. All vocal functions are controlled neurologically; the laryngeal muscles position the larynx and achieve adduction of the vocal folds, the diaphragm and intercostal muscles raise subglottal pressure, the muscles of articulation adjust the length and shape of the vocal tract, and the middle ear muscles reduce the sensitivity of the ear just before the initiation of phonation — all in response to a neurological signal (Sataloff, 1992).

Physical Efficiency and Vocal Health

For all singers, knowledge of how to care for the voice is necessary for the instrument to be available and in good condition whenever it is needed. For professional singers, keeping the voice in peak condition is necessary for earning a living, and yet the demands of busy schedules, demanding repertoire and constant travel make that a difficult task.

In the area of physical efficiency and vocal health, there is a body of knowledge readily available to teachers, with recent publications on singing pedagogy making explicit what was in earlier works implicit in the whole approach to vocal technique — a concern for the maintenance of vocal health. Studies on vocal health for singers have produced prescriptions relating to maintaining hydration; managing general health, fitness and lifestyle; avoiding vocal strain and fatigue; and using good technique to achieve efficient voice use.

Voice Classification

Voice classification is a subtle, complex matter, involving vocal range, weight, timbre, optimal tessitura (the range where a singer's voice is most beautiful and most easily produced) and register transition locations. These factors are determined by vocal fold length and thickness, the relationship of the larynx to adjacent structures, vocal tract length and configuration, thoracic dimensions, and the interplay of pectoral, epigastric and abdominal muscles. Higher voices have shorter vocal folds and vocal tracts, lower voices have longer vocal folds and vocal tracts. Hybrid classifications occur when long-necked singers have short vocal folds, producing a dark, high voice, or when short-necked singers have long vocal folds, producing a bright, low voice.

The discussion above details what the singing voice is and how it works. This comprises the content knowledge of singing. While this knowledge is essential for a voice teacher, it is essential that it be employed in the service of teaching different students, with different abilities, skills and experience. This requires pedagogical knowledge.

Pedagogical Knowledge

While singing teachers bring their own experiential knowledge of learning to sing to their work with students, this knowledge can now be complemented by research findings in a range of areas related to singing: skill learning, learning styles, the relationship between speaking and singing, practice and developing the self-regulated learner.

Singing as a Sensorimotor Skill

Singers need simultaneous training in both musical concepts and the sensorimotor skills that realise those concepts. This process presents particular difficulties. First, singers cannot hear themselves as others hear them. Second, voicing is accompanied by bodily sensations and singers must learn the particular body sensations associated with sounds that are aesthetically desirable and physically efficient.

"Skill is goal-directed, well-organised behavior that is acquired through practice and performed with economy of effort" (Proctor & Dutta, 1995, p. 18). There are three stages of skill acquisition: cognitive, associative and autonomous (Fitts & Posner, 1967). In both cognitive and associative stages, modelling and external feedback are important. Once the sensorimotor skills of singing have been acquired, the cognitive demands are reduced, freeing mental resources for musical and textual interpretation.

Teachers can help singers form an action plan by providing a task overview and directions using metaphors and mental images meaningful to the singer. The teacher needs to gauge when the singer is ready to learn a particular task, which then makes achievement of succeeding tasks possible. This is how singers move to the third, autonomous stage, becoming involved in a cycle of forethought, performance and self-reflection.

Skill acquisition requires information about performance during training and attention to perceptual information. While providing frequent information about performance (knowledge of results) during training may improve performance at that time, less frequent feedback seems to enhance longer-term learning (Verdolini, 1997, 2001). The timing of feedback is also vital: Havighurst (1952) referred to a "teachable moment", the optimal moment at which learning of a particular task is possible, making achievement of succeeding tasks possible.

Modelling and Feedback

Singing teaching is commonly based on a master–apprentice model, relying on good modelling and feedback, with modelling supplied by the teacher's demonstration or by using live or recorded performance. Singers receive feedback from both external or internal sources. External sources include the responses of audiences, teachers or colleagues. Internal feedback relates to body function and may be visual, tactile, auditory, kinaesthetic or proprioceptive.

Feedback that is specific, timely and meaningful to the student is a pedagogic necessity (Ericsson, Krampe, & Tesch-Römer, 1993; Chickering & Gamson, 1987). This involves the teacher making an assessment of the student's progress in relation to a goal or target, and also making an informed decision about the type, timing and frequency of feedback.

Chiviacowsky and Wulf (2002) found that allowing learners of a simple, sequenced, motor task the opportunity to decide when to receive feedback was more beneficial than externally controlling the timing of feedback, hypothesising that this enhanced the perception of self-control, which in turn enhanced learning. While teachers commonly use verbal feedback, unless the feedback is specific, the time spent talking has little effect on student learning (Juslin & Laukka, 2000).

The most important sense for singers may well be hearing, as auditory feedback allows the singer to match produced sound with intended sound. Both audition and audiation are crucial to pitch accuracy and resonance balancing. For those singing multiple styles, the ability to monitor the many stylistic differences as sound is invaluable. The mirror, the simplest visual feedback, has been used by singers for centuries. More recently, video recording and computer-assisted visual feedback have become widely available.

Student Learning Styles

Cognitive research in the past 25 years has brought wide recognition of the diversity of effective learning styles. Teachers need a range of teaching approaches to suit these diverse learning styles.

The work of Howard Gardner (1993) and collaborators (Kolb, 1984; Lazear, 1991) has investigated individual differences in profiles of intelligences and how these are linked to ways of learning. While people are attracted to domains related to their particular intelligences, success in a specific domain requires proficiency in a set of intelligences. For example, people with musical intelligence may be attracted to the domain of music, but for success in this domain they require proficiency in a set of seven intelligences. For a singer, these would include:

- verbal/linguistic — understanding order and meaning of words, memory and recall, story-telling
- logical/mathematical — abstract pattern recognition, discerning relationships and connections
- musical/rhythmic — appreciating the structure of music, schemes or frames in the mind for hearing music, sensitivity to sounds, recognition, creation and reproduction of melody and rhythm, sensing characteristic qualities of tone
- visual/spatial — active imagination, forming mental images
- bodily/kinaesthetic — control of "voluntary" movements, control of "pre-programmed" movements, the mind–body connection, expanding awareness through the body, communication through gesture
- social/interpersonal — effective verbal/non-verbal communication, sensitivity to others' moods, temperaments, motivations and feelings
- solidarity/intra-personal — concentration of the mind, mindfulness, metacognition (thinking and learning about knowing what you know), awareness and expression of different feelings.

Speaking and Singing/Language and Music

Both musical and linguistic intelligence are closely tied to the auditory–oral tract. Gardner (1993) defines auditory–oral musical intelligence as the ability to discern meaning and importance in sets of pitches rhythmically arranged and also to produce such metrically arranged pitch sequences as a means of communicating.

Essential to singing are both audition (hearing) and audiation (mental hearing or auditory imagery). "Audiation" is Gordon's (1993) term for mentally hearing and comprehending musical sound that is no longer present or that may never have been present. Speaking and singing involve a process of hearing, perceiving and remembering sound. This process forms a loop with the production of sound, dictating what is produced by the vocal apparatus.

It seems that visual feedback, in contributing to the learning of the motor skills of sound production, may well contribute to this process (Callaghan, Thorpe, van Doorn, & Wilson, 2003). Using real-time visual feedback in the development in school students of vocal pitch accuracy in singing, Welch, Howard and Rush found that the students "were able to extract meaning from the visual display and combine this with proprioceptive feedback from the voice mechanism to modify and develop their vocal pitch behaviours" (1989, p. 156).

Imagery and the Self-Regulated Learner

Zimmerman (1998) defined self-regulated learning as an open-ended process involving the learner in a cycle of forethought, performance or volitional control, and self-reflection. In this cycle, imagery plays a key role in forethought and volitional control (Isaac & Marks, 1994). Cumming and Hall (2002), when investigating the development of imagery skills in competitive athletes, found that when athletes were engaged in imagery for their sport they also enjoyed being challenged and felt that they were improving and becoming competent.

While traditional methods for learning to sing have relied heavily on auditory imagery, research in psychology and sports coaching suggests that for the bulk of the population this imagery is visual. Many students in our very visually-oriented society are more visually than aurally aware, and that visual awareness is part of the bodily–kinaesthetic intelligence that plays such an important part in singing. In talking about acting students, Barton (1997) claims that, at the introductory levels, the vast majority (often up to 80%) are visual learners; at more advanced levels more have become kinaesthetic or auditory learners. It is therefore important for singing teachers (who, as experienced musicians, may themselves think largely in sound) to be aware that using visual imagery and visual feedback to complement other types of feedback may achieve a better fit with the individual intelligence profile and ways of learning of many students, and enhance their acquisition of singing skills.

Practice and Song Learning

A number of studies exist on how practice affects motor learning. Generally, learning increases with the amount of time devoted to practice, and distributed practice is more effective than massed practice; that is, skills are best learned when practised for short periods, but often (Baddeley, 1997). Combining physical and mental practice is most effective in improving skill acquisition. While practice schedules and extrinsic feedback aid motor skill acquisition, for long-term learning, singers should rely on personal auditory images and sensory feedback of the vocal sound being produced, as performance situations may not provide any extrinsic feedback.

Learning songs requires the memory and physicalisation of musical and verbal text. Understanding vocal and musical patterns allows smaller, simpler patterns to be learned first, building to increasingly larger patterns. Silent rehearsal assists this process.

Pedagogical-Content Knowledge

> It may seem to many that every perfect singer must also be a perfect instructor, but it is not so; for his qualifications (though ever so great) are insufficient if he cannot communicate his sentiments with ease and in a method adapted to the ability of the scholar. (Tosi, 1723, p. 73)

> Simplification, not complication, should be the goal of all instruction. (Miller, 2004, p. 190)

While teaching relies on both content knowledge and pedagogical knowledge, what distinguishes experts from novices is the way experts bring these two types of knowledge together as pedagogical-content knowledge (Shulman, 1987), the capacity to transform content knowledge into forms that are pedagogically powerful yet adaptive to the variations in ability and background presented by the student, thus echoing Tosi's observation of 245 years earlier. This capacity requires teachers to reflect on their praxis, "Through reflection, [they] can surface and criticise the tacit understandings that have grown up around the repetitive experiences of a specialised practice, and can make new sense of the situations of uncertainty or uniqueness" (Schön, 1983, p. 61).

Singing teachers have always been concerned with voice, music and language, and how to convey to students knowledge of these elements in a way that allows them to be learnt as an embodied, holistic performance skill. The majority of teachers are, or have been, singers, so they bring to their teaching their own empirical knowledge of singing and, in a broader sense, performing. However, in dealing with students at different levels and with different learning styles, this craft knowledge can now be complemented by a wide range of knowledge accumulated through experimental and qualitative research in many disciplines.

Singing differs from other musical performance in that the performer *is* the instrument. The teacher's task is to bring together the content knowledge of voice with the pedagogical knowledge of how to teach a psychomotor skill in a way that promotes the most efficient learning of individual singers, with their individual bodies, brains and ways of learning. This requires understanding not only of the elements, but also of their dynamic interaction.

The Holistic Working of the Vocal Instrument

At the beginning of this chapter, the elements of the vocal instrument were outlined. Any part, or the overall coordination of all parts, of the instrument responds to the singer's general physical, intellectual and emotional state. Singer and teacher are concerned to achieve mastery of this instrument in order that it become a *musical* instrument, communicating musical, verbal and emotional meanings to an audience. For the singer, efficient body alignment and well-coordinated body use are essential to this task. For the teacher, an understanding of vocal anatomy, physiology and acoustics ensures that technical work is informed by principles of physical efficiency and vocal health, as well as providing the basis for fault diagnosis.

While teachers of singing cannot be expected to have detailed knowledge of pathologies and medications, they do need to be sufficiently informed and aurally aware to distinguish between poor vocal technique and possible vocal damage. They need knowledge of fitness and lifestyle management, both to maintain their own vocal fitness in what has been identified as a high-risk profession and to advise their students on such issues. They also need to be in contact with a wider network of professionals in related fields — teachers of spoken voice; body use professionals such as Alexander, Feldenkrais, Pilates, and yoga teachers; dentists and orthodontists; and otolaryngologists, speech therapists and voice care teams — with whom they can work and to whom students with vocal problems can be referred.

Body alignment and breath management affect lung volume, larynx height and tilt, and tracheal pull. All these affect laryngeal function, the voice source and the resultant sound, which needs to be aesthetically appropriate for the particular style and genre. Alignment of the head is particularly important, as it affects all postural reflexes. Because the larynx, hyoid bone and tongue base move as a unit, anything that alters their relationship to each other and to the sternum, spine and skull affects phonation. Head position must allow the sternocleidomastoid and scalene muscles to stabilise the neck and thorax, and allow the external muscles contributing to voice production (the strap muscles, cricopharyngeal and stylopharyngeal) to work efficiently.

Because the tongue is attached to the hyoid bone, from which the larynx is suspended, tongue position affects the larynx: extending the tongue raises the larynx and depressing the tongue lowers it. Tension in the jaw is undesirable in classical style, as it affects laryngeal position through the muscles connected to the hyoid bone. In some other non-classical styles, the jaw may be more firmly positioned by muscular activity.

Breath management involves gravity, elastic recoil and muscular activity, with body use affecting all these factors. Two common body use extremes have been labelled "belly-in" and "belly-out", or the "up-and-in" and "down-and-out" methods of support (Titze, 1994). The "belly-in" approach emphasizes maintaining a high, stable rib cage; the "belly-out" approach emphasises maintaining stable abdominal pressure. Neither extreme is ideal, since the physiology of respiration is complex and the many interrelated aspects of breath management may vary from singer to singer, depending on body type, and varying from one musical task to another and one genre to another. What is needed is a balanced coordination between the muscles of the abdomen, trunk and neck to suit different body types and meet different musical demands (Callaghan, 2000, pp. 36–39).

An important aspect of teaching is helping the singer achieve synchronised control between breathing and pitch muscles to meet musical demands in relation to pitch, loudness and duration. An indirect approach that addresses posture, audiation, breath management, onset and registration factors usually ensures that the musical demands are met.

Voice quality depends on the voice source spectrum, how that spectrum is filtered by the vocal tract and how the source and vocal tract resonances interact. Pedagogical concerns about resonance and articulation include production of a tone appropriate for the genre and musical context, vowel quality, vibrato and text articulation. Singers learn to tune formant frequencies through attention to vowel quality and the emotional motivation of the text, guided by the teacher's analytical ear. There are also computer software programs (e.g., Sing&See; Voce Vista) that give objective feedback on vocal acoustics.

Music, Language, Meaning and Embodiment

Singing is about music, language, meaning and embodiment. At a prosaic level, the human voice is a uniquely convenient, portable musical instrument that can be used in music education and group music-making at all levels. But at a poetic level, the human voice is the expression of who we are, and how we are in our environment. In *The Songlines*, Bruce Chatwin quoted Rilke: "Song is existence" (1987, p. 13). Chatwin's book relates how Aboriginal creation myths tell of the legendary totemic beings who wandered over the continent in the Dreaming, singing the world into existence. Chatwin postulated that the whole of Australia could be read as a musical score.

Vico held that it was typical of all languages that expressions referring to inanimate objects were "formed by metaphor from the human body and its parts and from human senses and passions" (quoted by Ruthroff, 2000, p. 37). Vico's New Science proposed that the early faculties of the mind must have "their roots in the body and draw their strength from it". He saw the origin of language as having begun "with signs, whether gestures or physical objects". Vico pointed out that for the Greeks, "logos" suggested not only language but also "things" (1968, p. 127f). So language in its early stages must have been "a fantastic speech making use of physical substances endowed with life" (quoted in Ruthrof, 2000, p. 36). Vico concluded that poetic speech preceded prose in the evolution of language. I suggest that music preceded poetry.

In song, music and language come together in expressing meaning through sound; and sound is like the self, sound is embodied. Meaning in both music and language comes from understanding, imagination and embodiment. Singing is about the self. The phenomenologist, Merleau-Ponty, spoke of "the emergence of the flesh as expression" and the body signifying "a certain landscape about me" (1968, p. 145).

It is clear from this discussion that the specialised body of knowledge and skills required of a singing teacher in the 21st century encompasses a wide range of material from voice science, performance, linguistics, neurology, cognition and psychomotor learning. Knowledge of this wide range of material and how it is best brought together in teaching different singers comprises the professional expertise of today's singing teacher. There are now tertiary courses on vocal pedagogy and professional bodies involved in continuing professional education, defining ethical behaviour and setting down general principles in relation to dealing with clients. Professionalism in singing teaching means using this expertise to enable our students to embody poetry, music and voice as a gestalt meaningful to them and to convey that meaning to an audience.

References

Baddeley, A. (1997). *Human memory: Theory and practice* (Rev. ed.). Hove, UK: Psychology Press.

Barton, R. (1997). Voice in a visual world: A neuro-linguistic programming perspective on vocal training. In M. Hampton, & B. Acker (Eds.), *The vocal vision: Views on voice* (pp. 81–92). New York: Applause Books.

Callaghan, J. (2000). *Singing and voice science.* San Diego, CA: Singular/Thomson Learning.

Callaghan, J., Hughes, D., & Power, A. (2009). Towards an interdisciplinary school curriculum in voice studies. In A. Power (Ed.), *Proceedings of the Joint Conference of XXXIst ANZARME Annual Conference and the 1st Conference of the Music Educators Research Centre, Akaroa, New Zealand* (pp. 41–48). Melbourne, Australia: Australian and New Zealand Association for Research in Music Education.

Callaghan J., Thorpe W., van Doorn J., & Wilson P. (2003) "Sing and See". In L.C.R. Yip, C.C. Leung & W.T. Lau (Eds.), *Curriculum innovation in music: Proceedings of the 4th Asia-Pacific Symposium on Music Education Research*. Hong Kong: Institute of Education.

Chapman, J.L. (2006). *Singing and teaching singing. A holistic approach to classical voice.* San Diego, CA: Plural Publishing.

Chatwin, B. (1987). *The Songlines*. London: Jonathan Cape.

Chickering, A.W., & Gamson, Z.F. (1987). Seven principles for good practice in undergraduate education. *AAHE Bulletin, 39*, 3–7.

Chiviacowsky, S., & Wulf, G. (2002). Self-controlled feedback: Does it enhance learning because performers get feedback when they need it? *Research Quarterly for Exercise and Sport, 73*(4), 408–415.

Cumming, J., & Hall, C. (2002). Deliberate imagery practice: The development of imagery skills in competitive athletes. *Journal of Sports Sciences, 20*, 137–145.

Dayme, M. (2009). *Dynamics of the singing voice.* Vienna, Austria: Springer-Verlag.

Ericsson, K.A., Krampe, R.T., & Tesch-Römer, C. (1993). The role of deliberate practice in the acquisition of expert performance. *Psychological Review, 100*(3), 363–406.

Fitts, P.M., & Posner, M.I. (1967). *Human performance*. Belmont, CA: Brooks/Cole.

Garcia, M. (1982). *Hints on singing* (B. Garcia, Trans.) (Rev. ed.). New York: Joseph Patelson Music House. (Original work published 1894).

Gardner, H. (1993). *Frames of mind: The theory of multiple intelligences* (2nd ed.). London: Fontana.

Gordon, E.E. (1993). *Learning sequences in music: Skill, content, and patterns — A music learning theory.* Chicago, IL: GIA Publications.

Havighurst, R.J. (1952). *Human development and education.* Philadelphia: David McKay & Co.

Hollien, H. (1974). On vocal registers. *Journal of Phonetics, 2*, 125–143.

Hollien, H. (1984). A review of vocal registers. In V.L. Lawrence (Ed.), *Transcripts of the twelfth symposium, Care of the professional voice, 1983*, Pt 1 (pp. 1–6). New York. NY: The Voice Foundation.

Isaac, A.R., & Marks, D.F. (1994). Individual differences in mental imagery experience: Developmental changes and specialization. *British Journal of Psychology, 85*(4), 479–498.

Juslin, P.N., & Laukka, P. (2000). Improving emotional communication in music performance through cognitive feedback. *Musicae Scientiae, IV*(2), 151–183.

Kolb, D.A. (1984). *Experiential learning: Experience as the source of learning and development.* Englewood Cliffs, NJ: Prentice-Hall.

Lazear, D. (1991). *Seven ways of knowing: Teaching for multiple intelligences.* Palatine, IL: IRI/Skylight Publishing.

McCoy, S. (2004). *Your voice: An inside view.* Princeton, NJ: Inside View Press.

Merleau-Ponty, M. (1968). *The visible and the invisible* (A. Lingis, Trans.). Evanston, IL: Northwestern University Press

Miller, R. (1986). *The structure of singing: System and art in vocal technique.* New York: Schirmer Books.

Miller, R. (2004). *Solutions for singers: Tools for performers and teachers.* Oxford, UK: Oxford University Press.

Nair, G. (2007). *The craft of singing.* San Diego, CA: Plural Publishing.

Proctor, R.W., & Dutta, A. (1995). *Skill acquisition and human performance.* Thousand Oaks, CA: Sage Publications.

Ruthrof, H. (2000). *The body in language.* London: Cassell.

Sataloff, (1992). The human voice. *Scientific American 267*(6), 108–115.

Schein, E. (1972). *Professional education: Some new directions.* Berkeley, CA: The Carnegie Foundation for the Advancement of Teaching.

Schön, D.A. (1983). *The reflective practitioner: How professionals think in action.* New York: Basic Books.

Shulman, L.S. (1987). Knowledge and teaching: Foundations of the new reform. *Harvard Educational Review, 19*(2), 4–14.

Sundberg, J. (1991). Vocal tract resonance. In R.T. Sataloff (Ed.), *Professional voice: The science and art of clinical care* (pp. 49–68). New York: Raven Press.

Thurman, L., & Welch, G. (Eds.) (2000). *Bodymind & voice: Foundations of voice education* (Rev. ed.). Collegeville, MN: The VoiceCare Network, the National Center for Voice and Speech, Fairview Voice Center, Center for Advanced Studies in Music Education.

Timberlake, C. (1990). Practica musicae: Terminological turmoil — The naming of registers. *The NATS Journal, 47*(1), 14–26.

Titze, I.R. (1994). *Principles of voice production.* Englewood Cliffs, NJ: Prentice Hall.

Tosi, P.F. (1987). *Observations on the florid song* (Galliard, Trans.; M. Pilkington (Ed.), London: Stainer and Bell. (Original work published 1742)

Vennard, W. (1967). *Singing: The mechanism and the technic* (Rev. ed.). New York: Carl Fischer.

Verdolini, K. (1997). Principles of skill acquisition applied to voice training. In M. Hampton, & B. Acker (Eds.), *The vocal vision: Views on voice* (pp. 65–80). New York: Applause Books.

Verdolini, K. (2001). Learning science applied to voice training: The value of being "in the moment". In O. Kähkönen (Ed.), *International Congress of Voice Teachers Congress book.* Helsinki, Finland: ICVT.

Vico, G. (1968). *The new science of Giambattista Vico.* New York, NY: Cornell University Press.

Welch, G.F., Howard, D.M., & Rush, C. (1989). Real-time visual feedback in the development of vocal pitch accuracy in singing. *Psychology of Music, 17,* 146–157.

Zimmerman, B.J. (1998). Developing self-fulfilling cycles of academic regulation: An analysis of exemplary instructional models. In D.H. Schunk & B.J. Zimmerman (Eds,), *Self-regulated learning: From teaching to self-reflective practice.* New York: The Guilford Press.

Chapter
3

Performers as Teachers: A Tertiary Perspective

Margaret Schindler

Conservatoires have traditionally appointed experienced performers to their classical voice faculties. Institutions recognise that performers bring to their teaching direct experience of the demands and requirements of high-level performance, as well as advanced musical, linguistic and stylistic skills. Mills stated unequivocally, "Performer–teachers fulfil a role within the culture of Western classical music that is crucial to the making of the performers of the future, and to the development of musical performance" (2004, p. 246). Within Australian tertiary institutions, performer–teachers remain the predominant teaching profile for the study of individual classical voice. Yet the impact on student learning remains largely unexplored. This chapter seeks to identify both negative and positive effects that the performer–teacher can have on the student learning experience, in the one-to-one studio learning environment and in performance, either through observation of teacher by student or through modelling, such as apprenticeship style performance experiences. In doing so, this discussion will also serve to identify both explicit and tacit performer knowledge, and the ways in which that knowledge shapes teaching and learning as well as student perceptions. The content of this chapter is drawn from interviews with students of the Queensland Conservatorium, Griffith University, Brisbane, and Australian tertiary voice teachers. The students have been quoted within this chapter and are referred to by their initials.

Context

In the field of classical voice, the traditional path has been for performers to maintain a career, retire from the stage and then teach (Miller, 1996, p. 28).

While this continues to be a common career trajectory, a growing number of performers are expanding their professional practice to include pedagogy. American voice teacher, Helen Swank, suggested "This is the period when, for the first time, voice teaching has become a professional entity in itself; not a lot of performers start teaching because they quit performing. There is now a different direction" (Blades-Zeller, 2002, p. 231).

Stanberg and Bennett (2006, p. 1), referred to the growth in the number of performers seeking to broaden their professional profile through teaching as a significant shift in identity profiles. Richard Miller suggested that the seasonal nature of employment for singers in America has led to an increased number of vocal pedagogues who concurrently pursue joint career paths (1996, p. 34).

This study found that voice teachers engaged at a tertiary level within Australia fall into three categories:

- Teachers who pursue full-time performance careers for a significant period of time, then retire from the stage to teach.
- Teachers who concurrently pursue both teaching and performance careers.
- Teachers who have had relatively short performance careers and long, illustrious teaching careers.

Within the context of this study, half the participants were active performer–teachers as described by the second category. The remaining participants were non-active performer–teachers represented by the first and third profile descriptions.

In light of changing professional employment for singers and the widespread perception of shorter singing careers, performer–teachers assume a key role in vocal pedagogy at a tertiary level. An environment of restricted university funding for the costly training of tomorrow's opera singers means it is necessary to identify and evaluate the role of the performer–teacher in institutional settings. The change in institutional governance, which came about in Australian institutions of higher education in the early 1990s and gradually throughout much of the world, led to the amalgamation of a majority of independent conservatoires with universities. Amalgamation arrangements have often prompted comment about the purpose of higher education given the generic, force-fit imposed on conservatories by universities (Schippers, 2007). This change to institutional culture altered the working profile and expectations of tertiary level performer–teachers. A shift in educational paradigms has also exposed the "untrained" status of performers who enter the teaching environment with no prior experience or formal training as teachers. Stephen Grant of Victoria College of the Arts (VCA) believes that "vocal teaching in some ways is maybe the most wildly divergent, in terms of approaches. Potentially the most out of date and out of touch teaching can take place in the context of tertiary vocal education" (SG). This perspective will be explored further, later in the chapter.

Duality of Performing–Teaching Roles

It is uncertain whether the two worlds do coexist in the same person simultaneously or whether the performer–teacher subjugates one role for the other at any given time. Persson (1994) suggested that the two roles of artist and pedagogue may be ascribed to the same individual but are, "different roles as well as different skills in different contexts" (p. 89), a view supported by voice teacher Janice Chapman: "They're separate and individual skills and talents and they're not naturally interchangeable. They're two separate strands" (JC).

Performer–Teacher Knowledge

Bearing in mind the synergies between performer–teacher roles and singer roles, it is useful to explore the perspective of performer–teachers in terms of knowledge, their contribution to student learning and the challenges they face within a tertiary institutional setting, as well as considerations for institutions themselves.

Blades-Zeller believed that "a performance background is essential to teaching excellence as without that first-hand knowledge and empathy, a teacher cannot truly identify and convey relevant information and insights to the student" (2002, p. 231). Richard Miller suggested that the process of performing and teaching requires the teacher to keep a "better check on his own singing; the teacher/performer concurrently teaches both himself and others" (1996, p. 34), a view supported by Janice Chapman when reflecting on her early years as a teacher:

> I was still singing and making explorations and mistakes myself, as a singer. And then going, "Come on Janice, you can work this out, what are you doing?" And then going from the feel of things, the sensation of things, and aligning that with the new knowledge I was getting. Had I not still been performing, that whole end of things wouldn't have happened. It's like I was still getting up there and doing it, and that for me was a very, very important part of how I was developing as a teacher. (JC)

In recent interviews with selected Australian tertiary vocal pedagogues, the following comments emerged in support of these views:

> I think that to know intimately and continually as much as possible what it feels like to sing at the optimal physiological, acoustic and emotionally expressive level is crucial. It increases the ability to empathise with what's going on in a singer's throat. That's a major tool for teachers. (RC)

> Teaching has helped my singing immensely. I'm obviously analysing the students every day, but I've been very lucky to be able to combine the two. (BR)

Greg Massingham also makes reference to the constant review and analysis performers conduct of their own singing and performance — overcoming their own shortcomings and bringing that knowledge to the teaching studio.

Aural Modelling as a Teaching Tool

In the vast reservoir of knowledge and experiences that performers acquire over an extended period of time, the role of modelling is frequently referred to, especially with regards to the utilisation of an aural library in teaching. Joseph Ward, reflecting on the high calibre of singers who served as quality models in his early professional days, notes that:

> When you consider the singers that were around: Del Monaco, Vickers, Leontyne Price, Callas, Tebaldi, all of those wonderful voices ... I got to hear those voices and those sounds have remained in my ears. The fact that one has standards of one's own ears makes you choosy about the sounds they (students) make. (JW)

Greg Massingham, speaking of hearing Sir Peter Pears, who would later become his voice teacher relates how:

> ... when I was 13, I heard his voice. I didn't know who he was. That was the Saint Paul on the road to Damascus moment for me, hearing his voice. So, in many ways, his voice was the thing that actually turned me to music as an art form. (GM)

> Someone who has sung at the Met has probably been a pretty superb singer at some stage in their life and has been around other superb singers. They are going to have something special to bring, an embodied knowledge of repertoire, a knowledge of working with other excellent young and experienced singers, experience of looking down someone else's gullet while they're doing it, experience of the huge variety there is in vocal technique. For instance, some people sing top notes with their mouths a foot open and some people don't open at all. (RC)

> I think it's important to expose oneself to the highest level of singing that one can possibly hear. We've noticed that if someone goes off to hear Renee Fleming or someone, they come back for the next lesson singing better. So there are definitely things that — whether that's the empathetic nervous system providing information or whether it's also just inspiration. I know for me, it was critical to have fantastic musicians to want to emulate. (SG)

Performer Skills as Distinct From Knowledge

The following section contains an inventory of performer knowledge drawn from interviews with leading Australian tertiary level voice teachers. All interviewees recognised an explicit set of skills that constitute a professional singer's craft. These included: a high level of vocal, linguistic, stylistic and musical proficiency; insightful interpretation, movement, acting, dance; a knowledge of platform and theatre etiquette; professional conduct including dress, entrepreneurship, negotiation of contracts, representation, image and self-promotion; and a knowledge of the basic geography of a theatre or stage and its negotiation. In the context of singer knowledge, these attributes are often taken for granted and not referred to directly in reflective observations about what singers know.

From interviews with 12 performer–teachers engaged at a tertiary level, five main clusters of conviction and constructs emerge:

Vocal Health and Wellbeing

- They know how to look after their voice, how much rest is needed, how much energy it takes to sing, what sort of diet to pursue, the types of restrictions one puts on oneself for the sake of a performance.
- They know how to negotiate long rehearsal periods and lengthy performance runs.
- They know how to sing with a cold or a sore throat.
- They understand the need to train properly.
- They know the challenges of travelling and singing, the effects of air conditioning, jetlag, fatigue and climactic changes on the voice and how to cope with the effect of hormonal changes on the voice and how to sing through that.

Emotional and Psychological Perspectives

- The need for psychological armour — just enough to protect yourself, but not so much that the audience can't get in.
- They know the joy of performing and the importance of that.
- They know viscerally what it feels like to fly, when something works beautifully.
- They know fear and failure.
- They understand performance anxiety and what happens to the voice under pressure.
- They understand emotional boundaries and performed emotion.
- They understand the personal psychological resources required to cope with the demands of professional life.
- They know the vulnerability inherent in performance.

Performer as Communicator

- Performers have an understanding of persona acquired through the performance process.
- They know how to adopt a persona that is out of the ordinary, serious, individual.
- They understand the difference in the internal experience of demonstrating something in the studio and actually engaging an audience.
- They know how to engage an audience.
- They know the physical and psychological freedom that comes with sound technique.
- They understand the transformative power of music.

Experiential Knowledge

- They know how to sing in difficult acoustics.
- They know how to follow a conductor.
- They have practical knowledge.
- They know the importance of the ears and the imagination.
- They understand motor learning.
- They know how to learn a role or individual piece of music.
- They know how to perform while coping with distractions, such as emotional issues, a bad acoustic, a terrible accompanist, conductor or orchestra.
- They know how to filter information.
- They know how to weather the loneliness and the isolation.
- They know how to deal with criticism from press, colleagues, conductors and so on.
- They understand that being a singer is a hard life.
- They know the anomalies that exist in singing, such as singers with crazy breathing techniques who sing extraordinarily beautifully.
- They know that there are different aesthetic values that people bring to singing ideals.
- They understand the variations that exist in performance — that even at the highest level there are people who sing remarkably badly as well as those whose work inspires.
- They understand the need to isolate oneself for adequate performance preparation.

The Importance of Self

- They know their own limitations, which makes them more open to analysis and continuous learning.

- They understand what it is to have a relationship with music.
- They know how to wear multiple hats.
- They understand the importance of individualism.
- They understand the need to take their music seriously, but not themselves seriously.
- They understand the need to strike a balance between technical proficiency and artistic integrity.

The way in which performers utilise this knowledge and experience, and apply it to the teaching process is largely dependent on their individual journeys. Formative experiences as a learner, early professional career, as well as ongoing activity as performer, teacher and researcher, serve to shape the pedagogical emphasis and the level of scrutiny a teacher applies to their own work and selves. "To be able to see other people with clarity, you have to see yourself with clarity" (personal interview with Neil Semer, 2008). Chapman concurred, "My own story is an integral part of the journey to my current philosophy and methodology" (2006, p. xvii).

Yet, it is widely recognised that an ability to perform does not ensure an ability to teach, "Not every great singer is necessarily a great voice teacher; such experience provides no guarantee for knowing (or caring) how to teach" (Blades-Zeller, 2002, p. 231). Miller cautioned institutions against the appointments of big name singers saying, "It would be detrimental to the teaching profession if great performing ability were to be mistaken for great ability in teaching" (1984, p. 42), although he concurred that the growing number of performer–teachers in America has improved the overall standard and national reputation for singing (1996, p. 28). This is a view echoed by Rowena Cowley, who stated that in Europe the traditional approach of passing on one's artistry remains the prevailing pedagogical model. Whereas in America, the recognition of the strengths in rigorous pedagogical courses underpinning performance training is the established norm and a key contributing factor to the high standard of singing in the US (RC).

The Role of the Teacher's Personal Journey as Pedagogical Stimulus

Interviews with Australian tertiary pedagogues revealed a large percentage of teachers who acknowledged a type of crisis — vocal, physical or emotional (or all three) — as being a key stimulus to their teaching strategies and critical rationale. A widely held belief that teachers who have worked through technical or personal difficulties are often better able to facilitate change in the teaching studio, is supported by Miller (1996, p. 29). "The worst thing that can happen to you is the best thing that can happen to you" (NS).

However, most teachers interviewed expressed a strong need to observe personal and emotional boundaries in managing the impact of their own personal experience on the learner.

> Having resolved one's own icky things personally and performing-wise, I feel a sense of responsibility to not visit my emotional world too strongly or inappropriately on students. (RC)

Throughout the course of interviews, still to be completed, it became clear that the adage "teach as you were taught" was not something that resonated with any of the voice teachers interviewed for this study. While acknowledging the influences of previous teachers as key influences at a particular stage of their development, a majority of teachers felt little or nothing of their current pedagogy could be traced to the methodology of their formative training; rather that through a carefully constructed vocal pedagogy based on practical experience, critical reflection and ongoing research, they had "created" a teacher from whom they would like to have learned, encapsulated in Janice Chapman's reflective question, "Where was I when I needed me?" (JC).

Challenges of Performer–Teachers in Institutions

Singers who become voice teachers with no professional training as educators, often with unidentified or unresolved issues as "failed" or "damaged" performers, can present challenges within an institutional setting.

> A lot of the time performers are very self centred ... they have to be if they're top notch. (JC)

> A lot of high profile artists have spent their lives performing. Often, they have dealt with a narrow range of technical issues specific to their own needs. Therefore, they lack a broad view of technique. Many are natural singers who functioned well in their youth because of their brilliant gift and had very few technical deficits. Then they begin to teach when their voices go into crisis and their career ends. (NS)

> I think some form of pedagogical understanding is critical, so that you're not imposing your own ideas or problems onto your students. (SG)

The performer–teacher runs the risk of bringing not just their experience and knowledge to the teaching and learning environment, but their "baggage" too. Identifying the constructive and potentially destructive elements that accompany performance knowledge and experience are a pedagogical concern. Susan Lee identified similarities with the field of dance education, "The most insidious of the problems are the ways in which unresolved personal issues with a career transition are communicated to the next generation" (1997, p. 39).

> One of the things I think is regrettable is that people who are teaching performers — and it's often performers who are teaching performers — are actually not always respectful of the teaching process or the fact that they are actually involved in an educational process. (RC)

> Schools of music believe they need the marquee appeal of famous singers' names on their teaching roster to attract students. In a more perfect world, they would do a more exhaustive search to see who really has a gift for teaching and developing students' technique and artistry. Bringing in famous singers for master classes, motivational speeches and question answering is great. However, the presumption that a great singer is a fine teacher without really investigating whether that is the case often doesn't yield the desired and presumed result. (NS)

Skilled Versus Unskilled Performer–Teachers

Issues surrounding a lack of formal teacher training of singer–teachers in Australian tertiary institutions are raised in the following discussion.

> Personally, I feel it's not okay not to be skilled in the ways you can be in order to teach. I have no illusions that a Masters degree is going to make somebody into a fantastic teacher. I hope that it will alert them to the fact that there is a body of knowledge and experience, and that they should continue to learn about it. I'd like to help them become familiar with that body of knowledge and to model an openness of mind. I'd like to see pedagogy students develop a point of view which is critical in a positive way of the information they come across and gives them some basis on which to be able to assess it. (RC)

> I remember that feeling of feeling terrified for at least the first semester. (GM).

However, Paul McMahon feels that performance credentials should remain the principal criteria for teaching appointments at tertiary level.

> I would be doubtful about the standard of vocal training that went on in an institution if it was appointing vocal teachers who a) weren't performers, but b) were there because they had some type of Master of Education degree or something like that. (PM)

Roland Persson's study (1994, p. 89) of a number of performance teachers at a renowned British music institution concluded that the lack of formal teacher training among performance staff disadvantaged and potentially damaged the student to such a degree that the student would be better served learning from "a gifted pedagogue than a musical maestro" (p. 89).

> If they're performers who have never taken an interest in what's going on around them, in their colleagues, or who have never done

> any teaching at all, quite often they're remarkably distant from the process. They really don't know how they do it themselves and they've never taken an interest in what goes on to make it happen. So I think that performers are not automatically teachers, although as a teacher you do benefit hugely from having been out there doing it. (JC)

Gaunt's study (2006, p. 1) of performance teachers engaged in one-to-one teaching at a tertiary level found that only a very small percentage of those teachers had received any training prior to commencement of teaching. Miller suggested that performers who want to teach should take the time to acquire an appropriate understanding of their instrument that "goes beyond their own personal performance acumen" (1996, p. 35). Furthermore, "If the teacher is an over-the-hill opera divo or diva, the student may pick up some tendencies it might be better not to have picked up" (Miller, in Blades-Zeller, 2004, p. 219). The advancements that continue to be made in the area of voice and voice-related disciplines have served to alter the way in which singers sing and the way singers teach. While this allows performer–teachers with a pedagogical emphasis aligned to enhanced cooperation and collaboration with other voice professionals to find greater credibility within an academic setting, it can polarise teaching styles if empirical methods are adhered to more closely. Voice teacher and researcher Janice Chapman supports this view (2006).

Words to describe sound and its production have been passed on further, written down, reinterpreted, understood/misunderstood and so on. With the scientific, anatomic, and multidisciplinary knowledge now at our disposal, I hope that the singing/teaching profession can agree to explore and use more common language.

The following comment from one of the world's greatest singers highlights the disregard for vocal pedagogy, which can prove problematic for tertiary institutions in appointing famous performers to their teaching staff. "There is a lot of hoohah goes on about it and one hears singers refer to 'the muscles of the throat.' I say that if I feel anything in my throat, it means I'm singing badly — either holding back or forcing the sound, or having something wrong with me" (Dame Joan Sutherland in Matheopoulos, 1991, p. 195). In qualifying this quote, it should be noted that Dame Joan Sutherland did not teach voice; however, she did on occasion, conduct masterclasses.

Challenges to Performer–Teachers in the Tertiary Environment

In interviews conducted with selected Australian tertiary level voice teachers, the challenges of working as a performer–teacher within an institutional environment were raised. Balancing the demands of a dual career was cited by those concurrently teaching and performing. These demands were most frequently in terms of time available for practice and preparation; however, several teachers also referred to the changes in persona required in transitioning between one role and the other. Performer–teachers seemed to recognise, however, the use of persona in creating professional identity, both in the teaching studio and on the stage, and that the ability of performer–teachers to utilise these roles as well as transition between them was a skill directly attributable to performance experience. Greg Massingham referred to a heightened affinity with persona and the ability to change it from student to student.

> ... the energy of the persona, whether it be sort of a little more earthy, as I might be with some students, more hands off with other students, who are emotionally vulnerable, or downright aggressive with people who need to pull their proverbial finger out. They are all hopefully personalities from the same source. (GM)

Teacher guilt emerged as a common experience for performers constantly striving to balance the demands of maintaining a meaningful and productive performance career with the demands of teaching and academic responsibilities.

> I should have been much more selfish. I would have given much better performances. I would have been a much better singer. I would have had more time to reflect on the performances and the whole environment of the performance, which in turn would inform my teaching. (GM)

Three themes emerged as central to the discussion:

Time Management

- The challenge of pacing oneself.
- Balancing the workload of teaching and performing.
- Juggling touring commitments with an academic timetable.
- Negotiating those aspects of performing that upset normal routine.
- The impact of a disjointed teaching schedule on student learning.

Institutional Constraints

- A lack of support or recognition of performer–teachers from tertiary institutions.
- The benefits they provide to teaching and learning in the form of institutional profiling and student recruitment.
- The demotivation of negative things institutions put in the way.
- Finding a way to disconnect from administrative demands when performances are pending.

- Tacit pressure to teach on the day of a performance (institutional expectations).
- Absence of mentorship programs for teachers of voice in Australian institutions — should follow instrumental models more of master teacher and apprentice in a bid to utilise the time of performer–teachers more appropriately

Challenge to Personal Psychical, Psychological and Emotional Resources

- Finding the physical energy and time to focus on performance and preparation.
- Frequent transitioning required, from self-focused performer to student-focused teacher.
- Shepherding one's energies to focus one's work not only on oneself, but on one's performing colleagues.
- The mental and physical demands of making up missed lessons owing to performance commitments.
- Balancing the duality of professional identity both personally and professionally.
- Guilt over apportioning time for performance preparation, being made to feel as though on is shirking one's responsibilities.
- Pressure to be invincible.
- Having to be protective of oneself, physically, mentally, emotionally, vocally.

Brenda-Jo Smith (2004–2005) supported these findings:

> Artists generally gather their powers for mental agility and artistic freshness outside the press of worldly routines. For many performers, solitude is the main source for mental and spiritual readiness. For these artists, the communal act of teaching was not seen as conducive to their work as performers. (p. 9)

Student Perceptions of Performer–Teachers

How do students regard the role of the performer–teacher and its impact on their learning experience at tertiary level? Interviews with tertiary vocal students conducted at the Queensland Conservatorium, Griffith University, uncovered a range of views expressing both positive and negative experiences of studying with a performer–teacher.

Having the opportunity to observe their teacher in performance and to be engaged in apprenticeship style performance settings were also two recurring themes recognised as benefits to student learning. Below is a list of responses solicited from students regarding the benefits of studying with a performer–teacher. These observations fell into three distinct categories:

Professional Credibility and Model of the Profession

- Students recognised the link between professional standing and teacher credibility.
- They appreciated that their teacher was well regarded by professional peers as being a good performer, good technician and reliable professional.
- They regarded their teacher as a model of professional behaviour and standards.
- Students believed that continued work as a performer lends greater integrity and generally liked the idea of having a teacher that is recognised to be a good performer and good all rounder.
- They appreciated the seriousness in which their teacher takes her role as a performer.
- Teacher has current knowledge of repertoire and its suitability.
- Teacher has a demonstrated ability to utilise professional contacts.
- Teacher is familiar with the current professional environment and opportunities for engagement, knows where things are at.

Experiential Knowledge, Current and Advanced Technical Knowledge

- Can transfer knowledge from stage to studio, share experiences.
- Can trust that she knows how to look after her instrument and herself.
- Has the ability to empathise with issues, such as nerves, memorisation, juggling everyday life and performing.
- Knows what's expected in a real situation.
- Understands that what happens in a studio isn't at all what happens when you're on stage.
- Benefits of studying with someone who has overcome technical hurdles.

Personal Attributes and Persona

- Students recognise the qualities of empathy, sympathy, realism, motivation are present in the teaching and learning exchange.
- Empathic elements in her presence … way of presentation makes her stand out.
- She knows what makes a professional.
- Understands how to isolate and address issues to do with performing in public.
- An ability to identify with performance issues.
- Maintains the mindset and charisma of a performer.

- Encourages interaction with other voice professionals as imperative to learning.

Students' perceptions regarding the type of learning that takes place through observation of their teacher in performance or in performing alongside their teacher were also explored. Students also commented that an ability to observe their teacher in performance was an affirmation of their learning path.

> I think they also see how much preparation is involved and how meticulous your preparation has to be, not just from a vocal perspective, but from a musical perspective ... they always come back and they say, "Whoa gee, we're so lucky to have you here". (BR)

Many students spoke of the learning that takes place from watching their teacher in performance as being like having a lesson. "It's important for a teacher to have sung or be a singer, because you've got to try out things. They have to work for you if you're going to be able to teach them to somebody else" Swank (2002, p. 197).

Negative Perceptions

There were few negative observations made by students in regard to learning from a performer–teacher. The only recurring negative comments centred on the impact of a disrupted lesson schedule, although a number of students also conceded that this promoted independent learning. It was felt that although their teacher was fair about making up missed lessons, there were specific times throughout the year, such as examination periods, when teacher absences were especially disruptive to learning. "I think sometimes for younger students in the early part of their course it can be a little unsettling, because I think they develop better if they have a fairly structured, regular sort of lesson" (student interview 2007). Students also qualified some of their positive observations regarding performer–teachers by recognising "that good performers aren't always good teachers and good teachers aren't always good performers" (student interview 2007).

Conclusion

Australian tertiary music institutions are required to carefully evaluate the role of performers within a tertiary setting. As increasing funding constraints are experienced, performer–teacher profiles, as well as traditional modes of transmission, are routinely brought into question. What is striking about the data examined so far, is the profound pedagogical resources contained in the complex layering of accrued performer knowledge and experiential perspectives identified through a process of enquiry, and made manifest in the teaching and learning experience via explicit and tacit exchange. Clearly, it is an important teaching model that invites closer examination to consolidate its pedagogical standing within the tertiary setting.

The elements that make up a holistic approach to teaching and performing are embodied in the performer–teacher. While there is no established model or framework for understanding how this works, this study highlights a growing adherence by performer–teachers to a comprehensive pedagogical approach in utilising their unique reservoir of knowledge to impact student learning.

It is hoped that ongoing investigation into this relatively unexplored aspect of the learning experience of tertiary level classical singing students in Australia will serve to enrich the current body of pedagogical literature and identify the Australian profile for teaching in this sector.

Acknowledgments

The author would like to acknowledge contribution of the following Australian teachers in the preparation of this chapter:

- Janice Chapman (JC) interviewed October 8, 2006.
- Rowena Cowley (RC) interviewed April 12, 2008.
- Stephen Grant (SG) interviewed January 5,2009.
- Gregory Massingham (GM) interviewed July 23, 2008.
- Paul McMahon (PM) interviewed September 12, 2008.
- Joseph Ward (JW) interviewed January 7, 2008.
- Barry Ryan (BR) interviewed January 7, 2009.

In addition, the author would like to acknowledge the contribution of New York-based teacher, Neil Semer (NS), interviewed April 7, 2008.

References

Blades-Zeller, E. (2002). *A spectrum of voices: Prominent American voice teachers discuss the teaching of singing.* Lanham, MD: The Scarecrow Press.

Gaunt, H. (2006). *One-to-one relationships: A case study of teacher's perspectives on instrumental/vocal lessons in a conservatoire.* London: Guildhall School of Music and Drama, London.

Lee, S.A. (1997). The artist as teacher: A psychological perspective. *Medical Problems of Performing Artists, 12*, 38–40.

Matheopoulos, H. (1991). Diva: Great sopranos and mezzos discuss their art. London: Victor Gollancz.

Miller, R. (1996). On the art of singing. New York: Oxford University Press.

Miller, R. (1984). The great artist as teacher. *The NATS Bulletin, 41*(1), 42.

Mills, J. (2004). Working in music: Becoming a performer-teacher. *Music Education Research, 6*(3), 246–261.

Persson, R. (1994). Concert musicians as teachers: On good intentions falling short. *European Journal for Higher Ability*, *5*(1), 79–91.

Schippers, H. (2007). 'The marriage of art and academia: Challenges and opportunities for music research in practice-based environments'. *Dutch Journal of Music Theory*, *12*(1), 34–40.

Smith, B.J. (2004–2005). The performing teacher: The role of applied music in liberal arts education, Part two: The performer as a teacher. *NACWPI Journal*, *53*, 4–13.

Stanberg, A., & Bennett, D. (2006, February). *Performing a metamorphosis: A teaching performer or performing teacher.* Paper presented at the Guildhall Conference: The Reflective Conservatoire: Apprentices and Sorcerers? Guildhall School of Music and Drama, London.

Chapter
4

Eminent Singers' Recollections of Learning to Sing: The Importance of "Fit" Between Singer and Singing Teacher

Jessica O'Bryan

The model of one-to-one singing lessons is embedded in centuries-old tradition, and tacit and enculturated attitudes are commonly found in this learning and teaching mode. The impact of singing teachers on their pupils is documented in memoirs, biographies and documentaries, but it is only recently that researchers have begun to more closely examine the relationship between singer and teacher. A historical and biographical narrative analysis is a useful means of revealing the unexplored and implicit reliance singers place on their teachers, and helps to link current research with past practice. I undertook an autobiographical and biographical narrative analysis of four eminent singer biographies and autobiographies, embedding Riessman's definition of thematic analysis (2003) within this strategy. In particular, I examined the eminent Australian singer histories of Dame Nellie Melba, Dame Joan Hammond, June Bronhill OBE and Lauris Elms AM OBE, and developed themes employing Deci and Ryan's Self-Determination Theory (2000). Themes emerging from the analysis include relational aspects of trust, respect, support and friendship between teacher and singer. Other themes perceptible from the analysis are relationship codependency, power struggles, betrayal and misplaced loyalty. Sound pedagogical approaches and teacher expertise are also revealed to be vital to a singer's feelings of trust and respect towards their teacher. The themes emerging reveal the extent to which a singer may be dependent on their singing teacher, but also reveal the independence and self-reliance required by a young singer for future success.

> Luck plays such a great part in finding the right teacher and I thank my lucky stars that I fell into such good hands. But you must believe in your teachers and do what they say. (Lucia Popp: Matheopoulos, 1991, p. 147)

When I first read Lucia Popp's statement, I immediately agreed with its sentiment. It is indeed the lucky singer who does not experience a singing teacher lacking empathy, or one who teaches poor vocal technique, or who imparts incomprehensible ideas. It is also the lucky teacher whose student is quick to comprehend, who works hard and who is intrinsically motivated to succeed. This "fit" between teacher and singer, as Popp suggests, is an elusive ideal, and for every positive singer's story about their learning experience in singing, there are many more negative stories that paint a dire picture of the singing teaching and learning experience.

This chapter is concerned with unpacking singer attitudes and perceptions of their singing education experiences through a narrative thematic analysis of four eminent Australian singer biographies and memoirs. Analysis of biography and memoir is not new, but rarely have singer memoirs been examined closely as a means of revealing attitudes and philosophies about singing and singing teaching. Of the singers selected, Dame Nellie Melba, Dame Joan Hammond and June Bronhill OBE are deceased. Lauris Elms AM OBE at the time of writing was nearing 80 years-of-age. No biographies of Australian men were chosen for analysis, due to the paucity of biographical material available. The singers selected are representative of many Australian singer experiences throughout a 100-year period of Australian history, from approximately 1880 until 1990. The experiences recounted by each of the singers are in many instances similar, including their overseas study experiences, the financial assistance provided to them, their determination and hard work, and their early life experiences. Their comments about their singing teachers, however, reveal some markedly different experiences. It is these learning and teaching episodes that I have selected for analysis, employing Deci and Ryan's Self-Determination Theory (2000) to explicate some of the emerging themes.

The Classical Singing Teaching and Learning Experience

Writings about classical Western art singing and teaching span several hundred years. Tosi, in 1743, was one of the first to observe that:

> It may seem to many that every perfect singer must also be a perfect instructor, but it is not so; for his qualifications (though ever so great) are insufficient if he cannot communicate his sentiments with ease and in a method adapted to the ability of the scholar. (Galliard, 1987, p. 73)

These sentiments have not appreciably altered over the past few hundred years. Ease of communication, adaptability of teaching styles and the knowledge that a great singer does not necessarily make a great teacher are all sentiments expressed by singers and singing teachers today. Hines (1982) noted in the preface to his book *Great Singers on Great Singing* that:

> … this teacher–pupil relationship is critical, and it depends on the pupil's ingenuity as much as the teacher's. The pupil must have a facile mind that will lead him to experiment with his own inner vocal equipment, but that mind must always be subject to his teacher's critical judgment. (p. 15)

The teacher–pupil relationship is still considered important in the 21st century. Some conservatoires and music institutions seem to recognise the importance of "fit" of teacher to student, according to Presland, who noted in her 2005 study examining relationships between conservatoire students and instrumental professors, that:

> … relationships seem to work primarily because a great deal of time is put in to the matching of student to professor. Factors such as technical proficiency, musical maturity, personal independence, age, nationality, command of language and general personality are all considered carefully. (p. 246)

For singers, arguably their most significant learning relationship will be with their singing teacher. In Chapman's 2006 text *Singing and Singing Teaching*, McCarthy made the following observation: "When singers commit to learning, they offer themselves with the expectation that the teacher will enter into a relationship with them to develop and unfold their potential" (p. 156). This statement presents a number of critical concepts about the act of learning to sing: one is that singers commit to learning. This commitment to learning implies an intrinsic motivation to sing. This intrinsic motivation towards a selected goal is what Deci and Ryan (2000) considered a vital element in Self-Determination Theory, where they identify human needs as being "innate psychological nutriments that are essential for ongoing psychological growth, integrity, and well-being" (p. 228). Deci and Ryan identified three main needs in this theory as being competence "to engage optimal challenges and experience mastery or effectance in the physical and social worlds"; relatedness "to seek attachments and experience feelings of security, belongingness, and intimacy with others"; and autonomy "to self-organise and regulate one's own behavior" (p. 252). Singers who commit to learning have made a decision to develop their voice, and are moving from an intrinsic motivation to assistance from an extrinsic motivator — their singing teacher.

Another concept McCarthy presented in the earlier statement is that singers "expect" a beneficial learning and teaching relationship. This expectation can have both negative and positive consequences. As singing teachers, we rarely espouse a professional or business-like approach to our singing and learning transactions. However, singers are paying for a service that they may reasonably assume embodies expertise in the craft and art of singing. Schön (1983) wrote:

> Although the reflective practitioner should be credentialled and technically competent, his claim to authority is substantially based on his ability to manifest his special knowledge in interactions with his clients...Both client and professional bring to their encounter a body of understandings which they can only very partially communicate to one another and much of which they cannot describe to themselves. (p. 296)

This body of understandings may be substantially different between singer and teacher and it can be argued that it is the teacher's paid responsibility to discover and interpret them in order to meet the expectations of the singer. Likewise, singers may reasonably expect that the teacher will teach them the skills for which they have paid. If these expectations are not met, the relationship entered into may not succeed, with corresponding disappointment, and loss of trust and respect by both parties.

The other concept contained in the McCarthy sentence is the development of vocal potential. In Deci and Ryan's Self-Determination Theory, the desire for competence and autonomy are innate for the development of human psychological growth and wellbeing. It is the singing teacher's role to help develop the student's vocal potential, and the student must be allowed to feel competent and supported in this development. The student must also be capable of self-direction, and autonomous in decision-making processes about their voice. Without competency and autonomy, the singer is thwarted of these psychological needs, which "results invariably in negative functional consequences for mental health and often for ongoing persistence and performance" (p. 262). A singing teacher unable or unwilling to allow competency and autonomy in their student, is, at worst, risking poor psychological health of that student, as well as promoting an unhealthy reliance on the teacher.

McCarthy (2006) wrote that singers carry hopes "which may be rooted deep within the soul, and dreams. Some dreams will be disclosed — about repairing or strengthening vocal technique, or performing with presence — and other dreams may remain as secrets only to be revealed when the teacher has earned their trust and the right to share in them" (p. 156). These concepts of trust and respect are deeply embedded in both current vocal literature and emerging research, but are rarely explored. Deci and Ryan stated that a strong relatedness base "appears to provide a needed backdrop — a distal support — for intrinsic motivation, a sense of security that makes the expression of this innate growth tendency more likely and more robust" (p. 235). This need for security appears to be very important for singers, which might be explained in part by Kemp (1996), who wrote "the singer's instrument is personal, invisible, and very complex, and in a performance it is the vocalist's personality that is presented, together with any vocal defects that are perceived as belonging directly to him or her" (p. 173).

The voice is the speech centre, the prime mechanism whereby thoughts and feelings are articulated, and arguably the conduit to one's soul. McCarthy warned that "what happens between the singer and the teacher is therefore of great consequence" (p. 156). The consequence of a poor learning and teaching relationship on a singer may be profound. Many well-known singers write of early teachers who undermined their feelings of security and self-confidence through a cutting and dismissive attitude, or nearly ruined their voices through poor pedagogy. Birgit Nilsson recalled an experience with a singing teacher who had told her "'it doesn't matter if you have the best voice in the world if you have no brain, because it's really not for a farmer to become a singer'. I went home crying the first day. He was an impossible teacher. He had a poor technique ..." (Hines, 1982, p. 195). Feelings of incompetence by Birgit Nilsson were compounded by her teacher's dismissive attitude and poor pedagogy, and thwarted her need for competence that Deci and Ryan claim is innate to human psychological health, growth and wellbeing.

Deci and Ryan's Self-Determination Theory may be usefully applied to explicating the learning of classical singing, and to unpacking the narrative analyses contained in this chapter. The three main elements of the theory have been examined in the following biographical analyses: that motivation must be both intrinsic and extrinsic to the artist; that the artist must feel a sense of competence through positive reinforcement; and that the artist must feel autonomous, that is, independent and capable of self-direction.

Other relational themes include gratitude and reliance on singing teachers, suggesting relationships go far beyond the immediate vocal and psychological development of the singers. For some singers, respect for sound vocal pedagogy is paramount, whereas for others, the powerful connection to opportunities is the primary force for their choice of teacher. Whatever the preference, the relationship between singer and teacher is the lynchpin by which success is measured, and, therefore, a perfect "fit" must govern the choice of teacher to student. Some of this is based, as Popp states, on "luck" — being in the right place at the right time, such as Elms found. For others, having the right connections and knowing the right people is the deciding "fit" of teacher to singer.

The experiences recounted in these narratives are the personal views of the singers, from recollections spanning some fifty years. A hazard when analysing narrative is the potential difficulty in separating fact from fiction. Tactful omission may also shape the narrative, and memories may be distorted by time and distance from the event. However, Riessman (2003) reminds us that:

> ...narratives do not mirror, they refract the past. Imagination and strategic interests influence how storytellers choose to connect events and make them meaningful for others. Narratives are useful in research precisely because storytellers interpret the past rather than reproduce it as it was. The "truths" of narrative accounts are not in their faithful representations of a past world, but in the shifting connections they forge among past, present, and future. (p. 6)

In this analysis, singer perceptions and attitudes about singing teachers and teaching are of greatest import. By examining past practice and perceptions of these four eminent singers, we might identify common attitudes about singing teaching that are still evident today.

Dame Nellie Melba

Melba learnt from three singing teachers; her first, while a schoolgirl, was Madame Mary Ellen Christian, a Canadian mezzo-soprano with a short but brilliant career who had moved to Australia on medical advice. With her second teacher, Italian émigré Pietro Cecchi, Melba initially enjoyed a very warm relationship, later repudiated by harsh comments in her second autobiography. Melba's last teacher, and most famous, was Mathilde Marchesi.

Melba is variously written about as a vain, shallow, self-centered woman with stars in her eyes; Cargher claimed that "by our standards Melba was not a nice person" (Melba, 1980, p. v), but also admits that she "was capable of great generosity, both in helping young singers and ordinary folk in distress, that her faith in her protégés was usually misplaced" (p. x). This Janus-like quality of Melba may help to explain some of her surprising attitudes towards her teachers — particularly her savage harshness towards Cecchi, who, it is now generally acknowledged, was the real builder of Melba's silvery voice.

Cecchi is noted as "a middle-aged tenor with an impressive black moustache and a volatile nature who had ... studied singing at the Academy of Music in Rome" (Blainey, 2008, p. 15). He had arrived in 1871 and was quickly acknowledged for his skills as a teacher. Cecchi "... trained his singers in the bel canto way," although he "was not a disciple of the great

Manuel Garcia" (p. 16). Cecchi soon realised Melba's potential, noting that "She was very quick and clever, and studied very hard" (p. 16). Cecchi considered that he was to Melba a friend, ally and even confidante. He allowed her to take lessons from him when she had no means to pay him back, and Melba wrote to him from overseas prior to her lessons with Marchesi. He was clearly not the "small, dark, swarthy figure and bright avaricious eyes" (Melba, 1925, p. 8) of her final encounter with him that she spoke of in her last memoirs, which recounts a tale of him demanding financial compensation for the lessons given her.

Cecchi supported Melba both financially and as a friend until her departure overseas. He was also intended to be a guest soloist at her farewell concert. Apparently, "… in Melbourne it was observed that Cecchi was 'visibly swelling with pride'" (Blainey, 2008, p. 45) and at her final concert at the Melbourne Town Hall, his gift to her was a "gold laurel wreath tied with long white silk streamers, across which ran the golden inscription 'Presented to his pupil by Signor Cecchi'" (Blainey, 2008, p. 47).

Cecchi held Melba in very high regard, not only because of her ability to learn quickly and her work ethic, but because his reputation as a teacher was improved as a result of her success. This mutual benefit is quite common in singing teaching, but it is a double-edged sword. Such a relationship, based on a marriage of convenience, can have unforeseen consequences for both parties. In the case of Melba and Cecchi, the consequences were a blackening of Cecchi's name after his death. In the case of Melba and Marchesi, the consequences affected others.

Melba credited Marchesi for the quality of her voice. Mathilde Marchesi, at the time, was "the most powerful teacher in Paris, the opera capital of Europe" (Cargher, 1980/1925, p. viii) and Melba was loyal to her even after Marchesi died. Melba considered her one of the greatest artists she had ever known:

> She was not only a superb technician; she also had a burning spirit of enthusiasm which made one feel even when one was singing a scale that one was singing something beautiful. From the beginning she showed me how inferior all my other teachers had been. (Melba, 1925, p. 18)

She wrote:

> I could write pages about Madame Marchesi, for she was the first woman who really began my education. Not only was she my artistic mother — she was my guide and sponsor in other things as well. I knew nothing of life. (Melba, 1925, p. 18)

Melba certainly knew very little of Paris life, but she was 25 years of age, she had been married and had borne a son. She was hardly an innocent.

Melba mercifully ignored Marchesi's quirks, such as not washing one's hair or taking baths. Melba took many of Marchesi's other eccentricities to heart, however, such as not riding horses because Marchesi considered the activity "bad for the vocal cords" (Melba, 1980/1925, p. 20). Melba noted in her autobiography: "I know better now, but in those days her word was law, and I abided by it" (Melba, 1980/1925, p. 20). This domination of her students was Marchesi's strength, and also her weakness.

At 65 years-of age, Marchesi had experienced hostility from previous students and had not trained a star pupil for many years. Despite her lack of star pupils, Marchesi was a powerful woman in opera circles and in high demand as a teacher. Dame Elise Wiedermann in Melbourne gave Melba a letter of introduction to Marchesi, and this opportunity was not lost on the young singer. Melba's success was due, in great part, to the Marchesi connections. Radic (1986) wrote that "Melba was right to put her trust in this woman. The evidence was there that she could carry out her promises she made to her students. The price Melba paid was betrayal of Cecchi" (p. 45). Melba maintained her loyalty to Marchesi all her life, even as the senile old woman refused to believe that Melba was whom she claimed at their last meeting. Melba recounted that "she spoke to me no more, and I left the house feeling that I had lost one of my dearest friends, to whom I owed my deepest debt of gratitude, for she was indeed more than a mother to me. And I loved her" (Melba, 1925/1980, p. 21).

Elphinstone and Hancock (2005) wrote that Melba's loyalty to Marchesi blinded her to the "old woman's advancing years" (p. 51). After Melba's success, they noted, many Antipodean singers chose to study with Marchesi, but they came when she was well past her prime. Marchesi's tuition has been directly blamed for vocal difficulties faced by Amy Castles and Evelyn Scotney, and while Melba persisted in sending singers to Paris to study with Marchesi, so the problems continued. This loyalty may be explained in part by Melba's very great appreciation for Marchesi's strict teaching methods. She recalled that "she at least would have taught them that no one is an artist who has not taken infinite pains, that there is no other sure road to success, and that detail, detail, detail must be the rule by which their lives are guided" (Melba, 1925/1980, p. 216). Marchesi was also known to dominate her pupils "like a female Svengali" (p. 239) and Melba, despite her intelligence, determination and natural fire, may have accepted this position as one befitting a lowly Australian without many other options.

Melba's relationships with her teachers were marked by a number of features. First, Melba used her teachers as stepping-stones to success. Cecchi was acknowledged as one of the best teachers in Melbourne and Melba recognised this, even as a young woman barely out of school. Marchesi was a powerful influence in operatic circles and Melba used her wealthy family connections to gain access to this important teacher. Second, Melba befriended her teachers. She was a friend to Cecchi and leant on him in times of hardship, which he warmly reciprocated, and she considered Marchesi to be more than a mother and one of her dearest friends. Third, she felt an overwhelming sense of gratitude for the opportunities given to her, which saw her reward Marchesi to the point of error. Fourth, she trusted her teachers. She entrusted Marchesi with her voice, her vocal training and her career choices for, as she recalled when she had chosen to ignore Marchesi's advice about singing Brünnhilde, "... from the moment when the curtain went up and I began to sing, I knew that Madame Marchesi had been right and I had been wrong" (Melba, 1925/1980, p. 110). Melba credits Marchesi as having the strongest influence on her life.

The themes of loyalty, trust, respect, familial association and influence are characteristic of a number of singer biographies, although they are by no means the only features of the singer–teacher relationship. As has been noted in Melba's example, other marks of a singer–teacher relationship can include betrayal, contempt, poor pedagogical advice and loss of trust.

Dame Joan Hammond

Dame Joan Hammond attended the Sydney Conservatorium, learning singing and violin. Her singing teacher there was a Mr Spencer Thomas, about whom, apart from mentioning his name, she makes no comment. On graduation, Hammond joined a repertory company after graduation for £3 per week and enjoyed a happy time there, while also competing in the NSW Golf Championship. Her time in Australia seems characterised by consistent hard work and while she mentions that she continued her singing lessons, she does not mention with whom. This oversight does not seem deliberate, but it suggests a fundamental characteristic of Hammond's persona. She was an independent learner and teacher; personality was of little use to her if she did not learn the appropriate skills. It was the pedagogy that was important.

Hammond had commenced her travels to Europe with help from a golf fund, and she began daily lessons with a Frau Eibenschütz in Vienna, as well as having daily coaching sessions with a Herr Gomboz. Hammond, in her autobiography, made frequent mention of her repetiteurs and coaches — she appeared to learn as much from them as she did from any of her teachers. She was also aware over time of a lack of progress in her singing lessons with Frau Eibenschütz, and eventually resolved to change teachers:

> She was not one of the best known teachers by any mean...I knew that the extensions of my voice were not developing as they should, and I could see no point in spending money to remain vocally static.

> It was a tearful 'break-away', but it had to be done"(Hammond, 1970, p. 67).

Hammond's autobiography reveals a pragmatic woman whose choices were ultimately not dictated by strong loyalty towards her teachers, although she felt great love and affection for her friends and family. She refused to remain with teachers who wasted her time and money, and her lessons with tenor Dino Borgioli are particularly illuminating.

Hammond was introduced to Borgioli and his wife by an acquaintance in London. Lessons soon commenced four times per week, although Hammond was warned not to tell anyone that Dino was teaching her. Hammond soon "began to have doubts about his teaching", as her "throat muscles tired easily. This worried Dino, but the trouble soon passed and the voice began to develop" (Hammond, 1970, p. 73). Borgioli was a renowned tenor, and was performing in Salzburg, in Verdi's Falstaff. The Borgioli couple invited Hammond along as chauffeur in return for reduced lesson fees, and she admitted to learning a tremendous amount from attending rehearsals, having singing lessons and daily coaching sessions with Alberto Erede, who "was meticulous over the smallest details, and he was no clock watcher either. He went on and on — time was of no account; only the music. A session with him was most stimulating" (Hammond, 1970, p. 74).

Hammond's relationship with Dino Borgioli deteriorated during the Falstaff season, due in part to disagreements over a contract Hammond was due to start in Vienna, which Dino prevented her from fulfilling. She wrote, "once again, I was having great doubts about Dino as a teacher" (Hammond, 1970, p. 76). She was furious about the contract, and became ill. She wrote:

> I knew my voice was not as it should be. I have always known instinctively that nature is the surest, safest guide to voice training. If the cords become inflamed or the muscles tire easily, the voice is not being properly produced. I had reached a critical point. (Hammond, 1970, p. 76)

At this time, she was offered a Glyndebourne contract in the chorus, but refused it, despite vociferous arguments from the Borgiolis. Hammond wrote, "It was a confused time in which I felt I was being pushed hither and thither, often to no point and without any consideration for what I myself wanted" (Hammond, 1970, p. 77).

Hammond did not take kindly to the meddling of the Borgioli couple, despite their apparent generosity, and struck out on her own, accepting the contract at the Vienna Volksoper and graduating eventually to the Staatsoper. She noted that on her return to London, there was pressure from her friends and from Dino himself for her to have more lessons with him, which she did so grudgingly, out of a sense of loyalty to those who were helping her and out of fear of angering Dino's many supporters.

Characteristic of the Hammond and Dino Borgioli relationship was Borgioli's insistence that Hammond continue lessons with him, despite her repeated refusals. His fees were expensive and she disagreed with him "on the question of breathing"(Hammond, 1970, p. 85). As Hammond's success grew, so did Borgioli's reliance on teaching as a source of income, and the previous secrecy over lessons was now forgotten. Later in her memoir, Hammond recounted "my lessons with Dino had virtually stopped as they were beyond my means, and in any case breathing was still a bone of contention between us" (Hammond, 1970, p. 105). Hammond's particular vocal issues at this time included problems with breath management, and Dino's techniques were not successful for her. She was convinced that:

> … abdominal breathing was the best whereas Dino liked, not clavicular breathing, but a sort of relation of it which kept the breath high. After three or four lessons I felt my throat muscles tensing, and my voice tired quickly as a result of keeping the breath too high. (Hammond, 1970, p. 105)

While Hammond did not dismiss the Borgioli influence entirely, she made it clear from her autobiography that she was not a singer to be dominated by her teacher. She noted at this time "I had never been spoken to in such a way, neither did I think he had the right to impose his will on me" (Hammond, 1970, p. 76). This dislike of extrinsic control is a key characteristic of loss of autonomy. Clearly, Hammond did not appreciate this domination, nor did she enjoy the loss of competence that came with poor vocal technique. She chose to end the relationship.

After the war, Hammond met ear, nose and throat specialist Ivor Griffiths, whom she claimed was "both friend and saviour as far as my voice was concerned. If Ivor advised me to stop singing, I would stop — I had absolute faith in him" (Hammond, 1970, p. 149). This relationship proved to be a vital one for Hammond, for, after her experiences with Dino Borgioli, she placed no trust in singing teachers. In vocal disarray, due to poor habits and vocal misuse, she became an autodidact, learning vocal physiology and experimenting with scales and exercises until she knew "… what corrective measures to adopt, anywhere, at any time" (Hammond, 1970, p. 165). She would have weekly check ups with Ivor Griffiths to ensure she was not damaging her voice. Her voice rebuild took her three years "… spent in trial and error. There were times of progress and retrogression, of happiness and disappointment, according to the success or failure of my efforts towards self-mastery. It was engrossing and rewarding" (Hammond, 1970, p. 165).

Hammond's mistrust of singing teachers was well founded — in a later chapter, she recounted the story of hearing two young girls sing who were being taught appalling techniques by a young American teacher. She wrote that "There is so much charlatanism in the world of singing teachers, and here was a big fake before me" (Hammond, 1970, p. 183). Hammond clearly trusted only her own teaching, and, after many years of vocal unwieldiness, was probably right to do so. She claimed that it was not until 1950 that she erased all of her bad vocal habits: she was then 38 years of age.

Hammond's own experiences with her singing teachers coloured her opinion of singing teachers generally. She distrusted them and learnt to rely on her own proprioceptive abilities to diagnose and treat her vocal ailments with the help of a reliable ear nose and throat doctor. Unlike the experiences of other singers, her independent and inquiring mind proved to be her best counsel, and she warned against charlatans in her autobiography.

The no nonsense, independent attitude of this Australian singer towards singing teaching expertise is an attitude mirrored in the experiences of Melba, Bronhill and Elms. Each singer, as they became more secure in their vocal development and ability to sense good from bad singing, was able to make decisions about the worth and expertise of their teacher and to make changes where necessary. A singer must develop a near invulnerable sense of autonomy and competence that will manifest despite youth and inexperience, as is evident in June Bronhill's narrative.

June Bronhill OBE

June Bronhill's breezy autobiography reveals a very personal connection to each of her teachers. Her first teacher in Broken Hill, at 15 years-of-age, was Molly Carrack-Morgan, who was, according to Bronhill (1987), "quite a vicious old thing at times" (p. 26). Bronhill noted that she was unbelievably strict, particularly about diction and the phrasing of songs, and that over the years

> … so many people have commented on the things that this wonderful woman in Broken Hill taught me. They comment on my diction, on my phrasing, my sense of style and on the way I use the words so importantly and the way that I feel for the words. (Bronhill, 1987, p. 27)

Bronhill maintained a similar attitude towards each of her teachers, except for her first Sydney based teacher, Hector Fleming, who, she claimed "became a little free with his hands. I didn't like this but didn't know how to handle it" (Bronhill, 1987, p. 29). She was, at this time, having free lessons with Fleming, and "I thought I had to get away from all this because I was an innocent girl from Broken Hill and I didn't like men touching me up!" (Bronhill, 1987, p. 29). At the start, "All went well for quite a while" (p. 29)

Then, after she came third in the Sydney Sun Aria, Fleming, delighted with her success, started teaching her songs that were

> … too heavy for my voice. For instance, at the ripe old age of twenty, as I was then, he was teaching me to sing things like 'Ritorna Vincitor' from Aida and I knew that this was completely wrong for me — it was much too dramatic and heavy for my voice. (Bronhill, 1987, p. 29)

Bronhill's next teacher was the well-known Marianne Mathy. Bronhill wrote devotedly about the relationship she and Marianne shared, stating "she was unbelievable — half French, half German — a martinet. I got on very well with her, I suppose, partly because we were both Cancerians, and she felt a great love for me almost immediately" (Bronhill, 1987, p. 30). Bronhill's preparedness for her teacher's foibles is indicative of a student well able to look after herself, and one not intimidated by her teacher's personality. She commented "I thought she was pretty fantastic because I was … a pretty cheeky kid, and I knew how to handle things so that if she ever got stroppy with me, I would just laugh it off" (Bronhill, 1987, p. 30). This strong, independent streak seems indicative of many eminent singers and appears to be integral to the personality of an opera artist. She recalled, "I'd been told by lots of other students of hers that at some stage of the game she'd have you in floods of tears because 'she's so evil and wicked and nasty to you.' So I was prepared" (Bronhill, 1987, p. 30).

Bronhill recounted an anecdote where "I was getting so upset, with myself and with her because she was being so nasty to me. I pulled myself together. I looked at her and said 'you're not going to make me cry, you bloody bitch.'" Indicative of Bronhill's close and trusting relationship with Mathy was this permission to be strong and forthright. Mathy responded unexpectedly, "'Oh darling, this is wonderful. You have got ze temperament to become a good singer, to have a profession as a singer. I love you very dearly, you are good girl. Now go home — we won't work any more'" (Bronhill, 1987, p. 30–31).

Bronhill's refusal to break under pressure speaks in part to the great trust she placed in her teacher, and to her own indomitable spirit. She wrote affectionately of Mathy, who considered herself Bronhill's foster mother, and recounted a number of stories about this "extraordinary woman," including several about Mathy's mad, mercurial personality, her foibles, her predilections for her young male students, the demands she placed on everyone she knew, and, finally a sad tale of Mathy's decline and death. She recalled that "whenever I came back to Australia for any shows or work of any kind I always made sure that I worked with Marianne because she was such a fantastic singing teacher. What she didn't know about voice production was really not worth thinking about" (Bronhill, 1987, p. 37).

That Bronhill and Mathy shared such a close relationship is not unusual in the life accounts of singers. Mutual trust, respect and love are clearly demonstrated in Bronhill's loving portrayal of her teacher and in the account of Mathy's last days. Bronhill's warts and all portrait of this extraordinary person is a telling one. It suggests a co-dependent relationship — Mathy was a strong personality, but also a demanding one, who imposed herself on her willing disciples and seemed to need the adulation of her students. Bronhill noted this need for adulation without sentimentality, yet acknowledged the strong connection between them. Bronhill's last name is also a Mathy invention, as was Melba's invented surname a Marchesi requirement.

Bronhill's final teacher in London was the aforementioned Dino Borgioli, the same teacher who had taught Dame Joan Hammond. Bronhill claimed "when I arrived in London, my voice wasn't in very good condition because towards the end of my studies with Madame Mathy, she had become too technical for me" (Bronhill, 1987, p. 41). By technical, Bronhill is referring to physiological aspects of singing technique. She wrote, "She would talk about things like 'lifting the larynx'. Well, I hadn't a clue about how to lift my larynx … I had started to yell up around the top C area and my voice wasn't in the same good condition that it had been a year before" (Bronhill, 1987, p. 41).

Bronhill claimed she went to Borgioli on the strength of some recordings she had heard. She made up her mind that there was no one else who could teach her. She wrote, "he was a darling, gentle man and a gentleman. He reminded me incredibly of my father, with the same delicious sense of humour and warmth, and I think he sort of became my other Dad" (Bronhill, 1987, p. 41). This familial association was evidently important for Bronhill, but this attribution of parental features to a beloved singing teacher is also documented in other singer memoirs. She noted that Borgioli would not let her sing arias or songs for six months, until the voice was corrected, and he would not let her audition for opera companies until she had been learning from him for nearly two years. This proved to be the proper course for Bronhill, as in 1954 she was made principal soprano at Sadler's Wells. Bronhill wrote, "I continued to work with Dino, lovingly, until I went home to Australia in 1960. While I was there I heard the very sad news that he had died. I never did work with another singing teacher in London" (Bronhill, 1987, p. 41). Again, Bronhill acknowledged her close, loving relationship with her teacher: "I didn't feel that I could find anybody who could give me all the wonderful, instinctive tuition that Dino had given me … I will remember him for as long as I live. I loved him dearly" (Bronhill, 1987, p. 45).

Bronhill's account of her relationship with her teachers are marked by very warm, affectionate portraits of these people. While she was able to disagree with their pedagogy at times, she maintained strong feelings for them, and as an adult even attributed parental qualities to them, particularly towards Mathy and Borgioli. She maintained her lessons with Borgioli until his death when she was 31 years-of-age, and continued her coaching with Mathy in Sydney, which suggests a woman dependent on her teachers for guidance.

This tendency for singers to continue having lessons throughout their careers has been well documented and is a common element of the life of a working singer. As the voice is an internal instrument, and what singers hear can be different to the sound they are producing, external feedback is necessary; however, it also indicates a sense of relatedness and security that is integral to self-determination. Bronhill's perceptions of her teachers are in direct contrast to Hammond's, for although Bronhill's independence and feisty spirit are clearly in evidence, she experienced different relationships with her teachers and relied on them for more than singing technique. Loyalty and friendship were predominant features in these interactions, which can also be seen in Elms' recollections of her last singing teacher, Dominique and his wife Dolly Modesti.

Lauris Elms OBE

Lauris Elms wrote of two singing teachers. Her first teacher was Madame Wielaert, with whom she began lessons at age 18. She confessed, "Madame taught a method of singing which I now believe to be dangerous, at least for me … but she developed great strength and beauty in my voice at the right time" (Elms, 2001, p. 18). Elms studied with Wielaert for four years. Wielaert provided Elms with a number of singing opportunities and Elms' career was developing well. She wrote, however, that "… in my fourth year of singing, my throat grew hot and my voice tired quickly. I needed to find a new teacher before any permanent damage was done" (Elms, 2001, p. 27). Elms wondered how she could do this

> … without hurting Madame Wielaert, who had given me such a new direction to my life? She had changed my ambitions when she had unlocked my voice. She had made me aware of a pleasure I never knew existed, and that I had possessed an unknown gift. (Elms, 2001, p. 27)

This loyalty to a teacher is common, and so too is the despair felt when the relationship must be ended due to vocal problems caused by poor pedagogy.

Elms' story is not unique; Hammond and Bronhill likewise had to make these decisions when faced with poor pedagogy and vocal mismanagement. The distinction for Elms was that she realised the opportunities afforded her by Wielaert were life altering, and that she owed Wielaert a debt of gratitude that leaving for another teacher would not repay: "I owed her so much, yet I knew I would not be able to sing for long if I continued to sing in this way" (Elms, 2001, p. 28). Elms' decision to go abroad and study was a way out of the conundrum, and her chance meeting with Dominique and (an expatriate Australian) Dolly Modesti in Melbourne proved the perfect solution.

The tale of the Modesti couple is a remarkable one, which Elms described in detail in her autobiography. This couple, as a memorial to their dead children, decided to select one Australian singer that they would teach for free, for two years, in Paris. On this trip to Australia they found three. One of these singers was Lauris Elms. Elms travelled to Paris with the generous help of her father, who paid her a living allowance for the time she was away. Elms did not state whether her family could afford this expense, but as her parents were able to travel to Paris at the end of her second year in the French capital, one must assume that money was no object.

Elms recounted her lessons with Dominique Modesti by noting:

> I had to learn to sing again. He was wise in that he never actually said, 'I am going to completely alter the way you sing.' I realised later that this is what he did. Subtly and slowly I felt the sensation in my body and throat changing. (Elms, 2001, p. 40)

She commented, "Monsieur and Madame Modesti were always talking about 'the organ' which often made me giggle, but they were right. This is what singing felt like now, a great instrument lodged within my whole body" (Elms, 2001, p. 40).

She also wrote that "Occasionally M [Monsieur] Modesti would be enraged, and sometimes I would burst into tears with frustration and impatience" (Elms, 2001, p. 40).

These lessons benefited Elms enormously, and her performance career developed apace after two years of intensive training with the couple. She did not mention the Modestis frequently thereafter until late in her biography, when she writes of the recently deceased Dolly Modesti:

> this gallant and generous woman had been a profound influence on my life and on the lives of a dozen or more Australian singers. How fortunate we were who knew her, this strong, vigorous and beautiful woman who gave herself wholeheartedly to whatever she did. (Elms, 2001, p. 249–250).

As with the singers before her, Elms felt a debt of gratitude for the opportunities given her by her teachers. She was also aware of the pedagogical soundness of one teaching approach over the other, and made the necessary changes to her life to ensure that her voice stayed in good health. At one point, she revealed hesitation about travelling to Paris to study with these strangers, the Modestis, but she quickly learned to trust and respect this extraordinary couple, and this respect is made evident by the inclusion of their tale in her own. She attributed much of her success to her singing teachers, particularly with regards to the performance opportunities they provided her.

Conclusion

The importance of the support by a singing teacher for an emerging singer should not be underestimated, as has been revealed by this biographical analysis of four eminent singers — Melba, Hammond, Bronhill and Elms. The singing teacher is the lynchpin for success or failure with each singer. The "fit" must be right — both in a pedagogical and personal sense. Borgioli is a case in point. He was patently unsuitable for Hammond — at the time of her studies with him, he was still singing on the stage and his approach was very much that of the autocrat. His methods of singing did not suit Hammond and she railed against his dictatorial attitude. By the time Bronhill came to him, 15 years later, Borgioli's teaching approach was the very best style Bronhill could have wanted. Used to an autocratic teacher in Mathy, she was beguiled by his gentleness and gentlemanly behaviour. Borgioli's pedagogy was right for her — perhaps it had changed in the 15 years between Hammond and Bronhill — and his personality sat well with Bronhill's lively persona. This different reading of the same teacher is commonly noted in the singing literature — what is good for the goose is not necessarily good for the gander.

This biographical analysis of four Australian singers is a useful means of exploring the attributes of singing teachers and their relationships with their students. By unpacking the attitudes, perceptions and behaviours of these eminent singers, we can begin to comprehend the complexity of the relationship of a singer with their singing teacher. By applying Deci and Ryan's Self-Determination Theory to the relationships of these singers and their teachers, we can begin to understand the responsibility of the teacher to singer. Of relatedness, the teacher must provide a safe, trusting environment that allows singers to explore their vocal capacity and worth, and the teacher must communicate pedagogical concepts clearly and correctly to the singer. Of competence and autonomy, the vocal techniques a singing teacher promotes must be appropriate to the singer's vocal development and the teacher must allow the singer to feel competent and autonomous in the development of their craft.

A number of themes emerged in this analysis. The first was that of trust. While not every singer claimed to trust their teacher, they certainly felt no compunction about changing teachers if pedagogical or personal trust was broken.

The second theme was that of affinity. Each singer sought affinity with their teacher — in Hammond's case, she sought, and eventually found, affinity with a medical doctor, whom she felt could best help her in her quest for vocal rejuvenation. The others developed close bonds with their teachers, which were sometimes familial in quality. At other times, singers were loyal to excess, as in the case of Melba's blind loyalty towards an elderly and senile Marchesi.

The third theme was that of respect. Each of these singers claimed to believe in the teaching methods of at least one particular teacher, with the exception of Hammond, who felt betrayed by poor pedagogy and an autocratic teaching style. For the others, deep respect for the artistic practices of their singing teachers was reflected in their affectionate recollections of vocal techniques taught during singing lessons. Respect for the ethical and moral practices of the singing teachers were also held to be important, as noted in Elm's account of the Modestis, although it is worth noting that respect for artistic practice was considered in the main the more important factor.

A fourth theme emerging from this analysis is the power of the teacher to shape young singers' lives. This power was abused by people like Marchesi, whose domineering approach drove many students away, and whose senility in old age caused vocal havoc in young singers. Power to assist singers was used to positive effect by the Modesti couple, who provided young singers the means to develop their craft in a caring atmosphere. This power is one not readily admitted to by teachers, but if a teacher has career connections, the students who work hard and show ability may be rewarded with opportunities not afforded the lesser talents.

A fifth theme revealed is the gratitude these singers felt towards their singing teachers for providing them with self-belief, a sound vocal pedagogy, friendship, opportunities and a place in the operatic world, with the exception of Hammond, whose gratitude to her family and friends was most evident.

Finally, characteristic of each of these singers was their dogged determination, independent spirit and intrinsic motivation to sing — essential prerequisites for a life in singing, and certainly prime indicators for psychological growth and wellbeing as theorised in Deci and Ryan's Self-Determination Theory. Perhaps the reliance that each singer placed on either their singing teacher or medical specialist was a result of the sheer hard slog that each singer had to undertake to succeed. Perhaps their teacher was the one person who recognised the challenge of making a career of singing, and who provided a secure sanctuary for these eminent artists. Whatever the reasons, each of the singers profiled here found a mentor who helped them develop a career in singing. They found their "fit" of teacher or medical specialist, who helped them to develop their voices in a warm, caring and supportive environment. The relationship between eminent singer and their teacher was acknowledged by each to be a crucial factor in determining future success.

References

Blainey, A. (2008). *I am Melba.* Melbourne, Australia: Black Inc.

Bronhill, J. (1987). *The merry Bronhill.* Sydney, Australia: Methuen Hayes.

Deci, E.L., & Ryan, R.M. (2000). The 'what' and 'why' of goal pursuits: human needs and the self-determination of behavior. *Psychological Inquiry, 11*(4), 227–268.

Elms, L. (2001). *The singing Elms: The autobiography of Lauris Elms.* Sydney, Australia: Bowerbird Press.

Elphinstone, M., & Hancock, W. (2005). *When Austral sang: the biography of Florence Austral.* Adelaide, Australia: Hyde Park Press.

Hammond, J. (1970). *A voice, a life: The autobiography of Joan Hammond.* London: Victor Gollancz.

Hines, J. (1982). *Great singers on great singing.* New York: Limelight Editions.

Kemp, A. (1996). *The musical temperament.* New York: Oxford University Press.

Matheopoulos, H. (1991). *Diva. Great sopranos and mezzos discuss their art.* London: Victor Gollancz Ltd.

McCarthy, M. (2006). The teaching and learning relationship: Part 2. In J. Chapman (Ed.), *Singing and teaching singing.* San Diego, CA: Plural Publishing.

Melba, N. (1980). *Melodies and memories, with notes and a foreword by John Cargher.* Melbourne, Australia: Thomas Nelson Publishing. (Original work published 1925).

Presland, C. (2005). *Conservatoire student and instrumental professor: The student perspective on a complex relationship. British Journal of Music Education, 22*(3), 237–248.

Radic, T. (1986). *Melba: The voice of Australia.* Melbourne, Australia: Macmillan Australia.

Riessman, C.K. (2003). Narrative analysis. In M.S. Lewis-Beck, A. Bryman, & T. Futing Liao (Eds.), *The Sage Encyclopedia of Social Science Research Methods.* Thousand Oaks, CA: Sage Publications.

Schön, D.A. (1983). *The reflective practitioner.* New York,: Basic Books.

Tosi, P.F. (1987). *Observations on the florid song* (J.E. Galliard, Trans.). London,: Stainer and Bell. (Original work published 1743).

Chapter
5

Classical Voice Pedagogy in the Greater Newcastle Region of New South Wales: The Singing Teacher's Perspective

Paul McMahon

Qualitative research in voice education in Australia offers a valuable contribution to our understanding and perspective on singing teaching in the 21st century. As Creswell (2003) argued, such a study offers a valid exploration of a topic on which little has been previously written. Through the perspective of professional singing teachers, this chapter examines some current issues facing classical voice pedagogy in the Greater Newcastle region of New South Wales. The lack of empirical literature on this topic is somewhat surprising, given Greater Newcastle's status as the most populous regional centre in New South Wales and it's proud artistic tradition of choral and solo singing. As Creswell (2003) suggested:

> ... one of the chief reasons for conducting a qualitative study is that the study is exploratory. This means that not much has been written about the topic or the population being studied, and the researcher seeks to listen to participants and build an understanding based on their ideas. (p. 30)

In order to address this paucity of knowledge, the author undertook interviews with five eminent teachers in the Greater Newcastle region. The participants were chosen for their knowledge of the region, their experience of classical voice and their capacity to describe the trends and themes associated with teaching classical voice in this region. The participants in this study were: Christopher Allan, Jennifer Barnes, Craig Everingham, Rosemary Saunders and Ghillian Sullivan. Profiles of these participants can be found in Appendix 5A.

Context

The city of Newcastle is located at the mouth of the Hunter River, approximately 166 km north-east of Sydney. The Newcastle statistical subdivision, hereafter referred to as Greater Newcastle, includes the local government areas of Newcastle, Lake Macquarie, Cessnock, Maitland and Port Stephens (ABS, 2008). Figures in the 2006 census reveal the population of Greater Newcastle to be 517,496, making it the second most densely inhabited region of New South Wales (ABS, 2008). Given natural population growth and Sydney's urban sprawl, the Greater Newcastle region is becoming an increasingly attractive option for those seeking an alternative to the pressures of the metropolitan lifestyle. This study is timely, given the growth in demand for music education services likely to occur in the Greater Newcastle region in the near future.

Method

Semistructured interviews were conducted with the participants in November and December 2009. The interviews sought to interrogate the following five research questions:

- What are the collective strengths of classical vocal pedagogy in the Greater Newcastle region?
- What challenges face classical vocal pedagogy in regional Australia, and particularly within the Greater Newcastle district?
- The Greater Newcastle area contains a large pool of musically gifted youth of high school or pre-tertiary age. As classical voice pedagogues, how do we identify the next generation of classical singers and attract them to ongoing study of classical vocal technique and the literature of classical singing, with a view to establishing a career as a classical singer?
- In order to cater for the needs of classical voice students in the 21st century, what should tertiary music education in the Greater Newcastle region provide or modify in current vocal pedagogy practices?
- As classical voice pedagogues, how can we address issues presented by the region's geographical proximity to Australia's largest capital city?

The interviews were transcribed and coded, following standard analytical methods (Richards, 2005) and sections of text were labelled with a descriptive term, thus forming topics within the text that allow the researcher to draw understanding of the data (Creswell, 2003). Through consideration, reflection and analysis, the author now outlines below the major themes emerging from the data.

Findings

Theme 1: Strengths of Classical Voice Pedagogy in Greater Newcastle

The major positive attribute to emerge from the study related to the variety and experience of classical voice teachers in the region. Sullivan (2009), for example, suggests that tertiary and non-tertiary students, as well as beginner, intermediate and advanced singers of all ages, are catered for by the diverse skills of classical voice teachers in the region.

Saunders (2009) described the vocal program at the University of Newcastle as one devoid of "territorialism". That is, singing teachers are willing to work collegially, giving singing students access to the broad range of skills and perspectives within the vocal staff. Classical voice students at the University of Newcastle are not encouraged to view their singing teachers as "gurus" representing all knowledge and understanding. She suggests that this lack of "ownership" of students and willingness to share knowledge and ideas on repertoire is a great strength of the University's vocal staff.

Allan (2009) points to the scientific knowledge of physiology within the pedagogy of the region's singing teachers as an element that has raised the standard of classical voice teaching over the past 10 to 15 years. Everingham (2009) saw the high standard performance experience of classical voice pedagogues within the region as a positive for students; a number of teachers of classical voice outside the University of Newcastle system are highly experienced operatic performers with companies such as Opera Australia and Glyndebourne Festival Opera. Of those within the University system, Allan has significant choral and recital experience, while the author is a regular concert, recital and recording artist with orchestras, choirs and chamber music groups throughout Australia, New Zealand and Asia. The performance experience of teachers is a significant drawcard for prospective students, as the flourishing private studios of the classical voice teachers within the region attests.

Theme 2: Challenges Facing Classical Voice Pedagogy in the Greater Newcastle Region

A number of subthemes are apparent in this domain. The management of the changing voice, the balance of musical genres in schools, the role of sport in schooling (and society at large), quality performance opportunities, collegiality and funding were perceived as major concerns. The domain of the changing voice is dealt with in other chapters in this volume and elsewhere (See Thurman and Welch, 2000; Durrant, 2003; Gackle 1991, 2000), and will not be addressed in great detail here. The issues associated with the sociological challenges of puberty, particularly male voices, have also been dealt with elsewhere (see Hall, 2005; Harrison, 2007; Collins, 2009; Young 2009). The balance of musical genres in schools is an emerging issue nationally, and was found to be problematic in this area.

Balance of Musical Genres Within the School Music Curriculum

Allan, Barnes and Saunders discuss the necessity for well-balanced school music curricula and well-educated classroom music teachers. All styles and genres of music, be they classical, contemporary, country and western, jazz, rock or world, should have equal prominence in the curriculum, as recommended by Cain (2010) and Schippers (2010). It is therefore the music teacher's responsibility to encourage students to explore other musical styles, whilst recognising and guiding talented young singers towards vocal tuition and further study of classical music.

Barnes (2009) notes that the Hunter School of the Performing Arts recently presented Carl Jenkins' *The Armed Man: A Mass for Peace*. It is a work drawing on varied influences, including the 15th century French song, "L'Homme Armé," with music by the Italian Renaissance composer, Giovanni Palestrina (c. 1525–1594), Brazilian drum rhythms and the chant of the Muezzin, a Muslim call to prayer. This type of work offers school age students examples of the multifaceted nature of music; the way compositions draw inspiration from far ranging sources and the benefits of musicians and composers keeping an open mind.

Allan believes the generalised nature of the high school music syllabus in New South Wales lacks a specific relationship to classical vocal music. For instance, one of the criteria within the syllabus suggests the study of "An instrument and its repertoire". This offers great variety of choice and caters to a large number of students. Recent similar changes in the Queensland syllabus designed to broaden appeal have also resulted in students or their teachers often choosing an option that seems easy or familiar, such as the contemporary music genre, without extending themselves through other styles, such as folk music, lieder or arias. With the advent of the national curriculum in the next few years, it is conceivable that this trend will become the norm across the country.

Related to the question of genre is the emerging Disney generation in schools. The first Disney musical was *Snow White* in 1940 and the first generation to grow up with the modern Disney musical is now of university entrance age. Allan suggests that the Disney musical is well entrenched in the psyche of this generation, and the appeal of the singing and dancing in this style of musical is the logical place of focus for the creative energy of what he calls the "Disney" generation. There is a connection between this and the curriculum issues discussed earlier. School music teachers and teachers of voice can work together to identify talented singing students and offer them guidance toward styles appropriate for their voice, not just familiar styles, such as the Disney musical. Barnes has many students who begin studying with her as "non-classical" singers, yet she often encourages these students to incorporate elements of classical singing technique. Many of these students subsequently move on to discover a love of classical vocal repertoire.

Quality Performing Opportunities

Barnes retains a thriving private singing studio in the city of Newcastle and laments the region's lack of quality performing opportunities. Organisations such as Opera Hunter, Newcastle Festival Opera, Newcastle University Choir, the Newcastle Anglican Cathedral Choir, Hunter Singers and Hunter Kids Sing are valuable organisations; however, they cannot cater for the large numbers of young singers who wish to take advantage of quality performing opportunities. A breadth of quality performing opportunities will, according to Barnes, encourage students to remain in the area, rather than seeking opportunities elsewhere.

Along with opportunities to perform, classical voice students also require the opportunity to view high-quality performances in the Greater Newcastle region. Such performances, according to the participants in this study, offer the singing student encouragement, inspiration, the prospect of critical thought and the opportunity for self-analysis of their own singing technique. In comparison to metropolitan centres, Barnes sees the relative lack of high-quality performances as a major disadvantage for classical voice students throughout regional Australia, not just the Greater Newcastle area.

The not-for-profit organisation, Musica Viva in Schools, is the largest provider of music education programs across Australia. This program offers a mixture of live performance, practical teaching applications and in-service training for teachers linked to music and creative arts syllabi. However, as Barnes noted, groups such as the Australian Chamber Orchestra and The Song Company maintain regular subscription seasons in Newcastle, whereas Musica Viva, the largest presenter of chamber music concerts in the world (and parent arm of Musica Viva in Schools), also offers a regular program for the Hunter region with concerts in Newcastle. Few schools take advantage of the opportunities available through such organisations for concert experiences complimentary to those accessible within the school music curriculum.

Barnes herself became beguiled by music through a school performance of Rossini's Barber of Seville by members of The Australian Opera. This experience reinforced Sullivan's belief that the combination of characters, music and story telling within opera can be intoxicating for children and the emphasis of the story-telling angle is an essential way to captivate and educate the audience of tomorrow.

The opportunity to view and attend (and participate in) such performances will only be possible if new audiences are drawn to performances. Allan, Barnes and Saunders believe that classical music in general, and classical vocal music in particular, must actively engage the community in order to attract new and younger audiences. Barnes stated that the technology boom of the last 20–30 years has produced extensive growth within the entertainment market and the number of choices available to audiences. With an established audience, classical music largely stood still, while growing competition for the audience dollar and diversification of the entertainment market occurred around it. All participants believe that classical music, and classical vocal pedagogy must address the ageing demographic of classical music audiences. Everingham suggests that events such as vocal workshops by highly reputable performers and vocal teachers within schools at the Newcastle Conservatorium and at the University of Newcastle would help the study of classical voice become more encompassing for today's youth.

The prime example of this phenomenon was that of the Three Tenors bringing operatic favourites to worldwide audiences in the 1990s and the current commercial success of violinist, Andre Rieu. Reform of Australian school music education and the review of the perceptions and underlying cultural attitudes to classical music driven by the Australian media are more likely to generate long-term change, as opposed to the short-term hype generated by classical artists operating in pop culture.

Australian Culture According to the Media: Sport Versus the Arts

Everingham pointed to the lack of balance within Australia's cultural identity that is affecting classical music generally in Australia, and by association, classical voice pedagogy. The author suggests that the media plays an influential role in shaping and projecting Australia's cultural identity. Traditionally, Australian media proprietors have made large profits through aspects of sport and sporting sponsorship. The huge audience on tap through the major sporting arenas and through television makes sport a natural draw card for sponsors willing to pay the high price tag to advertise their products, in return for the large-scale exposure available to prospective customers. The comparatively small audience and lack of media exposure makes the arts unattractive to such sponsors and it is therefore in the interests of business and the media to promote Australia's sporting identity as the heart of Australian culture.

The lack of prominence given to the arts in the Australian mass media promotes ignorance of the classical music art form within our culture. The respondents are unanimous in their belief that a balanced approach by the media to reporting and promotion of the arts would introduce more Australian youth to classical music. This in turn assists the regeneration of audiences, underlines the work of pedagogues introducing classical music to younger generations and helps to redress the cultural balance within Australian society.

Collegiality Among Classical Voice Teachers

Some participants reject the view of Saunders expressed earlier (i.e., that singing teachers are generally colleagial), instead emphasising that a more collegial approach by pedagogues would achieve a higher standard of teaching, as well as offering students a more attractive educational experience. Some of the inhibiting factors include: a lack of willingness to share ideas, the need to protect one's own teaching studio for financial reasons, isolation through the wish to take credit for individual singing students who go on to become prominent professional artists and a closed attitude to pedagogy. Many of these attitudes find support in the current research literature of Gaunt, 2008; Mills, 2008 and McWilliam, Carey, Draper, & Lebler, 2006. Sullivan sees the potential for the exposure of students to a range of pedagogical approaches utilising the skills and expertise of each teacher. Sullivan also believes that such an approach by the classical voice teachers in the region would help raise the profile and the standards of classical voice pedagogy across the board, as well as turning out polished, advanced students ready to enter elements of the music profession.

Funding of Tertiary Music Education

The Australian tertiary education system has experienced a significant number of changes in the past 20 years. In relation to one-to-one teaching, the most significant aspect of regulatory control has been the decreasing level of government and private funding for tertiary institutions. The marriage of conservatoires with universities (Schippers, 2007; Draper & Harrison, 2010) has impacted directly on the delivery of classical voice pedagogy. A student working individually with a voice teacher is often seen by tertiary managerial staff as an expensive, outdated and unnecessary mode of teaching. This attitude affects the successful development of graduates as professional classical singers and remains a major challenge for pedagogues in less affluent or regional universities.

Small group vocal pedagogy is often offered as an alternative to individual teaching. The author's experience as a student and teacher reveals this manner of delivery as a form of pedagogy offering students the opportunity to assess the strengths and technical weaknesses in the singers within their group, as well as reflection on elements of their own technical knowledge. However, Glover (2001, p. 17) noted that singing is contextual — we sing differently in specific environments. Sociological research supports this argument; people often behave differently in groups than they do as individuals and singers behave differently in ensembles than they do as soloists (Daugherty, 2001, p. 70). While social cohesion is perhaps one element that is enhanced in a group setting, Harrison (2007) noted that one-on-one relational skills are the most significant in the teacher–mentor relationship.

Harrison (2005) also cautioned that economic concerns might override "musical considerations in teaching through the small-group format" (p. 12).

Participants in this study concurred with these views, noting the deficiencies for students in the development of technique and repertoire knowledge. Participants also expressed concerns about small group vocal pedagogy in relation to individual rapport, and dealing with self-conscious students.

Theme 3: Identifying and Supporting the Next Generation of Classical Singers

The third major theme extracted from interviews was the identification and supporting of classical singers of the future. Four subthemes were identified in the interviews: the role of schools, choral directors and voice tutors; student performance; exposure to school-based performance; and parental influence.

The Role of School Music Teachers, Choral Directors and Voice Tutors

School and community choral programs are essential in the development of all musicians. Harrison, Cowley, Connell, and Southcott (2008) suggested that "singing in a wide variety of contexts, including singing in schools, tertiary and community-based settings contributes to both economic and quality of life measures" (p. 1). Encouraging students to sing throughout their schooling and removing the stigma from singing at school would encourage talented singers to take their singing studies to a tertiary level and beyond. Choral directors can assist this process by exposing their students to contrasting genres of classical music through the performance of varied, high quality repertoire, while schools can facilitate the singing student's development by employing experienced, technically assured vocal tutors and by offering regular opportunities to perform solo and ensemble music in a nurturing, constructive environment. Saunders offers Newcastle Grammar School and Hunter Valley Grammar School as examples of two schools within the region offering private singing tuition as part of the curriculum. Less wealthy schools may not have this luxury; however, they have a responsibility to present a broad and flexible focus on contrasting musical genres.

Sullivan supported Allan's view that primary and secondary school music teachers play a vital role in the ongoing growth of classical vocal music in the Greater Newcastle region. Allan believes that school music teachers must ignite the passion for classical music within their students, as these teachers play an important role in shaping the thought processes of the next generation of musicians, while effective leadership by school music educators would also help nurture the next generation of classical singers. Everingham supported Allan's view that school music teachers, choral directors and voice tutors can set an example to students by making well-informed musical choices. When teachers offer an open mind about all styles and genres of music, students are often prepared to take an open-minded approach to less familiar styles, such as lieder, operatic arias or song cycles. Sullivan contended that once school music teachers become unafraid of classical vocal music, they will broaden their own musical horizons, as well as those of their students.

Allan suggests a more collaborative approach by singing teachers within the Greater Newcastle area would impact directly on students and their knowledge of repertoire. For instance, a combined concert featuring students from the studios of several different teachers may introduce lied, art song or operatic arias to students previously unfamiliar with such repertoire.

Opportunities for Student Performance

Saunders pointed to a strong performance culture within schools as an important step in fostering new vocal talent. She noted three essential ingredients in the cultivation of young vocal talent: encouragement to perform, opportunities to perform, and inspiration through the performances of other musicians. The National Review of School Music Education set participation in vocal programs for every Australian student as a priority. The review also recommended that students with talent in vocal music have access to extensive vocal music programs (Pascoe, Leong, MacCallum, Mackinlay, Marsh, & Smith, 2005).

Sullivan encourages school age singing students to participate in groups and community activities, such as Young People's Theatre or Newcastle Festival Opera, in order to raise their level of excitement for the art form and to help them build a network of like-minded friends. All the respondents agree that encouraging children to express themselves in musical and theatrical groups paves the way for music and theatre to become a natural part of adult life.

Education Through Exposure to Music Performance

All respondents point to the inspirational element of school visits by classical singers. Opera in Schools and Musica Viva in Schools programs are the types of series that offer entertaining, inspirational and educational performances for the next generation. Allan suggests that a collaborative approach between schools and organisations, such as Opera Hunter and Newcastle Festival Opera, would further enhance the local environment.

Sullivan believes the process of storytelling is vital in the education of young musicians. Introducing children and adolescents to the characters and stories within opera and theatre would help to capture their attention and imagination. She offered the example of Engelbert Humperdinck's *Hänsel und Gretel* (1893) as an opera that works beautifully for both children and adults alike. Allan believes singing teachers in the non-tertiary program at the Newcastle Conservatorium who perform regularly in the Greater Newcastle area would inspire the existing students and help to attract a vibrant, youthful culture of classical singing in the region.

Parental and Family Guidance

Love of classical music is often developed within the home (Barrett 2005; McPherson 2006; Welch, 2006). Allan pointed to the positive influence that immediate or extended family members can have on the musical tastes of the younger generation. Barnes supported Allan's view and pointed out that parental guidance within the home can form a non-threatening and nurturing environment for music making. If parents teach their children to have an open mind about music and support this by their own attitudes, children feel encouraged to keep an open mind about music that they find new or unfamiliar. Parental introduction of classical CDs or DVDs and gentle guidance can impact positively on young students.

Theme 4: Classical Voice Pedagogy in Tertiary Music Education Within Greater Newcastle

Given the first three themes, the fourth theme to emerge concerned the tertiary sector. Subthemes evident in this domain included funding, community engagement and an opportunity to enhance the tertiary experience.

Funding

Respondents commented on the significance of funding for tertiary music education. The necessity to attract new income streams within tertiary music education is paramount. It would protect one-to-one pedagogy, which all of the respondents agree is vital to building the technique of classical singers. Saunders suggests inviting successful professional singers to "give something back" to education by involvement, even if on an occasional basis, in master classes, question and answer sessions, and concerts to inspire the next generation of singers coming through the tertiary system.

All respondents agree that convincing management within universities that successful classical voices are "built, not bought" is of supreme importance. The author believes that the development of classical singing technique takes years of careful training, which, by its nature is expensive. A number of common trends emerged in relation to the decreasing levels of funding within tertiary music education. These included a loss of access by students to undertake:

- Lessons in stagecraft and movement.
- Training in foreign languages.
- Sessions with specialist vocal coaches.

- Performance of operatic scenes.
- Performance of fully staged operas with orchestra, stage lighting, sets and costumes.
- Community engagement/philanthropy.

Allan would like to see classical voice maintain a higher profile within the Greater Newcastle community through regular music festivals, singing competitions and master classes. By embracing relevant performing groups outside the university, the potential is there to form mutually beneficial partnerships for tertiary music education within the Greater Newcastle region. For instance, groups such as Newcastle Festival Opera offer university students opportunities to perform in fully staged operas with orchestra; an option not presently included as part of undergraduate or postgraduate study at the University of Newcastle. Sullivan suggests that such a relationship would also complement activities presently offered within courses, such as student recitals, thus expanding opportunities for new elective units of study.

With the aim of attracting private and philanthropic funding from individuals and organisations interested in fostering the next generation of classical musicians, it may be timely for tertiary music education within the Greater Newcastle region to invest in more concert performance activity within the broader community. Drawing audiences to tertiary level performances and taking music performance into the community would engage tertiary music as an active, relevant and vital part of the local community, and offer a platform to secure ongoing funds from non-government sources.

Enhancing the Tertiary Experience

An extensive range of scholarships would entice high quality students and enhance the tertiary education experience for all students. Saunders suggests that courses offering opportunities to perform at high profile events, such as the Newcastle University Chamber Choir in Channel 7's Battle of the Choirs, is another way of enriching tertiary music study.

Barnes advocated the more extensive use of technology within tertiary music pedagogy. For instance, supervised use of devices such as "YouTube" allows students immediate access to a variety of interpretations, performances and perspectives on repertoire. The tertiary system in the region would benefit from offering vocal pedagogues the opportunity to employ voice-specific technology within their teaching, such as voice spectral analysis software. Such software presents students with visual feedback on concepts relating to the singer's formant, vibrato and vocal timbre. This software also documents the characteristics of the student's vocal tone and offers an aural record of vocal lessons. Digital camcorders are another useful device giving students and teachers a visual record of vocal lessons and offering scope for analysis of pedagogy.

Theme 5: Greater Newcastle's Geographical Proximity to Sydney

The final theme to emerge related to the proximity of Newcastle to Sydney. Many singing students find major metropolitan centres such as Sydney enticing, while some parents see Sydney as the logical place for successful students. Classical voice pedagogy in the Greater Newcastle region has many positive aspects including location, access to metropolitan-based professionals, scholarships and lifestyle.

Geographical Location

Several teachers interviewed for this publication described the geographical location of the Greater Newcastle area as ideal. That is, close enough to Sydney to enjoy access to activities that the city has to offer, yet far enough away to enjoy an independent identity and unique lifestyle. For instance, the 2–2.5 hour drive from Greater Newcastle to the Sydney Opera House or City Recital Hall Angel Place makes attendance at evening performances feasible. Saunders suggests that the University of Newcastle could make attendance at a Sydney Opera House performance compulsory for all music students. Such events help open the collective eyes and ears of students, giving them a new and exciting educational experience in iconic surroundings.

Conceding that Sydney is an important market for young professional singers, Sullivan and Everingham believe that if local classical singing students receive a whole and complete progression from beginner to advanced studies, more students would choose to remain within the Greater Newcastle area. While close enough to provide easy access to Sydney, the Greater Newcastle region has none of the hustle and bustle of metropolitan centres. The relaxed pace and the lifestyle on offer makes the region an attractive proposition for students and professional musicians.

Access to Metropolitan Practitioners

Given the relative proximity of Greater Newcastle to Sydney, classical voice teachers in the region can maintain links and attract regular professional visits from highly skilled practitioners based in Sydney. Barnes offered pertinent examples from her own practice, in which she regularly invites coaches and repetiteurs from Opera Australia to visit her studio in Newcastle to undertake sessions with her students. She believes this practice offers her students a different perspective and fresh ideas. Everingham also comments on the value of master classes and lessons with experienced, professional artists.

In Sullivan's view, links with major performing arts companies and orchestras within Sydney and access to discount tickets would also benefit the Greater Newcastle student population. She maintains that local students need to aspire to greater heights than the standard available in their immediate surrounds and suggests that awareness of the standard in Sydney is one way of inspiring students.

Scholarships

A range of university scholarships for classical voice students would make the University of Newcastle more attractive to students from the region and would draw students from other metropolitan and regional areas, as well as from overseas. Allan suggests that wide publication of such scholarships is also necessary, as broad awareness of scholarships widens the net of potential university music students and ensures competitiveness with other institutions.

Lifestyle

Respondents commented on the relaxed pace of life and the ease of mobility within the Greater Newcastle region. Saunders believes that classical voice teachers could highlight to their students the strengths of the region and the benefits of the local lifestyle, including a lower cost of living than Sydney. In contrast to Sydney, Barnes believes the relatively small number of classical voice students in the region acts as an incentive, offering students the opportunity to participate as soloists in a significant number of local productions by musical societies and semi-professional groups that they would be unlikely to receive in Sydney or in larger centres.

Conclusion

Classical voice pedagogues within this study reveal their passion for singing and a unity of purpose in the desire to nurture, guide and support their students. Through this research, pedagogues also expose the substantial challenges facing classical singing pedagogy within the region and within Australian music education in general.

The five themes and numerous subthemes (strengths of classical voice pedagogy; challenges facing classical voice pedagogy; identifying and supporting the next generation of classical singers; classical voice pedagogy in tertiary music education; Greater Newcastle's geographical proximity to Sydney) are, with exception of the fifth theme, relevant across the sector.

The participants in the study see the range of experienced classical voice teachers working in the region as a significant strength, while Greater Newcastle's geographical proximity to Sydney presents both positive and negative implications for classical voice pedagogy. The positive aspects of this geographical relationship include the simplicity of travel to events in Sydney, the ease of access to Sydney-based professional music practitioners and the relaxed, friendly lifestyle for singing students and residents within the Greater Newcastle region. The negative aspects emerging within the data include the loss of potential tertiary students to Sydney through inflexible tertiary entrance criteria, the failure of the region's university to attract new students by recognising and utilising the performance profile of tertiary music staff, and a paucity of lucrative scholarships attracting high-quality singing students to Greater Newcastle for pre-tertiary and tertiary vocal study.

The strong themes within the data link research questions regarding the challenges for pedagogy, the identification of the next generation of classical singers and aspects of pedagogy within tertiary education, respectively. These themes include quality and balance within the school music curriculum, maintaining the needs of children who sing, confronting Australia's cultural identity, the aging audience for classical music, and the implications of declining funding for tertiary music programs, with it's subsequent impact on current and future school music teachers, classical singers, pedagogues and audiences.

Revelations within this chapter highlight the clear demands ahead for classical voice pedagogues throughout the Greater Newcastle region. Though the pathway to reform within the region's music education curriculum, cultural identity and tertiary music sector is not without obstacles, the dawn of the second decade of the 21st century brings the promise of challenging, stimulating times for teachers and students of classical singing.

References

Allan, C. (2009, November). Research interview by P. McMahon [Audio recording]. Classical voice pedagogy in Greater Newcastle, Newcastle, Australia.

Australian Bureau of Statistics. (2008). National regional profile: Newcastle (Statistical Subdivision). Retrieved December 15, 2009, from http://www.abs.gov.au/AUSSTATS/abs@.nsf/Latestproducts/11005Population/People12002-2006?opendocument&tabname=Summary&prodno=11005 &issue=2002-2006

Barnes, J. (2009, November). Research interview by P. McMahon [Audio recording]. Classical voice pedagogy in Greater Newcastle, Newcastle, Australia.

Barrett, M.S. (2005). Musical communication and children's communities of musical practice. In D. Miell, R. MacDonald, & D. Hargreaves (Eds.), *Musical communication* (pp. 261–280). Oxford, UK: Oxford University Press.

Cain, M. (2010, January). *From philosophy to practice: Evidence of diverse practices in the primary music classroom.* Paper presented at the CDIME 10 Conference, Sydney, Australia.

Collins. A. (2009). A boy's music ecosystem. In S.D. Harrison (Ed.), *Male voices: Stories of boys learning and loving music in Australia* (pp. 33–47). Melbourne, Australia: ACER.

Creswell, J.W. (2003). *Research design: Qualitative, quantitative and mixed methods approaches* (2nd ed.). Thousand Oaks, CA: Sage Publications.

Daugherty, J. (2001). On the voice: Rethinking how voices work in the choral ensemble. *Choral Journal, 42*(5), 69–75.

Draper, P., & Harrison, S. (2010). *Through the eye of a needle: The emergence of a practice-led research doctorate in music.* Manuscript submitted for publication.

Durrant, C. (2003). *Choral conducting: Philosophy and practice.* New York: Routledge.

Everingham, C. (2009, December). Research interview by P. McMahon [Audio recording]. *Classical voice pedagogy in Greater Newcastle, Newcastle, Australia.*

Gackle, L. (1991). The adolescent female voice: Characteristics of change and stages of development. *Choral Journal, 31*(8), 17–25.

Gackle, L. (2000). *Understanding voice transformation in female adolescents* (Rev. ed.). In L. Thurman, & G. Welch (Eds.), *Bodymind & voice: Foundations of voice education* (pp. 739–744). Collegeville, MN: Voice Care Network Publication.

Gaunt, H. (2008). One-to-one tuition in a conservatoire: The perceptions of instrumental and vocal teachers. *Psychology of Music, 36,* 215.

Glover, S. (2001). How and why vocal solo and choral warm-ups differ. *Choral Journal, 42*(3), 17–22.

Harrison, S.D. (2005). The Cave Project: Collaborative approaches to vocal education. *Australian Voice, 10,* 24–27.

Harrison, S.D. (2007). Where have the boys gone? The perennial problem of gendered participation in music. *British Journal of Music Education, 24*(3), 267–280.

Harrison, S. D., Cowley, R., Connell, K., & Southcott, I. (2008). *The role of singing in the broader music education landscape.* Melbourne, Australia: Music Council of Australia Knowledge Base. Retrieved from www.mca.org.au

McPherson, G. (Ed.). (2006). *The child as musician: A handbook of musical development.* New York: Oxford University Press.

McWilliam, E., Carey, G., Draper, P., & Lebler, D. (2006). Learning and unlearning: New challenges for teaching in conservatoires. *The Australian Journal of Music Education, 1,* 25–31.

Mills, J. (2008). *Instrumental teaching.* Oxford, UK: Oxford University Press.

Pascoe, R., Leong, S., MacCallum, J., Mackinlay, E., Marsh, K., & Smith, B. (2005). *National review of school music education: Augmenting the diminished.* Canberra, Australia: Australian Government.

Richards, L. (2005). *Handling qualitative data: A practical guide.* London: Sage.

Saunders, R. (2009, November). Research interview by P. McMahon [Audio recording]. Classical voice pedagogy in Greater Newcastle, Newcastle, Australia.

Schippers. H. (2007). The marriage of art and academia: Challenges and opportunities for music research in practice-based environments. *Dutch Journal of Music Theory, 12*(1), 34–40.

Schippers, H. (2010). *Facing the music.* New York, NY: Oxford University Press.

Sullivan, G. (2009, November). Research interview by P. McMahon [Audio recording]. Classical voice pedagogy in Greater Newcastle, Newcastle, Australia.

Welch, G.F. (2006). Singing and vocal development. In G. McPherson (Ed.), *The child as musician: A handbook of musical development* (pp. 311–329). New York: Oxford University Press.

Young, A. (2009) The singing classroom. In S.D. Harrison (Ed.), *Male voices: Stories of boys learning and loving music in Australia* (pp. 62–78). Melbourne, Australia: ACER.

Appendix 5A

Participant Profiles

Baritone *Christopher Allan* is an experienced performer and teacher of singing. He has sung with Opera Australia and The Song Company and regularly presents recitals of early music, lieder and English art song. As a teacher, his interests include the developing voice and the application of voice science within the vocal teaching studio. Christopher is currently completing his doctoral research on teaching methodology and the younger singer, and recently presented a paper on 'voice science and its application for the developing singer' at the National Early Music Association's conference held in the United Kingdom. Christopher is a Senior Lecturer in Voice at the University of Newcastle, New South Wales.

Soprano *Jennifer Barnes* began her solo career within oratorio and studied opera with Josephine Veasey in London as a recipient of the Doris Smith Scholarship. Her operatic performances include principal roles with Opera Hunter, Opera Queensland, Sydney Metropolitan Opera, Sound Construction Company, Sydney Festival and Opera Australia. A career highlight includes the role of the Valkyrie Grimgerde in the State Opera of South Australia production of Wagner's Ring Cycle in 2004. Barnes holds a PhD and her research is published in the Journal of the Acoustical Society of America and Acoustics Australia. She regularly presents workshops and master classes on performance anxiety and performance skills, and operates a thriving private teaching studio in Newcastle, New South Wales.

Baritone *Craig Everingham* studied at the University of Newcastle, the Sydney Conservatorium of Music and the Royal Northern College of Music in Manchester. While in the United Kingdom, Craig performed in a variety of oratorio and operatic works and taught singing in several institutions. Since returning to Australia, Craig has performed with many of the professional opera companies and he maintains teaching studios in Sydney and Newcastle.

Rosemary Saunders completed her music and teacher training at the Newcastle Conservatorium of Music. After teaching in both Newcastle and Canberra, Rosemary moved to Sydney to sing with The Song Company and later returned to Newcastle to join the singing staff at the Conservatorium. During this time, she also began teaching singing at Newcastle Grammar School and subsequently held the Director of Music position there for seven years. During this time, Rosemary completed her Master of Music (Choral Conducting) degree. She continues to sing with the vocal quartet, Waxing Lyrical, and with Sydney based ensemble, Cantillation.

Following a distinguished career singing principal roles in major European opera houses and frequent concert performances with leading orchestras and international conductors, soprano *Ghillian Sullivan* returned to her native Australia to become a regular guest artist with Opera Australia and other major Australian companies. Recognised as a fine dramatic actress and an excellent comedienne, Ghillian has some 40 leading roles in her repertoire, as well as an extensive knowledge of art song and concert repertoire. Her role as the Artistic Director of Newcastle Festival Opera sees Ghillian focus on the direction of opera and the translation of opera libretti, as well as mentoring young singers and instrumentalists in opera and concert productions. Ghillian also teaches voice production in Brisbane, Sydney and Newcastle, and is regularly invited to direct operatic productions for leading Universities.

Chapter 6

Singing Teaching and Science: An Ancient Symbiosis

Sally Collyer

As far back as the 13th century of Jerome of Moravia and John of Garland (Timberlake, 1990), perhaps even as far as Ancient Greece, singing teachers have subjected their teaching to systematic enquiry. Each generation has critically re-examined accepted wisdom and developed new concepts, drawing on information emerging from all fields of endeavour. In turn, the observations of luminaries, such as Garcia II, Vennard and Miller, have informed and challenged disciplines as diverse as acoustics, education, laryngology, neurology and psychology. Teaching and science have always formed a dynamic symbiosis, a mutually beneficial partnership between two very different creatures. This chapter explores this symbiotic relationship between singing teaching and science. It begins with a cautionary tale of how misconception can arise and linger, a timely reminder for today's singing teacher who must tread a fine line between remaining open-minded and avoiding quackery in a host of unfamiliar disciplines. The tale reminds us, too, how errors can act as a catalyst for better understanding and further research. The chapter then turns to the thorny issue of how today's singing teacher can stay abreast of the accelerating body of interdisciplinary knowledge. Three examples are used: acoustic analysis and the beautiful voice, nonlinear phonation theory and contemporary singing, and respiratory analysis and appoggio. These examples highlight the challenge, as well as the exciting potential, for singing teachers in accessing and integrating cutting-edge science into pedagogy, which is traditionally dominated by the master–apprentice model, and personal experience as singers. The chapter concludes with an overview of the challenges and opportunities that face teachers and their professional associations (such as ANATS) in establishing a model of professional development to meet the needs of the 21st century teacher.

Once Upon a Time ...

... in a land far, far away, an article appeared in a journal for singing teachers. Unusually, it came with a warning label, which began:

> The content of this article, although of a controversial nature, presents a fresh viewpoint in the centuries-old search for an explanation of the laryngeal function in the formation of pitch. It would be premature to predict its impact upon the profession. (Husson, 1956, p. 12)

The article was called “A New Look at Phonation: Multiphase Conduction in the Recurrent Laryngeal Nerve During Phonation” (Husson, 1956), and it appeared in the *NATS Bulletin* of the US-based National Association of Teachers of Singing. The article was a translated résumé of a communication from Dr Raoul Husson of the Sorbonne to the French Society of Phoniatrics on October 24, 1951. The communication outlined the neurochronaxic theory, which proposed that vocal-fold vibration was controlled not by airflow, but by neural activity. An action potential travelled from the brain, via the recurrent laryngeal nerve, to the transverse fibres (or aryvocalis) of the thyroarytenoid muscle, opening the glottis. Fundamental frequency was determined by the number of action potentials per second, to a maximum firing rate of 500 Hz (slightly above B4, the B above middle C). Above 500 Hz, there was a phase shift in firing, so fibre bundles fired alternately, which overcame the limitation of firing rate. At c.1000 Hz, another phase shift occurred. Husson noted the upper limit of the female chest voice at 500 Hz and the shift to whistle register above c.1000 Hz, and attributed these to phase shifts in muscle firing. Most significantly, breath was not essential for vocal-fold vibration, merely the means by which vibrations were made audible. The vocal folds did not need exhalation in order to open and close. Husson cited a range of studies that supported this theory. A photograph of the great soprano, Mado Robin, reminded readers that these findings were corroborated by studies of her voice, amongst others. Husson concluded (in translation): “The pitch of the voice is fixed by the frequency of the rhythmic activity of certain elements of the encephalon” (Husson, 1956, p. 13).

As the warning label said, the proposition that the vocal folds vibrated by themselves was indeed controversial. The prevailing view was that the voice was an aerodynamic instrument. Although muscular activity was a key factor in regulating pitch, loudness and timbre, the vocal folds could not make themselves vibrate and certainly not at the frequencies easily achieved in speech and singing. The maximum firing rate of nerves (the chronaxie) was simply too slow, and Husson’s claim of a maximum firing rate of 500 Hz was astounding. In short, to vibrate, the vocal folds needed airflow. Thus, the neurochronaxic theory was a storm in the field of phoniatrics.

The article's warning label went on to make clear that the Research Committee had deliberated a great deal over whether to bring this work to the attention of singing teachers, and enormous care had been taken to ensure that both the résumé and its translation were faithful representations of Husson's proposition. The Committee's dilemma was obvious. If the theory were correct, it heralded a major shift in our understanding of phonation, and singing teachers deserved to know; but if it were wrong, as its many critics maintained, presenting science only to have it debunked would be a major blow to the ever fragile relationship between science and singing, and might close many teachers' minds to science in the future. In the end, the Committee placed their faith in the reasonableness of the average singing teacher and published.

The next issue of the *NATS Bulletin* contained an explanatory article called "Some Implications of the Husson Research" by the incomparable William Vennard (1957). He repeated the warning that "voice teachers are not qualified to take sides in a highly scientific controversy" (p. 4). He also noted that Husson's other writings recognised the role of breath and muscle adductive force in sustaining phonation. Vennard likened the firing of the aryvocalis fibres to spark plugs that "ignited" vibration. Caveats established, he then outlined the theory's potential contributions to singing teaching. There were many. The idea, of pitch being controlled by neural impulses originating in the auditory cortex, accorded beautifully with the teaching concept of hearing the note in one's head before singing it. The challenge of mentally hearing one pitch against a background of conflicting pitches explained the greater difficulty of singing dissonant intervals than consonant. And so on. But the most important implication was for voice registers. Transitions at c.500 Hz and c.1000 Hz matched changes into head and whistle registers, and validated the use of the term "falsetto" by Manuel Garcia II for both male and female voices above the chest register, later restated as "mixed" for the female voice.

On the other hand, Vennard's article was not a wholesale endorsement of Husson's work. He noted several questions raised by the theory. If pitch is a function of neural and not muscular activity, why does pitch lower when the singer is pressed gently on the thyroid cartilage? Or rise when pressed sharply in the epigastrium? What about vibrato? Nevertheless, Vennard concluded that the neurochronaxic theory added "a new factor to our speculations" (1957, p. 32).

But did it?

It certainly excited interest. Following demands for more information on "this subject [that] has stimulated more eulogistic letters to date than any previous feature" (Husson, 1957, p. 6), the next *NATS Bulletin* published another translated article by Husson, "The classification of human voices"

(1957, p. 6–11). The editorial preface effusively declared that the neurochronaxic theory had solved the problem of classifying voices. The article itself noted the failure of attempts to classify voices by vocal-fold length, body type and gender stereotyping. Building on the neurochronaxic theory, a singer's voice classification was shown to be determined by the maximum firing rate of the individual's recurrent nerve; that is, the point at which the aryvocalis fibres shifted to firing in phased groups, which determined the upper limit of the chest register. Furthermore, other work had shown that the chronaxie of the recurrent laryngeal nerve was well estimated by that of the medullary spinal nerve innervating the sternocleidomastoid muscles. Classifying voices was now simply a matter of measuring the sternocleidomastoids. The classification established "all the tonal characteristics of the human voice" (Husson, 1957, p. 9) and had been verified on 110 opera singers and students, including, of course, the great Mado Robin, whose picture adorned this article as well. The higher the chronaxie, the higher the voice category. Husson conceded that this classification was based only on pitch, not on timbre or intensity, and that it reminded us that voice types are a continuum rather than a series, but the results clearly proved this "definitive and rather spectacular solution of the old problem of voice classification" (Husson, 1957, p. 11).

The following month, the neurochronaxic theory was "the most exciting topic of discussion" at the International Voice Conference in Illinois, United States (Van den Berg, 1958, p. 6). However, one conference paper "shook the faith of many in the Husson conclusions," as the editor of the *NATS Bulletin* later described it (Van den Berg, 1958, p. 6). The paper was by Janwillem Van den Berg, a pioneer of the myoelastic-aerodynamic theory, and it was reproduced in the *NATS Bulletin* a year later. The paper was a beautiful example of explaining complex concepts to the layperson. It began with a potted history that reminded us that our understanding that phonation results from vocal-fold vibration was a relatively recent development. Next, it comprehensively rebutted the neurochronaxic theory — neurologically, anatomically, physiologically and aerodynamically — and the interpretation of scientific observations that gave rise to it. The paper then described the key elements of the myoelastic-aerodynamic theory of phonation which prevails to this day. This description was exquisite in its clarity and conciseness, introducing key concepts such as nonlinear coupling that are still being unravelled more than 50 years later.

The neurochronaxic theory was conclusively rebutted, and with it went the one-stop voice classification system. Still, the theory continued to exert an influence, because, in fact, the time was not so very long ago and the place not far away at all. After all, what is a theory? As the saying goes, a theory is only the best explanation currently available, ready to be updated or even ditched completely when a better explanation comes along. Van den Berg's (1958) potted history described how knowledge grows: incrementally, cautiously and even haphazardly. Even as Van den Berg dismantled the neurochronaxic theory and the observations that underpinned it, he made the point:

> Enough of these controversies, however, not without admitting the great progress of our knowledge induced by all these investigations. Everybody will immediately recognise the high spirit, courage and originality necessary to undertake experiments under such difficult conditions. (p. 10)

Nearly four decades later, Aatto Sonninen, another major critic of the neurochronaxic theory, praised Husson's daring and the galvanising effect his work had on the consolidation, and further study of vocal-fold anatomy, physiology and neurology. Sonninen wrote that the 1950s "scientific war" reaffirmed:

> ... that the bold and unprejudiced framing of questions — possibly leading to erroneous conclusions — is not dangerous, something to be feared ... however, a scientist must always aim at confirming in all respects the validity and reliability of his observations. (Wendler, 2010, p. 1)

Occasionally, the idea that the vocal folds are capable of self-vibration resurfaces in singing pedagogy. One source is a chapter in Husler and Rodd-Marling's *Singing: The Physical Nature of the Vocal Organ*. First published in 1965, by which time the neurochronaxic theory had already been dismissed, the chapter was retained in the 1976 revised edition and the 1983 reprint and states in part:

> In objective research on the voice, the following is now generally accepted: *it is not the outflowing breath that sets the vocal folds vibrating* ... (1983, p. 55, italics in original)

A footnote acknowledging criticism of the neurochronaxic theory makes an interesting observation:

> Should no substantiation be found for this concept ... it remains for us a pedagogic fiction of exceptional value in training voices. (1983, p. 56)

The Moral of the Story

The history of the neurochronaxic theory encapsulates many of the complexities inherent in the relationship between science and singing. These complexities are not unique to singing pedagogy; they reflect the ambiguity of the place of science in our society generally. By the end of the 19th century, the Victorian era had bequeathed to society an enthusiasm for "scientific method" as the stamp of worth. Singing pedagogy was not immune. To claim that one's teaching was "based on scientific principles" was a must for credibility, even if the claim might not quite withstand close scrutiny. But, since *scientia* simply means "knowledge," *science* can mean different things to different people and, indeed, different things to the same person depending on the circumstances. In fact, it could be argued that the Victorians bequeathed us an enthusiasm less for science than for technology, for gadgets and widgets.

Social reflections on the Victorian era from a 20th century perspective were not greatly flattering. Ironically, for an age that saw sweeping changes, the 19th century is often seen as repressed and regressive. Yet teachers tend to agree that the birth of singing science — or at least of singing technology — began with Manuel Garcia II's development of the laryngoscope. In 1854, the age of *singing pedagogy based on scientific principles* began.

Singing teachers reached out to a host of scientific disciplines, and scientists were eager to assist, especially the medical fraternity, though this reflected more the limitations in the available technology of other disciplines than any lack of interest. To this day, new disciplines can turn to singing only as their technology makes it feasible to do so; the enormous advances of vocal-tract imaging by scientists such as Brad Story (2008) awaited the development of magnetic resonance imaging technology to a critical minimum capacity. The keen interest of science was and is more than just the chance to rub shoulders with great singers or do hair-raising things to them in a laboratory. Singing lies at the heart of evolution and development. A lesser subject would have elicited a frantic wave of examination, a flurry of papers and pronouncements, until — as the saying goes — there was nothing left but the feathers and the pack moved on. But the passing parade of scientific disciplines did not, in fact, pass at all. It stayed, and has stayed ever since, because the answers were unexpected and fascinating. By the end of the 20th century, the Victorian view of science as the mainstay of relentless human progress had taken rather a beating, but by and large, science — and technology, with which it is often confused — had become an inextricable part of life and work (terms also often confused).

What Can Science Teach Teachers?

In these early years of the 21st century, it is largely taken for granted that voice science is an important part of singing pedagogy. That is not to say that this situation is without its critics, such as Thomas Hemsley (1998) and Peter Harrison (2006). The rejoinder that those without research training do not understand the nature of scientific investigation is superficial. It is also hard to dismiss the criticism of those who do have research training, such as Stephen Austin (1998), whose doctoral work in "hard-science" acoustics investigated the effects of subglottal resonance, yet who holds the view that voice science has added nothing other than corroboration to historical practice.

Perhaps it is the Australian experience, the notorious "tyranny of distance", or even remnants of the infamous Australian cultural cringe, but I know many singing-teacher colleagues who disagree. Indeed, my own experience has been quite different, in a myriad of ways. To give just one example, a teacher of mine one day suggested that I try using "imploded consonants". Despite our best efforts in every way imaginable, the understanding of how to sing an imploded consonant stubbornly refused to transfer from teacher to student. I found I was not alone in my inability to grasp and implement the concept but, sadly, those who could grasp it could not straddle that great divide to help us. There was occasional success, but it was random and confusing, and eventually the idea fell by the wayside. Some years later, I came across the well-known (in voice-science circles, that is) technique for subglottal pressure estimation devised by Smitheran and Hixon (1981). In brief, pressure in the mouth measured during the stop portion of the stop-plosive /p/ is a reliable estimate of subglottal pressure during the subsequent vowel, under certain circumstances. Reading through those circumstances, I recognised them as the criteria for an imploded consonant and understood what had eluded me— the technique was occasionally difficult with a subject "who shows a substantial degree of neuromuscular involvement in the orofacial region" (Smitheran and Hixon, 1981, p. 146). Facial muscular tension, externally invisible but very obvious to me, had been the culprit, and the harder I had tried, the worse it had gotten. However, this insight led further. I became very aware of the tendency in Australian English (and, later, in certain other cultures and languages) to drop pressure during consonants, to "under-voice" consonants and to compensate by over-enunciating. Since the technique highlighted the close relationship between pressure (wherever that might be) during the consonant and subglottal pressure during the ensuing vowel, and since beginning singers tend to compensate for insufficient subglottal pressure by increasing flow rather than pressure, the relationship between consonant formation, legato and timbre was apparent and readily applicable in the studio. A whole series of exercises gained new meaning.

Science is also a valuable ally in weeding out fallacy from our historical legacy, such as a literal interpretation of sinus-tone theory. In fact, it may be modesty that precludes Austin from acknowledging the substantial contribution of his work on subglottal resonance to recognising that register transitions are not simply a matter of the balance between the cricothyroid and thyroarytenoid muscles, as expounded in many historical writings. These examples are not to suggest that science holds all the answers or that imagery (in all its fascinating forms) is outdated. In fact, the most rigidly accurate literal description of what does what in singing is still an image, a concept, when we actually come to doing it. For the singer, an accurate image has no inherently greater validity than the wildest fantastic vision of pink sheep in purple fields. We tend to believe that an accurate image will be more likely to render improvement, but ultimately the test of an image's validity is whether it helps that singer sing better. The singer is concerned only with his or her personal *how*. The situation is quite different for the teacher, because he or she must identify *what* needs doing in order to begin establishing *how* it is to be done for this individual singer. Unless the teacher can draw on a base of fundamental principles to guide technical development in individual circumstances, training becomes an endless and confusing stream of tips and tricks.

Goal and Process

To return to the criticisms of Thomas Hemsley (1998) and Peter Harrison (2006), there is valid concern that the very effect of establishing an objective, quantitative investigation renders it unmusical. Apart from constraints imposed by technological limitations, which do recede each year but which in many disciplines are still substantial, scientific investigation is based on isolating the performance as far as possible from all influences other than the one being studied. The researcher is always acutely aware that "the 'Conclusions' giveth, but the 'Material and Methods' taketh away" (Spodick, 1975, p. 593). The situation is deliberately artificial, but that does not necessarily render it inapplicable, any more than the artificial situation of lesson and rehearsal renders them inapplicable to performance in an auditorium with an audience. Method and interpretation are crucial. What critics often overlook is that there are substantial similarities in goal and process between science and performing, and between science and pedagogy. All seek to establish a body of knowledge (generalised in the case of science and pedagogy, personalised in the case of the singer) from observations made on multiple individuals (including those outside the "study pool" or "studio list", such as the sight and sound of acknowledged master singers on stage, in recording, in rehearsal and in masterclass: *All hail the age of recording and YouTube*!). The scientist reviews the knowledge base, the literature, identifies the problem and selects from a wide range of options those means by which to investigate this problem. The results are discussed in light of the literature, then a report on the work is submitted to the peer-review process, which generally means that two or three anonymous reviewers test the report and, thus, the study for its validity and reliability in all aspects. If the report passes the peer review process (whether in its original form or revised), the results become part of the collective knowledge base, available for others to rely on and develop in subsequent studies. And so the cycle repeats. The teacher likewise draws on a wide knowledge base, including scientific and pedagogical literature, personal experience and the experience of colleagues, and information gleaned from observation and inquiry of *this singer*, to identify the next step and a range of means by which to approach *this issue* with *this singer*. The outcomes are also integrated into the teacher's personal experience. Vigilance and self-reflection are imperative, for thus far these are the only means by which the teacher can identify an error in logic or understanding. But how does one know what one doesn't know? Here is where professional networking becomes invaluable for the singing teacher, the chance to discuss outcomes and exchange information with colleagues. More rarely, the teacher might be persuaded to go into print, so the outcomes contribute to the pedagogical literature and reach a wider circle. The cycle repeats; it is flexible, but progressive. There is an additional factor in the equation — the singer, who is guided by the teacher, but must still remain an interactive participant, receiving and providing feedback, refining understanding and developing his or her personal technique. A singer who merely receives lacks self-efficacy and is never able to leave the nest, but the technique does not need to be applicable to any other singer.

Handling Failure

A major difference between science and teaching/singing is the reintegration into the knowledge base of "failures", or what science calls "negative results". The hypothesis of a scientific study — the expected outcome — is carefully derived from a gap, an apparent anomaly or an uncertainty in the existing knowledge base. The format is usually along the lines of, "Because we know A and B, we hypothesise that, if we do C (and, so far as possible, *only* C), we will get D". If the outcome is indeed D, then that confirmation becomes part of the foundation for other studies. If, however, the outcome is not D (perhaps it is E or Q or even 9!), this negative result could indicate a flaw of reasoning in the hypothesis or it might identify an anomaly or even an error in the knowledge database that could become the catalyst for an entirely new area of study and understanding. This is why critics of the neurochronaxic theory could sincerely applaud the role of Raoul Husson in expediting development of the myoelastic-aerodynamic theory and of our understanding of neurology in phonation.

For teachers, on the other hand, a negative result (an idea, tool or method that fails to elicit the intended result) is simply a dead end, perhaps modifying how the individual teacher uses the technique in the future, but rarely with the wider dissemination and influence given to successful outcomes. Unlike the peer-reviewed publication of the study, there are few mechanisms by which negative outcomes within the studio can be returned to the pool of knowledge to refine our *collective* understanding of the circumstances in which a given teaching tool or method is likely to be ineffective. Time pressure is one limitation — a singing lesson is for the development of the singer, not for the improvement of pedagogy. More significantly, the studio is a messy place in which to make reliable observations. It abounds with multiple threads of spoken and unspoken communication, of nuance and of history, unlike the theoretically sterile environment of the laboratory, where an individual factor can be isolated and its influence objectively measured. Sadly, it is very difficult to harness the wealth of information inherent in the studio failure. On the other hand, the circumstances under which an approach does *not* work are critical to the refinement of its application. How is this information to be harnessed?

Defining Science

The difference in the treatment of negative results by science (notwithstanding the ongoing debate about publishing null outcomes) and by teaching raises the question, just what is "science"? There can be a perception that it requires some sort of equipment, perhaps a white coat, and certainly a graph or two showing trends and statistical significance. At the other extreme, it might consist of nothing more than a lot of reading and watching. Or, as Antonio Damasio (1999) put it:

> As a student of mind and behavior I turned a pastime — curiosity about the minds of others — into a professional activity, which simply means that I was obsessive about it and took notes. (p. 84)

Both descriptions omit the key attributes of science — that it is "knowledge ascertained by observation and experiment, critically tested, systematised and brought under general principles, *esp* in relation to the physical world" (Science, 1998, p. 1478).

Critical testing makes it possible for Sonninen to declare that an erroneous conclusion is not dangerous and for missteps, such as the neurochronaxic theory, to enhance rather than hamper progress. The primary basis of critical testing is the peer-review system, described earlier. It is not a flawless system and it is weighted to favour the status quo but, generally speaking, a paper appearing in a reputable peer-reviewed journal has made it through the rites of passage into the collective knowledge base. The process is slow and painstaking. Some papers can take two years of review and rebuttal before they are published (or rejected). As the neurochronaxic theory showed, the process is slow because it must be thorough. Once findings are published, they become part of the collective knowledge. If the findings are in error, it may be years before the error is discovered, by which time the studies that rely partly or wholly on the earlier findings might be flawed or lost completely. Think back to Husson's (1957) formulae for voice classification, which was so enthusiastically welcomed: are these formulae invalid because the underlying theory was wrong or the measurements were flawed, or might there still be something valuable yet to be uncovered? Publications also have a way of resurfacing. In the past 10 years, I have met two teachers who had read about self-vibration in Husler and Rodd-Marling (1983) and who admonished me for not teaching it in my courses. To my knowledge, one teacher still teaches the neurochronaxic theory to her singers, apparently finding it "a pedagogic fiction of exceptional value in training voices" (Husler and Rodd-Marling, 1983, p. 56).

For science, the goal of all this testing, systematising and "principling," is to develop a theory. Earlier, I noted that a theory was, crudely speaking, the best explanation we have so far. This overlooks its far more important, indeed its critical, function as a means of predicting what *has not* yet been observed or, even more excitingly, what *cannot* yet be observed. The more clear and cohesive the theory, the more reliable and nuanced are its predictions of what will occur and the circumstances under which it will not. Singing teachers who want to understand and not merely chant the wisdom of past generations, and in turn contribute to their own, their colleagues' and their students' progress, rely every day on scientific theories that they have encountered and sought to master, often valiantly, in their quest for professional development. These theories allow us to predict the timbral effects of lowering the larynx, of lying down, of introducing nasality. It is the means by which we comprehend register transition, adductive force, singer's formant and mucosal wave. However, it is in the incorporation and development of newly relating, even newly forming, disciplines — such as motor learning and the study of consciousness — that the most exciting opportunity for advancing pedagogy lies: the gradual construction of a theory on singing teaching itself from which predictions at an individual, studio level can be made. The daunting, but exhilarating, challenge for singing pedagogy is to establish the means by which all forms of knowledge, including the fleeting and intangible that constitute so much of singing and of singing teaching, can be incorporated in a persistent, rigorous and objective self-scrutiny.

Mechanical Teaching

For many, such a bald statement conjures up Orwellian nightmares of mechanical, functional learning, delegated to a software program or coming to a plasma TV near you. Again, the distinction must be made between technology and science, and between the teacher's means of understanding how one *does* sing and the teacher's means of understanding how one *learns to* sing. A scientific approach to teaching means that every assumption is rigorously tested, systematic connections are made, principles are derived and then these are further tested, systematised and refined. The process is continuous and all-encompassing — no cherished belief or devoutly held viewpoint is above examination. It is not enough to say, "I know this works" without ruthlessly examining why, especially if the usual reason is demonstrably false. A case in point is the time-honoured directive to inhale through the nose as if smelling the scent of a flower. Some teachers maintain that this raises the soft palate, yet that would close the velopharyngeal port and stop airflow through the nose. The point is not to abandon an effective technique because the current explanation is flawed, but to seek out the true explanation and in the meantime admit the unknown, even at the risk of appearing uninformed against more confident but less rigorous colleagues, and even if only for the sake of a duty of care to the singers in your studio who will one day be teachers.

It should be acknowledged that many fear that knowing too much about singing will spoil its mystique. It is a common enough view, amusingly highlighted in Daniel Levitin's surprising commentary that Gordon Sumner (the singer, Sting) was very reluctant to observe the results of his brain scan in a study of music (Pochmursky, 2010). Sting's concern was indeed that such knowledge might destroy the mystery of his creativity, perhaps like the proverbial centipede who could no longer dance after the beetle enquired which leg went first. Ian Judge (2001) noted that, "The price of knowledge is dissatisfaction". On the other hand, knowledge in any endeavour offers an appreciation of achievement not recognisable to the layperson. At a personal level, this must be ultimately a matter for the individual. However, once the responsibility for training other voices is assumed, the teacher, like all professionals, must commit to taking every opportunity for professional development. Whatever the attitude to science, the luxury of ignorance is never an option for a professional.

Hot Topics

Assuming that the teacher wants to be on the cutting edge in singing pedagogy, where is that edge at the moment? As the story of the neurochronaxic theory illustrated, it is everywhere and nowhere. That is to say, the fascination that singing exerts on other disciplines means that almost every discipline imaginable, including studies of all creatures that phonate, can have a link to singing. To list them all would be impossible and in fact would be outdated even before it reached the page, but the following contains notes on three of these frontlines.

Acoustic Analysis and the Beautiful Voice

The holy grail of acoustic analysis has always been to define a beautiful voice in terms of its acoustic characteristics. Like all holy grails, this continues to elude pursuers. The problems are twofold. First, measurements that are simple enough to be readily applicable are too simple to encompass the complex meaning of the word "beautiful". Even the well-known singer's formant cluster (Sundberg, 1987) has undergone re-evaluation. Once thought to be exclusive to male and low-female voices, the question has arisen whether it might be a factor in the difference between a lyric and dramatic voice in female opera singers (Barnes, Davis, Oates, & Chapman, 2004). The assumed relationship between the singer's formant and the perceived professional standard of the singer has not held (Mitchell & Kenny, 2004). One possibility for perceived vocal standard is how smoothly the spectral balance (an acoustic measure, being the relative energy in low and high partials) changes with changing sound level (Collyer, Davis, Thorpe, & Callaghan, 2009), but it is only a suggestion, and Husson's voice classification formulae remind us not to jump to conclusions, however tempting and intuitively reasonable they might appear.

Second, the key word in the preceding was "perception". Robison, Bounous, and Bailey (1994) published an interesting study of baritones and female belt singers. Yet 16 years later, we still have no agreement on the definition of "belt". In fact, getting experienced listeners to agree on assessments is remarkably difficult (Kreiman, Gerratt, & Precoda, 1990). Although the research method can be adapted to increase reliability, the difficulty casts doubt on how reliable listeners are in real-world situations, such as audition panels and competition judging, a sobering thought (Collyer, Kenny & Archer, in press). And without reliable perceptual analysis, defining the beautiful voice acoustically remains a distant dream.

Nonlinear Phonation Theory and Contemporary Singing

Singing teachers of my generation have grown up with the linear theory of phonation, which says that the voice you hear is a product of the noise made by the vocal folds and the filtering effects of the vocal tract (Sundberg, 1987). The neglected twin of linear theory has been nonlinear theory, not actually a different or conflicting theory as this might imply, which was alluded to by Van den Berg in his rebuttal of Husson's work: "minor difficulties might arise when the pitch produced at the glottis comes near the pitch of the resonators" (Van den Berg, 1958, p. 11). Nonlinear refers to what occurs when the source is affected by the characteristics of the filter (Titze, 2004). The idea that nonlinear phonation might be much more common than was previously thought has major implications for our understanding of vocal-fold vibration, particularly because many of our observations have used a technique called inverse filtering, which presumes a linear context. To recall that familiar warning, "It would be premature to predict its impact upon the profession" (Husson, 1956, p. 12).

However, one of the most exciting aspects is the proposal by Ingo Titze that nonlinear phonation may be one of the major differences between classical and contemporary voice and, indeed, may be the reason why some rock singers, particularly, can sustain apparently hyperfunctional vocal behaviour without harm. Science of course progresses more slowly than we, impatient teachers, would prefer (Titze, 2008), but the speed of communication has certainly improved since 1958. Teachers who would like to know more about the implications of nonlinear theory can follow developments through such online resources as Ingo Titze's presentation at PAS4 (2009a) and a video clip uploaded to Youtube (2009b).

Respiratory Analysis and Appoggio

Singing pedagogy has long been aware that respiratory behaviour in singing is highly individual (Hixon, 1991). Although a trained singer is more consistent than an untrained singer in how he or she breathes for singing, lung-volume use and chest-wall kinematics (changes in the ribcage and abdominal dimensions that underpin lung-volume change) are as unique as a signature (Collyer, Thorpe, Callaghan, & Davis, 2008). On the other hand, singing literature over the years has tended to be increasingly prescriptive about kinematic behaviour, such as Richard Miller's (1996) detailed description of appoggio. Reconciliation of this dichotomy is hampered by current technical limitations in respiratory measurement. After all, kinematics is a dimensional measurement that can imply but cannot report muscular activity, for which techniques such as electromyography are needed; and one of the leaders in utilising electromyography to study respiratory muscle activity in singing is Viggo Pettersen (2005). To add to the confusion, trained singers have a complicated relationship with respiratory control — when given a directive to change their abdominal behaviour during a phrase, they could alter behaviour at the start of the phrase, but by the end of the phrase they had reverted to habit, although they *thought* they were following the directive (Collyer, Kenny, & Archer, 2009).

Keeping Up to Date

To look into the maelstrom of cutting-edge science can be quite frightening. It can leave the teacher feeling that there is no sure footing on which to build a teaching method. It is important to remember the historical treasure-trove of singing teaching, the vast and varied pedagogical literature that spans centuries and to which valuable additions and refinements are constantly being made. The renowned William Vennard, who brought to NATS members the work of great scientists, such as Husson, Van den Berg and Sonninen, and whose most famous pupil was the legendary Marilyn Horne, wrote in the preface to his book still revered today, *Singing: The Mechanism and the Technic* (1967):

> There are those teachers who feel that applying science to an art is quackery, but I believe that our only safeguard against the charlatan is general knowledge of the most accurate information available. (p. iii)

But if a singing teacher wants to remain up to the minute in singing pedagogy, how is this to be done? Of course there is the ever-present challenge of limited time. Sadly, I can offer no answer for that (and would be grateful to hear anybody else's solutions). However, there are many means by which a teacher can keep up to date with trends. First and foremost is active membership of his (or her) professional body. One can always be a passive member, turning up only for events and a little conversation, but active membership offers so much more. Although formal networking opportunities can be useful, informal networking is much more dynamic and flexible, and there is no better source of informal networking than your local teaching association committee. Related organisations, such as the Australian Voice Association, aim to bring together professionals from related — and even distant — fields. Many other organisations, such as the Australian Music & Psychology Society, hold regular speaker sessions where researchers can present their latest work.

The internet has brought a wealth of information into the studio. That brings its own problems, of finding the time and sorting the good from the ordinary or downright dangerous, but the opportunities for accessing information (such as Titze, 2009a, 2009b) are wonderful. There are dedicated discussion groups, such as VocaList (www.vocalist.org), and most professional associations run an online discussion forum (e.g., www.anats.org.au). It should not be overlooked that books and journals remain the most accessible resource for many. Most university libraries offer lending facilities to the general public, and the public library can be a veritable treasure-chest.

However, accessibility is not just a matter of obtaining a copy. To be truly accessible, a teacher needs to be able to assess the worth of what is being proposed, for, after all, there is good science and bad science, just as there is good teaching and bad teaching. If — perhaps, when — another neurochronaxic theory arises, how will singing teachers avoid being taken for a ride? Familiarity with the discipline in question is very helpful, and workshops by practitioners who straddle the divide between science and singing are valuable. As more and more singing teachers take up the research challenge, that divide is bound to reduce, to the benefit of all. A healthy scepticism is also a valiant shield; as the saying goes, if it looks too good to be true, it probably is. Of course, the quality of research is a problem throughout the science community, particularly the misapplication of statistical methods that can make something appear significant when it is not. And a little knowledge of the history of singing science is a major asset for spotting a dodgy proposition — good ideas never spring from nowhere.

Ultimately, the challenge for the singing teacher is the enormous breadth of topics to be spanned. This chapter has discussed the challenges in keeping up with scientific developments affecting pedagogy. Of course, science is only a part, and in many ways a small part, of the professional development of a teacher. A singing teacher must be competent across an enormous range of areas, including repertoire, styles, languages, performance trends, teaching methods, curriculum or examination requirements, and administration. It is an enormous demand to add to this an expectation that he or she will incorporate a little light reading in "teach yourself respiratory plethysmography"! There is an urgent need for the professional bodies to address the content and delivery of professional development to their members, which particularly takes into account that most singing teachers have undergone no specialist training, but have evolved as singers or pianists. However, the possibilities have never been so promising as now to continue this ancient symbiosis.

References

Austin, S.F. (1998). Confessions of a golf-playing voice scientist. *Australian Voice, 4*, 1–4.

Barnes, J.J., Davis, P., Oates, J., & Chapman, J. (2004). The relationship between professional operatic soprano voice and high range spectral energy. *Journal of the Acoustical Society of America, 116*, 530–538.

Collyer, S., Davis, P.J., Thorpe, C.W., & Callaghan, J. (2009). Fundamental frequency influences the relationship between sound pressure level and spectral balance in female classically trained singers. *Journal of the Acoustical Society of America, 126*, 396–406.

Collyer, S., Kenny, D.T., & Archer, M. (2009). The effect of abdominal kinematic directives on respiratory behaviour in female classical singing. *Logopedics Phoniatrics Vocology, 34*, 100–110.

Collyer, S., Kenny, D.T., & Archer, M. (in press). Listener perception of the effect of abdominal kinematic directives on respiratory behavior in female classical singing. *Journal of Voice.* Accepted for publication October 15.

Collyer, S., Thorpe, C.W., Callaghan, J., & Davis, P.J. (2008). The influence of fundamental frequency and sound pressure level range on breathing patterns in female classical singing. *Journal of Speech, Language and Hearing Research, 51*, 612–628.

Damasio, A. (1999). *The feeling of what happens: Body and emotion in the making of consciousness.* London: William Heinemann.

Harrison, P. (2006). *The human nature of the singing voice: Exploring a holistic basis for sound teaching and learning.* Edinburgh: Dunedin Academic Press.

Hemsley, T. (1998). *Singing and imagination: A human approach to a great musical tradition.* Oxford, UK: Oxford University Press.

Hixon, T.J. (1991). *Respiratory function in speech and song.* San Diego, CA: Singular Publishing.

Husler, F., & Rodd-Marling, Y. (1983). *Singing: The physical nature of the vocal organ: A guide to the unlocking of the singing voice* (Rev. ed.). London, UK: Hutchinson.

Husson, R. (1956). A new look at phonation: Multiphase conduction in the recurrent laryngeal nerve during phonation (J.T. Perkins, Trans.). *NATS Bulletin, 13*(2), 12–13.

Husson, R. (1957). The classification of human voices (E. Robe, Trans.). *NATS Bulletin, 13*(4), 6–11.

Judge, I. (2001, September 5). Mornings with Margaret Throsby. Interview by M. Throsby. ABC Classic FM.

Kreiman, J., Gerratt, B.R., & Precoda, K. (1990). Listener experience and perception of voice quality. *Journal of Speech and Hearing Research, 33*, 103–115.

Miller, R. (1996). *The structure of singing: System and art in vocal technique.* New York, NY: Schirmer.

Mitchell, H.F., & Kenny, D.T. (2004). The effects of open throat technique on long term average spectra (LTAS) of female classical voices. *Logopedics Phoniatrics Vocology, 29*, 99–118.

Pettersen, V. (2005). *From muscles to singing: The activity of accessory breathing muscles and thorax movement in classical singing* (Unpublished PhD thesis). Norwegian University of Science and Technology and University of Stavanger, Norway.

Pochmursky, C. (Writer and Director). (2010, January 12). The musical brain [Television broadcast]. Melbourne, Australia: Special Broadcasting Service.

Robison, C.W., Bounous, B., & Bailey, R. (1994). Vocal beauty: A study proposing its acoustical definition and relevant causes in classical baritones and female belt singers. *NATS Journal, 51*(1), 19–30.

Science. (1998). In S. Anderson, L. Corey, K. Cullan, S. Flackett & A. Grandison, *Chambers dictionary.* Edinburgh, UK: Chambers Harrap.

Smitheran, J.R., & Hixon, T.J. (1981). A clinical method for estimating laryngeal airway resistance during vowel production. *Journal of Speech and Hearing Disorders, 46*, 138–146.

Spodick, D.H. (1975). On experts and expertise: The effect of variability in observer performance. *American Journal of Cardiology, 36*, 592–596.

Story, B.H. (2008). Comparison of magnetic resonance imaging-based vocal tract area functions obtained from the same speaker in 1994 and 2002. *Journal of the Acoustical Society of America, 123*, 327–335.

Sundberg, J. (1987). *The science of the singing voice.* Dekalb, IL: Northern Illinois University Press.

Timberlake, C. (1990). Practica musicae: Terminological turmoil: The naming of registers. *NATS Journal, 47*(1), 24–26.

Titze, I.R. (2004). What is meant by nonlinear and interactive in voice science? *Journal of Singing, 60*, 277–278.

Titze, I.R. (2008). An appeal for patience and long suffering by singing teachers in their assessment of the value of voice science. *Journal of Singing, 64*, 593–594.

Titze, I.R. (2009a). *Pitch-vowel-register interaction in singing* [Video clip]. Fourth International Conference on the Physiology and Acoustics of Singing (PAS4-09), held on January 7–10, 2009 in San Antonio, TX. Retrieved from http://dlat.utsa.edu/Accordent/Static/UTSAxDigitalMedia+Download/JNix_PAS2008Conference/download.htm.

Titze, I.R. (2009b). *Ingo Titze's tip for tired voices: Grab a straw!* [Video clip]. Retrieved from http://www.youtube.com/watch?v=asDg7T-WT-0

Van Den Berg, J. (1958). On the myoelastic-aerodynamic theory of voice production. *NATS Bulletin, 14*(4), 6–12.

Vennard, W. (1957). Some implications of the Husson research. *NATS Bulletin, 13*(3), 4–5, 26, 27, 32.

Vennard, W. (1967). *Singing: The mechanism and the technic.* New York: Carl Fisher.

Wendler, J. (2010). In memoriam: Aatto Sonninen. *Journal of Voice 24*(1), 1.

■ ■ ■ ■ ■ ■ ■ ■ ■

Chapter
7

You Want Me to Think About What?! A Discussion About Motor Skills and the Role of Attentional Focus in Studio Voice Teaching

Adele Nisbet

Traditionally, singing teaching has relied on a teacher's content knowledge (Shulman, 1999) and performance experience to credit good teaching. Many vocal-method books appeared from notable teachers, such as Caccini, Mancini, Tosi, Garcia and Lamperti, but their focus was primarily on defining good singing, describing what the singer was expected to do, and with little thought to the methods for teaching the techniques they advocated (Stark, 1999). In certain singing circles even today, it is often assumed that being a good performer means you can teach. Intuition rather than pedagogical knowledge has often informed the tactics used in the exemplary singing studio (Brown, 1996). But for all the successes of past eras, it is fair to question whether singing teachers have been aware of theories that might better direct their pedagogical behaviour and assist in planning the work with their students. Concepts worthy of consideration are implicit/procedural and explicit/declarative learning, because the acquisition of both forms of knowledge is crucial for the singer. However, theories about how singers ultimately acquire their technique seem poorly defined in relation to studio teaching and learning, and certainly do not seem to drive the practice. This chapter looks at motor skill acquisition as a basic function of learning to sing and at the teaching of singing in light of the principles of attentional focus, which support the acquisition of motor skills for singing.

The Context

In many fields, Australia punches above its weight, and singing is certainly one of them! As I write this chapter, the Aussies at the 2010 Winter Olympics are making their presence felt. And I'm beginning to think that skiing and singing are not such distant cousins if we consider the physical skills and the courage required for top level performance in both fields. The number of notable classical singers that Australia has produced must surely attest to the existence of some marvellous singing teaching. This idea can't be formally confirmed or denied, but all singing teachers know of colleagues whose reputations grew as their students won competitions; they must have been doing something right! As a teacher of classical singing and a lecturer in vocal pedagogy, one question is constantly with me — apart from having an excellent ear, what do I need to know or do to be the best singing teacher I can be? How can I help my students be the best singers they can be? This is not a question exclusive to me, or to classical singing, but at present I am focusing on who and what I know. This chapter shares some of my explorations of this question.

Over the past 50 years, teachers of singing have increasingly integrated content knowledge about the physiology, acoustics and biomechanics of the voice into their studios (Vennard, 1973), with many tertiary institutions presenting specialist courses in vocal pedagogy to ensure singing students are also aware of this information (Verdolini, 2002). Singers and singing teachers in the 21st century have the best opportunity to hold accurate "content knowledge" (Shulman, 1999, p. 64) about the physiology and anatomy of the voice. This content knowledge is now firmly incorporated into the discourse of many singing studios in Australia, but often without an understanding of its pedagogical efficacy. There has been little reflection on or sharing of how we teach — the actual process of teaching and learning — as opposed to what we teach. Nor has there been much significant collection and codification of the existing "wisdom of practice" (Shulman, 1999, p. 68) within singing studios, so it is not surprising that there appears to be little empirical research specific to this topic. In many contexts, teaching practices with little explicit theoretical foundation are designated as "folk pedagogies" (Bruner, 1999, p. 6). Teaching practices within traditional singing studios are embedded in folk pedagogies; however, if we can also embed practice in educational and psychological theory, we can surmount the personality cult that often drives the popularity of a singing studio, and thus give any teacher, regardless of their charismatic or intuition quotient, the opportunity to excel at their job.

Learning to Sing

Simply put, vocal technique is a biomechanical action involving the management of the breath mechanism combined with the engagement of laryngeal and pharyngeal responses to make (phonate) and enhance (resonate) vocal sound, followed by the employment of articulation for communication. Any singer needs a high level of self-perception to integrate the awareness of the action and the sensory experience during the learning process. Oren Brown (1996) maintained, "It isn't so much a matter of making sounds as it is a matter of learning how to let sounds happen" (p. xiii). Letting sounds happen often means avoiding focus of attention on the biomechanics of the physical act of singing. A current lack of scholarly inquiry specific to singing and the acquisition of motor skills recommends this as a new and worthwhile line of investigation, which I have begun to follow. Schmidt and Lee (2005), whose central focus is human movement, recognised that

> … the use of the voice, whether by the vocalist in an opera, or the student learning a new language, is also a motor task, as the sounds are controlled by muscular activity of the vocal apparatus … The potential applications for the principles discovered in the field of motor control are present in nearly every aspect of our lives. (p. 6)

Richard Miller, arguably the preeminent vocal pedagogue of the 20th century and inspirational to much scientific research into the anatomy and physiology of the voice, was honoured in the *Journal of Singing* by Paul Kiesgen (2007), who said of him, "While providing solid information on the reasons behind his technical approach, Richard always has understood that people need to be led to feel the coordination of good singing by indirect means" (p. 263). My exploration of literature from the domain of sports psychology has revealed a growing body of research on the acquisition and development of motor skills and has opened up some critical leads about what might best support the teaching and learning of singing, despite a scarcity of scholarly inquiry specific to singing. Interpolating the process of acquiring motor skills for singing from the general theories of motor learning therefore appears eminently reasonable.

To sing in the *bel canto* tradition of classical music is to engage in a unique and complex activity, at the basis of which is a level of physicality capable of transformation into artistic expression and communication. To achieve a level of expertise, a singer must engage not only in the affective domain out of which the creative arts flourish, but also acquire the highly refined physical technique necessary for the vocal challenges of the performance. Thus, "… the artist must be gifted not only with that indefinable something that we call the inspiration of creation, but also with the required vocal technique" (Arbitbol, 2006, p. 347). Vocal technique involves conscious and unconscious knowledge. Singing is a gestalt made up of a complex web of affective, cognitive and perceptual operations. All human beings have the capability to sing; supervised training and extended effort called "practice" (Ericsson, 2001) has been shown to nurture this capability into skill and ability, which at its highest level of expertise is lauded in performance. In the artistic performance of an expert singer, technique is something that is inferred.

> Once a singer's muscle systems are trained athletically ... he or she can work without conscious control during performance conditions ... The opera and concert singer needs his or her full attention for artistry and performance and only when problems occur is there any need for awareness ... (Chapman, 2006, p. 58)

There are many skills that contribute to an expert vocal performance — communication, musicality, histrionic and linguistic abilities, but the physicality of the activity is central to an autonomous vocal technique. Bel canto principles identify vocal tone — "much of the expressive power of song lies in the voice itself" (Stark, 1999, p. xxv) — as the initial tool of the singer. A singer needs a high level of self-perception to integrate the action and the sensory experience resulting from the action during this learning process. As Brown (1996) would have us understand, letting sound happen rather than imposing overt control is fundamental to establishing optimal vocal tone; this often means avoiding attentional focus on the biomechanics of the physical act of singing. Researching this idea has led me to uncover some interesting and potentially valuable insights for singing teachers.

Perceptual Motor Learning Theory

Motor learning is defined as "a set of internal processes associated with practice or experience, leading to a relatively permanent change in the capacity for skilled behaviour, a state sometimes termed *habit*" (Schmidt & Lee, 2005, p. 320). Verdolini, in a collaborative treatise with Ingo Titze (manuscript in preparation) proposes her own definition, modelled on that put forward by Schmidt and Lee, "Motor learning is a *process*, which is *inferred* rather than directly observed, which leads to *relatively permanent changes* in the *potential* for motor performance, as the result of *personal practice or exposure*" (manuscript in preparation).

Schema Theory for perceptual motor learning (Schmidt, 1975) offered an explanation for what happens after the executive of the brain has initiated the generalised motor program in response to the internal "go" signal that initiates motor activity. Adams (1971) had earlier recognised the perceptual and cognitive elements in motor processing, and his theory paved the way for greater theoretical refinement from Schmidt (1975), Fischman and Oxendine (2001), and Schmidt and Lee (2005). Sherwood and Lee (2003) suggested that the construct of cognitive effort, defined as "the mental work involved in making decisions" (Lee, Swinnen, & Serrien, 1994, p. 329) needed to be central to Schmidt's Schema Theory (1975) and Schmidt subsequently supported this inclusion. More recently, Shea and Wulf (2005) described the general program and the discrete parameters of an action as fluid and developmental, capable of revision and transformation under the best practice environment. Giovanni Battista Lamperti, a distinguished vocal pedagogue from the 19th century, introduced the same idea, but without any knowledge of motor programming, when he described "singing by reflex" (Brown, 1957):

> There is a relationship, psychological and physiological, between the desire to sing and the body, similar to that between the necessity to sneeze and the muscular system ... The network of nerves in this "inside skin" are connected with the brain. They keep the singer informed as to what is taking place in these cavities, and finally anticipate and control the vocal process. (p. 35)

Schmidt's Schema Theory (1975) for the development of perceptual motor skills proposed the existence of two states of memory that issue intrinsic instructions to control our actions — recall memory and recognition memory. Schmidt described recall memory as being responsible for the character of a movement, written in the language of the nervous and muscular systems of the performer's body. Kinaesthetic awareness, at the point of anticipating an action, is part of recall memory, but when the effect or outcome of the action is evaluated, it aligns with recognition memory. The two states of recall and recognition memory are central to the way singers acquire their skills. At the moment, when a singer thinks about making the sound, the set-up of the voice is activated by a prephonatory "motor system", which is activated through neuromuscular engagement; this is the recall memory working. The recognition memory then engages a pattern of feedback , proprioceptive clues — pressure-sensitive receptors in the subglottic mucosa, stretch-sensitive receptors in the laryngeal musculature, mechano-receptors in the joints of the larynx and articulators, and auditory clues — awareness of the tone and tuning of the resultant sound (Stark, 1999).

Motor programming theory endeavours to address the underlying question about how abstract knowledge turns into practical action. For the singer, this means bridging the gap between the idea of singing and actually singing. The physical coordination required involves the complex breathing mechanism, the vibratory mechanism, the articulators and the resonators, all of which have movable and responsive parts. Clarke and Davidson (1998) described the physical body and the movements involved in the production of sounds as inextricably linked to the musical sounds produced by a singer. They also believe that it is naïve to disassociate the emotional from the physical, because the expressive impetus has been shown to engage the body for the creation of the sound. Primal sound associated with human emotional response, evidenced in the earliest recorded history, is testament to this fundamental link between human feeling and vocalising (Arbitbol, 2006; Brown, 1996; Chapman, 2006). A strongly-held notion about refined and artistic singing from the 18th and 19th century also aligns at a related level with this belief.

> Expressivity in singing can be strongly linked not only to the structure of the music or the meanings of the texts, but also to the manner in which the voice is used ... Vocal technique was considered to be inseparable from matters of musical style. (Stark, 1999, p. 154)

On the one hand, the influence of such ideas could be responsible for the bias in pedagogical material on "what to teach" with little on "how to teach". On the other hand, the promotion of musical and dramatic expression may be the ultimate focus of attention, which allows the singer's motor programs to be learned and refined without interference. Verdolini (manuscript in preparation) seems to be the only author producing scholarly comment on motor skill acquisition and singing. She summarised a set of five facts that apply to singing:

- Motor learning for singing is a set of processes.
- Motor learning for singing is not directly observable.
- Motor learning for singing is relatively permanent.
- Motor learning for singing creates capability.
- Motor learning for singing results from practice and exposure.

First, motor learning should be seen as a developmental process, not an imposed structure. The exact nature of that process is still being defined, but the focus needs to be on outcomes rather than the inferred activity that delivers the outcome. This relates to the second fact — that motor learning cannot be directly observed, but can be seen in the change of exhibited behaviour and the outcome. The intrapersonal process of learning to sing is crucial, all singers needing a strong self-awareness.

Third, definitive motor learning has only occurred when the action takes on an habitual character. A temporary shift in vocal performance during a single lesson or coaching does not imply learning; only long-term observation will judge whether retention and transfer of skills has occurred.

The last two facts recognise that once a singer has acquired the general motor skill through repetition and practice, the ability to respond to the detailed vocal demands of more difficult repertoire will become more reliable, as moving between recall memory and recognition memory also becomes unconscious. Experience facilitates learning, turning capability into ability, that is, doing it, not just thinking about doing it.

These five facts describe how the abstraction of singing is transformed into reality through the responses of the singer. A singer doesn't need to understand all this theory behind the performance, but a teacher who understands will be better equipped to support the singer's vocal development. Overarching these five facts is the assertion that "cognition is clearly involved in motor control and learning" (Verdolini, manuscript in preparation), aligning with the revised Schema Theory (Schmidt & Lee, 2005). In other words, the singer engages both conscious and unconscious thoughts to sing, but it is the nature and timing of these thoughts that will either support or hinder the learning process. Oren Brown knew experientially that "Singing requires thinking" (Brown, 1996, p. 183). I believe most singing teachers would concur with this idea! But to identify what sort of thinking and how and when it supports motor skill development in a singing voice is key to this discussion. Singing teachers would benefit from a clearer understanding of learning theory; the next section presents one relevant theory that specifically addresses motor learning.

A Developmental Model for Motor Learning

A three-phase model of motor learning developed by Fischman and Oxendine (2001) seems especially instructive, because it puts forward a pattern of three developmental phases applicable to a singer's acquisition of motor skills. This model, from educational psychology, sets out a logical continuum of learning, with the three phases being identified as cognitive, associative and autonomous.

Cognitive Phase

Novices are in the cognitive phase of motor learning, as they endeavour to learn what it is they have to do. The attentional focus is essentially subjective and for the compliant student, this phase is relatively short. Verdolini (2002) summarised this phase for singers as the "what to do" stage of learning to sing. For a singing teacher, the dilemma is how much information about "what to do" is too much or too little and when is it acceptable to load the student with this information? The cognitive phase is characterised in part by self-talk, both internal and external, as the singers guide themselves through the new process. However, motor learning does not rely on words. Motor learning actually commences unconsciously with listening and observation (Fischman & Oxendine, 2001), so verbalising information about the singing process has questionable value for "knowing about doing".

It is important for the continuing development of a singer that general motor skills are established during this relatively short cognitive phase, before additional parameters are added to performance tasks (Fischman & Oxendine, 2001). Novice singers might exhibit unsophisticated and approximate performance, constant loud singing with variable intonation; however, the skills become refined in the next phase.

Associative Phase

The associative phase of motor skill acquisition is much longer than the cognitive phase; it is when the learner must practise the motor skills to the point of accuracy and consistency (Fischman & Oxendine, 2001); Verdolini (in preparation) described this as the "how to do it" phase for the singer. Once the singer is aware of the whole body as the instrument, with appropriate alignment and ability to create efficient and supported vocal tone, attentional focus is less on the biomechanics, and the singer is beginning to demonstrate automaticity. The visual and aural senses are being replaced by the proprioceptive. Even though novices can experience proprioceptive cues, they may only employ the cues through recall memory, as they are usually not sensitive enough to associate the feelings with the outcomes. What this means is that novice singers may not have yet established reliable recognition memory of physical sensations for evaluating their singing. When a teacher says the sound is right, the novice singer may not be able to feel the difference. It is also a common phenomenon to find beginner singers comfortable with the physical sensations and sounds of their habitual voices, which can lead to a defensive reaction when a different physical coordination brings unfamiliar, therefore, uncomfortable sensations and produces different vocal quality that may be rejected as unpleasant (Chapman, 2006).

Attentional focus on new aspects of the singing process is a challenge in this phase of development. Sports coaches look to train anticipation, selective attention and visual search strategies (Fischman & Oxendine, 2001). Similarly, singing teachers need to guide singers' attentional focus to physical and emotional responses, coordination and varied tonal output. An associative-phase singer should be learning to use less interfering musculature, to maintain poise and therefore make fewer errors in tuning, move faster in melismatic passages, control the dynamic variation and become more consistent in all of these skills. Motor skills defined as closed, that is, those managed in a controlled environment, such as a singing studio, gain consistency in this phase, whereas open motor skills needed in an environment, such as a public performance, are initially less predictable. However, they should become more reliable and adaptive through this phase.

Autonomous Phase

Singers in the autonomous phase of motor skill development are able to perform using their vocal skills at an optimal level (Fischman & Oxendine, 2001). At this stage, very little conscious thought is needed for the motor skill component of the activity to succeed. The recall and recognition schema are highly developed and well established in the memory. True learning can be observed when there is a shift from reliance on cognition to trust in the motor skills (Schmidt & Lee, 2005). However, if that trust falters or the performer is distracted into giving attentional focus to physical action, the automatic performance responses will be disrupted. This has significant implication for the pedagogical approach of a singing teacher working with advanced performers. It also suggests that if the singer has established a secure automaticity, he can sing well despite any bad direction he may be given. A highly developed kinaesthetic awareness seems to be the hallmark of an advanced performer, so that he is able to concentrate on many things other than vocal technique. Using selective attentional focus during the autonomous phase has two purposes — to maintain the highest skill level and to inspire and motivate toward further refinement (Fischman & Oxendine, 2001).

It is a mistake to assume that little improvement can be achieved after the autonomous phase has been reached. In fact, it seems that experts who develop greater professional skill and kudos do so by constant re-engagement with the cognitive and associative stages of learning (Ericsson, 2004). Many top professional singers revisit their teachers for help in maintaining or developing their skills. Do we assume that all teachers working with advanced performers understand either consciously or unconsciously the optimal processes of this interaction? Do some singing teachers intuitively know how to work with advanced singers, but are not as effective with novices — and vice versa? What might happen to our teaching style if we were more aware of the phases of motor skill development?

Teachers need to adopt a fluid approach to instruction through the three phases of motor skill development (Glaser, 2000), adapting instructional methods as competency increases and performance improves. Instruction should move from an interactive phase of external support, through a transition of increased apprenticeship that encourages self-reliance, into self-monitoring and self-regulation when the learner is able to take full responsibility. A recent collection of studies (Poolton, Masters, & Maxwell, 2005; Maxwell, Masters, & Eves, 2003; Maxwell, Masters, Kerr, & Weedon, 2001) confirms that implicit/procedural knowledge is acquired independently from explicit/declarative knowledge. The recommendation from these studies is that initial work with a performer should establish the implicit/procedural knowledge as habit, before imposing explicit demands onto the working memory. Singers who perform material that demands histrionic and even choreographic complexity before they have established the habitual vocal skills inevitably seem insecure, incompetent or at worst untalented.

For novices, the learning and then the enacting of motor skills requires coexistent, but different, neurological responses — the performance is different from the practice session and consistency is variable. This is particularly noticeable with amateurs for whom the success of a performance often requires a "rise to the occasion" nervous energy element. The more advanced the performers, the more reliable the level of automaticity; they are able to access established schema and do not necessarily differentiate between a learning pattern and a performing pattern. Ultimately, the professional singer achieves a consistency and is secure in the knowledge that the high level of skill attained in rehearsal anticipates the desired outcome for the performance. Different types of cognitive effort assist motor skill acquisition at all levels of development. Experienced performers who are refining their skills access both implicit and explicit memory through cognitive processing, recognising and recalling past and familiar action as required (Squire, 1987). It is obvious that there are real differences between a novice and an experienced performer, therefore an effective teacher would look for different instructional approaches for the different phases of development.

> ... what is important is not only the task that is to be learned but also what strategy is implemented during learning, which in turn reflects what memory system is engaged. Under some circumstances the strategy that is engaged is not optimal for solving a task. (Squire, 2004, p. 174)

Motor Learning and Attentional Focus

Having briefly explored the theories that underpin motor learning, I became interested in identifying specific modes of discourse to support the teaching and learning of motor skills in the singing studio. Anecdotally, attentional focus would seem to be implicated in the process of learning and controlling vocal technique. A singer's technique is a complex combination of skills producing vocal sound. The voice is suspended in the skeletal and muscular framework of the body, and is subject to alteration as a result of any change to this framework. Change can be deliberate, part of technique required for pitch and rhythm patterns, dynamic variation, intermittent or continuous flow of sound and the delivery of language. Change can also happen when motor skills are not secure. The dilemma for all singers is the invisibility of their instrument and the temptation to impose direct control. Focus of attention is often drawn to the vocal source, especially if a singer is being introduced to the physiology of the voice at the same time and it may be that this disadvantages successful engagement with the autonomic system that serves technique. The predicament of control and autonomy while learning to sing is:

> ... that much of motor learning can be seen as a dance between them [controlled and automatic]. The wrong application of one or the other process in training, at the wrong time, probably can undermine the most brilliant biomechanically-based intervention model. (Verdolini, manuscript in preparation)

Through the work of Gabriel Wulf (2007) in particular, attentional focus is identified as a crucial factor associated with motor learning. Attentional focus can be defined as either internal/intrinsic or external/ extrinsic, close or distant, both physically and emotionally. There is growing evidence through numerous studies in human movement (Hodges & Lee, 1999; Wulf, Hob, & Prinz, 1998; Wulf & Prinz, 2001; Wulf & Weigelt,1997; Wulf, 2007), that using instruction to direct attention to the biomechanics of the task disrupts both performance and learning. This statement seems so counter-intuitive for teachers of singing. "Learning can be greatly enhanced if references to the performer's movements are avoided as much as possible and if their attention is instead directed to the desired movement effect" (Wulf & Prinz, 2001, p. 657). Attention to the physiological facts will not necessarily result in a positive outcome for motor learning or performance. "Evidence is accumulating to support the premise that presenting a performer with a large explicit knowledge base through learning is, paradoxically, not the most productive method of acquiring skill" (Poolton, Maxwell, Masters, & Raab, 2006, p. 89). However this depends on the place of the performer, along the developmental continuum. Poolton, Masters and Maxwell (2005) reiterated that

> Early experiences of environments that constrain hypothesis testing (and the associated dependence on working memory) allow procedural control unhindered by later accumulation of declarative knowledge. In other words, after a brief period of errorless learning, movement control may remain independent of working memory, despite subsequent periods of explicit learning. (p. 375)

Herein lies a vital cue for effective teaching and learning of singing; in the first stage of learning, knowing explicit information about the coordination of the "bodymind" (Pert, 1997) for singing would appear to be useful, but only to support a performer's first goal of establishing the implicit/procedural knowledge of vocal technique. This involves attention to sensory information, but without intentional doing. Verdolini (2002) suggested that singing teachers who engage primarily in verbal discourse — in other words those of us who talk too much — often overlook this form of teaching and learning. A teacher should deliberately be drawing a singer's attention to sensation, so that sensation becomes the guide for the action rather than attention to explicit/declarative information.

Nissen and Bullemer (1987) suggested that while "… learning does not necessarily require awareness of what one is learning, it may still be the case that learning, regardless of how it is measured, does require that the performance of the task be attended" (p. 5), highlighting the need to be compliant or committed to the learning process. Curran and Keele (1993) suggested that the concept of awareness is "highly subjective and problematic" (p. 18), but Verdolini responds to this challenge by coining the phrase "a non-analytical way of *being in the moment*" (2002, p. 48), to allow a singer to access this awareness or unconscious process. In the studio, a teacher needs to identify pedagogical tools, such as auditory models and visual ideals for tone quality, models for alignment or articulation, that guide a singer's attentional focus to uninhibited physical response. A teacher can employ physical action or manipulation to focus a singer's attention on the physical sensations, such as breath compression, resonance or pelvic alignment. Actions such as these deliver procedural knowledge that can then inform the singer's own error detection and technical development, especially in the cognitive and associative phases of development.

One of the key concepts behind external focus for the performer is not merely the distraction from the biomechanics of singing, but the deliberate attention to the effects of the singing. Explicitly, "directing attention to movement effects related to the movement form seems to be more beneficial than focusing on more remote effects that are not directly related to the movement technique" (Wulf, McNevin, Fuchs, Ritter, & Toole, 2000, p. 237). There is a growing acceptance that significant advantages exist for performers if they develop a strong external focus that distracts their inherent need to intervene in the automatic motor process (Wulf, Shea, & Park, 2001; Wulf, Weigelt, Poulter, & McNevin, 2003; Wulf, 2007). Ultimately, a singer must learn to trust unconscious responses rather than employ attention for conscious technical control. One of the mantras of Oren Brown (1996) appears to recognise the importance of trusting the unconscious processes of learned behaviour — Think : Let : Trust. "*Thinking* is necessary to create the proper conditions. If you have trained your *thinking* and done your practice, you can *trust* the result if you will just *let* it happen" (p. 36).

This section has given a brief account of the growing body of work on attentional focus and motor skill acquisition. Now follows a summary of principles under a framework of five headings, taking authority from the eminent work of Gabriel Wulf (2007), to apply to the discourse within a singing studio.

Applying Principles of Attentional Focus and Motor Learning to the Singing Studio

Primary Principles

Our motor system functions best when it is unhampered by attempts to consciously control movement. Focusing on the movement effect, rather than the movement itself, is more useful and efficient, that is, better coordinated, more accurate and with faster delivery. When the movement effect is given greater distance from the body movement, the benefit appears to be more pronounced. "Learning can be greatly enhanced if references to the performer's movements are avoided as much as possible and if their attention is instead directed to the desired movement effect" (Wulf & Prinz, 2001, p. 657). A comprehensive reading of studies in human movement reveals growing support for this as a principled approach to the teaching and learning of motor skills. For a singer, movement effects involve different degrees of externalisation as a particular element of vocal technique is addressed; this needs to be more closely defined.

However, here is a familiar story of how a singer's skills can be supported or disrupted by a change of attention and the distanced effect. In a resonant recital hall a singer receives distant audio-feedback from the space, which then allows greater trust in the automaticity of the vocal system; the performance feels easy to the singer and the effect is impressive for the audience. But in a space lacking sympathetic resonance, the audio feedback is reduced to a minimum, bringing the focus of the vocal sound back to the singer's body. This can create anxiety and make a singer engage in unnecessary work to produce the vocal sound; the performance can feel like hard work and the muted result for the audience can also reflect that. However, if a singer in an unsympathetic acoustic has arrived at a level of automaticity, and can rely on the learned kinaesthetic coordination rather than be distracted by the closeness of the body movement effect, the performance will succeed. Novices will have greater difficulty managing such a situation, because their automaticity is not likely to be secure and the conditions commonly degrade their current coordination.

Teaching Principles

In order to speed up automaticity, a performer should be encouraged, as early as possible, to execute movements "as if they are automatic". This implies the sort of "thinking" that Neil Semer (personal communication, March 26, 2010), New York voice teacher, refers to as "being present" rather than allowing distractions to destabilise the motor system. Studies in various sports have shown instruction that engages the "distance effect" is a robust concept in support of motor skill development — it seems this may reasonably apply to singing also. A singer has a number of "distance effects" from which to choose, such as core postural support, resonance sensations, tone quality and acoustic feedback, musical direction and shape, and drama and characterisation.

When there is no object involved in an activity, (singing and sprinting share this characteristic as opposed to golf and pole vaulting), metaphors and analogies can take the focus to the effect rather than to the action itself. Counter-intuitively, motor learning and performance have been shown to be negatively affected by instructions about body movement. In a study in which no instructions prior to practising the motor skill were given, these participants gained better results, that is, learned more effectively than the others who had been given detailed instructions about the movement pattern (Hodges & Lee, 1999). Anecdotally, direct physical instruction is often used in preparation to sing, either by a singing teacher or as part of self-talk by a singer, resulting in attention to the biomechanics of the task. However, the degree of success delivered by this approach for singing is still to be confirmed, given that the distance effect may still be present in certain cases.

Singing teachers who focus on the musical and emotional outcomes of a performance may instinctively know that they are also facilitating technical development. To prepare to sing, a performer needs to engage some cognitive process to set up the action — the unconscious element of this engagement gradually develops towards a desirable automaticity. However, if a singer continues to consciously draw on preparation thoughts as concurrent instruction during a performance, the motor program is likely to be disrupted. Another story — a singer of limited experience has not prepared sufficiently for a public performance and experiences real technical discomfort that matches his musical insecurity as he overloads his working memory to get through the performance. Reflecting on singing after a performance to allow the bodymind to edit the process before attempting it again, is a habit that will enhance the learning process.

There has been some research into the use of imagery or analogy as a teaching tool inducing visualisation of either an action unable to be observed or the effect of that action in relation to singing (Dunbar-Wells, 1997), but not with specific qualification to the development of motor skills. Careful and colourful narrative on the part of a teacher may well induce the implicit skills needed for the action, without undue attentional focus on the physical process (White & Hardy, 1995). Singing teachers who have used imagery or metaphor to draw attention to either sensory information or the effects of the actions may have discovered the value of this approach. Anecdotal reports suggest that some singing teachers use this device intuitively and effectively, thus supporting the singers' motor skill development. An instruction, such as "stop thinking about it — just do it" (Gray, 2004, p. 52), seems to support automaticity, but the performer may often react in the opposite manner, anxiety causing thought, therefore attention onto the process. Superficially, advice to reduce either emotional pressure or cognitive load may seem appropriate, but the small amount of research on this topic shows that a performer is likely to react in a subjective manner "specifically opposite to the intent" (Janelle, 1999, p. 213). This is a familiar story from the singing studio. Habitual external focus facilitates objectivity and automaticity, allowing consolidation, expansion and refinement of the vocal technique.

Developmental Principles

Novices, as they try to understand "what to do" need to pay attention to the details of their actions in order to facilitate the learning process. This often makes their singing temporarily worse. However, the use of the "distance effect" to focus on outcomes related directly to the actions is the principle that should consolidate motor learning and assist development toward automaticity. For a novice, once a simple task is mastered, no additional advantage from external focus will be evident, because the motor skill is already controlled automatically (Wulf, 2007). In the early stages of learning singing, specific guidance, either physical or verbal, helping to minimise errors and stabilise the complex coordination of singing will avoid the cognitive stress of problem solving later on. By establishing errorless action from the beginning, the patterning remains as a learning outcome (Wulf, Shea, & Whitacre, 1998).

Singing teachers have wanted so often to share all their knowledge of how the voice works with their student singers. Paradoxically, "evidence is accumulating to support the premise that presenting a performer with a large explicit knowledge base through learning is … not the most productive method of acquiring skill" (Poolton, Maxwell, Masters, & Raab, 2006, p. 89). For a novice, stimulus cues, which collect as rich internal representations of how things are working, are more valuable than an extrinsic knowledge base. A novice singer should be encouraged to recognise kinaesthetic messages that align with the teacher's description of events. Ziegler (2002) summarised the dilemma:

> Teachers and coaches who provide too much information during the initial stages of learning risk shifting the attentional focus of the learner from the style needed to respond to a cue (narrow external) to one that provides information overload and interferes with skill execution (broad internal). Stimulus cueing assists a student or athlete in the initial stages of learning, after which skill refinement, strategy, and advanced applications can be taught. (p. 29)

A novice singer is likely to be working on exercises using simple note patterns and addressing less complex technical tasks overall. A teacher's choice of repertoire for a novice generally reflects this low complexity level and allows an early singer to experience the satisfaction of successful performance. In contrast, an expert singer, relying on automaticity, will experience a disrupted performance if attention is directed to physical action. However, there is evidence to suggest that an advanced performer, not yet expert, but committed to developing more refined skills, is able to successfully focus on "high-level effects;" that is, the overall outcome that triggers all the submovements necessary to achieve a highly skilled outcome.

Optimal focus of attention seems to change throughout the developmental phases, but despite the importance of this indicator, this is still to be confirmed by specific studies (Wulf, 2007). A novice singer will begin to learn about "what is" as perception is heightened with deliberate audiation, cognition and observation. A teacher's task is to employ instructional language and behaviour that most effectively assists the sensory information that effects "what is," but does not draw attention to the process. Knowledge of how the bodymind and voice works is useful, but only as a foundation to support a performer's first goal of establishing the implicit/procedural knowledge that is vocal technique. Attention to sensory information without intentional "doing" supports the singing process. Maybe voice pedagogues and voice teachers should consider that separating the time and place for "learning about singing" and "learning to sing" may offer real advantages!

Retention and Transfer Principles

Permanency of learning is evidenced in the ability to retain and transfer the learned knowledge or skill. The effects of adopting an external focus when practising a motor skill are not just temporary, but benefit this retention and transfer. Therefore, singers should focus on the effect that corresponds to the highest level of control that is presently feasible for them, given the difficulty of the task and their experience with the task. For each student, the teacher must be discerning enough to choose repertoire that will be at once both challenging and successful, and avoid that which may be too difficult for the student's current stage of development.

In performance, advantages can be created for a singer if external focus is employed with complex and challenging repertoire, relative to the current level of development; it is possible that a singer, performing under such conditions, can consolidate the necessary technical skills through this experience. Singers practised in external focus are likely to have greater confidence that the set of skills they have established will be autonomously engaged for each new performance. We all know of singers who have developed their careers not in a formal educational setting, but by engaging in lots of performing. Employing this strategy can offer developmental advantages aligned with the vast experience seen in experts who demonstrate the reliable automaticity lacking in a novice (Boronat & Logan, 1997). It is worth noting, however, that most singers reach a point in their development when guidance from a teacher is really valued and necessary to confirm the implicit knowledge acquired.

Feedback Principles

Feedback has always been a basic teaching tool in the voice studio; however, attentional-focus principles challenge the nature and efficacy of the feedback commonly employed. It now seems that feedback that directs attention to the effect of the action rather than the action per se creates a context for successful motor learning and that feedback inducing external focus is most useful when delivered post-performance. Externally focused feedback can be delivered concurrently with performance, although for a singer this must be visual, because to sing while trying to listen to aural feedback creates cognitive confusion unhelpful on all levels — a teacher, conductor or stage director shouting at a singer during a rehearsal is an extreme, but not unfamiliar, example. Performers themselves often notice immediate changes in their own performance as a function of their attentional focus, which can be regarded as intrinsic feedback — this intrinsic feedback, provided it also has an element of external focus, is a useful tool for motor learning (Wulf, 2007).

Verbal feedback that makes reference to or describes the physical process appears to have similar implications to instructing a singer about the physical process — under certain conditions, the focus may be too close for any benefit. It has also been shown that when either instruction or feedback are employed at the wrong point in a performer's development, the outcome does not support the creation of stable and reliable motor skills (Wulf & Prinz, 2001). Intrinsic concurrent feedback can be usefully employed when singers watch themselves in the studio mirror — a standard practice in all good singing studios. Biofeedback, with the introduction of real-time computer programs and video display, is a growing phenomenon both in sport and in singing, and although this is sometimes concurrent, it can often be delayed when the captured images are replayed for review later. However, internally focused feedback delivered concurrently only serves to confuse and degrade the learning experience. It is important to be able to judge the level of cognitive overload that may be induced in the process of delivering concurrent feedback, because too much thinking will disrupt the automaticity achieved with external attentional focus and put unnecessary demands on the working memory. A singer needs to leave all judgement of a current performance until it is over. Then the most helpful focus for a singer is on the extrinsic successes and failures of the performance itself, not the intrinsic coordinations of the body. So there is enough evidence to suggest that the way a singing teacher employs feedback can affect a singer's performance, either positively or negatively— on the positive side, informed use of feedback reinforces motor learning.

Concluding Thoughts

Holding a big-picture vision of my role as a professional singing teacher has lead me to investigate the fascinating topic of the role of motor skills in studio voice teaching. Knowledge about focus of attention and its role in the acquisition of motor skills is shaping the discourse in my studio. My strong commitment to pass such research on to the next generation of singing teachers is also compelling.

From the Australian commentary box at the Winter Olympics, Alisa Camplin, about to witness the finals of the Freestyle Woman's Skiing said something along the lines of "All the girls need to do now is trust their bodies; they've done the hard work necessary, now they must get rid of their heads and go for it". Singers in performance need the same approach. Further research is needed to help us better understand the theory behind the singer's development of physical skills. However, even now, the rare wisdom of that eminent teacher, Oren Brown, takes on greater significance, "It isn't so much a matter of *making* sounds as it is a matter of learning how to *let sounds happen*" (Brown, 1996, p. xiii). To "*let sounds happen*" would appear to align with the laws of practice that have been the topic of this discussion— motor learning flourishes when a singer's attentional focus is distanced from the biomechanics of singing.

References

Adams, J.A. (1971). A closed-loop theory of motor learning. *Journal of Motor Behaviour, 3*, 111–150.

Arbitbol, J. (2006). *Odyssey of the voice.* San Diego, CA: Plural Publishing.

Boronat, C.B., & Logan, G.D. (1997). The role of attention in automatization: Does attention operate at encoding, or retrieval, or both? *Memory & Cognition, 25*(1), 36–46.

Brown, O.L. (1996). *Discover your voice: How to develop healthy voice habits.* San Diego, CA: Singular Publishing Group.

Brown, W. (1957). *Vocal wisdom: Maxims of Giovanni Battista Lamperti.* Whitefish, MT: Kessinger Publishing.

Bruner, J. (1999). Folk pedagogies. In J. Leach, & B. Moon (Eds.), *Learners & pedagogy* (pp. 4–20) London: Paul Chapman Publishing.

Chapman, J.L. (2006). *Singing and teaching singing: A holistic approach to classical voice.* San Diego, CA: Plural Publishing.

Clarke, E., & Davidson, J. (1998). The body in performance. In W. Thomas (Ed.), *Composition, performance, reception: Studies in the Creative Process in Music.* Aldershot, UK: Ashgate Publishing Company.

Curran, T., & Keele, S. (1993). Attentional and nonattentional forms of sequence learning. *Journal of Experimental Psychology: Learning, Memory, and Cognition. 19*(1). 189–202.

Dunbar-Wells, R. (1997). *The relevance of metaphor in voice teaching: A comparative study of sinus tone production and vocal cord theories* (Unpublished doctoral dissertation). University of Reading, UK.

Ericsson, K.A. (2001). The path to expert golf performance: Insights from the masters on how to improve performance by deliberate practice. In P.R. Thomas (Ed.), *Optimising performance in golf* (pp. 1–57). Brisbane, Australia: Australian Academic Press.

Ericsson, K.A. (2004). Deliberate practice and the acquisition and maintenance of expert performance in medicine and related domains. *Academic Medicine, 79*(10), (S70–S81).

Fischman, M., & Oxendine, J. (2001). Motor skill learning for effective coaching and performance. In Williams, J. (Ed.), *Applied sport psychology: Personal growth to peak performance.* Mountain View, CA: Mayfield Publishing Co.

Glaser, R. (2000). Cognition and instruction: Mid, development, and community. *Journal of Applied Developmental Psychology, 21*(1), 123–127.

Gray, R. (2004). Attending to the execution of a complex sensorimotor skill: Expertise differences, choking and slumps. *Journal of Experimental Psychology: Applied, 10*(1), 42–54.

Hodges, N., & Lee, T. (1999). The role of augmented information prior to learning a bimanual visual–motor coordination task: Do instructions of the movement pattern facilitate learning relative to discovery learning? *British Journal of Psychology, 90*(3), 389–403.

Janelle, C.M. (1999). Ironic mental processes in sport: Implications for sport psychologists. *The Sport Psychologist, 13,* 201–220.

Kiesgen, P. (2007). How Richard Miller changed the way we think about singing. *Journal of Singing, 63*(3), 261–264.

Lee, T., Swinnen, S., & Serrien, D. (1994). Cognitive effort and motor learning. *Quest, 46,* 328–344.

Logan, G.D. (1988). Towards an instance theory of automatization. *Psychological Review, 95,* 492–527.

Maxwell, J., Masters, R., Kerr, E., & Weedon, E. (2001). The implicit benefit of learning without error. *The Quarterly Journal of Experimental Psychology, 54A*(4), 1049–1068.

Maxwell, J., Masters, R., & Eves, F. (2003) The role of working memory in motor learning and performances. *Consciousness and Cognition, 12,* 376–402. Retrieved from www.elsevier.com/locate/concog

Nissen, M., & Bullemer, P. (1987). Attentional requirements of learning: Evidence from performance measures. *Cognitive Psychology, 19,* 1–32.

Pert, C. (1997). *Molecules of emotion: Why you feel the way you feel.* New York: Simon & Schuster.

Poolton, J., Masters, R., & Maxwell, J. (2005). The role of working memory in motor learning and performance. *Human Movement Science, 24*, 362–378. Retrieved from www.elsevier.com.locate/humov

Poolton, J., Maxwell, J., Masters, R., & Raab, M. (2006). Benefits of an external focus of attention: Common coding or conscious processing? *Journal of Sports Sciences, 24*(1), 89–99.

Schmidt, R.A. (1975). A Schema theory of discrete motor skill learning Psychological Review, 82, 225–260. Retrieved from http://gateway.ut.ovid.com/gwl/ovidweb.cgi

Schmidt, R. (2003). Schema Theory after 27 years: Reflections and implications for a new theory. *Research Quarterly for Exercise and Sport, 74*(4), 366–376.

Schmidt, R., & Lee, T. (2005). *Motor control and learning: A behavioural emphasis* (4th ed.). Champaign, IL: Human Kinetics.

Shea, C., & Wulf, G. (2005). Schema theory: A critical appraisal and re-evaluation. *Journal of Motor Behavior, 37*(2), 85–101.

Sherwood, D., & Lee, T. (2003). Schema Theory: Critical review and implications for the role of cognition in a new theory of motor learning. *Research Quarterly for Exercise and Sport, 74*(4), 376–382.

Shulman, L. (1999). Knowledge and teaching: Foundations of the new reform. In J. Leach & B. Moon (Eds.), *Learners and pedagogy* (pp. 61–77). London: Paul Chapman Publishing.

Squire, L.R. (1987). *Memory and brain.* New York: Oxford University Press.

Squire, L.R. (2004). Memory systems of the brain: A brief history and current perspective. *Neurobiology of Learning and Memory, 82*, 171–177.

Stark, J. (1999). *Bel canto: A history of vocal pedagogy.* Toronto, Canada: University of Toronto Press.

Vennard, W. (1973). *Developing voices: From the studio of William Vennard.* New York: Carl Fischer.

Verdolini, K. (in press). Motor learning principles. In I. Titze (Ed.), *Vocology.* Iowa City, IA: National Center for Voice and Speech.

Verdolini, K. (2002). On the voice: Learning science applied to voice training: The value of being "in the moment". *Choral Journal, 42*(7), 47–51.

White, A., & Hardy, L. (1995). Use of different imagery perspectives on the learning and performance of different motor skills. *British Journal of Psychology, 86*(2), 169–176.

Wulf, G. (2007). Attention and motor skill learning. Champaign, IL: Human Kinetics.

Wulf, G., Hob, M., & Prinz, W. (1998). Instructions for motor learning: Differential effects of internal versus external focus of attention. *Journal of Motor Behaviour, 30*(2), 169–179.

Wulf, G., McNevin, N., Fuchs, T., Ritter, F., & Toole, T. (2000). Attentional focus in complex skill learning. *Research Quarterly for Exercise and Sport, 71*(3), 229–239.

Wulf, G., & Prinz, W. (2001). Directing attention to movement effects enhances learning: A review. *Psychonomic Bulletin & Review, 8*(4), 648–660.

Wulf, G., Shea, C., & Park, J-H. (2001). Attention and motor performance: Preferences for and advantages of an external focus. *Research Quarterly for Exercise and Sport, 72*(4), 335–344.

Wulf, G., Shea, C., & Whitacre, C. (1998). Physical-guidance benefits in learning a complex motor skill. *Journal of Motor Behaviour, 30*(4), 367–380.

Wulf, G., & Weigelt, M. (1997). Instructions about physical principles in learning a complex motor skill: To tell or not to tell ... *Research Quarterly for Exercise and Sport, 68*, 362–367.

Wulf, G., Weigelt, M., Poulter, D., & McNevin, N. (2003). Attentional focus on suprapostural tasks affects balance learning. *The Quarterly Journal of Experimental Psychology, 56A*(7), 1191–1211.

Ziegler, S. (2002). Attentional training: Our best kept secret. *Journal of Physical Education, Recreation and Dance, 73*(9), 26–31.

Chapter 8

Knowledge and Skill in Teaching Registers: A Reflection on Practice

Rowena Cowley

Teaching and learning singing in the 21st century is strongly influenced by the growth of research into vocal function as well as by pedagogic traditions. This chapter begins by observing some major interactions between voice science and vocal pedagogy. It comments on the research methodology most common in voice science, and outlines some bases for qualitative approaches to the study of teaching practice in the singing studio, in particular the use of action research.

Studio teachers are challenged by this knowledge of singing function to examine their own practice. In this chapter, an example of action research aims to explore the degree to which the concept and terminology in the author's teaching reflect evidence-based knowledge of vocal function in teaching female vocal registration, and to reflect on the implications of the findings for her teaching practice. The research questions are: to what extent do I use the concepts and terminology of evidence-based knowledge of vocal register function in the studio? How do I use written materials to interpret and transmit the sensations and sounds of good singing?

Two data sources, on teaching and on evidence-based concepts, provide material for the study. The source of data on teaching is a section from a summary of instructions written by the author and provided to members of her studio in 2007. The source of evidence-based concepts is a necessarily limited literature review of current voice science on female vocal registers. Findings on concepts and terminology from the two sources will be compared, and similarities/differences discussed. Indications for change in the author's teaching practice and possible further research are identified.

The Partnership Between Vocal Pedagogy and Voice Science

Voice science can be described as a complex intersection of many different fields that augment the centre: anatomy, physiology and acoustics. Brewer (1989) identified a list of 36 scientific disciplines that are associated with the study of voice. Voice science has a long and honourable tradition of empirical research, particularly strong in the past half-century, producing replicable results based on the experimental model. Von Leden (1990) and Sundberg (2003), for instance, reflected on the cumulative effects of research on the singing voice. In a wryly amusing multimedia presentation, Wendler (2008) paid tribute to a number of researchers of European and United States origin who are or were also singers, including Husson, van den Berg, Schutte, Seidner, Sundberg, Sataloff and Titze. These researchers have often generated collaborations with singer/teachers.

Singing teachers have responded by integrating voice science-generated knowledge into their teaching, often working as part of interdisciplinary teams. A number of important pedagogues writing on pedagogy in the 21st century have addressed the relationship between voice science and pedagogic practice (Callaghan, 1998, 2000; Thurman and Welch, 2000; McCoy, 2004; Sell, 2005; Chapman, 2006). Some, for example Callaghan (1998, 2000) and Chapman (2006), have contributed to voice science research. Each in their own way has addressed the issue of translating knowledge of vocal function into pedagogic explanations that work in the studio for a range of learners.

Ways of Knowing About Teaching Singing

There is, however, room for reflection on the relationship between researcher/performer/teacher knowledge about voice function and the function, work or art of a teacher (Macquarie Dictionary, 1981, p. 1275). Interaction with voice scientists has led to a comparatively lesser concentration on the issues which present through the process of voice teaching itself. Other components of the singer/teacher's domain provide different models for research. Vocal repertoire and style is examined by musicologists (Elliot, 2006) and music performance by music psychologists (Gabrielsson, 2003). Music education provides mixed method research approaches that can help singers and teachers examine studio practice in a critical light.

Music education research has valued qualitative approaches to research for their rich verbal, visual and audio data in naturalistic settings, such as that of the singing studio. Patton (1990) distinguished between the underlying extremes of scientific or basic research and qualitative research in the following way:

> The purpose of basic academic research is to generate theory and discover truth, that is, knowledge for the sake of knowledge. The

> purpose of applied research and evaluation is to inform, enhance decision making, and apply knowledge to solve human and societal problems. (p. 12)

The idea that research into teaching should be applied implies the potential for changes in practice. To this end, teachers of singing have much to gain from reflecting on their own practice and utilising developments in action research over recent decades. Action research, originating in the work of Kurt Lewin (1948), involved the identification of a problem, fact-finding, planning, executing and evaluating a step before taking another step and repeating the process. Some of its permutations in music education can be found in Bresler (1995), in Davidson (2004) and in McCain (2008). Action research "is based on the close interaction between practice, theory and change" (Bresler, 1995, p. 16).

Action research includes reflective practice. The theories of Argyris and Schön (1974), and Schön (1983) led to ideas about how a professional, in the practice of their work, could validate their own experience:

> The practitioner ... reflects on the phenomenon before him, and on the prior understandings which have been implicit in his behaviour. He carries out an experiment which serves to generate both a new understanding of the phenomenon and a change in the situation. (Schön, 1983, p. 68)

Qualitative researchers, and reflective practitioners in particular, must balance critical ability with awareness of the influence of the researcher's "values, attitudes, perceptions, opinions, actions, feelings, etc" (Cohen, Manion, & Morrison, 2000, p. 239). However, potential gains from learning from one's own practice may benefit both students and teachers of singing, and the music they express. With this in mind, a model for a singing teacher's action research might be found in the Figure 8.1.

A Small-Scale Action Research Project in the Singing Studio: A Teacher Reflects

Introduction and Aims

It takes a certain amount of courage to reflect on one's own teaching, in whatever form. This brief action research project aims to explore the degree to which concept and terminology in my teaching reflects evidence-based knowledge of vocal function in teaching female vocal registration, and to reflect on the implications of the findings for my practice. Two sources of data — an extract on registers from a document written by me for my studio in 2007, and a necessarily limited literature review of current voice science on female registers — provide materials for comparison of the ideas behind and ways of transmitting information on vocal registers in the

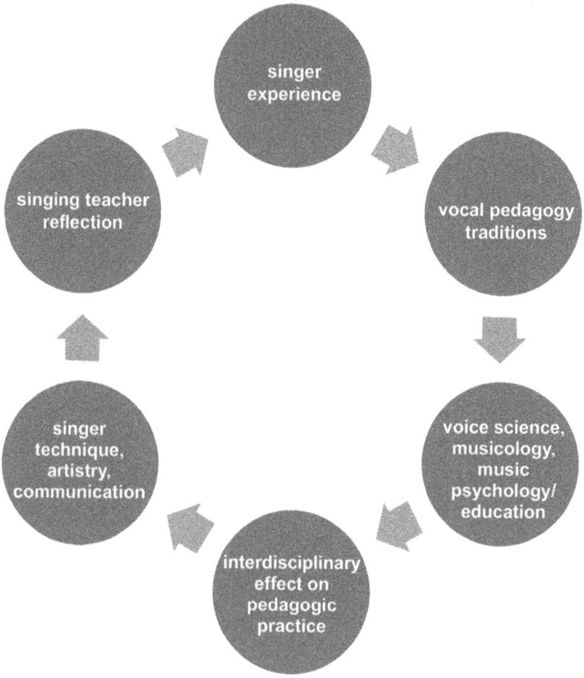

FIGURE 8.1

Reflective cycle for teaching/learning singing in the 21st century.

studio. Findings may contribute to further stages in my own reflective cycle and be of benefit to fellow practitioners.

Research Questions

The study responds to the following questions: to what extent do I use the concepts and terminology of evidence-based knowledge of vocal register function in the studio? How do I use written materials to interpret and transmit the sensations and sounds of good singing?

Literature Review: Voice Science on Registers

Definition

Current methods of investigation, such as "laryngoscopic, electrophysiological, acoustic, auditory or proprioceptive observations" have added to the store of knowledge about vocal registers, but that knowledge remains incomplete (Roubeau, Henrich, & Castellengo, 2009, p. 426). In the absence of definitive explanations of the sources of register, most writers refer to the perceptual evidence that they exist. Sundberg is blunt on the topic:

> Unfortunately, there is no generally accepted clear definition of the term register. The most common description is that a register is a phonation frequency range in which all tones are perceived as being produced in a similar way and which possess a similar voice timbre. (Sundberg 1987, p. 49)

Researchers have recognised that there are perceptual, acoustic, physiological and aerodynamic elements to vocal registers (Hollein, 1983). There remains, however, debate as to whether registers are primarily based on "underlying laryngeal mechanical principle" or defined "on the basis of sound voice quality" (Henrich, 2006, p. 7). Some difficulties with definitions arise from differences in means of investigation, types of singers studied, and the professional perspectives and terminologies of the researchers (Roubeau, Henrich, & Castellengo, 2009).

Number and Nomenclature

There is considerable variation in nomenclature used for registers (Large, 1972; Henrich, 2006). An example of medical nomenclature is that of the Collegium Medicorum Theatri (CoMeT), which proposed a numbered system of register labels, from the lowest to the highest (Hollein, 1983), but there remain many references to historical/pedagogic terms. The most commonly discussed number of registers is two for male voices (modal and falsetto) and three for female voices (chest, middle and head) (Sundberg, 1987). In recent literature reviews of register research, three modes of laryngeal function are identified, and a number of traditional register names categorised according to these modes (Henrich, 2006; Roubeau, Henrich, & Castellengo, 2009).

Register Boundaries

The "break" or transition between perceived registers is also much debated (Large, 1972); however, some common findings exist. The transition can be described as an area of perceptual change in males at 320 Hz and females at 353 Hz (Keidar, Hurtig, & Titze, 1987). Other researchers acknowledge a common involuntary transition for males and females in the vicinity of 300–350 Hz (approximately D4 to F4) (Titze, 1988, 1994; Sundberg, 1990; Vilkman, Alku, & Laukkanen, 1995). The transition between middle and upper regions of the female voice is placed by Miller and Schutte (2005) in the range between D5 and F5, and the transition into the flageolet at B5 to C6.

Physiology

There is general agreement that successful register transitions depend on a gradual change in ratio between thyroarytenoid dominance for lower and cricothyroid dominance for higher frequencies, but that there is a likely influence of subglottal resonance on vocal fold vibration, such that an involuntary register change may result (Hirano, 1988; Titze, 1994; Vilkman, Alku, & Laukkanen, 1995). At the common male/female register transition ("the primo passaggio of females and the secondo passaggio of males"; Vikman, Alku & Laukken, 1995, p. 71) vocal fold vibration changes from the deeper vertical vocal fold contact and longer closed phase associated with thyroarytenoid dominance to a mode in which the vibrating mass and thickness of the vocal folds is reduced, the cricothyroid is dominant and the open phase is longer (Vilkman, Alku, & Laukkanen, 1995; Miller & Schutte, 2005).

The soprano flageolet or whistle register is a spectrally and perceptually distinct area of the voice (Walker, 1988). This upper register of the female singing voice exhibits two sections. The first is typified by pitches around G5, "that segment where the first formant closely matches the fundamental frequency on all vowels" (Miller & Schutte, 1993, p. 211). Above that, in the flageolet or whistle register typified by pitches around D6, "reduced vocal fold oscillation" is likely (Miller & Schutte, 1993, p. 212).

In recognition of singers' kinaesthetic sense associated with register, Sundberg studied the chest wall vibrations in phonation caused by subglottal pressure, and suggested that Pacinian receptors "offer a means of obtaining tactile feedback for phonation at low fundamental frequencies," that is, below the female chest to middle register transition at 300–350 Hz (Sundberg, 1990, p. 50). This interaction between vibration and sensation is also found in the acoustics of registers.

Acoustics

Acoustic and perceptual measurements rely on two types of hearing, one of which is objective and can be quantified, the other subjective and descriptive (Keidar, Hurtig, & Titze, 1987). Acoustic phenomena are generated in the larynx and in the resonance cavities (Roubeau, Henrich, & Castellengo, 2009) as well as affecting the function of vocal fold vibration.

1. Supra-glottal resonance. There is considerable evidence that supraglottal resonance acts on the voice source (Large, 1972; Titze, 1994). Oncley (1973) distinguished between the muscular coordinations in register and the resonance phenomena which he called "lifts" or formant shifts, which are vowel and quality related, and which he demonstrated at about G3, then about C4, Eb4, Ab4 and E5. He suggested that these are common to male and female voices, varying with individual vocal tract size and shape. "Heavier" registers have greater energy in higher harmonics, including singer's formant in male and low female voices, resulting from a fairly long closed phase and steep slope of closing. Lighter registration, such as falsetto, has fewer high harmonics, shorter closing phase and less steep closing slope (Hirano, Hibi, & Sanada, 1989). The timbre transition between head and chest, notably the primo passaggio and the secondo passaggio in males and females, "is characterized by an abrupt quality change that results from loss or gain of high-frequency sound energy at the source" (Titze 1988, p. 183). These characteristics invite speculation about singer subjects' technical development and/or aesthetic choices. For instance, a recent study of the passaggio from the middle voice to the upper voice in sopranos found that in the region of C#5 to G#5, female singers exhibited characteristics such as wider lip/jaw openings, raised tongue, elevated uvula and widening of the pharynx, but "almost no systematic modification of the vocal tract distances" (Echternach et al., 2010, p. 136). Interaction between singer percept and acoustic evidence is likely in the extreme upper range. The soprano flageolet/whistle register is both "the pitch at which it is no longer expedient to adjust the first formant upward to match the fundamental frequency" (about B5 or 988 Hz) and the result of reduced vocal fold oscillation. The tendency of F1 and F2 to converge at A5 "apparently causes considerable tension". This tension is "released" at B5, "where the effort to raise F1 to the level of F0 (here 988 Hz) is abandoned" (Miller & Schutte, 1993, p. 210).

2. Sub-glottal resonance. It is likely that "acoustic pressures below the vocal folds can be phased in such a way that they contribute, constructively or destructively, to the intraglottal driving pressures of the vocal folds and therefore to register transitions (Titze, 1994, p. 263). Titze identified two pairs of favorable and unfavorable subglottal resonances (at 306 Hz and 510 Hz, and 146 Hz and 204 Hz, respectively), with an additional constructive interference at 1530 Hz (Titze, 1994, p. 266).

Aerodynamics

Large's 1972 literature review referred extensively to research findings in support of a role for respiratory factors in registral control. Rubin, LeCover, and Vennard (1967), for instance, confirmed that airflow is greater in falsetto register. Register transition in both male and female voice may be affected by differing strategies in chest (thyroarytenoid-dominant) and falsetto (cricothyroid-dominant) registers. In falsetto, the longer opening phase is counteracted by supraglottal "back-pressure," whereas in chest register, the open phase is too short for this to take effect and is replaced by increased adduction. The female transition, taking place relatively low in the range, requires less adduction and subglottal pressure than the male transition in the same frequency range (Miller & Schutte, 2005).

Register Equalisation

Registers are a physiological/acoustic fact and cannot be removed, but "it is important to conceal registers or their effect by training the student to equalize or balance the different sound qualities" (Hollien, 1983, p. 3).

Titze recommended several strategies for smoothing registral transitions. With decreasing thyroarytenoid (TA) activity, coordination of vocal fold adduction and lung pressure can smooth the transition into cricothyroid (CT) dominance with rising pitch. In particular, adductory control can smooth registers "when the vocal folds are driven harder by subglottal formant pressures at specific pitches". Titze recognised that "differential control of two intrinsic laryngeal muscles is one of the most difficult tasks of all voice training" (Titze, 1994, pp. 272–273).

It is likely that trained singers use "smaller strain" for a given pitch than untrained singers, and that "this might imply a tendency to avoid an excessive increase in stiffness, leading to a register break in the high-pitch range". In addition, "the so-called covering of the voice most likely means using a mixed register in which falsetto and chest register qualities coexist and the voice source is richer in harmonics even at higher pitches" (Vilkman, Alku, & Laukkanen, 1995, pp. 71–72). In slightly different terminology, mixed register can be seen as an area of the voice that can be sung in either laryngeal mechanism 1 (chest register) or mechanism 2 (light register), according to singer choice (Castellengo, Chuberre, & Henrich, 2004).

Many researchers have made considerable efforts to relate their work to pedagogic practice. A recent example is the use by Roubeau, Henrich, and Castellengo (2009) of pedagogue Richard Miller's register terminology. Researcher/singer Donald Miller, with colleague Harm Schutte, made an interesting comment on the relationship between voice science and pedagogy:

> One can imagine two distinct purposes for writing on the working of the singing voice. One is to arrive at a verifiable, scientifically correct description of its acoustic and physiology. The other is to explain it in terms that help the singer and the teacher to more effective practice. (Miller and Schutte, 2005, p. 290)

Method

This action research study aims to explore the degree to which concepts and terminology in the author's teaching reflect evidence-based knowledge of vocal function in teaching female registration. The source of data on teaching ("the pedagogic text") is a section from a summary of instructions written by myself and provided to members of my studio in 2007. It is assumed that this written record (the "pedagogic text") is an accurate record of my teaching concepts and terminology at that time, as captured in written form. The source of evidence-based concepts is the preceding literature review. Both sources deal only with female classical voices, with the vocal range of A3 to C6. Voice science and pedagogic terminology and concepts will be identified and examined against each other to discover the ways in which I use written materials to transmit information about singing. Findings on concepts and terminology from the two sources will be compared, similarities/differences discussed, and implications for changes in practice and further research identified.

Demographics

I am a soprano, with a career in (mainly) concert performance. I have taught voice full-time for 15 years, and pedagogy for the past 10 years. The core of my teaching is with tertiary students, primarily, but not exclusively, with female classical singers who are undergraduate and graduate voice and opera students. Most of my students are in their mid-twenties. More advanced students are professionals in opera and music theatre at a national and international level.

Pedagogic Textual Data

In the extended pedagogic text, sections on posture, breathing and phonation, precede a discussion of vocal register as shown in Table 8.1.

Findings

Table 8.2 refers to a number of issues that are directly related to concepts in voice science.

Table 8.1
Pedagogic Text on Registers

Concept/Skill	Discussion
Register	This is an area of voice quality, determined by the length and thickness of the vocal folds and some acoustic/resonance factors. Historic register terms include chest and head voice (reflecting referred sensations of vibration in the head for high pitches and chest for lower pitches). Speech pathologists use modal and tilt, and others speak of shortener/lengthener. Higher register terms include male falsetto (breathy high range) and female whistle or flageolet register (above C6). Lower register terms include Strohbaß (males only). The number of registers is also debated. Most agree that there are two predominant registers, chest and head. The third register is usually some form of mixed or middle register. There are adjustments of sensation every four to five tones.
Sound concept	There is a strong element of singer hearing or ability to imagine sound in registral work, so it's important to know how the various registers sound. Listen to good singers, and also to young singers who haven't yet mastered the adjustments. Both can help you imagine what would feel right in your throat. Be prepared to experiment, calmly.
Sensation	The change in sensation singers notice in different pitch areas often causes them to "flinch" or close the vocal tract and airway and drop support, just when optimal function of these is needed most. The following strategies may help overcome this natural reaction.

Continued over

Table 8.1 (CONTINUED)
Pedagogic Text on Registers

Concept/Skill	Discussion
Strategies	Blend from the top down, as it's easier to gradually add muscle mass than to gradually shed it. Make sure posture is optimal, breath low and vocal tract open. Keep the tone forward and palate broad, air flowing, sustain the vowel. Calmly teach yourself to apply extra low support and extra awareness of open vocal tract when you feel the change of sensation coming on. You will need to be patient and positive with yourself.
Passaggii	The main register change or transition for all voice types is in the area encompassing C4 (middle C) to F4. This is the area where the shortener muscles (TA) must give way to a dominance of lengthener muscles (CT) smoothly in order to avoid a "click" or obvious change in quality. Most female singers are aware of areas of transition at the top of the treble clef (D5 to F#5), as well as at B5 to C#6. Most males are aware of areas of transition from B3 to D4 and again at D4 to F#4. Adjustments of sensation are even more frequent. Remember that these vary according to voice type, technical skill and musical/textual context.
To access the higher, thinner fold adjustments	Keep the tone forward, use a forward vowel, such as [i], "yelping" or "puppy sounds", speak in a very high pitch (just be prepared to lose your dignity!), imitate a "bad soprano" (speaking high with very open vocal tract), use an "ü" or darker vowel (covering) to keep the vocal tract open at the back or the oral pharynx and sustain the low larynx (within reason). Don't worry if the higher pitched sensation is of a "thin" sound. That's probably correct. Most of these strategies cause a sensation of vibration in the head (the whole skull), of no connection to the throat. Learning to let the latter "go" is important.
"Open at the back, closed at the front"	It's essential to keep "open" in the larynx and pharynx, and once this is well established, you will find it helps to keep the registers aligned (and larynx stable) to keep the front of the mouth relatively closed for all vowels. This may feel a bit contrived at first, but if you are feeling the air flowing and sensation in the skull, you should be able to do this with an absolutely loose jaw and tongue.
To access the lower ranges	Keep the tone forward, and increase the vocal tract space and downward support (don't let the jaw pull back and close off the space). The low larynx should be sustained. Depending on your concept of speaking voice range, you may find it useful to speak then sing. People often notice a sensation of "flattening out" in the extreme low range — this can be helped by a strong concept of breadth in the larynx tube. This helps to avoid "engaging" the throat, and encourages working with the sensation of "resonance" only. The [a] vowel is more helpful than [i] here.

TABLE 8.2
Comparison of Voice Science and Pedagogic Text: Concept and Terminology

Concept	Voice science	Pedagogic text
Definition	• Registers exist and are perceptually evident. • There are perceptual, acoustic, physiological and aerodynamic elements to vocal registers. • Concepts vary with exploratory methods, types of subjects, professional orientation.	• "Register is an area of voice quality, determined by length and thickness of the vocal folds and some acoustic/resonance factors". • Register is also a "sound concept — there is a strong element of singer hearing or ability to imagine sound in registral work".
Number and nomenclature	• Numbers and names vary with professional orientation. • Most common number is two main registers for male voice and three for female voice. • Nomenclature includes historic/pedagogic terms.	• Nomenclature varies with professional orientation. • "The number of registers is … debated." • "There are two predominant registers, chest and head." • These reflect "the sensations of vibration in the head for high pitches and chest for lower pitches." • "Higher registers include falsetto, and female flageolet/whistle," the latter above C6. • "The third (major) register is usually some form of mixed or middle register."
Register boundaries	• Findings on register transitions vary. • Titze (1988) described four transition points, with the common register transition in males and females following D4. • Miller and Schutte (2005) placed the transition into the female upper voice from D5 to F5, and into flageolet at B5 to C6.	• "The main register change or transition for all voice types is in the area encompassing C4 (middle C) to F4." • "Most female singers are aware of areas of transition at the top of the treble clef (D5 to F#5), as well as at B5 to C#6." • "The third register is usually some form of mixed or middle register" • "Adjustments of sensation are even more frequent."

TABLE 8.2 (CONTINUED)
Comparison of Voice Science and Pedagogic Text: Concept and Terminology

Concept	Voice science	Pedagogic text
Physiology	• Lower pitches in both male and female voices are associated with thyroarytenoid dominance, shorter and thicker vocal folds, deeper vertical vocal fold contact and longer closed phase. • Higher pitches are associated with cricothyroid dominance, longer folds with reduced vibrating mass, longer open phase. • Female upper voice contains two distinct sections (see Miller & Schutte, 1993, 2005), which are identifiable with spectrographic evidence, and probably involve reduced vocal fold oscillation.	• The physiology of registers is not included under "registers," but briefly described in the pedagogical text under "pitch" as follows: "long and thin vocal folds (lengthener or cricothyroid dominant) produce high pitches, short and thick (shortener or thyroarytenoid dominant) [vocal folds] make low pitches. Thickness of the vocal folds depends to some extent on registral/vocal quality choices". • The area encompassing C4 to F4 "is the area where the shortener muscles (TA) must give way to a dominance of lengthener muscles (CT) smoothly in order to avoid an … obvious change in quality".
Acoustics	• Acoustic phenomena are related to physiological function. • Supraglottal resonance acts on the voice source. • There is evidence of "lifts" or formant shifts that are vowel and quality related at musical intervals of a third to a fifth throughout the voice (Concley, 1973). • Heavier registers have greater energy in higher harmonics, including singer's formant, fairly long closed phases, and a steep slope of closing. • Soprano upper range (from F5) is characterised by the tendency of F1 and F2 to converge on the spectrum. • Subglottal resonance may affect vocal fold vibration by contributing negatively or positively to register transitions.	• There are "acoustic/resonance factors" associated with register. • Perceptual aspects of register includes "sound concept — there is also a strong element of singer hearing or ability to imagine sound in registral work". • "There are adjustments of sensation every four to five tones". • These sensations "vary according to voice type, technical skill and musical/textual context". • "Most female singers are aware of areas of transition … [at] D5 to F#5, as well as at B5 to C#6". • "Don't worry if the high pitched sensation is of a thin sound. That's probably correct."

TABLE 8.2 (CONTINUED)
Comparison of Voice Science and Pedagogic Text: Concept and Terminology

Concept	Voice science	Pedagogic text
Aerodynamics	• There are airflow adjustments in, for instance, falsetto register. • The register transition in females requires less adduction and subglottal pressure than the male at the common register transition as it occurs low in the range.	• "Most of these strategies cause a sensation … of no connection to the throat." • "Learning to let the [throat] 'go' is important." • "Keep the tone forward and palate broad, air flowing, sustain the vowel."
Register equalisation	• Registers cannot be removed but can be concealed. • A balance of subglottal pressure and adduction can facilitate lessening of vocal strain and the gradual release of the TA muscle. • Middle or mixed voice can be a co-existence of falsetto and chest qualities (associated with "covering") or a choice by the singer of a laryngeal mechanism associated with chest or with falsetto.	• Sound concept: "It's important to know how the various registers sound. Listen to good singers". • "To access the higher, thinner fold adjustments, keep the tone forward, use a forward vowel such as [i], 'yelping' or 'puppy' sounds , speak in a very high pitch …use an 'ü' or darker vowel (covering) to keep the vocal tract open at the back [of the pharynx] and sustain the low larynx (within reason)". • "To access the lower ranges, keep the tone forward and increase the vocal tract space and downward support … The low larynx should be sustained." Speaking voice may be a reference point. [a] may be helpful. • "Remember that [passaggii] vary according to voice type, technical skill and musical/textual context." • "Calmly teach yourself to apply extra low support and extra awareness of open vocal tract when you feel the change of sensation coming on." • "Blend from the top down … make sure posture is optimal, breath low and vocal tract open. Keep the tone forward and palate broad, air flowing, sustain the vowel". • "It's essential to keep 'open' in the larynx and pharynx … it helps to keep the registers aligned (and larynx stable) to keep the front of the mouth relatively closed or all vowels" • "Be prepared to experiment, calmly".

Note: All quotes referred to here are from Table 8.1.

Discussion

There are many similarities and some differences between pedagogic text and voice science concepts and terminology. The pedagogic text definition of registers draws on the historical (perceptual) definition originally found in Garcia's work. It refers to some basic physiological factors, but does not mention, for instance, open/closed phase or spectral slope. Further reference to vocal tract and aerodynamically mediated aspects of register identification would be more complete. However, identification of "sound concept" or singer audiation of registral qualities is an important pedagogic tool that relates to traditional perceptual definitions of register.

The number of registers described in the pedagogic text is in line with much of the voice science literature — identifying two main registers serves both male and female voices without undue complication. Mention of the third or middle register reflects ongoing discussion in voice science literature of the functional basis of this concept. Some alternate register names are supplied in the pedagogic text as a means of clarifying terminology encountered in other studios and pedagogic literature. Recognition of the importance of sensation in singer perception of registers is reflected in the pedagogic use of historical terminology.

The pedagogic text descriptions of register boundaries closely resemble findings in voice science, which themselves are variable, possibly according to the skill of the subjects studied (a factor not always sufficiently recognised in voice science research literature). The pedagogic statement that "these [boundaries] vary with voice type, technical skill and musical/textual context" reflects the fact that trained singers can make choices about the registral mix used for a particular phrase based on perceptions of efficiency and voice quality, and on expressive and stylistic purpose.

Voice science provides fairly consistent descriptions of the physiology of register based on the ratio of TA or CT dominance and on patterns of vocal-fold vibration. The pedagogic text refers only briefly to the physiology of registers, as the functional basis of pitch is described elsewhere in the document. It is consistent with voice science in the description of intrinsic laryngeal muscle function in each register and in the major passaggio, but does not refer to vibratory differences between the registers or to the functional basis of flageolet register. The pedagogic aim is to keep description of vocal fold function closely associated with perception of voice quality, as the latter is more likely to be under a singer's perceptual control.

The association of physiology with acoustic factors in registers is recognised in both voice science and the pedagogic text. The interaction between supraglottal/subglottal resonance and voice source vibration is not discussed specifically in the pedagogic text. Singers are, however, advised of the need for stability of vocal tract shape and "support" when changes of sensation prompt unwanted muscular adjustments. It is possible that these unwanted muscle movements ("flinches" in the pedagogic text) originate in part from the body's reaction to acoustically unhelpful resonances. Vocal tract stability and appropriate breath support, in turn, may assist in facilitating fine adjustments of glottal adduction and subglottal pressure, which are a necessary response to the enabling or disabling effects of resonance factors on the voice source.

Acoustic factors are a probable source of other important sensations associated with registers. Oncley's concept of "lifts", which vary with vocal tract size and shape, for instance, is a likely source of the pedagogic description of singers' "changes of sensation every four to five tones". Further attention is drawn to the sensations of female upper register, where a common singer response to initial good singing that the sound is "thin" may result from the interaction of F0, F1 and F2 at these pitches. The experience of "thin" sound may intensify at the transition into the flageolet/whistle register as a result of reduced vocal fold vibration.

At the lower passaggio, it seems likely that subglottal resonance may exacerbate singers' difficulty with smooth register transition, but this can be mitigated, as indicated earlier, by careful adductory control and airflow. This is an example of an "aerodynamic" aspect of register function. The pedagogic text advises "a sensation … of no connection to the throat" of learning to let the throat "go", with air flowing. These are strategies that are designed to reduce adduction of the vocal folds, allowing them to make the muscular and vibrational adjustments necessary for register change.

It is not surprising that the most extensive writing about register equalisation is from the pedagogic text — studio teachers need to find solutions for the singers with whom they work. Voice science offers advice based primarily on the balance of subglottal pressure with glottal adduction and changing vocal fold vibration activity associated with TA or CT dominance, facilitated by such strategies as vowel modification or "covering".

The pedagogic text recognises the importance of the perceptual element — audiation, sensation and perceived voice quality based on coordination of the vocal instrument are the bases of register management. Key physiological concepts for achieving the desired coordination are postural alignment with co-contraction of the diaphragm and abdominal muscles to facilitate open vocal tract and optimal laryngeal efficiency during phonation, and the gradual release of TA dominance in favour of CT dominance as the pitch rises. Concepts related to acoustic factors are mostly perceptual — awareness of bone-conducted sensation in facial, cranial and chest wall bones, and soft tissues, as well as what is heard as voice quality by the singer and teacher.

Selection of a CT or TA dominant voice quality can be assisted by strategies such as those listed in Table 8.1. Many of these strategies aim at relative stability of vocal tract and vertical laryngeal position throughout the range, as well as control of adduction and subglottal pressure. Vocal tract stability and appropriate breath support facilitate free and minimal jaw and articulator movement, with gains in clarity of vowels and consonants at most pitches, and "covering" as an indirect result of laryngeal stability.

Such strategies depend on a singer's ability to reproduce voice quality and associated sensation. Changes in these sensations are an important means of alerting the teacher and singer to finely calibrated changes in pitch and vocal quality. To a singer with increasing skill, they function as a signaling system for the minor adjustments of vocal tract shape, vocal fold adduction and airflow, which will produce optimal vocal quality.

In this context, register transitions are minimised, and registral/voice quality choices can be made with reference to musical style, textual meaning and expressive purpose.

Conclusions and Further Research

This action research study has provided me with reflections on one form of pedagogic input on registers used in my singing studio. It is a challenge to write clearly about vocal technique, and in this case the written text was always intended as a reminder of studio practice for my own students. Without further research into student responses to this input, it is not possible to assess to what extent these pedagogic prompts are useful to students. Nevertheless, with a keen practice-based awareness of the range of singer/learner's needs, it is clear to me that attempting to write down one's pedagogic approach is a salutary part of clarifying teaching process.

The pedagogic text does derive mostly from evidence-based concepts drawn from voice science. Reference to register definition, number and nomenclature, boundaries, physiology, acoustics, aerodynamics and register equalisation are congruent with voice science. Descriptions of laryngeal and vocal tract functions are quite close to those found in voice science, though necessarily less detailed in the brief document for student singers found in Table 8.1. The close alignment of accessible description with evidence-based functional knowledge is an aspect of my teaching I can continue to develop in the light of ongoing research.

Some notable omissions from the pedagogic text are fuller recognition of the role of acoustics and aerodynamics in the definition of register, descriptions of patterns of vocal fold vibration in registers and the interaction of supra- and subglottal resonance with vocal fold vibration. Discussion of acoustic factors in general is approached in the pedagogic text through their effect on sensation. There is room for more clarity on this in my teaching, possibly through using some form of real-time acoustic feedback in the studio.

It is not surprising that the other main difference between voice science and pedagogic text in this study is in the provision of strategies for register equalisation. It is the teacher's responsibility to find ways to stimulate coordinations that enable singers to reproduce desired sound in a given artistic situation. Besides verbal explanation or written text, these include kinaesthetic, auditory and visual feedback, imagery, the use of gesture and vocal modelling. Singing teachers also rely on their own experience of excellent vocal function, and on their ability to intuit a student's vocal function based on sound. All of these provide opportunities for action research or mixed method research approaches as suggested by Figure 8.2. Action research theory implies the application of findings to real world problems by continuing the reflective cycle. Such a reflective cycle can further stimulate change in my own teaching and perhaps inspire other 21st century teachers and singers to critically examine their practice.

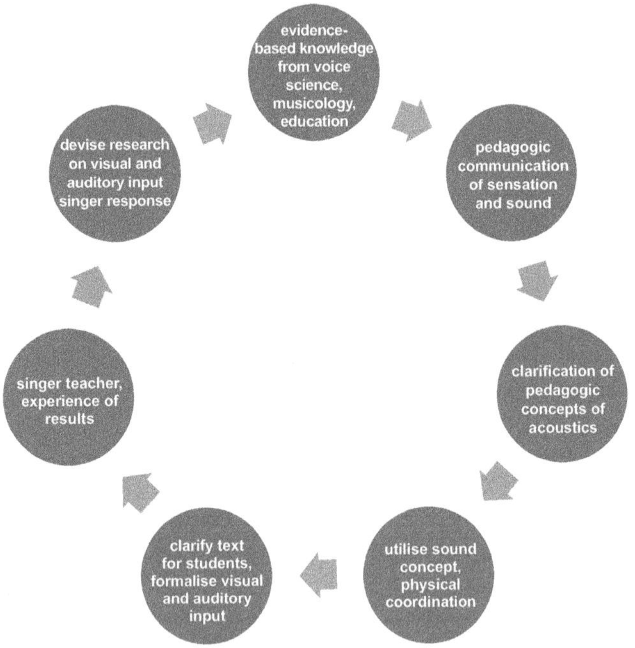

FIGURE 8.2

Actions for change in personal pedagogic practice.

Acknowledgment

The author would like to thank Professor Anna Reid for reading drafts of this chapter.

References

Argyris, M., &. Schön, D. (1974). *Theory in practice.* San Francisco, CA: Jossey-Bass.

Bresler, L. (1995). *Ethnography, phenomenology and action research in music education.* Retrieved from http://www-usr.rider.edu/~vrme/v8n1/vision/Bresler_Article_VRME.pdf

Brewer, D.A. (1989). Voice research: The next ten years. *Journal of Voice, 3*(1), 7–17.

Callaghan, J. (2000). *Singing and voice science.* San Diego, CA: Singular.

Callaghan, J. (1998). Singing teachers and voice science — an evaluation of voice teaching in Australian tertiary institutions. *Research Studies in Music Education, 10,* 25–41.

Castellengo, M., Chuberre, B., & Henrich, N. (2004). Is voix mixte, the technique used to smoothe the transition across the two main laryngeal mechanisms, an independent mechanism? *Proceedings of the International Symposium on Musical Acoustics* (pp. 1–4). Nara, Japan: ISMA2004.

Chapman, J.L. (2006). *Singing and teaching singing.* San Diego, CA: Plural.

Cohen, L., Manion, L., & Morrison, K. (2000). *Research methods in education* (5th ed.). New York: RoutledgeFalmer.

Davidson, J. (2004). *The music practitioner.* Burlington, VT: Ashgate.

Delbridge, A. (Ed.). (1981). *The Macquarie Dictionary.* McMahons Point, Australia: Macquarie Library.

Echternach, M., Sundberg, J., Arndt, S., Mark, M., Schumacher, M., & Richter, B. (2010). Vocal tract in female registers — a dynamic real-time MRI study. *Journal of Voice, 24(2),* 133–139.

Elliot, M. (2006). *Singing in style.* New Haven, CT: Yale University Press.

Gabrielsson, A. (2003). Music performance research at the millennium. *Psychology of Music, 31*(3), 221–272.

Henrich, N. (2006). Mirroring the voice from Garcia to the present day: Some insights into singing voice registers. *Logopedics Phoniatrics Vocology, 31,* 3–14.

Hirano, M. (1988). Behaviour of laryngeal muscles of the late William Vennard. *Journal of Voice, 2*(4), 291–300.

Hirano, M., Hibi, S., & Sanada, T. (1989). Falsetto, head/chest, and speech mode: An acoustic study with three tenors. *Journal of Voice, 3*(2), 99–103.

Hollien, H. (1983). A review of vocal registers. In V.L. Lawrence, *Transcripts of the 12th symposium: Care of the professional voice* (pp. 1–7). New York: The Voice Foundation.

Keidar, A., Hurtig, R. R., & Titze, I. (1987). The perceptual nature of vocal register change. *Journal of Voice, 1*(3), 223–233.

Large, J. (1972). Towards an integrated physiologic-acoustic theory of vocal registers. *The NATS Bulletin, 28*(3), 18–36.

Lewin, K. (1948). In G.W. Lewin (Ed.), *Resolving social conflicts: Selected papers on group dynamics.* New York: Harper & Rowe.

McCain. (2008). The characteristics of action research in music education. *British Journal of Music Education, 25*(3), 283–313.

McCoy, S. (2004). *Your voice: An inside view.* Princeton, NJ: Inside View Press.

Miller, D.G., & Schutte, H.K. (2005). 'Mixing' the registers: Glottal source or vocal tract? *Folia Phoniatrica Logopedia, 57*, 278–291.

Miller, D., & Schutte, H. (1993). Physical definition of the flageolet register. *Journal of Voice, 7*(3), 206–212.

Miller, R. (2004). *Solutions for singers.* New York: OUP.

Oncley, P.B. (1973). Dual concept of singing registers. In J. Large (Ed.), *Vocal registers in singing: Proceedings of a symposium* (pp. 35–44). The Hague, The Netherlands: Mouton.

Patton, M. (1990). *Qualitative evaluation and research methods* (2nd ed.). Newbury Park, CA: Sage Publishing.

Roubeau, B., Henrich, N., & Castellengo, M. (2009). Laryngeal vibratory mechanisms: The notion of vocal register revisited. *Journal of Voice, 23*(4), 425–438.

Rubin, H., LeCover, M., & Vennard, W. (1967). Vocal intensity, subglottic pressure and airflow relationships in singers. *Folia Phoniatrica, 19*, 393–413.

Schön, D. (1983). *The reflective practitioner.* London: Temple Smith.

Sell, K. (2005). *The disciplines of vocal pedagogy: Towards an holistic approach.* Burlington, VT: Ashgate.

Sundberg, J. (1990). Chest wall vibrations in singers. *Journal of Research in Singing, 13*(2), 44–51.

Sundberg, J. (2003). Research on the singing voice in retrospect. *TMH-QPSR, 45*, 11–22.

Sundberg, J. (1987). *The science of the singing voice.* DeKalb, IL: Northern Illinois University Press.

Thurman, L., & Welch, G. (Eds.). (2000). *Bodymind and voice.* Collegeville, MN: The VoiceCare Network.

Titze, I. (1988). A framework for the study of vocal registers. *Journal of Voice, 2*(3), 183–194.

Titze, I. (1994). *Principles of voice production.* Englewood Cliffs, NJ: Prentice-Hall.

Vilkman, E., Alku, P., & Laukkanen. (1995). Vocal fold collision mass as a differentiation between registers in the low-pitch range. *Journal of Voice, 9*(1), 66–73.

von Leden, H. (1990). Pioneers in the evolution of voice care and voice science in the United States of America. *Journal of Voice, 4*(2), 99–106.

Walker, J.S. (1988). An investigation of the whistle register in the female voice. *Journal of Voice, 2*(2), 140–150.

Wendler, J. (2008). Singing and science. *Folia Phoniatrica et Logopaedica, 60*, 279–287.

Chapter
9

Vocal Registration in Young Voices — A Balancing Act

Elizabeth Willis

Recent scientific research is validating concepts of vocal registration that have been a part of singing teaching for centuries. Issues concerning registers are being clarified, and the implications for vocal health when natural registration is overridden (what McCoy [2004] termed "register violation") more clearly understood. For Miller (1986), vocally healthy voice-use requires integrated, dynamic balance between two predominant laryngeal muscle groups, resulting in smooth transitions between registers — the aesthetic aim for the *bel canto* musical style. Register transition notes (passaggi) and vocal timbre are prescriptive of voice-type. In contrast, musical styles, such as yodelling and country-and-western rely on strong register differentiation. Titze (1988, 1994) identified two modes of register transition — changes in fundamental frequency and in spectral balance — and noted a major timbral passaggio consistently around 300–350 Hz [E4] for both men and women. But is this the situation with young voices? Changes in tracheal length, laryngeal size, and in vocal fold structure and length occur during adolescence. The acoustic changes that result are explored through the work of Gackle (2000, 2006) for girls, and Cooksey (1977a, 2000) for boys. The development of pitch-breaks around 392–494 Hz (G4–B4) and weakness in the lower vocal range around 262 Hz [C4] of some girls during Gackle's Phase 11A, and the "Blank Spot" that is an indicator of boys in Cooksey's "Newvoice" stage (between Stages III and IV of Tanner's 5-stage indicator of pubertal change) are explored as the genesis of adult registration. Strategies are discussed for teaching vocal registration concepts and management.

One of my most cherished possessions was found in an antique bookstore; a small book, entitled *Jenny Lind: Her Vocal Art and Cadenze.* Written in 1894 by Rockstro, and complete with handwritten dedication and letter from Madame Lind's husband and associate artist, Otto Goldschmidt, it was intended as "a record and analysis of the 'Method' of the late Madame Jenny Lind" (p. i).

This small book showed the Swedish nightingale possessed a formidable technique. At the height of her artistic powers, her voice was described as "soprano drammatico", but it had great flexibility capable of brilliant fioriture and cadenze, which Lind gained only through disciplined practice. Her full vocal range was two- and three-quarter octaves, from B3 [247 Hz] to G6 [1568 Hz], but it was not always so. She began her artistic career at a very early age, appearing as an actress or singer in 22 professional performances at the age of 13. By the age of 21, she had performed the roles of Euryanthe, Pamina, Julia (in Spontini's *La Vestale*), Alice (in *Robert Le Diable*), Donna Anna, Lucia and Norma (Pleasants, 1966, p. 199). In the spring of 1841, when she was 21, a provincial tour left her chronically hoarse. Concerned, she travelled to Paris, and sought lessons with Manuel Garcia. The book tells us that "under this unrivalled Maestro di Canto", she studied diligently for 11 months from August 1841 until the summer of 1842; by which time she had learnt "all that it was possible for any master to teach her" (Rockstro, 1894, p. 6). Rockstro continued that she left Garcia, possessing "a rich depth of tone, a sympathetic timbre" and "a bird-like charm in the silvery clearness of its upper register". Yet to Jenny Lind herself, the voice never fully recovered from the early overexertion in Sweden. Although praised for her ability to blend across the vocal registers, she always felt that the notes F4 to A4 (349 to 440 Hz) "never became quite right" (Rockstro, 1894, p. 11).

Why should Jenny Lind's vocal range between F4–A4 (349–440 Hz) be so affected? Is this effect universal? Acoustically, vocal registers can be defined as "a group of like sounds or tone qualities whose origin can be traced to a special kind of mechanical (muscular) action" (Reid, 1983, p. 296). To Hollien (1974), a vocal register was "a totally laryngeal event; it consists of a series or a range of consecutive voice frequencies which can be produced with nearly identical phonatory quality" (pp. 125–143). However, Titze (1988) felt that registers were not totally a laryngeal event, but that resonance was also involved — that the ricochet of subglottal and/or supraglottal resonance back to the glottis, but out of phase with the vocal fold vibrations, would also affect registration. Consequently, both the dimensions of the trachea and vocal tract would be involved, and register transitions could be both learned or involuntary in reaction to acoustic pressures.

Register breaks or cracks were abrupt vocal timbral changes that occurred over identifiable crossover frequencies of acoustic adjustment (Thurman, Welch, Theimer, & Klitzke, 2004, p. 37). Titze also considered that registers were a perceptual event — that the listener was equally important (Titze, 1994, pp.253–254). He identified two modes of register transition — one by periodicity (or changes in fundamental frequency [pitch]), and the other by timbral adjustment (changes in spectral balance), and he wondered why a major timbral passaggio is consistently around E4 (300–350 Hz) for both men and women (Titze, 1988, p. 188).

Physiologically, we know that muscles work in pairs — one muscle does the work (the agonist muscle), whereas another controls the action (the antagonist muscle). Vocal registration is managed by shifting workloads between agonist and antagonistic muscle groups in a dynamic, flexible response to task requirements. With the voice, the two main muscle groups are the thyroarytenoid muscle group and the cricothyroid muscle group. The thyroartenoid muscle group, which singing teachers also call "heavy mechanism", is most active during low range and speech. The vocal folds have a greater closed quotient, which results in a vocal timbre that is also called "chest voice" by singing teachers. The cricothyroid muscle group, called "light mechanism" and "head voice" has a smaller closed phase and is responsible for higher range. In a further refinement, Miller (1986) specified these natural register change points (or passaggii) as important indicators of voice-type for bel canto singing style. Sopranos, according to Miller, have the primo passaggio from the thyroarytenoid group (heavy mechanism) to heavy-light mix range (voce mista) around E-flat 4 (311 Hz), and the secondo passaggio from mix-range to light mechanism around F#5 (740 Hz). In male voices, the situation is similar, with the position of the passaggii assisting voice classification. However, vocal problems can arise at these passaggii, particularly around the primo passaggio. In bel canto style, a smooth passaggio transition is the most aesthetically pleasing — a blending of registers, so that the timbral differences are minimised. In other musical styles, such as yodelling, the aesthetic requirement is an abrupt timbral change from one register to another. Vocal problems arise when one muscle group is asked to do the work normally undertaken by the other muscle group — what McCoy (2004) called a register violation — and this is possibly what had happened to Jenny Lind.

The vocal muscular system in children is not the same as in adults. Laryngeal shape, size and position in the neck in newborns and children are all different to the adult larynx. At birth, the lower border of the cricoid cartilage of the larynx sits at a level between the second and third cervical vertebra. The larynx slowly descends in relation to the vertebral column, until between the ages of 15 and 20 years, when the lower border of the cricoid cartilage sits level with the sixth cervical vertebra. After this, it continues a slower descent in relation to the cervical vertebrae throughout life (Zemlin, 1988, pp. 174–175). Hirano, Kurita, and Nakashima (1983) also identified changes affecting vocal fold length and structure. At birth, the vocal folds are 2.5–3.0 mm in length, and grow to 17–21 mm in males and 11–15 mm in females. This is achieved by changes in both cartilaginous and membranous lengths of the vocal fold, and changes in their ratio to each other. Hirano et al. (1983) found that it is the membranous part of the vocal fold that has flexibility, and that the increased ratio of the membranous part over the cartilaginous section in adults is one reason they have greater vocal control than children. Vocal fold structure in itself changes from two to three layers. In the newborn, a two layer-structure is observed, with no ligamentous structure evident. By adulthood, this has developed to three layers, the top layer being the epithelium and superficial layer of the lamina propria, the middle layer being the intermediate and deep layers of the lamina propria (vocal ligament), and the bottom layer being the vocalis muscle. The membranous portion of the vocal fold has elastic fibres at each end — the anterior and posterior maculae flavae. This three-layered structure matures during adolescence, adding length and bulk to the folds, which affects acoustic output (Hirano et al., 1983, pp. 22–43; Titze, 1994).

Are vocal registers present is children's voices? Research indicates that registers and passaggii are present in children's voices, but are less perceptually apparent because of the pitch-range and timbre in which children speak and sing. A study by McAllister, Sederholm, and Sundberg (2000) asked five child-voice specialists to assess voice range profile recordings of 15 10-year-olds, nine boys and six girls. Voice range profiling (VRP) is a technique that uses differences in sound pressure levels between softest and loudest notes over the full vocal range to establish an individual's voice contours, which can then be drawn as a phonetogram. Six of the child subjects formed a control group of normal voices, and a register change was detected in this group at a mean fundamental frequency around B4 (511 Hz), 25% higher than in the voices of adults. This difference in pitch between these children and adults was attributed by McAllister et al. (2000) to differences in tracheal length. In addition, a small number of children were heard to have a second transition almost an octave higher, at a mean frequency just above A5 at 902 Hz. These perceptual results were confirmed in the phonetogram results.

In his book on child voice, Phillips (1992) simplified the register challenge. He stated that there are three adult vocal registers — lower, middle and upper. Lower is C2–C4 (65–262 Hz), middle is C4–C5 (262–523 Hz) and upper is C5–C6 (523–1047 Hz). The child voice is similar to the female voice, with the low register being G3–C4 (196–262 Hz), the middle adjustment register being C4–C5 (262–523 Hz) as in the adult voice, and the upper register being C5–G5 (523–784 Hz) with a possible extension to C6 (1047 Hz). In the middle adjustment register, F#4 (370 Hz) is the point at which there is a 50/50 balance between the registers. This may be the case with child voice, but is oversimplified for adolescent voice when the change to adult voice is both timbral and, particularly for boys, frequency-based. At this stage, the register areas change to align more closely with Titze's observation that the major timbral changes occur around E4 (300–350 Hz) in all voices (Titze, 1988, p. 188). Gackle (2000, p. 817) also noted that there is a period in the voice-change of some young girls, Phase IIA, when sung pitches below E4 (330 Hz) are not possible — that is, that they cannot access their chest-voice range. These observations indicate changes in both vocal tract and vocal folds, as noted by Titze (1994).

Studies of register variations in adolescent singing voices are rare. In his theory of voice transformation in male adolescents, John Cooksey (1992) undertook the major work of classifying the stages of male voice change. This work stands as the best guide to teachers today, and his stages of change are given in Table 9.1.

Cooksey's research indicated that the boys' voices moved down like "a 'slinky', moving down the steps of a stairway" (Cooksey, 1992, p. 10). This "eclectic theory" included the concept of a "Blank Spot", pitched on average between C4–F4 (262–349 Hz), as a phenomenon of "Newvoice" (previously known as "New Baritone") stage. This is an area of the boys' voice where tone production is either difficult or impossible, and is the classic "broken voice", a term to which Cooksey strongly objects (Cooksey, 2000, pp. 828–829). A study by Harries, Hawkins, Hacking, & Hughes (1998) confirmed this Blank Spot appears between Stages 3 and 4 of Tanner's 5-stage indicator of pubertal change (Tanner, 1975). They found that the

Table 9.1

Cooksey's Stages of Male Adolescent Voice Change With Average Speaking Fundamental Frequency Ranges

Stage of change	Average speaking fundamental frequency range
Unchanged	220–260 Hz (A3–C4)
Midvoice 1	220–247 Hz (A3–B3)
Midvoice II	196–233 Hz (G3–A3)
Midvoice IIA	175–185 Hz (F3–F#3)
Newvoice	131–165 Hz (C3–E3)
Emerging adult voice	110–139 Hz (A2–C#3)

sudden drop in pitch did not correlate to changes in vocal fold length, but rather to changes in vocal fold structure and mass. Changes in the vocal tract had been noted previously — the increase in length and width of the neck, and the subsequent lowering of the larynx (Polgar & Weng, 1979), growth of the paranasal sinus and atrophy of the adenoids (Weiss, 1950) — all of which resulted in a longer vocal tract and larger resonance chamber. Pedersen, Møller, Krabbe, Munk, and Bennett (1985) used phonetograms to assess the acoustic result of these physiological changes, and found the Blank Spot around D4–E4 (294–330 Hz) in the voices of boys aged 14.6 years. More recently, Fuchs et al. (2007) researched predictors of voice change by studying the jitter (instability in pitch), shimmer (instability of amplitude), noise component and changes in speaking fundamental frequency of boys' voices. This research found that vocal instability appeared in the speaking voice on average seven and five months before the appearance of the Blank Spot. The Willis and Kenny (2008) longitudinal study of twelve 13-year-old boys used glides over the total vocal range, and confirmed that the Blank Spot is part of a sequential process. Pitch-breaks first appeared very low in the vocal range, around D3–F#3 ([145–189 Hz]; average weight of boys: 46.6 kg; average speaking fundamental frequency: F3 [178 Hz]), then very high (around C6 [1036–1058 Hz]; average weight: 48.61 kg; average speaking fundamental frequency: F#3 [188 Hz]). The speaking fundamental frequency indicates that this occurs in Cooksey's Midvoice IIA. Note the slight rise, rather than lowering, in speaking fundamental frequency when the high pitch-break is present. Another area of weakness then sometimes developed around A4–C5 (438–510 Hz), when the speaking fundamental frequency was around D3 (146 Hz; average weight of boys: 56.06 kg). This was either concurrent with, or followed by the development of the long-term midrange gap identified by Harries et al. (1998). In the Willis and Kenny (2008) study, the average Blank Spot developed around C#4–G#4 (278–427 Hz; average weight of boys: 56.06 kg; average speaking fundamental frequency: around C#3 [139.18 Hz]). Two observations should be made: the first is that the vocal ranges in which pitch-breaks occur are similar to those that singing teachers know as register transition points. The second is that the initial, very low pitch-break may help to explain the "Year 8 bass", as the phonational gap limits the inflectional pitch-range and around the speaking fundamental frequency. The wide variation between boys in rate and severity of change means that individual differences must be taken into account. For some, phonational gaps greater than an octave develop. The Willis and Kenny (2008) research indicated that boys are very aware of these vocal changes, and avoid the embarrassment of pitch-breaks during speech (or what some boys call "testepops") at all costs. One other phenomenon needs comment. Fuchs et al. (2007) noted that the noise component in speaking voices just prior to change is very low. Those of us who teach these young voices know that this is the time when our young singers often sound best — musically developed young singers with a warmer, richer timbre, just prior to the development of the Blank Spot. It must be remembered that the process is sequential — that the tessitura (or pitch-range in which the voice phonates most easily) for boys in Midvoice IIA is C4–E4 (262–330 Hz), which is the same range as the Blank Spot of Newvoice. Figure 9.1 is an example of the changeable pitch-range of the Blank Spot over one year for a subject in the Willis and Kenny study (2008), with voice-range, speaking fundamental frequency and weight also detailed.

And what about girls? Because girls' voices do not change as dramatically as the boys, there is less research about them, and longitudinal studies are

Subject 26-Phonational gap ('Blank Spot') - 5 times over 1 year

	1	2	3	4	5
—◇— Max GFo	875	935	979	1011	887
—△— GapFin	675	352	404	431	447
—▲— GapStart	459	292	240	224	228
—◆— Min GFo	175	123	103	95	99
—✳— SFo	210	163	133	142	131
‥●‥ Weight	50.7	52.7	53.9	54.9	56.6

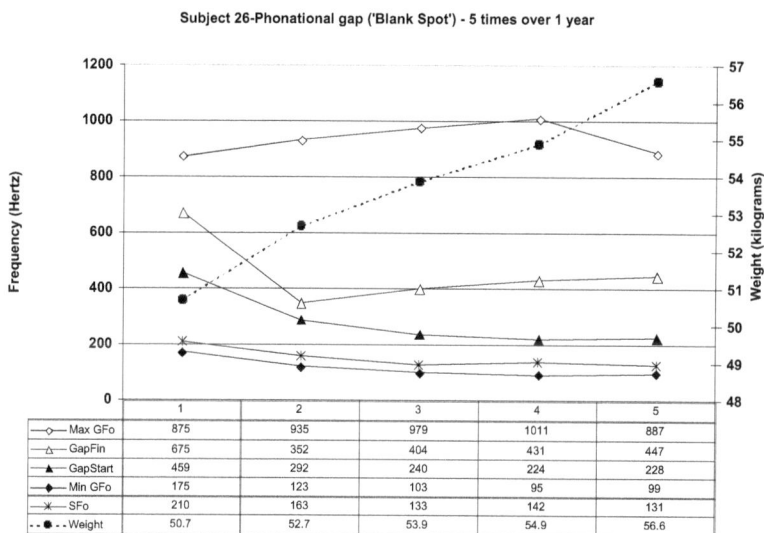

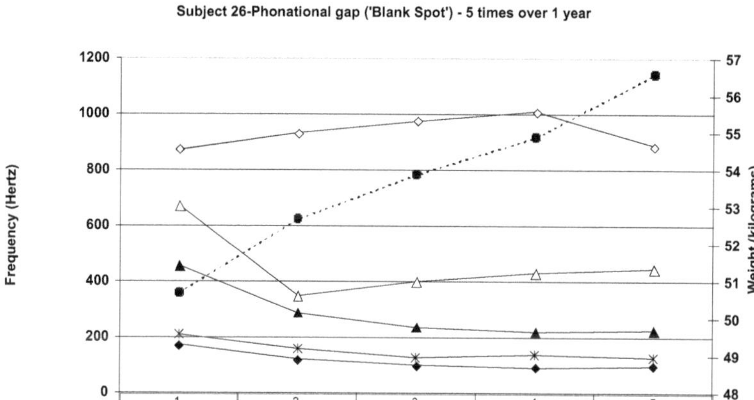

FIGURE 9.1

Subject 26 — the phonational gap or Blank Spot is an area in the vocal range that does not phonate easily. Cooksey identified that on average it is from C4 (middle C) to F4 (262–349 Hz), and appears as an indicator of boys in their Newvoice stage. In their study of 13-year-olds, Willis and Kenny (2008) found these Blank Spots are highly variable over time, and can be considerably wider than a perfect fourth. For Subject 26, the phonational gap was from A#4–≈E5 (459–675 Hz) at Time 1. It narrowed to D4–F4 (292–352 Hz) at Time 2 before expanding to be an octave wide at time 5 — A3–A4 (228–447 Hz). Simultaneously, the speaking fundamental frequency and minimum glide note dropped almost an octave from A3 to C3 (210–131 Hz). Subject 26's weight gain over the year was from 50.7 kg at Time 1 to 56.6 kg at Time 5.

even rarer. Lynne Gackle, established a sequence of voice change events similar to the boys (Gackle 2000, pp. 814–820, 2006, pp. 28–37). The phases of female voice change she identified are given in Table 9.2.

Register breaks are not apparent in Phase I, but in Phase IIA, a register transition break can occur around G4–B4 (392–494 Hz), the same range that was difficult for Jenny Lind. During this stage, Gackle reported that some girls have difficulty with their lower range, with pitches around middle C (C4-262 Hz) losing power. Breathiness is evident in the tone, due to an incomplete closure of the glottis caused by varying growth-rates (such glottal chinks persist in adulthood, and are the norm rather than the exception. A study by Södersten and Lindestad (1990) found them in 86% of the phonation of adult females). In Phase IIB, the register break at G4–B4 (392–494 Hz) remains, and another can develop around D5–F#5 (587–740 Hz) — what singing teachers know as the secondo passaggio. Gackle described the voice as warmer in the low range, but it can "flip" into a breathy, more childlike "flutely" quality when transitioning into the higher register around the primo passaggio. By Phase III, the voice is more even across the registers, although register breaks still occur around the secondo passaggio, a quality more typical of adult female voices. Gackle's is a universal model applicable to all girls, which may explain the differences found between it and a study by Decoster, Ghesquiere, and Van Steenberge (2008) of 17 girls (aged 9.9–16.11 years) from the Antwerp Cathedral Choir who were an auditioned group. This study found that despite the presence of considerable individual differences between the girls, the Gackle model for speech data was accurate. However, the Gackle model for singing during different developmental phases was limited in comparison to the abilities shown by the members of the Antwerp choir, probably reflecting the choristers' status as both auditioned and trained. Decoster et al. (2008) noted that the repertoire chosen for the girls to sing was often higher than their upper frequency limit, a situation that McKinney (1982, p. 121) described as potentially pathological, as it promotes the development of vocal nodules. Data from the Willis and

TABLE 9.2

Gackle's Phases of Adolescent Female Voice Change With Average Speaking Fundamental Frequency

Stage of change	Average speaking fundamental frequency range
Phase 1 prepubertal	260–290 Hz (C4–D4)
Phase IIA pubescence–premenarcheal	245–275 Hz (B3–C#4)
Phase IIB pubescence–postmenarcheal	222–275 Hz (A3–C#4)
Phase III young female–postmenarcheal	210–245 Hz (A3–B3)

Kenny study (unpublished) showed that some girls displayed a frequency-break pattern similar to boys. For girls, the low-range pitch-breaks were around C3–F3 (132–175 Hz), followed by very high-range pitch-breaks around A-flat6 (1638–1702 Hz), then a lower pitch-break around B-flat5-B5 (943–991 Hz) developed before the voice settled into the adult secondo passaggio around E5–F#5 (659–740 Hz). As with the boys, these changes occurred around the time of rapid weight-change.

What constitutes best teaching practice for managing the inherent weaknesses in different stages of development of young voices? One can only respond — the basics, ideally taught before voice-change. Good posture, low breath support and clear forward resonance and diction are the most helpful tools for these young voices. In my opinion, good posture is paramount, as it facilitates both low breath support, and the dynamic interaction between the thyroarytenoids and the cricothyroid groups of muscles. Low breath support assists both in supporting the voice, and in the mitigation of performance anxiety. For boys, clear, forward resonance assisted by more articulated diction ("tip of the tongue, the teeth and the lips!") is the most useful tool in Cooksey's Stage IIA and Newvoice classifications. At this time, the speaking voice lacks projection and is unreliable, due to Blank Spot interference with the speaking voice range. Clear consonant production does not rely on pitch and is a vital tool in a young man's armoury for communication.

It is important to involve the boys in the process — a vital component of what Thurman (2000, pp. 188–301) described as "human-compatible learning". Establish each boy's speaking fundamental frequency by asking them to count backwards from 20. Choose a syllable to extend (e.g., the "4" of "14"), and pitch-match this to the piano — this will give an approximate speaking fundamental frequency. Because of the work of Cooksey (1977b, 2000) and Harries (1998), we know that boys grow in growth-spurts, with each spurt lowering the speaking fundamental frequency by about a third.

To ascertain voice-range, ask the boys to vocalise both descending glides ("from as high as possible to as low as possible") and ascending glides ("from as low as possible to as high as possible"). Is there a recurrent pitch-break? How much of the falsetto range is still accessible? For some boys, particularly those unaccustomed to singing, the falsetto will seem to have disappeared. As the voice settles for these boys, work from the speaking fundamental frequency outwards, gradually reintroducing a wider pitch-range. For the boys who still have a falsetto range, the recommendation is to exercise heavy and light mechanisms separately, until the two can be linked together (Phillips, 1992, p. 225). Use the descending vocal glide to work on this.

There may be resistance to exploring this high, light mechanism range, as boys associate it with a more feminine sound, but it is important to keep the agonist/antagonist mechanism operational. Work to energise the tone through consonants. This can be through call and response, with the teacher using a plosive consonant like "k" or "ch" in a rhythmic pattern, which is then copied by the student(s); or in a classroom situation, use a plosive consonant to the rhythm of a known song (e.g., "Happy Birthday") — work this as a round or against the rhythm of another known song to develop focus, concentration and audiation (the ability to think music — a vital skill for singers). Guiding rule — let the boys know the exercises have a serious intent, even though they are fun!

The initial analytical work is best done without girls present, but gradually involving the girls in the process as the year progresses assists them to understand the voice-change process. Always work to develop a supportive environment (Barham & Nelson, 1991, p. 11). Cooksey also suggested keeping a progress sheet so that the boys recognise that voice-change is an ongoing process. This can also be done in the private studio where it is easier to focus on a boy's strengths while also working on his weaknesses. Choose repertoire very carefully — repertoire with a narrow range, but that is still intellectually and musically challenging — and be prepared to change key every week. For the classroom teacher, the complexity is that every boy is at a different stage of change, but work to accommodate individual differences musically.

For girls, the challenges are different, as a usable voice range remains intact. At the stage when high range decreases, and the low range becomes warmer, with greater ease of phonation (Gackle's Phase IIB), some girls believe they are altos. This is possibly the stage when a Jenny Lind would push her heavier sound too high. It is important to explain that the high range will return, to insist that both high and low ranges be exercised, and not to classify the voices too early into soprano and alto. In a youth choir situation, try using "emerald" and "ruby" instead of the traditional classifications, and choose equal-voiced and crossing-part repertoire. Also be aware that a musically literate girl in a choral situation should be classified according to natural vocal range and timbre, rather than as an alto because she reads music and can hold a part! Pushing the heavier quality too high is the particular danger for these young voices. To correct this, I believe all girls must be able to differentiate heavy and light mechanism. An exercise to do this is for the teacher to sing E4 (330 Hz) first in light mechanism (associated with hands held palm-downward, forefingers aligned, then gently bouncing the forefingers together using a slightly circular movement to simulate the gentler, lateral-medial action that occurs at vocal fold level), then heavy mechanism (with palms facing and pressed firmly together, representing the more closed quotient ratio of the vocal folds at glottis level). Use of the hands in this way gives students a better understanding of vocal fold activity, makes students more observant of the conductor's hands, and encourages a better head–neck relationship as the students subconsciously adjust their posture to counterbalance the weight of their lifted hands by moving the weight of their head to a more supported position over the spine.

The concept of balanced use of thyroarytenoid and cricothyroid muscle groups can be taught with Indian arm wrestling — very useful for demonstrating the dynamic flexible flow between muscle groups necessary for good vocalisation. Agonist and anatagonist muscle use is explained with the assistance of good plastic anatomical models. Parts are allocated — either teacher or student is the thyroarytenoid muscle group, and the other the cricothyroid muscle group. The concept of agonist and anatagonist muscle use is experienced in moments of flexible arm-wrestling, and passaggii identified as times of power-balance between the muscle groups. This is an excellent exercise when teaching registration concepts in an individual or small groups setting, but if you try it with larger groups of 12- to 14-year-olds, you are more courageous than I am!

Understanding the concept of balanced register use is one thing — developing the kinaesthetic skill to achieve varying vocal timbres is another. Thurman et al. (2004, p. 44) recommend the use of pitch-glides, sirening and "yoo hoo" calls in the context of storytelling to develop the neural networks necessary for singing in higher registers. With all young singers and in a choral situation, Haasemann (1992) used the idea of barking first as a Pekinese, then as a larger and larger dog, finally barking as a St Bernard. Thus, the concept of registers is taught in an imaginative, non-gendered way. Haasemann's books and video on group vocal technique are highly recommended as a source of exercises to teach not only registers, but other aspects of vocal technique imaginatively, efficiently and effectively (Haasemann & Jordan, 1992). For more mature voices, McKinney referred to the need to "line up the registers" (McKinney, 1982), and, for the male voice, to use the falsetto to do it. Further analysis of the literature shows two underlying principles for register consistency and balance for more mature singers.

The first principle is diaphragmatic activity and strong, but flexible breath support in response to the changing demands of different registers. This can be taught by the use of mezza di voce — exercises based on crescendo/decrescendo; this simultaneously disciplines breath support and vocal fold adduction. McKinney (1982) also recommended an exercise that starts softly in falsetto above the passaggio range, then to sing down the scale over a perfect fifth with a gradual crescendo into the passaggio area, then to decrescendo on the ascending 5-note scale. We know that Vennard (1967) used this exercise; his student, mezzo-soprano Marilyn Horne, described it in some detail in her discussion with Jerome Hines (Hines, 1990, 38–139). For the 17-year-old Horne, Vennard began with exercises over the range

E5–A4 (659–440 Hz), then extended them over a wider vocal range. For her, the sensation of ascending from heavy — to mixed to light — mechanism was "like an hourglass" or "like two pyramids, one upside down", their tips touching each other.

The second principle is vowel modification (that is, dropping the jaw for high range notes — for example, the vowel sound [i:], as in "me" moves closer to an [ɑ:] as in "father"; and as the pitch moves lower into chest range, shortening and brightening the closed, long vowels — for example, [i:] moves towards [I] as in "mitt"). These exercises, which always proceed from light to heavy mechanism, establish a balanced workload between the two muscle groups — particularly important for young voices.

These are a few suggestions to teach register awareness. It is our challenge as teachers to maintain the vocal health of our students, whatever the musical style. Ensuring a balanced use of vocal registers is an important part of this challenge.

References

Barham, T.J., & Nelson, D. (1991). *The boy's changing voice.* Miami, FL: CPP/Belwin.

Cooksey, J.M. (1977a). The development of a contemporary, eclectic theory for the training and cultivation of the junior high school male changing voice: Part 1, existing theories. *Choral Journal, 18*(2), 5–14.

Cooksey, J.M. (1977b). The development of a contemporary, eclectic theory for the training and cultivation of the junior high school male changing voice: Part II, scientific and empirical findings: some tentative solutions. *Choral Journal, 18*(3), 5–16.

Cooksey, J.M. (1977c). The development of a contemporary, eclectic theory for the training and cultivation of the junior high school male changing voice: Part III, developing an integrated approach to the care and training of the junior high school male changing voice. *Choral Journal, 18*(4), 5–15.

Cooksey, J.M. (1992). *Working with the adolescent voice.* St Louis, MO: Concordia Publishing House.

Cooksey, J.M. (2000). Voice transformation in male adolescents. In L. Thurman, & G. Welch (Eds.), *Bodymind and voice — Foundations of voice education* (pp. 718–738, 821–841). Collegeville, MN: The VoiceCare Network.

Decoster, W., Ghesquiere, S., & Van Steenberge, S.(2008). Great talent, excellent voices — no problem for pubertal girls? *Logopedics Phoniatrics Vocology, 33*, 104–112.

Fuchs, M., Fröehlich, M., Hentschel, B., Stuermer, I.W., Kruse, E., & Knauft, D. (2007). Predicting mutational change in the speaking voice of boys. *Journal of Voice, 21*(2), 169–178.

Gackle, L. (2000). Female adolescent transforming voices: voice classification, voice skill development and music literature selection. In: L. Thurman & G. Welch (Eds.), *Bodymind and voice — Foundations of voice education* (pp. 814–820). Collegeville, MN: The VoiceCare Network.

Gackle, L. (2006). Finding Ophelia's voice: The female voice during adolescence. *Choral Journal 47*(5), 28–37.

Harries, M.L., Hawkins, S., Hacking, J., & Hughes I. (1998). Changes in the male voice at puberty: Vocal fold length and its relationship to the fundamental frequency of the voice. *Journal of Laryngology and Otology, 112*, 451–454.

Harries, M.L., Walker, J.M., Hawkins, S., Williams, D.M., & Hughes, I.A. (1997). Changes in the male voice at puberty. *Archives of Disease in Childhood, 77*, 445–447.

Haaseman, F., & Jordan, J.M. (1992). *Group vocal technique*. Chapel Hill, NC: Hinshaw Music.

Haaseman, F., & Jordan, J.M. (1992). *Group vocal technique: The vocalise cards*. Chapel Hill, NC: Hinshaw Music.

Hines, J. (1990). *Great singers on great singing*. New York: Limelight Editions.

Hirano, M., Kurita, S., & Nakashima, T. (1983). Growth, development and aging of human vocal folds. In D.M Bless & J.H. Rose (Eds.), *Vocal fold physiology: Contemporary research and clinical issues* (pp. 22–43). San Diego, CA: College-Hill Press.

Hollien, H. (1974). On vocal registers. *Journal of Phonetics, 2*, 125–143.

McAllister, A., Sederholm, E., & Sundberg J. (1997). Perceptual and acoustic analysis of vocal registers in ten-year-old children. In A. McAllister (Ed.), *Acoustic, perceptual and physiological studies of ten-year-old children's voices* (PhD thesis). Department of Logopedics and Phoniatrics, Karolinska Institute, Huddinge University Hospital, Sweden.

McCoy, S. (2004). *Your voice: An inside view.* Princeton, NJ: Inside View Press.

McKinney, J.C. (1982). *The diagnosis and correction of vocal faults.* Nashville, TN: Broadman Press.

Miller, R. (1986). *The structure of singing: System and art in vocal technique*. New York: Schirmer Books.

Pedersen, M.F., Møller, S., Krabbe, S., Munk, E., & Bennett, P. (1985). A multivariate statistical analysis of voice phenomena related to puberty in choir boys. *Folia phoniatrics, 37*, 271–278.

Phillips, K.H. (1992). *Teaching kids to sing.* New York: Schirmer Books.

Pleasants, H. (1966). *The great singers: From the dawn of opera to our own time.* New York: Simon and Schuster.

Polgar, G.,& Weng, T.R. (1979). The functional development of the respiratory system. *American Review Respiratory Diseases, 120*, 625–695.

Reid, C.L. (1983). *A dictionary of vocal terminology: An analysis.* New York: Joseph Patelson Music House.

Rockstro, W.S. (1894). *Jenny Lind: A record and analysis of the "Method" of the late Madame Jenny Lind-Goldschmidt.* London: Novello, Ewer & Co.

Södersten, M., & Lindestad, P-Ă. (1990). Glottal closure and perceived breathiness during phonation in normally speaking subjects. *Journal of Speech and Hearing Research, 33*, 601–611.

Tanner J.M. (1975). Growth and endocrinology of the adolescent. In I.L. Gardner (Ed.), *Endocrine and genetic diseases of childhood and adolescence* (14–64). Philadelphia, PA: W.B. Saunders.

Thurman, L. (2000). Human-compatible learning. In L. Thurman, & G. Welch (Eds.), *Bodymind and voice — Foundations of voice education.* Collegeville, MN: The VoiceCare Network, pp. 188-301.

Thurman, L., Welch, G., Theimer, A., & Klitzke, C. (2004, October). *Addressing vocal register discrepancies: an alternative, science-based theory of register phenomena.* Second International Conference on Physiology and Acoustics of Singing, National Center for Voice and Speech, Denver, CO.

Titze, I.R. (1988). A framework for the study of vocal registers. *Journal of Voice, 3*, 183–194.

Titze, I.R. (1994). *Principles of voice production.* Englewood Cliffs, NJ: Prentice Hall.

Vennard, W. (1967). *Singing: The mechanism and the technic.* New York: Carl Fischer.

Weiss, D.A. (1950). The pubertal change of the human voice. *Folia Phoniatrica, 2*(3), 125–159.

Willis, E.C., & Kenny, D.T. (2008). Relationship between weight, speaking fundamental frequency, and the appearance of phonational gaps in the adolescent male changing voice. *Journal of Voice, 22*(4), 451–471.

Zemlin, W. (1988). *Speech and hearing science: Anatomy and physiology.* Englewood Cliffs, NJ: Prentice Hall.

Chapter 10

Building Voices and Concepts: Thirteen Annotated Vocal Exercises for Studio and Choral Rehearsal

Noel Ancell

As both voice teacher and choir director, I constantly monitor the vocal development of each of my singers. Continuously listening to individuals and watching their posture and body language enables me to detect and correct errors early. Thus, simple mistakes or technical blunders may be prevented from turning into bad habits by "practising" faults that may slow improvement and possibly threatening long-term vocal health.

Constant correction and reminders from a teacher gradually empower each singer to monitor him or herself, and in due course singers assume responsibility for correcting aspects of their technique. This becomes apparent when, after several reminders, just a significant look from the teacher to an individual is enough to produce in that singer a change in midsong (and sometimes an acknowledging facial expression). In the choral rehearsal, my singers are encouraged to acknowledge mistakes with a quick raise of the hand to signify that they know what they have done wrong and know how to fix it.

However, for singers to achieve their vocal potential through this process, they must have access to the technical tools that will give them control over their instruments. These tools are, first, the understanding of what constitutes a successful technical manoeuvre and, second, how it should feel. Further, they need to relate their own experiences of the act of singing to the language used by the singing community at large. This is complicated by the fact that both voice teachers and choir directors use metaphorical language.

Debate has raged (and will, no doubt, continue) between the proponents of such picturesque language and those who maintain that all conversations about vocal technique should be in scientific language, but there can be little doubt that language that takes account of the perceptions of the singer (rather than the demonstrable "truths" of anatomy and physiology) can be helpful. Knowing its name and function will not help us to control the diaphragm, for example, because it functions in a counter-intuitive way.

Vennard's warning (1967) is still true:

> Scientific language is inadequate in teaching an art, and we fill out the inadequacy with poetic imagery. As long as we do not confuse fancy with fact, this can be a means of finding truths which are as yet beyond our understanding, but which may nonetheless have practical usefulness. The only thing to avoid is word magic. To worship the image instead of the Reality is idolatry, and yet in our profession there are many such worshippers. Pupils have a superstitious faith in the language of their teachers and decry other teachers who say the same thing with other figures of speech. (pp. 147–149)

Recent work by Skoog (2004) and Gullaer, Walker, Badin, and Lamalle (2006) cautiously endorsed what has long been the practice of studio voice teachers. Building on Vennard, however, Miller (1996) warned:

> Attempting to superimpose one's own physical imaging on another person is generally less than successful. When teacher and singer later agree as to what the imaginative language may mean as it pertains to established function, there is then a role for imagery, even in the technical aspects of singing. Unfortunately, much studio *technical* imagery remains a mystical language, one the student is unable to penetrate … Teacher-imposed technical imaging often unintentionally produces complications that interfere with good vocalism. (pp. 4–5)

We have been warned! However, my experience suggests that it is possible to supply each singer with constructive and monitorable experiences that reconcile the Reality with their physical sensations. By controlling each experience and discussing singers' perceptions, it is possible to guide them towards and then to habituate the commonly used language. In this way, each singer gradually acquires a repertoire of actions or gestures together with the language to discuss their perceptions with others. As Miller (1996) pointed out, the order of events is important:

> After the singer has learned to coordinate [technical issues], an image may be useful in unifying those functions. The superimposition of

> imagery on the student beforehand may bring more confusion than assistance. (p. 4)

These things are most easily done with individuals in the voice studio, but it is quite possible to achieve them in the choral rehearsal. In both situations, I rely heavily on a relatively small number of exercises to put each singer in touch with perceptions of voice. Using these exercises regularly in a consistent way and supported by appropriate verbal commentary builds concepts and firmly establishes physical techniques.

The conductor must, therefore, become as familiar with each voice in his or her care as must the studio voice teacher. This takes time and sensitivity — as well as technical knowledge — and requires a trusting and mutually supportive attitude amongst the choristers. It also requires considerable time to be spent working at technical exercises, such as those I enumerate later. But, at least to some degree, the process must continue while working on repertoire. This may be more feasible in repertoire with a small number of parts or in more transparent textures (such as polyphonic works) that facilitate listening both by conductor and teacher.

Over time, in my experience, the singers develop an interest in each other's triumphs as well as their problems, and the listening they apply to each other helps them to develop their understanding as well as their technique. The individual's efforts should always be seen as contributing to the team's overall sound, not as a way of establishing a pecking order. Useful by-products of this kind of mutual appreciation include mentorship by more experienced and skilled singers of those less so and a more "democratic" approach to the assignment of parts or even solos.

Without guidance, each individual may form perceptions of vocal usage that do not resonate with others' ideas. A young singer may, for example, have found a way of dealing with a register change that works for her, but she cannot explain it in a way to which her peers can relate. Worse, because she has no way of testing her method against techniques sanctioned by tradition and or voice science, she may turn this into a bad habit that will restrict further development.

Perceptions of space, tension and resonance are crucial to the building and critique of vocal technique. Regular use of well-understood exercises facilitates in students the growth of consciousness about vocal elements and enables the teacher to discover how each student interprets and uses pedagogical concepts. Both in the studio and the rehearsal room, I encourage singers to examine and comment on their perceptions of their own and others' efforts. I make them aware of constant scrutiny, both by me and by other singers, and I try to reward good results as well as correct poor ones. This takes time, but is well worth it. Often what is being acquired is as much attitude as technique.

At the risk of labouring the point, the "method" I am advocating only works if three conditions are in place:

1. The exercises must be repeated frequently. Repetition "conditions" singers so that the desired behaviours eventually become automatic and unconscious.
2. They must be practised with absolute consistency. Variations are likely to confuse and slow down the rate at which the techniques are absorbed. By establishing a particular way of approaching each technical goal, the technique can then be referred to in other contexts, such as successfully negotiating a difficult interval, or achieving unified vowel colour.
3. The teacher must monitor every attempt to ensure that the result is successful. This may be difficult in large rehearsal groups, but is worth doing and will reward the extra effort by producing choristers with a common understanding and a unified approach to vocalism.

I regularly use the 13 vocal exercises that follow, some original, some invented by other teachers and some adapted from the work of others. I use them extensively in the "warm-up" that precedes other work in a lesson or rehearsal, but insist that singers regard them as just as important as the "real" music (sometimes even more so!). I present them under headings that relate to areas of vocal pedagogy, not necessarily in the order each student may encounter them. Obviously, different exercises are appropriate for different situations, but the following have widespread applicability and continue to work well for my singers.

Breathing (and Posture)

I expect my singers to gain facility with what Richard Miller (1986) calls "an amazingly uniform concept of breath management in the international Italianate school" (p. 23) — Appoggio. This is not simply a particular method of breathing, but involves posture, coordination and musical application. It assists with the shaping of phrases as well as ensuring their length. Crucial to good breathing is good posture, which can be encouraged by example, explanation and physical adjustment. Typical among the language I use to remind singers of what they have discovered are phrases such as "Don't lose altitude", "High here and here" (indicating the bend in the sternum and the back of the top of the head), and "Ribs up and out".

Such turns of phrase are not delivered without some prior discussion and, preferably, some demonstration of their meaning and effectiveness. Working with individuals to establish physical "correctness" is important, as is the use of monitoring techniques, such as the use of fingers to feel which muscles are operating, or dropping the bottom to facilitate good alignment of the spine. For example, young or inexperienced singers are instructed to pant like a dog or simply execute "a row of hisses" (see Exercise 10.1).

Exercise 10.1: Row of Hisses

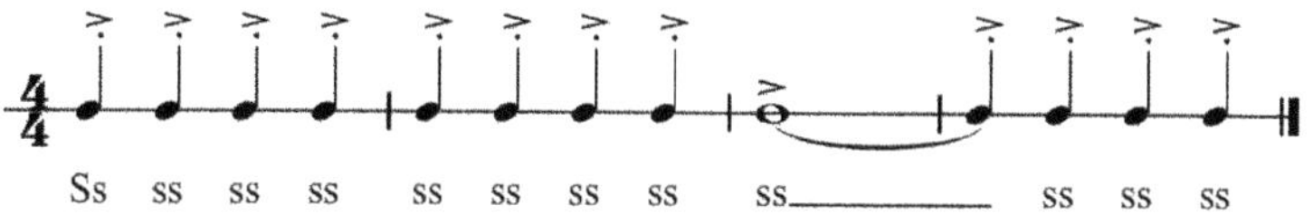
Ss ss ss ss ss ss ss ss ss ss ss ss ss

The teacher demonstrates how to start — by hissing forcefully, but staccato, at a rate of about MM = 112. As they copy this, most students will discover that one can do this for a considerable period of time apparently without stopping for breath. Those who do not must be helped to allow release of the muscles between each exhalation and the next. It is an exciting moment when they realise that breath is automatically renewed if the singer allows this to happen. It does not require thought and certainly does not need any shoulder movement — indeed, shoulder movement and heaving of the chest are strictly forbidden and (usually) easily eliminated with the help of a mirror or a partner.

Further practice, provided it is carefully monitored and supported with discussion and explanation, leads to the discovery of the role the external oblique muscles play in "supporting" sound (in this case just the hiss of air against the teeth). Next, what I call the "release breath" is revealed as a relaxation of most of the muscles of the abdomen — labelled the "SPLAT breath" by Chapman (2006, p. 42–3) (of course, the major muscle that does not relax at the moment of breathing in is the diaphragm, but the student has no control over this and should not try). Provided the rib cage is appropriately held up and out, air will come "as a free gift from the atmosphere". Singers with an understanding of physics can discuss how the difference in pressure between chest and the atmosphere will produce movement of air and even how changes in chest volume produce pressure changes according to Boyle's Law — pressure and volume are inversely proportional (Zemlin, 1988). Singers are encouraged to maintain what I call the "gesture of inspiration" constantly while in singing mode. Adequate breath eventually comes without thought. It must never be an exercise in "hunting and gathering"!

The final phase of good breathing technique is applying it to musical expression. The release breath should also be a preparation for singing the next note. This depends on support throughout the last note of the previous phrase and works just as the hissing exercise does. Even in the early stages of learning appoggio technique, singers should make this connection. I tell my singers that breaths connect, rather than separate, phrases.

Flexibility

The greatest obstacle to good singing is tension in the wrong place and/or at the wrong time. Singers discover as they improve their breathing for singing that some tension is absolutely necessary, provided it is appropriately and flexibly applied. However, an early stage of any vocal warm-up should include routines that allow the singer to relax at least the neck and shoulders, muscles controlling the lower jaw and articulatory apparatus, such as the tongue and lips.

A crucial early concept for inexperienced singers of all ages is what I call "Tongue Obedience". Just as a young dog learns first to sit and stay, so awareness of the tongue is best dedicated to sitting it relatively low and forward in the mouth, perhaps just touching the bottom front teeth. Few beginning singers have a clear idea of what the tongue looks like; discovering how large its "root" is will provide powerful motivation for keeping it as relaxed as possible. Of course, the tongue has a vital part to play in the formation of different vowels, but low and relaxed is an important "default" position to learn early.

The following five exercises are particularly appropriate for "warming up".

Exercise 10.2: Nanana

♩ = 80
Na na na na na na na na na na na na na,
Na etc
etc...

I normally use the notes of a major scale for this exercise, so differentiating between major and minor seconds is important and requires careful tuning.

- Both ascending and descending scales are used for the starting note, but the pattern of the exercise remains the same.
- The [a] vowel requires the teeth to be quite far apart — at least two fingers' width. The initial [n] involves the tongue briefly touching the alveolar ridge. The tongue must then drop to the floor of the mouth and the lower jaw drop to open the mouth. The teacher must check for sufficient mouth opening and relaxed tongue.
- Some singers try to open their mouths (and often succeed) by keeping the lower jaw still and raising their upper teeth. This is achieved by tensing muscles at the back of the neck and should be avoided at all costs!
- I encourage singers to exaggerate vertical movement of the jaw in order to loosen the whole musculature of the neck and in some cases ask them to slowly rotate their heads from side to side to reduce tension further.

- One breath is enough for each pattern, and singers are encouraged to use a "release breath" both to complete each pattern and prepare the next.

Exercise 10.3: Many Men

Ma - ny ma - ny ma - ny ma - ny ma - ny ma - ny ma - ny men.

This is similar to Nanana, but the words now mean something, which may lead to a healthily humorous approach that can be enhanced by changing some of the "many"s to "money"!

- Exaggerated jaw movement is a regular feature of my warm-up exercises for the reason outlined previously.
- This exercise uses two different vowels, requiring more sophisticated use of the tongue. I insist on the [e] and [I] vowels, but many singers will try to use [ɛ] (or even [æ]) and [i]. While solo singers should be helped to achieve the best solution for their personal diction, in choral contexts uniformity is important.
- The two consonants involve not only the tongue, but also the lips in closure for the [m].

Again, a good grasp of major tonality will help this exercise.

Exercise 10.4: Rocking Triads

Ee-aw ee-aw etc...
Ee...

This is a more demanding exercise than those above, as it requires very clear differentiation between vowels.

- The teacher should listen for, and discourage, hard "glottal stop" onsets (or releases).
- I use this gradually rising by semitones. Thus, the triad remains a major one, but the exercise could also be used to practise minor triads.
- The teacher must listen carefully to ensure the vowels are correct, especially as rising pitch requires vowel modification, and should check jaw, lip and tongue position.

Exercise 10.5: Ho!

Heavy and accented ♩ = 76
Ho ho ho ho ho ho ho ho ho ho ho, Ho ho ho ho ho ho ho ho ho ho ho, Ho...

This is a demanding exercise designed to strengthen the external oblique muscles and to reinforce the routines of the appoggio technique. It can be exhausting!

Shoulders should not be used, either for breathing in or for attacking the sound.

- Air may be taken in unconsciously at any time between notes, but gasping is discouraged.
- While a complete ascending and descending set of this pattern is feasible, it should be followed by an exercise allowing more relaxed musculature, especially of neck and jaw.

Vowels — Placement, Modification (and Identification)

Although this can be a vexed question amongst vocal pedagogues, I maintain that it is helpful for singers to develop awareness of the sensations of resonance produced by different vowels. Terms commonly used by singers to talk about their perceptions of tone include space, focus, bright, dark and so on. I encourage my singers to hone their perceptions, helping them to understand the similarities as well as the differences between vowels, and I sanction the use of terminology commonly found in the literature and in use by reputable vocal pedagogues.

Often, because of the linguistic environment in which singers have been raised, they find it difficult to differentiate between sounds they hear. My own background, in which the "closed" [e] was more prevalent than the open [ɛ], made my early experiences of Melbournian speech quite painful, and I have been fighting the ubiquitous [ɛ] ever since! I have found calling one the "egg" vowel and the other the "air" vowel helpful, but in some cases I have to resort to asking singers to pretend they are New Zealanders to get the desired result! I encourage my singers and in particular my choirs to use 13 vowels when singing in English as contained in the sentence:

> Two Chooks Crow for Hot, Dark Rum: At Worst Their Eggs Will Please.

Most singers will agree that the first few are generally referred to as "back" vowels, whereas the last are considered to be "forward". These terms enshrine the commonly held perception that resonance for particular vowels seems to be located in particular areas within or around the vocal tract. I encourage singers to regard the list as a road map of vowels — those closest together are most similar and there is a gradual change of character from one end of the list to the other. I also encourage singers to discuss the "shapes" that they perceive for their resonating spaces; it is often possible to move towards a shared way of thinking about specific vowels and, particularly, how to prepare appropriate resonance spaces for a change of vowel.

Of course, we all know that vocal sound originates in the vibration of the vocal folds and that the resonance spaces we set up with mouth and other hollow areas amplify the sound to audible levels. It seems that the larynx responds to the preparation of resonating spaces by producing frequencies appropriate to those spaces.

Exercise 10.6: Oo oh ah (Range extension)

My introduction to Exercise 10.6 was at the hands of my first voice teacher, Donald Munro.

At first, this exercise facilitates understanding of resonance placement: [o] feels further "forward" than [ʊ], and [ɑ] is further forward still. But, as the pitch is raised, the stretch required to provide sufficient resonating space for [ʊ] increases, whereas the adjustments needed to change the vowel from [ʊ] to [ɑ] are in a comfortable direction and allow consolidation and increased focus for the more forward sounds.

It provides the opportunity to develop beautiful legato singing between release breaths that may be one, two or more bars apart. Gentle and gradual range extension is also a possible outcome by gradually raising the pitch, but the teacher must watch for distortion of the face and mouth that could indicate faulty technique, and ensure that upward extension is not excessive.

Exercise 10.7: Koo raw mah veh shi

Exercise 10.7 is designed to encourage several outcomes. I generally use it one syllable at a time to begin, concentrating on the correct placement and "feel"

for the varying pitch. Over time, the singers learn that they can control what spectrum of frequencies their larynges supply only by controlling the resonating spaces. It is as though the larynx can only "read" space, not words.

- The first and third notes should feel the same, but singers who find they are different need help to ensure uniformity.
- The exercise is repeated a semitone higher, gradually working towards the highest notes of the singer's range.
- Good legato should be maintained.
- The [k] of koo, made by the meeting and parting of the back of the tongue on the velum, sets up space appropriate for the long ("telescope-like") resonance of [ʊ]. A rolled [r] initiates the extra support needed for the ascending interval and provides time to prepare extra space. [m] concentrates resonance forward at the lips and reminds the singer that most descending intervals need forward placement. I encourage strong voicing of the [v], again assisting forward focus, while the "fish-mouth" (Ehmann & Haasemann, 1981, p. 137) that results from the [ʃ] both places the vowel forward and prevents spreading.
- When all five vowels are used, there is an elegant progression between the syllables, each helping to prepare the next.
- The teacher monitors, and corrects when necessary, vowel shape and placement, always listening and watching for good phrase shaping and competent release breathing, especially between each repetition and the subsequent (higher) one.

Onset

Exercise 10.8: Onset

Exercise 10.8 was invented by Richard Miller (1986 p. 13–14), who presented it as an essential step in the acquisition of basic technique. Specifically, it is

designed to coordinate attack and release with the correct breath control techniques of appoggio. Its stimulation of the support musculature also helps to develop vibrant tone quality.

Its main purpose, however, is to ensure clean onset of vibration of the vocal folds — what is generally referred to as "free flow phonation" (Miller 2008, p. 52) — and avoiding "pressed" phonation, which reduces the beauty of tone and may, ultimately cause lesions on the folds.

- The singer should avoid both breathy attack and hard "glottal" onset, the latter in particular being monitored by the teacher. Audible pre-phonatory sounds, such as a hum or a grunt, should also be discouraged.
- The opportunity should always exist for air to enter the lungs after each pitch level (indicated by commas in the notation), but I do not insist on a breath at every comma. If the "gesture of inspiration" is properly maintained, the lungs will accept air as and when necessary. Good appoggio facilitates replenishment of the air supply as a "free gift from the atmosphere".
- The descending scale fragment is limited, allowing careful control of vowel shape and placement, while the relatively extended time spent on the lowest note of each pattern allows the singer to think about and prepare the appropriate spaces for the first (and higher) note of the next pattern.
- While Miller allows "any vowel", I use only [ʊ], [ɔ], [ɑ], [æ], [e] and [ɪ] in that order on each pitch before moving to the next pitch.
- Depending on the individuals involved, I commence this exercise for treble voices with the first note around G4 and gradually raise it to E5 or higher. Changed male voices can complete the exercise an octave lower, although young baritones in particular may not be able to deal with a starting note higher than C4 (middle C).
- Freedom, beauty and easy control should be the aim. Visible tension in throat, shoulders, face (or even hands!) indicate problems that must be addressed.

Passaggio

Exercise 10.9: Loo-law

I have found Exercise 10.9 to be particularly helpful for boys' changing voices. Especially, regular practice can assist to prevent and even remedy the "holes" that sometimes appear in the changing voice around D4 to G4. I explain to the singers that different muscle groups learn to cooperate in sharing the work of making the basic vibrations, which then must be resonated to produce good (and free) vocal tone.

The exercise begins in falsetto, and should be sung quite quickly, without thinking too much about tone quality — and not thinking at all about register. Each voice will change registers in its own time, which may change from phrase to phrase. On no account should a singer "decide" where a register change is to occur — the whole point is for the voice to find its own "comfort zones" — which may well be different on different days! Immediately on finishing the first phrase, repeat a semitone lower, gradually descending until the whole phrase is sung in modal register.

Four guidelines should be observed rigidly: (a) each phrase must be completed on one breath; (b) the lower jaw should be as loose and "active" as possible, producing adequate mouth opening; (c) separate the quavers descending to the bottom note; and (d) join the bottom note to the following top note.

Exercise 10.10: Far Away

Exercise 10.10 has proven to be effective in encouraging female singers into their lower register; that is, below the primo passaggio.

The [f] helps to reinforce the notion of forward placement that is necessary when descending in pitch. Singers often "swallow" or "dig for" their low notes, creating harmful tension in the throat, particularly by inhibiting the function of the muscles (e.g., cricothyroid) on which accurate tuning depends.

- Violent register shifts should be discouraged, the ideal being a smooth transition that is not noticed by anyone, but singer and teacher. Generally, the more forward the sensation of resonance, the less likely is a heavy change.
- The teacher monitors appropriate mouth opening and encourages relaxed neck and throat muscles.

Exercise 10.11: Passagio

I learned Exercise 10.11 from Anton Armstrong, when he was working with the National Honour Choir at the 2001 Brisbane Choralfest. It is excellent for boys in the early stages of voice-change, but I also use it for adult males in the choral situation.

- It should be sung very slowly and very softly with no weight applied to the voice.
- It should be very legato.
- The aim is to make as beautiful a sound as possible.
- The teacher should monitor for signs of tension (which may manifest itself as much in the hands and arms as the face and throat) and help singers to relax.
- No attempt should be made to force a register change at any point; the singer must accept what happens, even if a register shift happens at one pitch in the hum and somewhere else when singing "loo". Falsetto may be used as needed.
- Starting around E3, the exercise should be repeated, ascending a semitone at a time, until the top note is well above the second passaggio. I generally take the singers up at least to F#4.

Tonality

I am a convinced "Solfegist", encouraging the use of solfa syllables (and Curwen handsigns with my younger singers) and using a moveable doh to inculcate a strong sense of tonality and good intonation. Attention to vowel shape assists in attaining in-tune singing and also directs singers' attention to the differences between the ways particular vowels are pronounced by different speakers. Routines that practise scales and intervals are an essential element in all my teaching and lead in due course to fluent reading of music. With the youngest singers — and sometimes with older ones who are willing to try the method — I use solfege in the early stages of learning all new music. I also use it to correct passages of known music that show intonation problems. Differentiating between major and minor intervals (and scales) is an important area where consistent and regular practice helps to habituate the conventions of western musical culture. This can be an important element in any vocal warm-up.

Exercise 10.12: Ascending and Descending Seconds

Oo ah oo ah etc...
Ah oo ah oo etc...

I use Exercise 10.12 in warm-up, to drill several concepts. In addition to differentiating major and minor seconds, it subtly establishes a strong understanding of the major triad. Attention should be paid to vowel placement, particularly as the exercise is steadily raised in pitch, and the teacher watches and listens for good appoggio.

Exercise 10.13: Me, oh my!

Me oh my oh me oh my oh me oh my oh me oh my oh
me oh my oh me oh my oh me oh my oh me!

Exercise 10.13 is another warm-up. It can be done in one breath or, for less experienced singers, provided with a "comfort stop" breath at the dominant. Once thoroughly learnt, it is a useful way of drilling solfege, but my favourite use is as an expressive medium. The exclamation "Me, oh my!" can mean many different things and singers are encouraged to act out satisfaction, frustration, anxiety, affection and urgency, amongst many other human moods or states. The singers often want to invent their own, and youngsters enjoy doing the exercise in a way they have invented for a partner who has to "guess" what is being expressed. It is a useful way of reminding singers that technical expertise is of little benefit unless we use it to make our music more expressive and more meaningful to audiences.

In conclusion, this collection of exercises is not exhaustive of the ways in which I encourage singers to grow their abilities, but it provides a core that can help each singer to develop both a sound vocal technique and the shared experience to build further development. The key to their use is a knowledgeable and attentive teacher whose ears are constantly evaluating and whose consistent attention to detail keeps the student steadily developing the best habits, strongly based on voice science as well as artistic excellence.

References

Chapman, J.L. (2006). *Singing and teaching singing: A wholistic approach to classical voice.* San Diego, CA: Plural Publishing.

Ehmann, W., & Haasemann, F. (1981). *Voice building for choirs* (B. Smith, Trans. Rev. ed.). Chapel Hill, NC: Hinshaw Music.

Gullaer, I., Walker, R., Badin, R., & Lamalle, L. (2006) Image, imagination, and reality: On effectiveness of introductory work with vocalists. *Logopedics Phoniatrics Vocology, 31*(2), 89–96

Harrison, Scott D. (Ed.). (2009). *Male voices: Stories of boys learning through making music.* Melbourne, Australia: ACER Press

Miller, R. (1986). *The structure of singing: System and art in vocal technique.* New York: Schirmer Books.

Miller, R. (1993). *Training tenor voices.* New York: Schirmer Books.

Miller, R. (1996). *On the art of singing.* New York: Oxford University Press.

Miller, R. (2000). *Training soprano voices.* New York: Oxford University Press.

Miller, R. (2004). *Solutions for singers: Tools for performers and teachers.* New York: Oxford University Press.

Miller, R. (2008). *Securing baritone, bass-baritone, and bass voices.* New York: Oxford University Press.

Phillips, K.H. (1992). *Teaching kids to sing.* New York: Schirmer Books.

Sataloff, R.T. (Ed.). (2006). *Vocal health and pedagogy, Volume 1: Science and assessment* (2nd ed.). San Diego, CA: Plural Publishing.

Skoog, W. (2004). Use of image and metaphor in developing vocal technique in choirs. *Music Educators Journal, 90*(5), 43–48.

Smith, B., & Sataloff, R.T. (2006). *Choral pedagogy* (2nd ed.). San Diego, CA: Plural Publishing.

Sundberg, J. (1987). *The science of the singing voice.* Dekalb, IL: Northern Illinois University Press.

Titze, I.R. (1994). *Principles of voice production.* Englewood Cliffs, NJ: Prentice Hall.

Vennard, W. (1967). *Singing: The mechanism and the technic* (Rev. ed.). New York: Carl Fischer.

Zemlin, W.R. (1988). *Speech and hearing science: Anatomy and physiology* (3rd ed.). Englewood Cliffs, NJ: Prentice Hall.

Chapter 11

Music Theatre Voice: Production, Physiology and Pedagogy

Tracy Bourne, Maëva Garnier and Dianna Kenny

Most of the scientific research on singing voice has focused on classical and operatic singing. While music theatre and contemporary voice are growing in popularity within western musical culture, less is known about safe and effective training methods, aesthetics and vocal health for students of these vocal styles. A number of recent developments in voice science for this style, collectively known as Contemporary Commercial Music (CCM), offer evidence-based research to assist teachers in finding their way through the maze of conflicting information and opinion. In particular, voice qualities such as "belt," "mix" and "legit" that are used in music theatre vocal styles involve very different laryngeal behaviours and vocal tract adjustments compared to those used by classical singers. The differences are greatest around the transition area between the two main laryngeal mechanisms, perceptually described as "chest" or "head" registers. Findings so far suggest that classical vocal training methods may not be appropriate for music theatre voice at pitches near the register transition. In this chapter, we will present findings from a survey of expert music theatre voice teachers, conduct a broad review of current scientific literature on the music theatre voice, followed by an examination of recent research on vocal registers. We will discuss the relevance of these findings to music theatre voice teaching in a practical sense and will make some recommendations on approaches to voice training and health.

What is Music Theatre Voice?

Music theatre voice is a style within the broader field of CCM, previously described as "non-classical" music (LoVetri, 2008, p. 60), and includes vocal qualities described in the professional industry as "belt" and "legit".

The belt sound may have originated in the early 20th century with vaudeville "coon shouters", such as May Irwin, Stella Mayhew, Ethel Levey and Sophie Tucker, who sang in a style parodying African-American women (Banfield, 2000). In 1930, Ethel Merman made belt famous when she sang the final C5 (C above middle C) of *I've Got Rhythm* for 16 bars in a loud "chest voice" without amplification over a band of brass, reeds and drums (Grant, 2004). Her performance earned her multiple encores, prompting George Gershwin to visit her during the interval and advise her never to take a singing lesson (Flinn, 2009, p. 33).

The growing importance of plot in the American musical of the 1940s and 1950s led composers to write melodies that were lower in pitch and more restricted in vocal range, so that the text could be more easily understood. At the same time, composer/writer teams, such as Rodgers and Hammerstein, wrote more realistic characters, often requiring performers to place vocal expressivity before beauty. Celeste Holm, who first created the role of Ado Annie in *Oklahoma* (Rodgers & Hammerstein II, 1943), sang Schubert's "An die Musik" for her audition, but was asked if she could also sing in a more "untrained voice". She produced what she described as her "hog call" and got the role (Osborne, 1979).

The music theatre sound changed radically with the introduction of the rock musical in the 1960s and 1970s. Lead roles in musicals, such as *Hair* (MacDermot, Rado, & Ragni, 1967) *Jesus Christ Superstar* (Lloyd Webber & Rice, 1971) and *Rent* (Larson, 1994), required strong contemporary singers that had the stamina for eight shows a week. More recently, the musical, *Wicked* (Schwartz & Holzman, 2003) extended the technical requirements of the female belt sound, requiring an F5 in the song, "Defying Gravity".

The legit vocal quality is grounded in the classical tradition, arising out of the popularity of operetta in the early 20th century (LoVetri, 2008). Early music theatre singing from the beginning of the 20th century was almost all classical, although the tessitura was generally lower and the range more restricted than for operatic repertoire. The music theatre legit sound was most popular in the musicals of the 1940s, 1950s and 1960s, but has generally declined in use since then. It is still a required sound for some roles in music theatre productions, such as Johanna in *Sweeney Todd* (Sondheim & Wheeler, 1979) or Fabrizio in *Light in the Piazza* (Guettel & Lucas, 2003).

This chapter will report on responses from a survey of experienced music theatre pedagogues from Australia, United Kingdom, United States and Asia about current industry definitions and methods of training. Current knowledge on the vocal health risks for music theatre voice will be discussed and a review of scientific literature on the physiology and acoustic characteristics of music theatre vocal qualities will be presented. A summary of research on vocal registers and laryngeal mechanisms will be followed by a discussion of registers in the music theatre voice, and the implications for vocal health and training. Finally, the article will offer specific recommendations, including an evaluation of the appropriateness of classical methods for teaching the music theatre singing voice.

Do We Need a Pedagogy for Music Theatre Voice?

In the past decade, the demand for training in music theatre singing styles has grown and singing teachers are now seeking specific training methods for this style. In 2001, the president of the National Association of Teachers of Singing (NATS) reported that a workshop in that year on the music theatre and belt voice attracted over 300 members from eight countries and 46 states from the United States. "It was thought that this might have been the largest workshop registration in NATS history" (Delp, 2001, p. 1). A survey of Victorian members of the Australian National Association of Teachers of Singing (ANATS) in 2006 showed a similarly high level of interest amongst members for workshops on music theatre vocal techniques (Caire, 2006). A survey of 139 singing teachers from the United Kingdom and the United States reported that 91% of respondents taught CCM vocal styles, but only 45% had any specific training for teaching this style (LoVetri & Means Weekly, 2003). A follow-up survey of 145 singing teachers in the United States that asked questions about training background and experience found that only 19% of music theatre voice teachers were assessed as having training appropriate to teaching this style (Weekly & LoVetri, 2009). A total of 58% of respondents indicated that their training methods for classical voice and music theatre voice were completely different, while 31% reported some differences in their training methods, 7% taught these styles similarly and only 4% taught both styles the same way. An Australian survey in 1998 found that tertiary singing teachers of music theatre or contemporary commercial styles were more aware of current scientific knowledge of the voice than their classical colleagues (Callaghan, 1998). There is no known research on pedagogical differences between these teacher populations.

Perceptions of Expert Studio Teachers of Music Theatre Voice

The first author conducted a semistructured interview with 12 expert teachers from Australia, Asia, United States and United Kingdom in order to gather more information about the knowledge and practice of expert teachers, and their perceptual understandings of the physiological and acoustic qualities of belt, legit and mix in the music theatre voice. All teachers were music theatre voice specialists and taught at tertiary institutions and/or private studios for professional music theatre singers in Broadway, the West End, or the professional Australian Industry.

Respondents described belt as a chest or thyroarytenoid[1] (TA) dominant sound with "forward," "twangy" vowels. They articulated a range of belting styles, suggesting that there may be more than one type of belt sound. Responses suggested that there was confusion amongst teachers when defining male belt, although the majority of teachers asserted that men can belt in their higher range, generally at pitches where they may choose to sing in "chest" or "falsetto". Incidentally, this was also the pitch range where 11 of the 12 teachers agreed that women belted. Most teachers agreed that belt may have vibrato, is generally loud, and may use nasality as a character choice.

Respondents all agreed that legit is a more classically based vocal quality, with a brighter and "twangier" sound than the classical voice. They suggested that for women, legit is cricothyroid[2] (CT) or "head" register dominant, whereas for men, it generally remains in chest or TA dominant production. Vowels are brighter and "twangier" than classical vowels.

Most respondents described "mix" as a sound that balanced chest (thick vocal folds) and head register (thin vocal folds). At the same time, teachers expressed their frustration with the term, suggesting that it lacked clarity: "I don't use the word 'mix'. I still don't know what mixing is" and "I don't use the word mix even though it is employed a lot in the profession, for this simple reason: All good singing is a mix, so to me it's a redundant term".

Results from the survey suggest that the management of vocal registration in music theatre singing appears to be a big concern for all teachers, and followed two contradictory lines of opinion on the use of chest register in the belt sound: (1) that belt is defined as chest register taken up in pitch, past the usual point of transition into 'head' register; or (2) that belt should not be produced in this way, because it is vocally damaging to do so. Many of the teachers reported their discomfort with the term "chest voice", and used other terms instead, such as "chest register", "chest register dominant", "TA dominant" or "thick folds".

Music Theatre Voice and Vocal Health

Singing teachers have long expressed concern about the inherent risk of music theatre singing. Note these three quotes that cover a 50-year time span:

> This technic is characterized by a loud, "thick" and unpleasant quality, and an extremely limited range of about one octave. It is the type of phonation employed exclusively by the "coon-shouter" or "jazz singer" and cannot, for a moment, be considered as real singing. (Stanley, 1929, p. 60)

> Another singer is out of a show with a ruptured blood vessel on a vocal cord! ... you can blame it all on chest voice and belting ... Singing with the greatest amount of unnecessary tension is called chest voice; singing with a little less is called belting. (Howell, 1978, p. 14)

> To argue that some singers belt and survive has all the weight of observing that some people smoke three packs a day, live to eighty, and die of causes other than cancer, emphysema, or heart attack (Osborne, 1979, p. 65)

Miles and Hollien (1990) conducted a review of literature and a survey of experienced teachers and researchers about the belt voice. Their findings indicated a high level of concern amongst teachers about the inherent risks of singing in this style and concluded that "it appears well established that the singer who belts frequently experiences vocal pathology" (p. 66). Miles and Hollien further stated that there was little evidence to indicate why belt had a reputation for being unhealthy, or information about other factors that may have also led to vocal injury, such as poor vocal training or susceptibility to vocal damage in the singer.

In fact, research on vocal health for the music theatre and belt voice is hard to find. Lawrence (1979) suggested that common pathologies for "belters" included signs of hyper function, including reddening of the edges of the folds and oedema, and vocal fold polyps and nodules as well as tired and tender neck muscles resulting in "vocal weakness and loss of vocal control, loss of volume and vocal fatigue" (p. 28). However, this study provided no quantitative or comparative data to indicate how prevalent these injuries are amongst music theatre performers and how these rates compared with other types of singers. Only one study to date has compared the vocal health of professional opera, contemporary and music theatre singers. It found no significant differences between groups in terms of vocal impairment, disability or handicap (Phyland, Oates, & Greenwood, 1999).

In the past decade, North American teachers appear to be less critical of the aesthetic and health of the belt sound. The NATS' *Journal of Singing* has published a number of articles on the belt voice over the past decade arguing that it is a valid and reasonably "safe" vocal style if taught properly (Balog,

2005; Burdick, 2005). Robert Edwin, as Associate Editor of the *Journal of Singing*, has written and commissioned a series of articles that describe the sound, the look and feel of belt (Edwin, 2000, 2002, 2003, 2004, 2005, 2006). The American Academy of Teachers of Singing (AATS) has also published an article "Promoting Vocal Health in the Production of High School Music Theatre" including suggestions for avoiding or reducing the risks that young singers may face in amateur music theatre productions (AATS, 2004). Australian singing publications demonstrate some support for the training of music theatre voice through the publication of a number of articles in *Australian Voice* (Bartlett, Winkworth, & Callaghan, 2002; Collyer, 1997; Wilson, 2003). However, the majority of research is still weighted heavily towards classical voice.

The Science of Music Theatre Voice Production

There are a number of studies examining the distinct physiological and acoustic differences in the production of the belt sound. From this research, we can describe belt as typically produced with a high larynx and tongue, narrower pharyngeal space and high lung pressures (Lawrence, 1979; Miles & Hollein, 1990; Sundberg, 2000), although there are singers who may be able to produce this sound with a relatively low larynx and wide pharyngeal space (LoVetri, Lesh, & Woo, 1999). The vocalis, or thyroarytenoid, muscle activity is dominant over cricothyroid muscle activity, resulting in strong glottal adduction with the vocal folds closed for a larger percentage of the vibratory phase than for classical singing. There are not many studies specifically addressing breath use and support in the belt voice, although subglottal pressures have been shown to be higher in the production of belt than for classical sounds (Bjorkner, Sundberg, Cleveland, & Stone, 2006).

Belt voice has a weaker fundamental frequency and comparatively low energy in the upper partials of the sound compared with the operatic sound. 'Belt' also has higher sound pressure levels and higher 1st and 2nd formant frequencies (Sundberg, Gramming, & LoVetri, 1993). Singers appear to adjust their vocal tract shape in order to "tune" the first formant to the frequency of the second harmonic in the sound spectrum, contributing to the loud, "bright" quality of this sound (Bestebreurtje & Schutte, 2000).

Only one article to date has measured the acoustic qualities of the legit sound in comparison to belt, describing it as a falsetto mode of vocal fold vibration with a high first formant that is slightly below the 2nd harmonic, producing a light, open sound that facilitates easy comprehension of the sung text (Schutte & Miller, 1993).

The only study of the music theatre mix sound compared a single subject demonstrating mix, belt and operatic sounds. Mix quality was a combination of the other two qualities, with high upper harmonics and higher 1st and 2nd formants as in belt production, and lower subglottal pressure with moderate sound pressure level (SPL; an objective measurement of loudness in decibels), as with operatic production (Sundberg, Gramming, & LoVetri, 1993).

Belt and the Vocal Registers

Given the concern and uncertainty around the use of chest register in the belt voice, it is worth examining current research on vocal registers. In particular, what is chest register, how does it relate to belt, and what are the inefficiencies or risks to performers singing in chest or belt?

Vocal registers are defined perceptually by pitch ranges of homogeneous vocal timbre. While the speech community largely agrees on the existence of three registers (pulse or vocal fry, modal or chest, and falsetto), the singing community is still very much divided on the number of registers, their names and how they should be defined (Henrich, 2006). Registers are underlined by different modes of vocal fold vibration and vocal tract adjustments. In particular, four "laryngeal mechanisms" (labelled M0–M3) have been defined physiologically (Roubeau, Henrich, & Castellengo, 2009). Mechanisms M1 and M2 are most commonly used in speech and singing, and are characterised by fundamentally different muscle adjustments:

- Laryngeal mechanism 1 (M1) has thick vocal folds; that is, a higher vibrating mass of the folds than in M2. This is due to the coupling of the vocalis within the vocal fold. The vocalis muscle is dominant over the cricothyroid muscle.
- Laryngeal mechanism 2 (M2) has thinner folds; that is, less vibrating mass than M1. This is due to the decoupling of the vocalis within the vocal fold. The folds are more stretched, due to the dominance of cricothyroid muscle activity over thyroarytenoid muscle.

These different glottal configurations have an effect on the pattern of vocal fold vibration; in M1, the folds vibrate over their whole length with vertical phase difference. The amplitude is greater. The closed phase is longer than the open phase and is generally in the range of 30–80% of the vibratory cycle (Henrich, d'Alessandro, Doval, & Castellengo, 2005). In M2, the folds vibrate with lower amplitude and no vertical phase difference. The open phase is always longer than the closed phase; that is, greater than 50% of the vibratory cycle.

Differences in glottal vibration can be observed to some extent through indirect and non-invasive methods, such as electroglottography (Henrich, d'Alessandro, Doval, & Castellengo, 2004).

Thus, chest register may be produced by mechanism M1, whereas falsetto register (men), and head register (women) may be produced in mechanism M2. As M1 and M2 share an overlapping pitch range between E3 (165Hz) and F#4 (370Hz) for male voices, and G3 (196 Hz) to G4 (392 Hz) for female voices, singers can choose to vocalise in either M1 or M2 depending on the intended vocal quality.

As yet, there is no published research on laryngeal mechanisms in the contemporary or music theatre voice. However, a number of inferences can be made from the available evidence. Research on the belt voice that defines laryngeal behaviour as a long closed phase, with thick vocal folds, and strong adduction with dominant vocalis or thyroarytenoid muscle activity (Bjorkner, 2008; Estill, 1988; Miles & Hollein, 1990; Sundberg, Gramming, & LoVetri, 1993), suggests that belt voice is in mechanism M1. Most expert teachers also support this definition (Bourne & Kenny, 2008), even when they express confusion about the relationship between belt and chest. Furthermore, Schutte and Miller (1993), and Bestebreurtje and Schutte (2000) support the pedagogical theory that belt is chest register taken to higher frequences than would be usual for classical singing (Bestebreurtje & Schutte, 2000; Schutte & Miller, 1993). There have been no studies that describe the laryngeal behaviour of the legit quality in the music theatre voice. However, it is frequently associated with the head register by teachers and some researchers, which suggests that this is a M2 mechanism.

Expert teachers define mix as a blending of chest and head registers; however, recent research on classical mix voice does not support this theory. It seems that singers in this quality either sing in mechanism M1 or M2 for a given pitch, while also adjusting their vocal tract and laryngeal open quotient so that the overall sound quality imitates that of the alternate mechanism (Castellengo, Chuberre, & Henrich, 2004; Lamesch, Expert, Castellengo, Henrich, & Chuberre, 2007; Miller & Schutte, 2005).

These findings suggest that male and female music theatre singers need to develop a flexible approach to their technique in order to produce the broad range of sounds required in the music theatre profession. A female singer may produce a belt in mechanism M1, a legit in mechanism M2, and a mix quality by disguising the transition between mechanisms through careful resonance adjustments. Male singers are more likely to sing in M1 for most of their vocal range, so register management may not be such an issue, except in the upper notes of their range, where choices would need to be made about which mechanism to use, depending on the intended vocal style.

If belt is a quality produced in mechanism M1, what does this tell us about the vocal health risks for this style? M1 is a mode of production that has strong forces of glottal adduction, with high subglottal pressures. Many medical specialists and voice therapists have expressed concern about the long-term effects of singing in this manner, particularly at high levels of intensity. However, predicting vocal strain and quantifying vocal effort may not be as simple as measuring glottal adduction and open/closed quotients. Bjorkner (2008) compared male music theatre singers with male operatic singers. She found that the degree of pressed phonation was similar in both groups, even though subglottal pressure and closed quotient were higher in the music theatre singers. It is also possible that some teachers teach a style of belt that has a relatively high open quotient and a low level of volume, which may be less effortful for the singer (McCoy, 2007).

Recommendations

Training for music theatre singing should include the following:

- Women need to practise in both chest register (for belt) and head register (for legit), as well as with a seamless register transition (for mix). Although the teacher and student may perceive the mix sound to be in a middle register, this is not physiologically correct.
- Men may move between classical and contemporary styles in their training and repertoire more easily than women, because they sing in laryngeal mechanism M1 for most of their range. However, they need to be more flexible in their higher pitch range when making a choice to sing in either belt voice or classical voice. Men need careful guidance in the development of their higher pitch range for contemporary singing in order to prevent excessive vocal tension that may be associated with the production of the loud, bright qualities of belt.
- Teachers should encourage students to develop bright and forward resonance qualities for belt and mix as well as a more balanced timbre for legit. The "back" or "covered" sound typical of the classical vocal style is not stylistically appropriate for musical theatre singing. Exercises that promote twang and forward vowels can assist students to develop this quality in their sound.
- Classical vocal training may offer some advantages to music theatre singers in the improvement of their technique when:
  - disguising the vocal break between mechanisms. A prime purpose of classical vocal training is to reduce the audibility of the register "break" for both male and female sounds. Exercises that assist singers learning to "balance registers" may be appropriate for music theatre singers learning to sing in mix.
  - learning to sing in M2 at speaking pitch in legit quality. Many classical voice teaching methods encourage female classical singers to sing

in their head register for most of their pitch range. Exercises that encourage singers to bring the head register lower in the range may assist in the production of the female legit voice.

- Classical vocal training is not likely to be useful for students learning to produce the belt sound. Female music theatre singers need to be able to sing in M1 at relatively high frequencies in an efficient and aesthetically pleasing manner, whereas female classical singers are actively discouraged from singing in their chest register as much as possible. Male contemporary singers need to be able to sing M1 at relatively high pitches in belt production with ease while maintaining a loud volume, whereas male classical singers are generally encouraged to transition into M2, lower in their pitch range.[3]

Summary

The evidence suggests that music theatre singers need to be versatile and flexible in their vocal choices. They need to be able to produce sounds that are distinctly in mechanism M1 and M2, as well as sounds that blend the transition point between these mechanisms. When singing in belt, women may need to be able to maintain M1 production at higher pitches than they would need to for classical singing. Male singers may also need to maintain mechanism M1 for belt quality in their upper range. Music theatre singers need to be able to produce bright and relatively loud sounds, as well as the more balanced, warm sounds of legit and mix qualities. Vocal health is of concern for teachers and singers, but there is very little evidence-based information on how singers can produce music theatre qualities efficiently and safely.

Endnotes

1 The thyroarytenoid muscle connects the thyroid and arytenoid cartilages; shortening and thickening the vocal folds as it contracts. The chest register is associated with this muscle function.

2 The cricothyroid muscle connects the cricoid and thyroid cartilages; lengthening and thinning the vocal folds as it contracts. The head register is associated with this muscle function.

3 Although we wonder if some operatic tenors may be producing some of their very high notes in a quality that has similarities to the belt sound. There is no evidence to support such an idea; this is only a subjective observation.

References

American Academy of Teachers of Singing. (2004). Promoting vocal health in the production of high school music theater. *Journal of Singing, 60*(3), 223–225.

Balog, J.E. (2005). A guide to evaluating music theater singing for the classical teacher. *Journal of Singing, 61*(4), 401–406.

Banfield, S. (2000). Stage and screen entertainers in the twentieth century. In J. Potter (Ed.), *The Cambridge Companion to Singing* (pp. 63–82). Cambridge, UK: Cambridge University Press.

Bartlett, I., Winkworth, A., & Callaghan, J. (2002). Voice and performance profiles of working contemporary commercial singers: Implications for voice care. *Australian Voice, 8*, 68–71.

Bestebreurtje, M., & Schutte, H.K. (2000). Resonance strategies for the belting style: Results of a single female subject study. *Journal of Voice, 14*(2), 194–204.

Bjorkner, E. (2008). Musical theatre and opera singing — Why so different? A study of subglottal pressure, voice source, and formant frequency characteristics. *Journal of Voice, 22*, 533–540.

Bjorkner, E., Sundberg, J., Cleveland, T., & Stone, E. (2006). Voice source differences between registers in female musical theatre singers. *Journal of Voice, 20*(2), 187–197.

Bourne, T., & Kenny, D. (2008, September). *Perceptual descriptions of legit and belt voice qualities in music theatre.* Paper presented at the Australian National Association of Teachers of Singing (ANATS): Sing into Spring, Perth, Australia.

Burdick, B. (2005). Vocal techniques for music theater: The high school and undergraduate singer. *Journal of Singing, 61*(3), 261–268.

Caire, J. (2006). *Survey of Victorian ANATS members* (unpublished membership survey).

Callaghan, J. (1998). Singing teachers and voice science — An evaluation of voice teaching in Australian teaching institutions. *Research Studies in Music Education, 10*(June), 25–41.

Castellengo, M., Chuberre, B., & Henrich, N. (2004). *Is 'voix mixte', the vocal technique used to smooth the transition across the two main laryngeal mechanisms, an independent mechanism?* Paper presented at the Proceedings of ISMA, Nara, Japan.

Collyer, S. (1997). The classical teacher and belting. *Australian Voice, 3*, 37–41.

Delp, R. (2001). Now that the belt voice has become legitimate ... *Journal of Singing, 57*(5), 1–2.

Edwin, R. (2000). Apples and oranges: Belting revisited. *Journal of Singing, 57*(2), 43–44.

Edwin, R. (2002). Belting: Bel canto or brutto canto. *Journal of Singing, 59*(1), 67–68.

Edwin, R. (2003). A broader Broadway. *Journal of Singing, 59*(5), 431–432.

Edwin, R. (2004). Belt yourself. *Journal of Singing, 60*(3), 285–288.

Edwin, R. (2005). Contemporary music theater: Louder than words. *Journal of Singing, 61*(3), 291–292.

Edwin, R. (2006). These are not your great grandfather's vocalises. *Journal of Singing, 63*(1), 77–79.

Estill, J. (1988). Belting and classic voice quality: Some physiological differences. *Medical Problems of Performing Artists, 3*, 37–43.

Flinn, C. (2009). *Brass diva: The life and legends of Ethel Merman*: Berkeley, CA: University of California Press.

Grant, M.N. (2004). *The rise and fall of the Broadway musical.* Boston, MA: Northeastern University Press.

Guettel, A., & Lucas, C. (2003). *Light in the Piazza* [Musical].

Henrich, N. (2006). Mirroring the voice from Garcia to the present day: Some insights into singing voice registers. *Logopedics Phoniatrics Vocology, 31*, 3–14.

Henrich, N., d'Alessandro, C., Doval, B., & Castellengo, M. (2004). On the use of the derivative of electroglottographic signals for characterization of nonpathological phonation. *Journal of the Acoustical Society of America, 115*(3), 1321–1332.

Henrich, N., d'Alessandro, C., Doval, B., & Castellengo, M. (2005). Glottal open quotient in singing: Measurements and correlation with laryngeal mechanisms, vocal intensity, and fundamental frequency. *Journal of the Acoustical Society of America, 117*(3), 1417–1430.

Howell, E. (1978, April 14). Chest voice-belting. *Equity News.*

Lamesch, S., Expert, R., Castellengo, M., Henrich, N., & Chuberre, B. (2007, August). *Investigating 'voix mixte': A scientific challenge towards a renewed vocal pedagogy.* Paper presented at the Proceedings of the 3rd Conference on Interdisciplinary Musicology (CIM07), Tallin, Estonia.

Larson, J. (1994). *Rent* [Musical].

Lawrence, V. (1979). Laryngological observations on belting. *Journal of Research in Singing, 2*, 26–28.

Lloyd Webber, A., & Rice, T. (1971). *Jesus Christ Superstar* [Musical].

LoVetri, J. (2008). Contemporary commercial music. *Journal of Voice, 22*(3), 260–262.

LoVetri, J., Lesh, S., & Woo, P. (1999). Preliminary study on the ability of trained singers to control the intrinsic and extrinsic laryngeal musculature. *Journal of Voice, 13*(2), 219–226.

LoVetri, J., & Means Weekly, E. (2003). Contemporary commercial music (CCM) survey: Who's teaching what in non-classical music? *Journal of Voice, 17*(2), 207–215.

MacDermot, G., Rado, J., & Ragni, G. (1967). *Hair* [Musical].

McCoy, S. (2007). A classical pedagogue explores belting. *Journal of Singing, 64*(5), 545–549.

Miles, B., & Hollein, H. (1990). Whither belting? *Journal of Voice, 4*(1), 64–70.

Miller, D.G., & Schutte, H.K. (2005). 'Mixing' the registers: Glottal source or vocal tract? *Folia Phoniatrica et Logopaedica, 57*, 278–291.

Osborne, C. (1979). The Broadway voice part 1: Just singin' in the pain. *High Fidelity, 29*(1), 53–65.

Phyland, D.J., Oates, J., & Greenwood, K.M. (1999). Self-reported voice problems among three groups of professional singers. *Journal of Voice, 13*(4), 602–611.

Rodgers, R., & Hammerstein II, O. (1943). *Oklahoma!* [Musical].

Roubeau, B., Henrich, N., & Castellengo, M. (2009). Laryngeal vibratory mechanisms: The notion of vocal register revisted. *Journal of Voice, 23*(4), 425–438.

Schutte, H.K., & Miller, D.G. (1993). Belting and pop, Nonclassical approaches to the female middle voice: Some preliminary conclusions. *Journal of Voice, 7*(2), 142–150.

Schwartz, S., & Holzman, W. (2003). *Wicked* [Musical].

Sondheim, S., & Wheeler, H. (1979). *Sweeney Todd: The demon barber of Fleet Street* [Musical].

Stanley, D. (1929). *The science of voice.* New York: Carl Fischer.

Sundberg, J. (2000). Where does the sound come from? In J. Potter (Ed.), *The Cambridge Companion to Singing* (pp. 231–247). Cambridge, UK: Cambridge University Press.

Sundberg, J., Gramming, P., & LoVetri, J. (1993). Comparisons of pharynx, source, formant, and pressure characteristics in operatic and musical theatre singing. *Journal of Voice, 7*(4), 301–310.

Weekly, E.M., & LoVetri, J. (2009). Follow-up contemporary commercial music: Who's teaching what in nonclassical music? *Journal of Voice, 23*(3), 367–375.

Wilson, P. (2003). Sinful modern music: Science and the contemporary commercial singer. *Australian Voice, 9*, 12–16.

Chapter 12

Reflective Journaling in the Singing Studio

Cathy Aggett

This chapter investigates the effectiveness of reflective journaling as a pedagogical learning and teaching tool for use in the singing studio. The chapter has three parts. It begins by discussing reflective practice, reflective and reflexive journaling, and describes the author's reflective journaling process for a musical performance. The second section presents writing from a mezzo-soprano and a soprano's (the author) viewpoints when engaged in short and long-term reflective journal writing during the preparation of Australian art songs for public performance. Entries from the journals are given to show aspects of different levels of critical thinking present, and related to musical examples from the repertoire. The entries are analysed using categories of reflective thinking based on Mezirow's (1991) levels of reflection (adapted by Kember et al., 2000). The third and final section focuses on aspects of reflective journaling relevant to the singing studio and a pedagogical approach to learning repertoire, discussing how the analysis of different levels of reflection can encourage deeper learning in the studio context and details some of the drawbacks of reflective journaling. A range of questions are posed to stimulate all levels of reflective action that can be applied to assist the learning and teaching process in the singing studio.

In her article, "Making a reflexive turn: Practical music-making becomes conventional research", Jane Davidson suggested that:

> … in the western art tradition performance is typically a more presentational than a reflexive activity … [urging] practitioners to begin to consider their own musical and performance processes and examine why certain elements which contribute towards creating a

> rehearsal or performance occur and how they may be different. (Davidson, 2004, p. 134)

This chapter considers the process of preparation for vocal performance by investigating the effectiveness of reflective journaling as a pedagogical learning and teaching tool in the singing studio through a review of the practice of two singers involved in research into Australian art song. Reflective journaling is being used as an educative tool by practitioners in many fields including pre-service teaching, nursing, clinical and psychological practice, all providing enhanced potential for learning and teaching. The results are applicable in the one-to-one environment of the singing studio. As a practitioner–researcher with a passion for Australian art song and an interest in finding ways for singers and singing teachers to learn and perform the repertoire more easily and effectively, I believe reflective journaling has played an integral part in my own teaching and learning process. This chapter has three parts. It begins by discussing reflective practice, reflective and reflexive journaling and the reflective journaling process of the author for a musical performance. The second and main section presents the viewpoints of a mezzo-soprano and a soprano (the author) who engaged in short and long-term reflective journal writing during the preparation of Australian art songs for public performance. Entries from the journals are given to show aspects of different levels of critical thinking present, and related to musical examples from the repertoire. The entries are analysed using categories of reflective thinking based on Mezirow's (1991) levels of reflection (adapted by Kember et al., 2000) as a means of discussing focused practice-based journaling for performance. Finally, the chapter draws together the earlier sections by proposing a model of reflective journaling that could be used by both singers and singing teachers when approaching the discovery of new song repertoire. This is undertaken by examining how such an approach can assist performers and studio teachers through a pedagogical frame that encourages reflective journaling and discusses how the analysis of different levels of reflection might encourage deeper learning in the studio context. It is hoped these preliminary findings may act as a means to spark discussion amongst the singing community in the area of reflective practice through reflective journaling.

Reflectivity

Reflective thought is considered to constitute "… active, persistent, and careful consideration of any belief or supposed form of knowledge, in light of the grounds that support it and the further conclusions to which it tends" (Dewey, 1933, p. 9).

As a practitioner–researcher, my own reflective writing over the past four years has taken the shape of writing a reflective journal in which I have recorded my thoughts, reflections and ideas for improvements on my rehearsals, recordings and subsequent performances of more than 33 Australian art songs. Initially, I began journaling because I was asking students in my music studio, including singers, to journal. Since that time, reflective journaling has become integral to my rehearsal process, the constant cycle of practicing, journaling, recording, reflecting, practicing, journaling and reflecting (the process of which is graphically presented in Figure 12.1), with much of the writing having a reflexive focus, informing my final performances. McPherson and Zimmerman (2002, p. 237) described this type of self-regulation as cyclical, as feedback obtained from prior performance helping the learner (performer) to adjust their performance and future

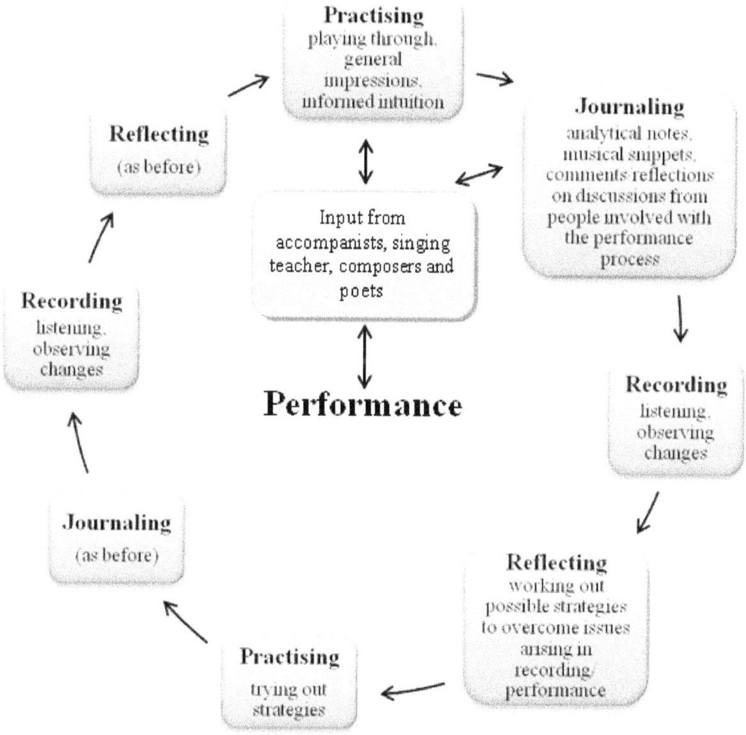

FIGURE 12.1

A graphic representation of Aggett's (a soprano) cyclical reflective journaling process in preparation for a musical performance.

efforts. This approach has strong resonances with the establishment of Rink's (1990) notion of informed intuition, which guides the process of performance analysis by "accru[ing] with a broad range of experience and … [that which] may exploit theoretical and analytical knowledge at the 'submerged level of consciousness'" (p. 324).

In the research environment, the result is practice-based research from both reflective and self-reflexive perspectives, using journaling to inform the performance process. In the studio, a similar multifaceted approach can be a strong teaching and learning tool. Reflection is involved with the notion of learning and thinking, where "we reflect in order to learn something, or we learn as a result of reflecting" (Moon, 2004, p. 186). Reflective journaling about one's practice can be viewed as a learning exercise in self-assessment (Gillian & Hendrika, 1995; Paris & Paris, 2001).

Journaling and Reflective and Reflexive Professional Practice

The terms "reflective" and "reflexive" are both used in the literature, in some instances interchangeably, yet it can be useful to understand the difference between the two terms. "Reflective practice" is used by Schön (1987, 1991) to depict practitioners reviewing their actions and the knowledge that informs them. The terms "reflection-*in*-action" and "reflection-*on*-action" were coined by Schön, the former occurring during rehearsals when strategies were suggested by either performer and enacted upon, and the latter when a singer is reviewing journaling entries plus recordings and performances. Reflective journaling is used by practitioners in the fields of pre-service teaching (Francis, 1995; Hourigan, 2009; Towell, Snyder, & Poor, 1995), library students (Tilly, 1996) and music therapy (Barry & O'Callaghan, 2008, p. 59), as an educative tool to investigate the way in which they practice their craft. Journals are used as a means to foster self-learning and encourage the development of the reflective practitioner (Lyons, 1999). The idea of reflective journaling as a pedagogical strategy to effectively enhance self-awareness was introduced by Hampton and Morrow (2003) when teaching civil engineering in a United States military academy, integrating its use throughout their courses.

In music education, singer and teacher Lotte Latukefu (2009) fosters peer learning and self-reflection through the use of journaling in a tertiary music setting to teach classical singing in groups. Students are encouraged to become self-regulated learners by using journals to reflect on their vocal development over a period of three years, with the singing and spoken voice lecturers providing the transfer of knowledge and peers offering additional feedback in classes. In research focused on Australian art song, singers have detailed their performance preparation through a combination of reflective journaling on recordings of rehearsals and performances to inform the reflection process, including the application of practical strategies (Aggett, 2009b, 2010). Reflective practice is enhanced through self-assessment comments from contemporary tertiary music students in journals in a tertiary setting, devised to provide students with the means to become their own teachers, with situations similar to Latukefu's work where peers are involved in the feedback process (Lebler, 2007). To encourage engagement with Asian-Pacific music, composer Diana Blom with classroom teacher Anne Bischoff involved a class of upper primary students in a focused composition module over a term, which included the use of a shared student process journal, with entries by all students, designed to encourage reflective thinking (Blom & Bischoff, 2008).

Reflexive journal writing is used to generate and integrate new understandings and extend practice by music therapists working in an oncological clinical placement. These include seeking an understanding of contextual influences on practice, connecting theory and practice, self-evaluation and supervision, and understanding the usefulness of music therapy (Barry & O'Callaghan, 2008, p. 59). These authors believe reflexive journaling can help to "develop insight, self-awareness and analytical thinking" (p. 61).

Reflexivity is focusing on one's own actions and their effects on others, situations, and professional and social structures (Bolton, 2005, p. 10); it is about understanding how research is affected, in terms of outcomes and process, by one's own position as a researcher (Fox, Martin, & Green, 2007, p. 186). In the singing studio, the singing teacher is acting as the researcher, reflecting on his or her singing as a professional, extending the knowledge drawn from this reflection to students, other professionals or performers involved in the performance process. My own role in this article is exactly this — a singing teacher and singer who is using reflective thinking to research the topic, with this same reflexive activity, as encouraged by the teacher's students, to be expanded on further. Researcher reflexivity can be further explained as "the capacity of the researcher to acknowledge how their own experiences and contexts inform the process and outcomes of inquiry" (Etherington, 2004, pp. 31–32).

My work as a researcher–practitioner is reflexive in two ways. First, a large part of my research has involved reflection and reporting of other singers' reflections, responses, performances, interviews, feedback and work relating to their preparation of 20th and 21st century repertoire, including Australian art song (Aggett, 2008a, 2009a, 2009b). The second aspect of reflexivity is about my own vocal preparation work in this process (Aggett, 2007, 2008b, 2008c, 2010). While it is impossible to be totally impartial in one's views when reporting on such issues, especially when there is an emotional connection as a performer and as a teacher of performers, the constant struggle of which other reflexive researchers and practitioner–researchers report is always present in that one constantly seeks to find a balance between being self-aware and self-indulgent (Fox, Martin, & Green, 2007, p. 189).

Analysing Reflective Thought in Journal Entries

Reflective journal entries are a large body of text that usually require guidance and analysis to help draw out the key knowledge. As a means to assess whether students were engaging in reflective thinking during their courses and the depth of that reflection, Kember et al., (1999) used seven categories of reflective thought based on Jack Meizrow's (1991) work on reflective thinking. Six of these have been illustrated in Figure 12.2. The level of reflective thinking represented in the diagram increases from bottom to top, with categories shown on the same horizontal level regarded as being equivalent in reflective thinking. Meizrow separated non-reflective action from reflective action (Kember et al., 1999, p. 22), with non-action falling into the three areas of habitual action, thoughtful action and introspection (shown in Figure 12.2, shaded in grey).

Habitual action is action that has been learned before and can be performed automatically or with little conscious thought. These actions are usually not recorded in journals. An example of habitual action for a singer might be an effective breathing technique, once learned, even though a singer's breathing technique needs to be applied to each song and each phrase in a song.

Thoughtful action directs our attention to action that draws on previous meaning or learning schemes and can be described as a cognitive process. In a thoughtful action, such as playing a musical instrument, a performer may be drawing on such aspects as prior knowledge, analysing, evaluating, making

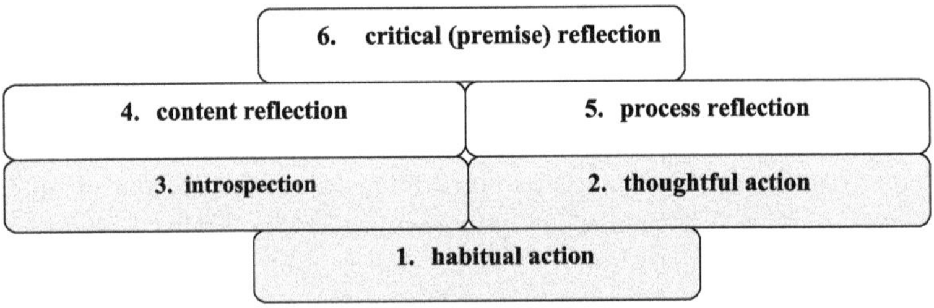

FIGURE 12.2

Categories of reflective thinking, increasing in reflection from bottom to top, with categories shown on the same horizontal level regarded as being equivalent in reflective thinking. Based on the work of Mezirow, adapted Kember et al., 1999, further adapted by Aggett (with permission).

judgements and discriminating, becoming what Schön called "knowing-*in*-practice" (Schön, 1991, p. 61). Through reflecting on knowledge-*in*-practice, a performer develops a greater understanding of an issue, trying out possible strategies in rehearsal by articulating feelings they have about it (p. 63). Introspection refers to an awareness of thoughts or feelings about ourselves. As there is no attempt to re-examine, test or validate previous knowledge, introspection is considered a non-reflective action (Mezirow, 1991, p.107).

Reflective action (which combines the final categories of Content, Process and Critical Reflection) is described as making decisions or taking action based on insights as a result of reflection, dividing reflective thinking into the three areas of content, process and critical reflection (Mezirow, 1991, p. 108). Content reflection is *what* we perceive, think, feel or act upon (p. 107). Process reflection is *how* we perform these functions of perceiving, thinking, feeling or acting and an assessment of our effectiveness in performing them. Premise (critical) reflection is where we become aware of *why* we perceive, think, feel or act as we do and the possible consequences of those actions (p. 108). Changes in perspective in the writing need to be noted for writing to be coded as premise reflection. If we accept that many of our actions are governed by a set of beliefs and values that have been unconsciously learnt within a particular context, then premise reflection requires a critical review of beliefs from conscious and unconscious prior learning and their consequences (Kember et al., 1999, pp. 23–24). As Kember et al. also decided, the political overtones of Mezirow's original interpretation of premise reflection are irrelevant in this discussion and have therefore not been considered. Reporting on work carried out to create a questionnaire to measure reflective thinking, Kember et al. adopted Dewey's definition and used the term critical reflection to replace premise reflection as the term has been more commonly used for this level of profound reflection and the term has also been adopted in this frame.

Approaches to Journaling — Short- and Long-Term Journaling

A practice-led project involving three singers (Aggett, 2008b) — a soprano, mezzo-soprano and a baritone — in the preparation and subsequent performances of specific Australian 20th and 21st century art songs required the singers to record their practise sessions, keep and reflect on practise journals, while choosing and adopting appropriate strategies as a means of improving their performances. The following discussion relates to the short and long-term journaling of two of the singers from the project — the mezzo-soprano and soprano (the author) — highlighting the reflective journaling undertaken.

Journaling During the Learning and Performance Stages — Long- and Short-Term Journaling

The mezzo-soprano's journal was written in two distinct sections over a six-month period. It detailed the preparation of five songs with a general focus on overall strategies to learn the songs. The entries in the first section of the journal had an emphasis on pitch, whereas the second section mainly contained strategies on the text and meanings of songs, with reflections to deal with these topics. As with many students who have participated in reflective journal writing exercises in different disciplines, including music, and discussed earlier, one of the biggest drawbacks of writing a reflective journal is the time it takes. While the mezzo-soprano's journal was brief, her entries showed an increase in the type of reflective writing from her first entries compared with those in the second section of her journal.

My journal (the soprano) detailed the preparation of 30 Australian art songs by 11 composers. When learning these songs for two major recitals, I decided to deliberately journal the journey, largely because I had found this approach to be helpful in the past. Initially, my journal entries were haphazard, other than including the date of entry, but as time progressed, the writing became more structured. Over a four-year period, the reflective nature of the entries developed as I became more comfortable writing my thoughts down and a structure emerged in the journal. The writing showed a gradual development in journaling to include analytical notes, personal comments, musical snippets, trials of appropriate techniques suggested by other singers and in the literature, and analyses of the songs where it helped to enhance the understanding. Also included were comments from discussions with people involved with performance process, including from my singing teacher, several accompanists and composers involved in the performance process.

Analysing Categories of Reflective Thinking in the Journals

As a means of discussing the content of the journals, Meizrow's (1991) levels of reflection, adapted by Kember et al., (1999) (see Figure 12.2) were adopted to analyse levels of reflective thought within the journals and how they relate to the music being prepared. The proposed journaling model (see Figure 12.3) that emerged and subsequent musical examples seek to give a reflexive perspective by linking the action (reflection) with the resulting process (practising, with the application of strategies) and outcome (performance) to provide an understanding of how writing and thinking, that is, research, can be affected by one's own position as a teacher and performer in terms of outcomes and process (Fox et al., 2007, p. 186). Kember added a sixth level of reflection to his model — content and process reflection —

however, this level of reflection has been removed in the model of analysis proposed in this chapter, as there was no evidence of joint content and process reflection found in the presented journal entries. Possible levels of reflection throughout the reflective journaling process can be seen graphically represented in Figure 12.3.

Writing any kind of diary or journal is a very private activity. Issues surrounding journal writing, therefore, include who the journal is for. Who will see it? Will it be marked? The author of any journal needs to feel free to express themselves in whatever way they choose, or there is no purpose in keeping the journal in the first place. The journal entries of the two singers presented in this chapter were not written to be marked or viewed by the public, so no preliminary ground rules were set with either author before

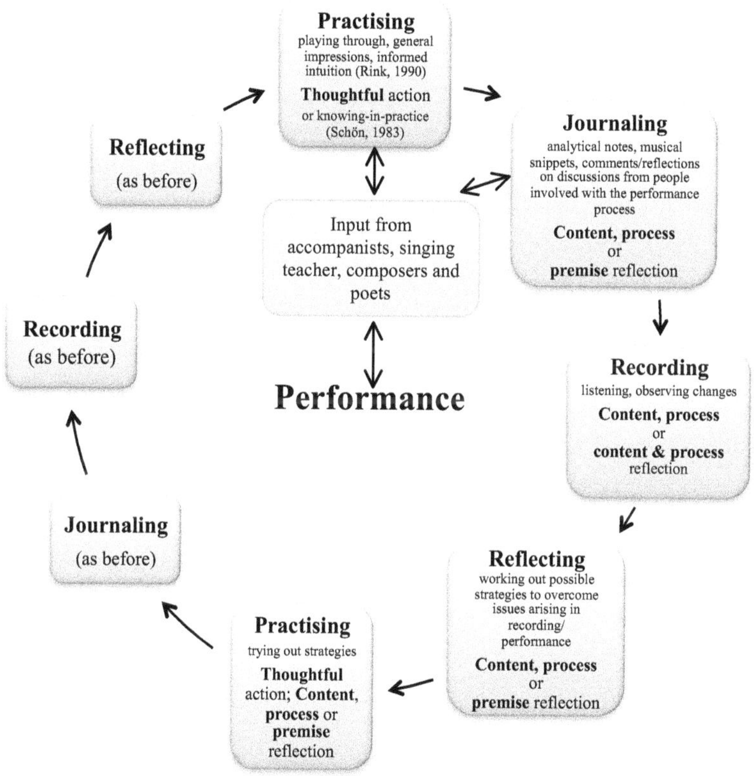

FIGURE 12.3

In this model of Aggett's cyclical reflective journaling process, Mezirow's (1991) levels of reflection (adapted by Kember et al., 1999) have been applied to each of the steps in the cycle. When practising, informed intuition (Rink, 1990) and "knowing-in-practice" (Schön, 1983) may also be used.

beginning the project, the journals were being written primarily for self-assessment. This is a different approach from that of many of the examples present in the articles previously discussed about journaling (e.g., Hampton & Morrow, 2003; Kember et al., 1999).

In the two singers' journals, Habitual action was not identified. This is performed automatically and was therefore less likely to appear in the journals.

Thoughtful action was recorded by both singers in the journals, particularly in relation to the cognitive processes evident during the experimentation, implementation, adaptation and subsequent reflection on the development of strategies applied in the learning of repertoire.
The mixed metre of Margaret Sutherland's song "You Spotted Snakes" (1940) — the first section (bb1–7) being in quadruple metre and the second section (bb8–15) alternating between quadruple and compound duple metre (see Figure 12.4) — caused the mezzo-soprano to reflect on its irregularity:

> … in the $^{5}4$ time, [which is] quite irregular, … a temptation [exists] to give the bar 6 beats, but you've got to keep going. [I] sang through … both verses, taking care with vowels and consonants.

The mezzo-soprano wrote in her journal that she "… needed rhythm strategies to assist with this challenge", these thoughtful actions involving

> … speaking the text in rhythm, while tapping the beat and singing the song slowly, gradually building up speed.

The similarity was noted twice in her journal between Sutherland's song and a song by Peter Warlock, titled "Sigh No More, Ladies" (1928, OUP), as both have a text by Shakespeare and alternating meters between $^{5}4$ and $^{6}4$.

Also thoughtful actions, the mezzo-soprano identified "our fairy queen" (bb6–7, Figure 12.5) as a section containing "difficult intervals" and "repeated [the section] over and over" again as a strategy to master it. The same section in the second verse, "do no offence," gained attention to:

FIGURE 12.4

"You Spotted Snakes" from *A Midsummer Night's Dream* by Margaret Sutherland, text by William Shakespeare, bb 8–11. © Antony Bunney.

FIGURE 12.5

"You Spotted Snakes" from *A Midsummer Night's Dream* by Margaret Sutherland, text by William Shakespeare, bb 6–7. © Antony Bunney.

> … distinguish the vowel 'o' between 'no' and 'offence' — especially with [the] low interval/change of register.

Another thoughtful action recorded by the mezzo-soprano was in relation to a strategy used by both singers, in this case in reference to the initial exploration of Martin Wesley-Smith's song "Climb the Rainbow" (1976, rev. 1992), text by Ann North, to "play a skeletal accompaniment while sight-singing the vocal line".

The soprano devised strategies to assist in the learning of the difficult rhythmic and atonal song "I'm Nobody" from Frogs by Nigel Butterley (2006), the composer describing its tonality as being "purposefully astringent," referring to the atonal melody that "clashes" with the accompaniment (24 October 2007). Aside from learning the pitch, which was the singer's (my) responsibility, rhythm was tied to the diction and ensemble in the song, making it an issue for both singer and pianist. Both found it easier to rehearse this together, prompting my thoughtful action comment that "… it's an organic thing, the more you get together — an osmosis. It takes time for things to grow … you can't practise this on your own".

A strategy occurring out of this process was to play all notes in a section/passage/beat as a chord while holding the sustain pedal down to familiarise the singer with the tonality, while singing the passage very slowly. This has become a favourite strategy of mine, whether the music is tonal or atonal. As example of how this was applied to the first three bars of the song is given in Figure 12.6.

Two instances of introspection were recorded by the soprano in the preparation of Betty Beath's cycle Towards the Psalms (2004). The first refers to the different tone colour being worked on for "The Lament of Ovid", where a "… different thought process" was explored to achieve the vocal tone (Figure 12.7).

FIGURE 12.6

"I'm Nobody" from *Frogs* by Nigel Butterley (1995). © Wirripang Pty Ltd, 2006. Text by Emily Dickinson, bb 1–3. Adapted by the composer with permission. Suggested chordal strategy to rehearse these bars written on the staves underneath the piano accompaniment.

Different vocal tones were explored on this note, both in rehearsal alone and with the accompanist, with reflective comments made on recordings of these sessions to "get in the zone," not only for this note, but for this whole section of the song.

The second introspective reflection refers to a register issue at the end of Beath's "Love Makes You See a Place Differently …", "…the last phrase is *so* hard for me — sits low in the register and is supposed to have a diminuendo on the last note — dreaming!" (see Figure 12.8).

FIGURE 12.7

"The Lament of Ovid" from *Towards the Psalms* by Betty Beath, text derived from the novel *Fugitive Pieces* by Anne Michaels. b23. © Wirripang Pty Ltd, 2004.

FIGURE 12.8

"Love Makes You See a Place Differently ..." from *Towards the Psalms* by Betty Beath. © Wirripang Pty Ltd, 2004. Text derived from the novel *Fugitive Pieces* by Anne Michaels. bb 48–51.

The mezzo-soprano identified some early content reflection in her preparation of Margaret Sutherland's "You Spotted Snakes" when she journaled of her preparation of some tricky intervals, "Sang through with full voice — perhaps too heavy ... Then sang with lighter sound — better for song".

This kind of reflection on the quality of the sound while practising reinforces the vocal quality that best suits the singer's voice and the music. The more specific you can become about your own sound and the qualities you want to express in music, the keener the ear becomes at analysing the quality of voice's timbres.

The mezzo-soprano found much to reflect on in "Climb the Rainbow" by Wesley-Smith, despite it being one of the easier songs in her repertoire for the recital. The following content reflection reveals a dialogue she journaled on the meaning of the text of the song and its connection to the variation in tempi:

> There was a lot of variation in dynamics and tempo in the song even though it seems so repetitive. My mind started to wonder what that's all about. It seems to be a journey of a relationship with someone — perhaps a lover or a partner. Each time the journey is taken (to climb the rainbow) is a different stage of the relationship. Rainbows are elusive, beautiful and intangible — it is impossible to climb, except in the imagination. So it's a metaphor for achieving a feat or a pleasurable experience.

Variation in tempi and dynamics occur throughout and within "Climb the Rainbow". The example in Figure 12.9 shows the climax of the song, the loudest section, with the signature glissando used throughout the song seen on the word "slide". Two versions of the song exist — an unaccompanied, solo version (the original, 1976) and this accompanied version, both of which require the singer to explore the contrasts the mezzo-soprano speaks of in her journal.

FIGURE 12.9

"Climb the Rainbow" by Martin Wesley-Smith (1976, rev. 1992). © Martin Wesley-Smith. Lyric by Ann North, bb 24–33.

Examples of content and process reflection occurred in the journaling by the soprano of Diana Blom's "Willow Flowers" from *Four Korean Songs (Sijo)* (1974). The song has a relatively constant high *tessitura*, beginning on a repeated F#5s and in the following two phrases (see Figure 12.10), where I found it:

> Very hard to 'drop down gently!' from F#4–A#3 pp … You want to/need to go into a heavier voice … Will need to work on that.

Working on enunciation of "willow flower drops" and the word "silent" prompted the entry "Think of the legato line, but the consonants are on that line too", both of these reflections being content reflection.

To achieve the goal of pitch security in the performance preparation of "Willow Flowers," the following thoughts expressed process reflection:

> I think it's one thing to sing these pitches in abstraction/by myself … I need to get with Diana … So more work with the piano, getting the notes that 'distract'!

Many of the songs I have performed in relation to my research of Australian art song often sit more in the range for a mezzo-soprano, despite the fact the scores may state they are written for a soprano, with little of the repertoire using the full soprano's range. Having said that, I blame myself for not having made wiser choices selecting repertoire or not refusing to sing some

FIGURE 12.10

"Willow flowers" from *Four Korean Songs* (Sijo) Systems 1–3, by Diana Blom. © Diana Blom. Poem by Yi Py nggi. Performed a tone higher than the original.

of the lower songs, simply because the notes were in my range — a common mistake of singers I often warn my own students against.

That little story precedes the one critical reflection found in either journal, in this case, the soprano's, following the performance of Diana Blom's "The Window" from *Four Korean Songs (Sijo)*. "The Window" is sung "senza misura" to the rhythm of the text, as it is in "Willow Flowers". The accompaniment is sparse and getting your notes is sometimes a challenge. It would be fair to say you feel very exposed in this song. The song was transposed up a tone from the original to accommodate my range, but even so, it really sat too low for me (Figure 12.11). I had wanted to do well in this particular performance, but physically, I wasn't well. Whether that was stress or nerves — I'll never know — all I do know is that my performance on the day was way under par:

> I think I learnt with the performance of this song that despite the fact you can sing the notes of a song, if they're *not* in your comfort range, you should listen to your heart/head and not perform them in public.

FIGURE 12.11

"The Window" from *Four Korean Songs* (Sijo) Systems 2 and 3 by Diana Blom. © Diana Blom. Poem by Yi Py nggi. Performed a tone higher than the original.

> Have enough professionalism to say, "no — this isn't right/doesn't suit my voice". Deep down in your heart, you *know* if the song is right for you and if you flirt with danger, one day — such as this — you're bound to be burnt. I think lessons were learnt here. I've made a promise to myself never to sing outside of my range again.

There are times as a performer when you would like to do the performance all over again. Of course, you cannot. What you can do, as both performers and teachers, is learn from the experience.

So What? Implications for Learning and Teaching Singing — A Pedagogical Frame to Assist Performers and Studio Singing Teachers

So is reflective journaling something you would do or implement as a performer or as a singing teacher in your singing studio? Do you need any special skills? The positioning of reflective journaling within a musically pedagogical frame to offer performers and studio teachers to assist in the learning of repertoire is the aim of this final section of the chapter. Guidelines will be proposed for those interested in implementing reflective journaling within their studios, the benefits and drawbacks of which are also outlined.

In the many references consulted on journaling, there was no shortage on suggestions as to how to begin to journal, recommending where you wrote on a page, how many pages, what kind of a book to write in, and so on. Unless there are reasons for prescribing a particular format, I would advise leaving it up to the performer/student as to what medium they wish to record their thoughts in. There are advantages in having an unstructured format, and perhaps even a loose-leaf arrangement, which can be portable, removed, or even torn out (something to be avoided). Hard-covered journals that free the writer to seek other surfaces to write on will also last much longer than flimsily covered journals (Moon, 2006, pp. 95–96). All of the literature is in agreement about one thing, however, that writing your thoughts down about an activity will enhance the learning (and reflection) process. You don't need any special skills to be able to journal — just the courage to put your thoughts down on paper and then come back and do it again. One of the most difficult things is probably that first entry you make. The reassuring thing about journaling is there are no mistakes and there are no rules. It's your journal, your writing and you can do what you like in it — say what you like in it. Once you understand that, there is a freedom that comes over you and you begin to write.

Conclusion

This chapter has positioned reflective journaling in a solitary (performer) and one-on-one (student–teacher) paradigm, compared with the documented classroom/tertiary/clinical/community practice so often reported on in the literature. Being able to control, monitor and decide on how you go forward with your preparation can be such a freeing experience — I highly recommend it to everyone. The models suggested in Figures 12.1 and 12.3 offer starting points for performers and teachers to begin and develop the process of reflective journaling.

In my own studio, reflective journals are used to assist students in their journey to self-awareness of their own ability of their singing (and in the performance of piano and violin, the other instruments I teach) and in taking ownership of their learning, guiding me to the areas they feel they need most assistance with. While it is impossible to be prescriptive in the way all songs are approached and having said there are no rules, the following aspects are identified as being helpful when using reflective journaling as a pedagogical tool in the singing studio and are given only as a starting place or guideline:

- four pages assigned for a song, beginning with its title; if used, start another four;
- include the date for every entry you journal;
- general impression of song recorded on first playing/singing, identifying any possible issues that might cause concern;

- sections journaled identified by bar numbers;
- where possible, solutions to problems or the steps in a process recorded along with any associated impressions;
- record (and video if possible) sessions regularly and reflect in the journal to inform the reflection process; and
- start by using a music exercise book as a journal, with the normal note pages on the outside to write reflections in and manuscript paper on the inside to jot down any notation/musical thoughts. This needs to be covered, though, as its flimsy. There are fancier options, of course, and I do own some — it is up to the individual.

As a performer, the journal then becomes a tool that can be used to hone and refine their performance, focusing on issues of concern, recording possible ways to overcome problems, reflecting on the success or not of an approach. If reflections of recordings are also added to the reflection process and these are also kept and looked back on, the performer has a stronger aural sense of their own sound.

For the singing teacher, journaling becomes a tool in the singing studio to assist singer and singing teacher to better communicate what is going on between lessons, what issues the singer is finding difficult and needs most help with and conversely, what aspects are working for them. As a teacher, we need to find ways to help the student overcome their difficulties and ensure that indeed, the aspects a student thinks they are doing correctly are indeed, being performed with no strain or stress. For those students who take to journaling and use it on a regular basis, the journal can reduce the amount of time spent by the teacher in the lesson trying to work out where the student is having problems and needing help. You can simply ask for the journal, check out what areas need your assistance and less time is wasted in the lesson — the journal becomes the "prescription pad" for the lesson!

As a means of giving the performer and singing teacher a guide to exploring and encouraging student use of journal writing, Mezirow's (1991) levels of reflection offer an understanding of different ways and levels of reflection that can be used. This method of analysis is not prescriptive; rather, a suggestion of how such an approach can be applied to journal writing. It would be rare that a studio teacher would set out to mark a student's journal unless written for a specific course or the teacher was linked to a conservatoire or teaching institution. As an independent studio teacher, I set my own goals and assist students in their goal setting, which will never include marking! Having said that, it is not about the marking of journals at issue here; rather, it is about equipping studio teachers with knowledge about reflective practice and, specifically, about reflective journaling, so they can best guide their students in their quest for more effective and higher goals in performance. Having an understanding of Mezirow's levels of reflections, and deliberately journaling at all of the levels, performers and teachers can either assist themselves or their students in the learning process, setting goals where they need to go in their learning/teaching with the next step of the performance process. Each level of reflection has its own inherent pedagogical implications for the teacher, and knowing where a student is at with their performance preparation can only help to enhance their teaching and their relationship with their student.

One way to encourage an exploration of all levels of reflection is through questions. For example, a question such as "How are you standing?" requires examination of a habitual action. The cognitive processes of thoughtful action may be stimulated with questions such as "Why are you performing the melody that way?" or discuss a recording of your performance and how prior learning can be implemented to improve it. Questions exploring the emotional connection of the singer to their performances may enhance introspective reflection. Content reflection may be stimulated by questions such as "How did you feel about your vocal technique in that phrase you just performed?" or "What do you think is the best way to approach … in your singing?" To stimulate the method or manner in which students think — process reflection — questions such as "How do you think/feel/when you perform x in the song?" may assist. While you cannot change a person's perception about an issue, to encourage them to become aware of why they think, feel or act a certain way — premise or critical reflection perhaps questions why they are thinking or feeling about a situation in a certain way — will stimulate some beginning thoughts.

The short-term journaling as detailed by the mezzo-soprano in the preparation of Australian art songs over a six-month period showed a gradual development in reflective writing to incorporate the application of overall strategies found to be most helpful to the singer, displaying thoughtful actions and content reflection in her journal entries. The soprano's journals, detailing the preparation of Australian art songs over a four-year period, focused on holistic impressions of songs, textual issues and strategies to address specific technical concerns within the repertoire. Thoughtful action, introspection, content reflection and critical reflection were all part of the journaling of the soprano, most likely a result of the longer time spent to develop the skill.

For performers considering implementing reflective journaling into their performance preparation, the benefits can include greater self-awareness, a deeper understanding of their performance practice, a greater understanding of their craft, targeted goal setting with measured outcomes and self-directed performance goals. For the studio teacher implementing reflective journaling in their teaching of singers encourages students in a greater self-awareness of their abilities; sets singers on a path towards self-education, with your guidance, with the teacher as mentor — the facilitator, if you like — may improve the performance output of students and may give insights into a student that have not been revealed in a lesson. Journaling can be a valuable reflective and reflexive tool when preparing difficult 20th and 21st century songs outside of the regular rehearsal techniques at a singer's disposal.

I have found reflective journaling to be of great benefit as both a practitioner-researcher, and as a studio singing teacher and teacher of other musical instruments. The lessons I have learned about myself as a musician, performer, singer and teacher through journaling have convinced me that reflective journaling is a very worthwhile pedagogical tool.

Acknowledgments

The author gratefully acknowledges the following copyright holders for allowing the inclusion of musical examples in the article: to Diana Blom for "Willow Flowers" from *Four Korean Songs (Sijo)*, to Antony Bunney, for "You Spotted Snakes" from *A Midsummer Night's Dream* by Margaret Sutherland, to Martin Wesley-Smith and Ann North for "Climb the Rainbow", and to Wirripang Pty Ltd for Betty Beath's The "Lament of Ovid" and "Love makes you see a place differently ..." from *Towards the Psalms*, and Nigel Butterley's "I'm Nobody" from *Frogs*.

References

Aggett, C. (2007, July). *A discussion of performer's analysis in relation to Gordon Kerry and Carolyn Masel's song Moonrise.* Paper presented at the Celebrating Musical Communities, ASME XVI, Perth, Australia.

Aggett, C. (2008a). Lotte Latukefu: A singer's journey in an Asian-Pacific cantata. In B. Crossman, & M. Atherton (Eds.), *Music of the spirit: Asian-Pacific musical identity* (pp. 191–206). Sydney, Australia: Australian Music Centre.

Aggett, C. (2008b, July). *Singer's strategies for performing and learning 20th century Australian art songs: 'I'm Nobody' from Frogs by Nigel Butterley.* Paper presented at the 28th World Conference of the International Society for Music Education, Bologna, Italy.

Aggett, C. (2008c, October). *Tessitura considerations in Peggy Glanville-Hicks' songs 'Stars' and 'Homespun Collars' from Five Songs (1944).* Paper presented at the Research Matters, College of Arts Conference, University of Western Sydney, Australia.

Aggett, C. (2009a). Songs for the boys: Five Australian art songs for the baritone. *Voice of ANATS, 22*, 4–7.

Aggett, C. (2009b, December). *Strategies for achieving performing excellence of twentieth and twenty-first century art song.* Paper presented at the International Symposium on Performance Science, Auckland, New Zealand.

Aggett, C. (2010, July). *Reflective journaling: A singer's path to performance.* Paper presented at the ISME Commission for the Education of the Professional Musician 18th International Seminar (CEPROM), Shanghai, China.

Barry, P., & O'Callaghan, C. (2008). Reflexive journal writing. *Nordic Journal of Music Therapy, 17*(1), 55–66.

Blom, D., & Bischoff, A. (2008). Creating 'a very fulfilled and wonderful piece': Asia-Pacific musics as an impetus for upper primary class composition. In M. Atherton, & B. Crossman (Eds.), *Music of the spirit: Asian-Pacific musical identity* (pp. 145–158). Sydney, Australia: Australian Music Centre.

Bolton, G. (2005). *Reflective practice. Writing and professional development* (2nd ed.). London: Sage publications.

Davidson, J.W. (2004). Making a reflexive turn: Practical music-making becomes conventional research. In J.W. Davidson (Ed.), *The music practitioner. Research for the music performer, teacher and listener* (pp. 133–147). Hants, UK: Ashgate.

Dewey, J. (1933). How we think: A restatement of the relation of reflective thinking to the educative process. Boston, MA: D.C. Heath.

Etherington, K. (2004). *Becoming a reflexive researcher: Using our selves in research.* London: Jessica Kingsley Publishers.

Fox, M., Martin, P., & Green, G. (2007). Doing practitioner research. London: Sage.

Francis, D. (1995). The reflective journal: A window to preservice teachers' practical knowledge. *Teaching and Teacher Education, 11*(3), 229–241.

Gillian, R., & Hendrika, M. (1995). Reflection-on-practice: Enhancing student learning. *Journal of Advanced Nursing, 22*(2), 235–242.

Hampton, S.E., & Morrow, C. (2003). Reflective journaling and assessment. *Journal of Professional Issues in Engineering Education & Practice, 129*(4), 186–189.

Hourigan, R.M. (2009). Preservice music teachers' perceptions of fieldwork experiences in a special needs classroom. *Journal of Research in Music Education, 57*(2), 152–168.

Kember, D., Jones, A., Loke, A.Y., McKay, J., Sinclair, K., Tse, H., et al. (1999). Determining the level of reflective thinking from students' written journals using a coding scheme based on the work of Mezirow. *International Journal of Lifelong Education, 18*(1), 18–30.

Kember, D., Leung, D.Y.P., Jones, A., Loke, A.Y., McKay, J., Sinclair, K., et al. (2000). Development of a questionnaire to measure the level of reflective thinking. *Assessment & Evaluation in Higher Education, 25*(4), 381–395.

Latukefu, L. (2009). Peer learning and reflection: Strategies developed by vocal students in a transforming tertiary setting. *International Journal of Music Education, 27*(2), 128–142.

Lebler, D. (2007). Student-as-master? Reflections on a learning innovation in popular music pedagogy. *International Journal of Music Education, 25*(3), 205–221.

Lyons, J. (1999). Reflective education for professional practice: discovering knowledge from experience. *Nurse Education Today, 19*(1), 29–34.

McPherson, G.E., & Zimmerman, B.J. (2002). Self-regulation of musical learning. A social cognitive perspective. In R. Cowell & C. Richardson (Eds.), *The new handbook of research on music teaching and learning* (pp. 327–347). New York: MENC: The National Association for Music Education.

Mezirow, J. (1991). *Transformative dimensions of adult learning.* San Francisco: Jossey-Bass.

Moon, J.A. (2004). *A handbook of reflective and experiential learning: theory and practice.* New York: RoutledgeFalmer.

Moon, J.A. (2006). *Learning journals: A handbook for reflective practice and professional development* (2nd ed.). New York: Routledge.

Paris, S.G., & Paris, A.H. (2001). Classroom applications of research on self-regulated learning. *Educational Psychologist, 36*(2), 89–101.

Rink, J. (1990). Review of Berry 1989. *Music Analysis, 9*(3), 319–339.

Schön, D.A. (1987). Educating the reflective practitioner (1st ed.). San Francisco: Jossey-Bass.

Schön, D.A. (1991). *The reflective practitioner: How professionals think in action.* Aldershot, UK: Ashgate.

Tilly, C.M. (1996). *Reflective journalling and fieldwork: A case study with library and information studies students at the Queensland University of Technology, 1994.* Brisbane, Australia: Education for Library and Information Services.

Towell, G.L., Snyder, D.W., & Poor, A. (1995). Listening to the past: Using student journals in a music education course. *The Quarterley Journal of Music Teaching and Learning, VI*(3), 18–29.

Zimmerman, B.J. (2002). Attaining self-regulation — A social cognitive perspective. In M. Boekaerts, P.R. Pintrich & M. Zeidner (Eds.), *Handbook of self-regulation* (pp. 13–39). Elsevier.

■ ■ ■ ■ ■ ■ ■ ■ ■ ■

Chapter 13

Breaking Through the Frames of Custom: A Sociocultural Approach to Learn Singing

Lotte Latukefu

This chapter will present a summary of the results from a series of studies carried out between 2003 and 2009 in the Faculty of Creative Arts at the University of Wollongong. These studies investigate a model of learning singing underpinned by the sociocultural theories of Vygotsky. A design-based research methodology was adopted in order to carry out the aims and purpose of the research. The conclusions reached in each of the studies informed the design of the sociocultural model of singing and also the development of educational principles that can act as a framework in which singing teachers can organise the content of their singing teaching. For teachers who are interested in curriculum renewal and review, the theoretical concepts of how students can learn using a different model of teaching will be useful as they develop their own models of learning suitable to their local context. This chapter also reflects on the desirability of aligning teaching and assessment with qualities such as reflection, critical thinking, responsibility and self-regulated learning in students.

> We teachers must make an intensified effort to break through the frames of custom and to touch the consciousness of those we teach. (Greene, 1995, p. 56)

Music conservatoires and universities are increasingly finding themselves under pressure from funding bodies to increase student-to-staff ratios. In a recent example, the Victorian College of the Arts in Australia is being forced to consider a new curriculum for 2011, which might include adopting a less intensive teaching model and increasing student-to-staff ratios. Their faculty dean, Sharman Pretty, spoke to the media about the shift in curriculum as a way of "contextualising training in the world of higher education that would 'empower' students' long-term learning and make them more competitive" (Trounson, 2009, p. 26). There is often a lack of alignment between a conservatoire's curriculum and pedagogical approach, and the learning outcomes relevant to a workforce destination. "Put bluntly, is our curriculum and traditional pedagogy setting students up for failure as 'lifelong' learners?" (McWilliam, Carey, Draper, & Lebler, 2006, p. 26).

Historically, the predominant relationship between teacher and student in vocal instruction has been described as a master–apprentice relationship, where the master is looked at as a role model and a source of identification for the student, and where the dominant mode of student learning is imitation (Jorgenson, 2000). Despite the negative connotations of imitation as a learning style, research by Davidson and Jordan, (2007) concluded that one-to-one teaching empowers student learning more easily than other approaches and should be encouraged. They qualify this, however, by acknowledging that,

> ... cultural and political agendas of various state education systems will impact upon how this teaching and learning develops in its various physical environments, and in whether the lessons remain one-to-one or group-focused, and how much responsibility is left with the student and his or her peers. (Davidson & Jordan, 2007, p. 742)

Even more challenging to the master–apprentice model is a European study exploring one-to-one teaching in an academy of music. It took Foucault's concept of discursive practice as a point of departure and found that academies of music are characterised by the extensive individualisation of teaching and learning available to the students, and a high degree of specialisation on the part of the staff and students. Despite the individualised organisation, however, academy teaching practices are highly institutional in their character. "The teaching is heavily bounded in the historical practices of music performance" (Nerland, 2007, p. 399). It is this bind with traditional teaching practices, especially the master–apprentice model, that makes it difficult to bring about change in the conservatoire.

Conclusions presented in this chapter, in the form of educational principles, are the result of a series of studies that were carried out in a seven-year period from 2003–2009 at the University of Wollongong (Latukefu, 2007, 2009, 2010). The conclusions were reached based on empirical evidence of how students learn singing, using Vygotskian (1978) notions of the zone of proximal development, mediated learning, scientific and everyday concepts, co-construction of knowledge, intermental to intramental learning and transformation of practical activity.

Context and Background

I teach singing in a faculty of creative arts at a non-metropolitan university in Australia. The pressure applied from my university faculty to change traditional one-to-one teaching to group-focused was the beginning of the present study. We had to think of different methods of delivering teaching to greater numbers of students. In the process, we considered the kinds of graduate qualities that we would expect our students to possess at the end of their under-graduate degree and these qualities informed the design of the interventions and the environment.

In 2001, the Dean of my faculty announced that the music department in which I taught singing would be amalgamated with the theatre department. There had been hints that this move was afoot, but once the decision was made, change was swift. It began at auditions, where students were chosen for their acting skills and their singing potential rather than their polished singing skills. The biggest change, however, occurred in the mode of teaching.

Overnight, my one-to-one lessons became small groups. I also had to cope with differing levels of skill and experience in students. Some students were interested in extending their voices and learning classically, others just wanted to be able to sing competently. The students were demanding, ambitious and desperate to work. They also were used to working in small groups from their acting training. I realised that if I were to survive, I had to make changes to the way I was teaching. By necessity rather than choice, I began to investigate educational theories of learning that might help me develop better ways of teaching singing in a non-traditional way.

Looking for Alternatives

In the United Kingdom, a study that explored changes made to teaching practices at conservatoires (Calouste Gulbenkian Foundation, 1965; as cited in Davidson & Smith, 1997) noted that the level of change at conservatoires has been very slow. The report made in 1965 showed that many conservatoires in the United Kingdom offered similar curricula from their opening (some of them had opened in the 19th century) up to the date of the report's publication.

In the United States, Vogel (1976) and Holden (2002) showed that there was something to be gained by introducing peer involvement to the teaching process. Holden (2002) argued that group lessons meant that teachers did not have to repeat themselves over and over and would therefore feel more motivated and invigorated in their teaching. He did not mention the benefits (Vygotsky, 1986) of students learning from each other. Vogel (1976) discovered that student learning benefited from the atmosphere created by "so many thoughts, concepts, and suggestions flying about" (p. 21). Forderhase (2007) carried out a study that investigated teacher attitudes to team teaching. Of the teachers surveyed, 71% said that they would co-teach a student if the other teacher and the student agreed. However, in the comment section provided in the questionnaire and filled out by 50 of 203 respondents, the largest group of comments showed teacher concern that exposure to more than one vocal teacher at a time would lead to confusion from students.

All of the studies mentioned dealt with an important aspect of my own research that encouraged peer learning and multiple perspectives. An article challenging conservatoires to be open to innovative pedagogical possibilities and alternative models of learning, opened up issues around the values and limitations of traditional pedagogy for students (McWilliam, Carey, Draper, & Lebler, 2006). The researchers documented a non-traditional instrumental learning model, which emulated the learning practices of popular musicians in the broader community. A structured reflective journal and an evaluative self-reflection described as a distinctive feature of the program acted to "add a layer of formal knowledge" (McWilliam, Carey, Draper, & Lebler, 2006, p. 29). Peer learning was valued over a master–apprentice learning model and the program was very successful, judging by student evaluations. This study provided useful data for developing the learning model in the present study, as it successfully incorporated sociocultural practices, such as peer learning, co-constructed learning, authentic learning and reflection.

Kamin, Richards, and Collins (2007) investigated the psychological, social and environmental influences on the talent development process of non-classical musicians. Of most interest in relation to my own study were their findings on peer influence. The writers found that for non-classical musicians, peer influence was exclusively positive, but both positive and negative for classical musicians. They suggested that this needed to be considered within the context of the domain if it is to be used.

Riggs (2006) developed a philosophical model for studio instruction based on flow theory, developed and researched by Mihalyi Csikszentmihalyi (1997). The model Riggs proposed, was concerned with development of the "whole" student to serve as a "philosophical supplement to studio instructors who may not have received much training in developmental issues, educational theories, or related facets of the psychology of learning and performance" (Riggs, 2006, p. 176). Riggs suggested that applied studio instructors move away from the master–apprentice model to one where the teacher is a co-constructor of knowledge. In response to Riggs' paper, Freer (2006) proposed situating her model "in a constructivist paradigm where instructional scaffolding becomes a dominant component of the teaching and learning process" (Freer, 2006, p. 227).

Chapman (2006) used the term "holistic singing" to describe her philosophy of singing. She developed a teaching model that provided useful tools for singing teachers. At the core of the nucleus or satellite are components she considered to be basic building blocks for the voice. They are primal sound, postural alignment, breathing and support. Her model developed from a linear one in which one part led to the next, to a model positioned in a way that allows the components to be revisited frequently from any other component. The components also interacted with each other directly, which corresponded to Vygotsky's ideas of learning being an organic and interdependent whole, rather than separate components (Liu & Mathews, 2005).

All of these proposals for alternative models had components that could be related to the present study. Many of them were concerned with content knowledge, rather than the process of learning, others did not relate solutions to a theoretical framework Reeves (2000). Finally, none of the studies produced educational principles that I could use to develop my own model.

Theoretical Framework

There were certain key concepts that I used in the development of the singing model. Vygotsky's (1978) theory of Zone of Proximal Development (ZPD) promotes the idea of a novice performing a range of tasks that they cannot accomplish on their own, but in collaboration with an expert are able to achieve. The emphasis is on the collaboration and eventual shared understanding that develops between the expert and novice. To reach the learner's ZPD, the expert's assistance should be slightly above the level of the learner's independent performance, but provide enough support to enable them to complete the task (Vialle, Lysaght, & Verenikina, 2005). According to Daniels (2008), Vygotsky discussed the ZPD in terms of assessment and instruction. Vygotsky was interested in assessing the ways in which learners make progress. He endorsed the notion that formal instruction, which moves ahead of the student's development, is in itself a source of development (Daniels, 2008).

> The formal aspect of each school subject is that in which the influence of instruction on development is realized. Instruction would be completely unnecessary if it merely utilized what had already matured in the developmental process, if it were not itself a source of development. (Vygotsky, 1987, cited in Daniels, 2008 p. 212)

Vygotsky's theory of concept formation is related to the theoretical view of learning as a socially and culturally mediated process, which brings together the individual experience of the learner and the wealth of the theoretical knowledge accumulated in society (Vygotsky, 1986). Spontaneous or everyday concepts refer to the individual practice; they are the result of spontaneous, empirical "generalization of everyday personalised experience in the absence of systematic instruction" (Karpov, 2003, p. 171). They are rich in personalised experience and well suited to working in a particular context. However, everyday concepts are inextricably tied to a learner's concrete experience; they are unsystematic, not easily transferable and not conscious. They are likely to include misconceptions and are "often wrong" (Karpov, 2003, p. 171).

Scientific concepts are acquired consciously, according to a certain system of formal instruction. They are generalised, systematic and are abstracted from concrete experience, and therefore are easily transferable from one context to another (Vygotsky, 1986). This formal instruction, however, relies on co-operation and collaboration with the teacher:

> The development of the scientific concept, a phenomenon that occurs as part of the educational process, constitutes a unique form of systematic cooperation between the teacher and the child. The maturation of the child's higher mental functions occurs in this co-operative process, that is, it occurs through the adult's assistance and participation. (Vygotsky, 1987, p. 168, cited in Daniels, 2008)

The acquisition of scientific concepts helps to mediate students' thinking and problem solving, and restructure their spontaneous concepts (Karpov, 2003). Student reflective writing about their practice is the process in which speech and practical activity converge in the development of intellect (Vygotsky, 1978).

> In the process of solving a task the child is able to include stimuli that do not lie within the immediate visual field. Using words (one class of such stimuli) to create a specific plan, the child achieves a much broader range of activity, applying as tools not only those objects that lie near at hand, but searching for and preparing such stimuli as can be useful in the solution of the task, and planning future actions ... Thus, with the help of speech children, unlike apes, acquire the capacity to be both the subjects and objects of their own behaviour. The speaking child has the ability to direct his attention in a dynamic way. (Vygotsky, 1978, p. 26, p. 36)

Singing teachers are concerned with individual development and although "Vygotsky's (1978) 'general genetic law of cultural development' asserts the primacy of social in development" (Daniels, 2008, p. 12) it also shows that he was concerned with individual development. While it is the interchange that occurs between individuals in the group that contributes to the learning, there is also a change that happens as the individual internalises the information. "An interpersonal process is transformed into an intrapersonal one. Every function in the child's cultural development appears twice: first, on the social level, and later, on the individual level; first between people (interpsychological) and then inside the child (intrapsychological)" (Vygotsky, 1978, p. 57).

Methodology

Singing is a skill that develops over time. In order to understand this development, we must observe the transitions that occur in individuals as they become more adept. One of the fundamental assumptions of a sociocultural approach according to Wertsch (1991) is that what is described and explained is human action. A component of the sociocultural approach is to analyse the process. "Genetic analysis in Vygotsky's approach is motivated by the assumption that it is possible to understand many aspects of mental functioning only if one understands their origin and the transitions they have undergone" (Wertsch, 1991, p. 19).

Vygotsky maintained that proper understanding of the role that the learning environment plays in the student's development must be approached from the point of view of the relationship that exists between the student and his or her environment at different stages of development (van der Veer & Valsiner, 1994).

This study used a design-based research methodology in order to carry out the aims and purpose of the research. Design-based research, also known as development research, is concerned with developing broad models of how humans think, know, act and learn (Barab & Squire, 2004). The paradigm evolved, according to Sandoval and Bell (2004), as a way to study innovative learning environments in classroom settings. The theory of design-based research evolved from the work of educational psychologists and also researchers involved in educational technology learning, who were concerned about bridging the gap between experimentation in laboratory studies and the messiness of the classroom (Bannan-Ritland, 2003; Barab & Squire, 2004; Brown, 2004; Collins, 1992; Design-Based Research Collective, 2003; Hoadley, 2004; Kelly, 2003; McKenny, Nieveen, & van den Akker, 2006; Reeves, 2000).

Design-based research methodology is defined beautifully by Wang and Hannafin (2005) as "a systematic but flexible methodology aimed to improve educational practices through iterative analysis, design, development, and implementation, based on collaboration among researchers and practitioners in real-world settings and leading to contextually-sensitive design principles and theories" (pp. 6–7).

The main focus in the development of the present singing model was the authentic environment of the classroom. For ethical reasons, it was not possible to have a control group of students who did not receive the intervention, nor was it feasible to try and develop a laboratory-based experiment to test how students learned singing. The context and the interventions had to reflect reality, but at the same time it was important to have a theoretical framework to reflect on so that the interventions were guided. The continuous analysis of data and documentation of process that was required from the methodology means that the findings were inextricably linked to the research process. Any other singing teacher wanting to use the theoretical principles that emerged from the design could see how they evolved. This is important, because not every singing course will ever be exactly the same. The circumstances will always be slightly different, but this methodology allows for multiple variables as part of the authentic development.

The students were consulted throughout the process, and subject evaluations and reflective journals collected at the end of each session were used to refine the next iteration of the design. Part of the process in design-based research methodology was to use conjectured theories on which to base the interventions. I had to find a theoretical framework with which to design the interventions. Vygotsky provided a way to respond to the central aim of my study. In particular, utilising his writings on scientific and everyday concepts and how children construct knowledge first interpsychologically and then intrapsychologically helped me conceptualise the design of interventions that were used.

Interventions Using a Sociocultural Approach

In the following section, I will briefly describe the interventions that were introduced into the singing course. Reflection and self-assessment were introduced to students in order that they "view changes in their immediate situation from the point of view of past activities, and they can act in the present from the viewpoint of the future" (Vygotsky, 1978, p. 36). Reflection engages learners in a meta-cognitive thinking process (Burwell, 2005). This meta-cognition helps them to think about what they need to do to improve (Parncutt, 2007). Students that acquire these meta-cognitive skills become more in charge of their own learning, thus becoming self-regulated learners. Students at University of Wollongong (UOW) made weekly reflections on singing development, but it soon became clear that hardly any students were journaling weekly, and the students were instead writing the entire journal the night before it was due in class. The journaling assignment was changed to reflect this and the students wrote a retrospective statement of their vocal development and the strategies they developed over the session (Latukefu, 2009).

One of the assumptions that contributed to the interventions was the benefit to be had from peer learning. The environment of the class was organised so that the teacher was a co-constructor with other students in the development of singing, rather than an authoritative figure with knowledge to transfer. In Latukefu (2009), I investigated transformation of the teaching environment from the traditional master–apprentice approach to one of peer learning and collaboration. To do this, I turned to Vygotsky's theory of the zone of proximal development, which relates strongly to intermental processes that occur between the teacher and student or between experienced students and their less advanced peers, before they internalise learning.

Vygotsky's theory of concept formation was vital when considering the relationship between the everyday concepts that students bring to class about how to sing and the scientific concepts that I teach. Vygotsky emphasised that both scientific and everyday concepts are essential for learning. He described the elaborate relationship between experienced-based and scientific concepts as follows:

> In working its slow way upward, an everyday concept clears a path for the scientific concepts and its downward development. It creates a series of structures necessary for the evolution of the concepts more primitive, elementary aspects, which give it body and vitality. Scientific concepts, in turn, supply structures for the upward development of the child's spontaneous concepts toward conscious and deliberate use. (Vygotsky, 1986, p. 194)

The pedagogical views of a singing teacher will have a great deal of influence on how vocal training is transmitted. How we transmit this knowledge is crucial and Vygotsky argued that direct transmission of scientific concepts was not the best method.

> Pedagogical experience demonstrates that direct instruction in concepts is impossible. It is pedagogically fruitless. The teacher who attempts to use this approach achieves nothing, but a mindless learning of works, an empty verbalism that stimulates or imitates the presence of concepts in the child. Under these conditions, the child learns not the concept but the word, and this word is taken over by the child through memory rather than thought. Such knowledge turns out to be inadequate in any meaningful application (Vygotsky, 1987, p. 170).

Despite the fact that teaching of vocal physiology has become reasonably common practice in Australia, there is ongoing debate amongst teachers on whether, and how, scientific concepts should be taught to enhance learning singing. I heard evidence of this when I attended a music conference in London in 2009 and witnessed a discussion by a panel of singing teachers from the Guildhall as to whether or not there is value in introducing scientific concepts to students. Some of the teachers argued that while it was necessary for them as teachers to understand scientific concepts, it was not necessary for students to be taught this information. In the present study, scientific concepts were introduced into the singing class as part of the authentic act of learning singing. Class time was spent drawing bodies on butcher paper and inserting body parts that were necessary for singing. Explicit connection was made to the roles each part played in singing.

Universities in Australia have all participated in the development of graduate qualities that describe the distinctive qualities of a graduate of the particular university. Peer assessment (Latukefu, 2010) was introduced as a means to encourage individual development of graduate qualities, such as critical thinking and responsibility, in students. The literature tells us that peer involvement in assessment has potential to encourage learning and develop assessment skills that will last a lifetime (Boud, 1989; Boud, Cohen, & Sampson, 1999; Falchikov, 2007). A review of literature and analysis of current practice found that there were relatively few music institutions that had formal peer assessment as part of their programs. Reservations about over-marking by students, extra workloads for staff and problems that arose when different instruments and genres were involved, were held by those that did use peer assessment (Blom & Poole, 2004; Daniel, 2004; Hunter & Russ, 1996; Searby & Ewers, 1997).

In the present study, students participated in developing assessment criteria that described what they considered to be high quality singing. These criteria were then used to peer assess. The performances were compared only with the assessment criteria and not with other students or with general improvement of a student. Students formed panels and the three students in the panel assessed another student in the class. Performances were discussed and marked, and written feedback was provided to the performer by the panel. The criteria developed by the students were used as a guide and the panel was asked to mark holistically rather than dividing up the criteria and giving each part a mark. Panel feedback was moderated by a staff member before being passed on to the assessed student. Student assessors were given support in the weeks leading up to the peer assessment through modelling or prompting by the teacher, but were not marked on how they assessed.

Data Collection and Analysis

The planned interventions were introduced over a few years and Table 13.1 provides a summary of the timeframe. Each intervention was treated as a

Table 13.1
Summary of Timeframe of Study

Year	Intervention	Purpose
2003	Pilot study	Investigate student reaction to being taught both singing and spoken voice as part of performer training
2004	Transformation of classroom environment	To encourage social interaction amongst students
2005	Introduction of reflective journals	To encourage critical thinking and informal self-assessment
2006	Formal introduction of scientific concepts into the spoken voice and singing voice course	To encourage students to self-regulate their own singing when they understand how their voice works scientifically in relation to their bodies
2008	Formal introduction of peer assessment	To encourage students to be able to judge quality in singing and foster a sense of responsibility for others

research project and data collected in a variety of ways (see Table 13.2). There were three different cohorts of students who took part in the research. The first cohort commenced in 2006, the second in 2008 and the third in 2009. The total number of participants who began the study was 90; however, some students dropped out of the course, so the numbers decreased. The students were all completing an undergraduate tertiary performance course. They were a mixed group of acting students, male and female, and some had prior singing training while others did not.

A variety of instruments were used to collect data. Table 13.2 describes each of these instruments, its purpose and how the data was collected. The instruments consisted of student reflective journals, questionnaires, focus groups, input from other staff members, and teacher and subject evaluations administered by the university. The questionnaires contained opened and closed questions, as well as Likert scales, and the teacher/subject evaluations were administered anonymously by the University as part of their own regular evaluations and the results provided to me at the end of each session. Teacher evaluations carried out at the end of each session were a major influence on refinements that were made to the model. Input from other staff members was in the form of discussions about subject development.

Table 13.2
Instruments Used to Collect Data

Instrument	Purpose of instrument	How data was collected
Student and teacher reflective journals	To gain an understanding of undergraduate singing students' perceptions of and interpretations of their bodily and singing experiences and the meanings, which they assigned them as well as the changes that happened. To add teacher perceptions and interpretations of the same experiences.	The journals were collected twice in a session from January 2006 until November 2009. Two full cohorts of students were involved in the collection and all gave permission for their reflections to be analysed.
Teacher's notes taken in class of student assessments and performances	To keep a record of ongoing vocal development in order to compare teacher perceptions with students' perceptions of the same time	Detailed notes of students' performances and assessments were collected for analysis
Teacher/subject evaluations	These were anonymous and therefore students could write freely and with honesty about the performance of the teacher and the course	University administered evaluations at the end of each session, with results provided to the teacher. Questions used Likert scales as well as open ended questions for comment by students.
Document Reviews	Documents provided a context for the model being developed	Documents included subject outlines from 2000 until 2007 as well as comparison of courses teaching music or drama around Australia
Planning meetings with other staff members	Used to reflect on and assess the progress of students and plan content of classes. Also to seek advice on matters pertaining to the theoretical framework.	Held at the beginning and end of the university session
Questionnaires	To find out music education background and any existing vocal problems as well as what students found useful about the innovations and any suggestions they had for improving them or dropping them	Administered throughout the study and at the end of projects
Focus groups	The groups were used to collaborate with students on the development of descriptors of quality that could be used in peer assessment	Discussions in focus groups were recorded and analysed

Table 13.2 (CONTINUED)
Instruments Used to Collect Data

Instrument	Purpose of instrument	How data was collected
Pilot study and pilot interviews	These informed the research questions being investigated in the present study and assisted with the final wording of interview questions in the main study	Carried out at the beginning of the study
Submission of manuscripts to international and national peer reviewed journals	The critical feedback from reviewers shaped both the manuscripts and the nex iteration of the design	Each research project was documented and submitted for publication. Comments fromt reviewers were used to inform changes in the design.

This study used Interpretative Phenomenological Analysis (IPA) to arrange and analyse the data from journals, questionnaires and class notes. IPA has its origins in health psychology (Fade, 2004); however, it has been adapted and used in music research (e.g., Bailey & Davidson, 2005; Coimbra, Davidson, & Kokotsaki, 2001; Holmes, 2005; Sansom, 2005). When the students at UOW wrote in their reflective journals about how their singing was developing, they interpreted and modified the meaning of things that were happening to themselves (Blumer, 1969). The ontological standpoint of the present study is that it is important to understand students' perceptions of and interpretations of their bodily and singing experiences, and the meanings that they assign them.

IPA is an interpretation by the researcher of the participants experience while at the same time an attempt to capture the quality and texture of the individual experience (Willig, 2001). By interpreting the data through constant reflection on the theories of social constructivism, it is possible to evolve explanations from the data in the forms of models or narrative (Chapman & Smith, 2002). Theories can be developed for the shared meanings that a group of individuals attach to the experience of developing their singing in a sociocultural environment and a case study approach can be used to develop an in-depth description of just one individual's experience (Fade, 2004). For example, the content of all the reflective journals was analysed individually and common themes emerging were noted and used to develop shared meanings for the group. These journals were an authentic part of the teaching method developed in the study to assist students to become self-regulated learners. Students reflected on their learning process and made comments on how their singing was developing. The journals were read carefully and any entries thought to be relevant to the research were highlighted. The themes that emerged summarised and captured the quality of the participants' experience of the singing development. The themes were then mapped against concepts of sociocultural theory, such as scientific concepts. Journals were also analysed, looking at individual development of students over the three years in the course. This singing development, which included identity construction, was documented and used for case studies (Latukefu, 2009).

Discussion

How Can the Research Help Other Practitioners?

The nature of a sociocultural approach, combined with development-research methodology, means that certain educational principles emerge from the constant reference back to theory. These principles are transferable to other contexts, even if the local context is different from the one where the principles were developed. The following section will discuss what principles emerged from the series of studies. Students self-regulate their own singing when they understand how their voice works scientifically in relation to their bodies.

It is already common practice in Australia to include scientific concepts as part of a range of teaching strategies. This study continues to support this and add to the knowledge that transmission of these concepts is best in an authentic manner and in combination with everyday concepts that students hold. The analysis of data collected from student journals showed how students developed their understanding of the scientific concepts as long as they were taught as part of the authentic learning experience not detached from it. The comment below, taken from a reflective journal, written after a class on body mapping, is typical:

> I found the concept of the inner working of my body and to actively recognise where they are and what they do to control various parts was an aspect of singing that I had rarely thought of before now. This whole body engagement has put singing in a different perspective for me. I must first understand the whole body and its mechanics so I can be aware of where things are and what they do so I can control them.

From a sociocultural perspective, scientific concepts cannot be simply assimilated in a ready-made form. They must undergo development in order to obtain individual meaning (Vygotsky, 1986). This development is carefully directed by the instructor in close connection to the individual characteristics of the learner. Unlike models of learning singing, which are often prescriptive of content, this model allows practitioners the flexibility to choose scientific concepts of singing that they will teach their students. As a teacher/researcher I am aware that singing teachers may adjust the types of scientific concepts they choose to teach depending on the student learning style and the context (Reid, 2001). The design principle in this case is not the type of scientific concept a teacher should use, but the fact that scientific concepts themselves can become a mediative tool for learning if combined with the everyday concepts students hold about singing.

An important characteristic of scientific concepts is their transferability. In the following excerpt from a student reflective journal, the student was excited when he realised that introducing scientific concepts into something he was already doing was helpful. He wrote in his journal:

> My voice was stronger, richer and more lively than our last gig. I was constantly aware of how I was using my voice and it greatly added to my performance. I ventured even further at times, throwing glottal pops into songs and experimenting with venturing from one extreme of my pitch to the other, swooping from my chest voice to my head voice. To summarise what I find to be the most valuable aspect of my singing progress and current practice is an increasingly deeper and more detailed awareness of my voice and my singing, which is become more instinctive.

Another excerpt from a student reflective journal showed that she found body mapping to be very useful, because she was able to transfer the scientific concepts she was learning about her body to other acting subjects:

> The body mapping was useful and immediately transferable because now when given instructions by various teachers, I am much more readily able to visualise what they are asking me to do in relation to what my body is required to do.

Interaction With Peers Motivates Reflection and Further Learning

The dominance of the one-to-one lesson in the conservatoire means that students don't get as much chance to learn from each other as they do using a sociocultural approach. Students in the study placed a high value on watching the development of others and learning with them. While advocating for the continued need for one-to-one lessons in the conservatoire (Latukefu, 2009), I questioned whether at an undergraduate level a balance between group teaching of concepts that are basic for vocal development and one-to-one lessons was more beneficial because of the peer learning culture that develops. Nielsen (2004) advocated more use of peer learning, and in the case of one student in this study, it was clear that listening to other students who were at a similar level, but a little more advanced, helped her hear things that were achievable. This is what she wrote:

> Every week in class I learn more about the amazing control singers have to have over their voices. The difference between the third years

> and us is just amazing and I can see that training and applying these techniques is quite a long term thing that will take many years but you will still always be improving (Latukefu, 2009, p. 129).

Transformation of Practical Activity Through Reflection Benefits Learning

In Latukefu (2009), I demonstrated that formal reflection by students about their vocal development and why things were happening assisted students in solving problems. It did this by providing students with an opportunity to diagnose a problem, think of a solution, carry out the solution through their practice and then refine the solution if necessary. Acquiring these meta-cognitive skills helps students to become more self-regulated learners and improves their practice as they can think about what they need to do in order to improve (Parncutt, 2007). In two case studies carried out (Latukefu, 2009), the students used their reflective writing as a way to synthesise the different perspectives they were getting from books and other classes. In a third case, the student journal writing became much more detailed once he had mastered the terms in which to express himself.

Singing Students Must be Able to Critically Discern Quality in Singing

A sociocultural approach to learning singing encourages students to become better self-regulated learners (Montalvo & Torres, 2004) capable of continuing with their learning after graduation (Falchikov, 2007). In order to achieve this, students must be capable of thinking critically about their own singing. The introduction of peer assessment into the course (Latukefu, 2010) was a strategy to try and encourage students to think about what constituted quality singing in others, which in turn made the students consider what constituted quality singing in themselves. Students completed a survey concerned with exploring their experience of peer assessment. Results suggested (Latukefu, 2010) the main benefit the students perceived from the exercise was that it helped them to reflect on their own practice by having to make the effort to interact with the criteria given in order to properly assess a peer. A couple of responses from students were:

> By assessing my classmates I found that during my assessment I was thinking critically and could therefore work to apply the things I had noticed lacking in previous assessments.
>
> I liked the ability to be able to discuss as a panel why and how the performance of the singer worked. Playing the assessor gave me an understanding what are the standards and criteria I need to full fill (sic) to be able to perform well in my own performance.

Peer assessment may not be the only way that students develop this ability to discern quality in themselves and others, but it was an effective strategy in the local context of a higher education degree. Students co-constructed the assessment related knowledge, which they were able to appropriate as their own and apply to self-assessment (Latukefu, 2010).

Multiple Perspectives are Important for Construction of Learning Singing

There is a culture of protection and possession of students that exists in many conservatoires (Jorgenson, 2000). This is exacerbated by the master–apprentice style of teaching that takes place, and many times as a student and also a teacher I have heard other teachers say that it is just too confusing for students to have different teachers tell them different things. Forderhase (1994) also found this a common comment in his study on vocal team teaching. In Latukefu (2007), I demonstrated how a sociocultural approach supported the case for multiple perspectives being extremely helpful to singing students, especially when the other teacher was a spoken voice teacher. In my own teaching journal, I describe an impromptu class visit from the voice teacher. It demonstrates a collegiality that contributed to helping with student learning.

> C (voice teacher) came to class today and worked with Barbara [pseudonyms are used]. Barbara has a huge operatic sound, which is much more mature than you would expect from someone her age and shows some worrying signs of things not being quite right. There is creakiness in the sound and also a bit of a wobble. Her pitch is often flat and singing always seems like such an effort for her. This effort distracts from the performance. Also, she does not glide smoothly when changing pitch or register, but tends to have a rather lumpy line. Mostly she sings loudly and without a lot of vocal colour change. I can hear this and we have tried different strategies to try and improve, but nothing seems to stick. C immediately asked her to stop trying to drop her larynx and instead sing using a soft twang. Barbara found this almost impossible at first, she could not sing softly and employ twang. Finally she got it and the change in her sound and performance was breath taking. For the first time she was able to sing freely, pitch was centered, there was no sign of wobble and she still projected beautifully. Also the creaky sound that was caused by pushing and therefore constricting disappeared altogether. She was able to concentrate on the meaning of the text and the character and it was the first time that her voice and the effort of producing her "sound" was not a distraction to the audience. I had not thought of this as a strategy probably because my own opera training with low larynx position

> is so strong. I was really happy that C had been able to help her so easily and she did it in a way that did not threaten me at all. She worked as a speechie [speech therapist] not a singing teacher and I think this was really thoughtful of her.

Conclusion

The different approaches and perspectives that the teachers brought to their work meant that students transferred the vocal work that they were doing from one class to the next with good results. A quote from one of the students' reflective journals showed how she was integrating the spoken voice work with the singing classes. She was transferring the vocal skills of anchoring, release of constriction and twang learnt in spoken voice class and applying them to her singing with what she perceived to be good results:

> I warmed up as usual and sang through two songs, *Auf Eines Altes Bilt* and *Ave Maria.* I practised using anchoring that we learned in spoken voice, particularly on the high notes, and found this quite difficult because of the isolations of the body required. While creating stability in the core of my body, I had to be careful to retain an open throat and avoid constriction. Also my breathing — while activating my back muscles, I had to be careful not to clench and strain my tummy muscles and keep my breath flow consistent. In spoken voice class we learnt about "twang" and practised it. L (singing teacher) was there and C (voice teacher) talked about using it in singing, just enough so as to create less strain on the voice, but so it doesn't turn nasal. The difference was amazing in our speaking voices and the ease with which volume was created by using natural twang was incredible (Latukefu, 2007 p. 12).

Who Benefits From This Knowledge?

For inexperienced teachers, the sociocultural approach provides insights into strategies that students develop for learning and this in turn can act as a framework in which they can organise the content of their singing teaching. For more experienced teachers who find themselves having to adjust the way they teach, because of economic pressures or as part of curriculum renewal and review, the theoretical concepts of how students can learn using a different model of teaching will be useful as they develop their own models of learning suitable to their local context.

Future Research

In 2009, I attended a youth opera festival in the Netherlands, where many debates were held about the role of conservatoire for modern musicians. A clarinetist attending the festival who works as a successful performing musician, although not with a symphony orchestra, swore that the only thing he really learnt to do well at conservatoire was play a beautiful "e" on his clarinet. It is alarming to think that this is his perception of learning at conservatoire. Now he is part of an independent wind ensemble that performs contemporary music, designs and implements music educational programs for schools, and devises and performs original works for children. I would hate to think that I might have students attending conferences and complaining that all they learnt in their degree was how to sing a perfect "e". We teachers must identify realistically what qualities we want our singers to have when they finish their undergraduate degrees and align our teaching with those qualities. That way we will be preparing our singers much better to go out into the real world.

References

Bailey, B., & Davidson, J.W. (2005). Effects of group singing and performance on a group of middle class and marginalised singers. *Psychology of Music, 33*(3), 269–303.

Bannan-Ritland, B. (2003). The role of design in research: The integrative learning design framework. *Educational Researcher, 32*(1), 21–24.

Barab, S., & Squire, K. (2004). Design-based research: Putting a stake in the ground. *The Journal of the Learning Sciences, 13*(1), 1–14.

Blom, D., & Poole, K. (2004). Peer assessment of tertiary music performance: opportunities for understanding performance assessment and performing through experience and self-reflection. *British Journal of Music Education, 21*(1), 111–125.

Blumer, H. (1969). *Symbolic interactionism perspective and method.* Berkley, BA: University of California Press.

Boud, D. (1989). 'The role of self-assessment in student grading', *Assessment and Evaluation in Higher Education, 14*(1), 20–30.

Boud, D., Cohen, R., & Sampson, J. (1999). 'Peer learning and assessment'. *Assessment and Evaluation in Higher Education, 24*(4), 413–426.

Brown, J.E. (2004). Moving towards excellence: Creating a teaching framework that challenges musicians to a pursuit of excellence. *Studies in Learning, Evaluation, Innovation and Development, 1*(1), 16–23.

Burwell, K. (2005). A degree of independence: Teachers' approaches to instrumental tuition in a university college. *British Journal of Music Education, 22*(3), 199–215.

Calouste Gulbenkian Foundation. (1965). *Making musicians.* London: The Gulbenkian Foundation.

Chapman, J.L. (2006). *Singing and teaching singing.* San Diego, CA: Plural Publishing.

Chapman, E., & Smith, J.A. (2002). Interpretative phenomenological analysis and the new genetics. *Journal of Health Psychology, 7*(2), 125–130.

Coimbra, D., Davidson, J.W., & Kokotsaki, D. (2001). Investigating the assessment of singers in a music college setting: The students' perspective. *Research Studies in Music Education, 16*, 15–32.

Collins, A. (1992). Towards a design science of education. In E. Scanlon & T.O. Shea (Eds.), *New directions in educational technology* (pp. 15–22). New York: Springer-Verlag.

Csikszentmihalyi, M. (1997). *Finding flow: The psychology of engagement with everyday life*. New York: Basic Books.

Daniel, R. (2004). Peer assessment in musical performance: The development, trial and evaluation of a methodology for the Australian tertiary environment. *British Journal of Music Education, 21*(1), 89–110.

Daniels, H. (2008). *Vygotsky and research*. London: Routledge.

Davidson, J.W., & Jordan, N. (2007). Private teaching, private learning: An exploration of music instrument learning in the private studio, junior and senior conservatories. In L. Bresler (Ed.), *International handbook of research in arts education* (Vol. 1, pp. 729–744). Dordrecht, the Netherlands: Springer.

Davidson, J.W., & Smith, J.A. (1997). A case of 'newer practices' in music education at conservatoire level. *British Journal of Music Education, 14*(3), 251–269.

Design-Based Research Collective. (2003). Design-based research: An emerging paradigm for educational inquiry. *Educational Researcher, 32*(1), 5–8.

Fade, S. (2004). Using interpretative phenomenological analysis for public health nutrition and dietetic research: A practical guide. *Proceedings of the Nutrition Society, 63*, 647–653.

Falchikov, N. (2007). The place of peers in learning and assessment. In D. Boud & N. Falchikov (Eds.), *Rethinking assessment in higher education learning for the longer term*. London: Routledge

Forderhase, J. (1994). Attitudes toward team teaching as an approach to vocal instruction. *The NATS Journal, 50*(3), 3–11.

Freer, P.K. (2006). Response to Krista Riggs, "Foundations for flow: A philosophical model for studio instruction". *Philosophy of Music Education Review, 14*(2), 225–230.

Greene, M. (1995). *Releasing the imagination: Essays on education, the arts, and social change*. San Francisco: Jossey-Bass.

Hoadley, C.M. (2004). Methodological alignment in design-based research. *Educational Psychologist, 39*(4), 203–212.

Holden, R. (2002). A new model of training the collegiate voice student. *Journal of Singing, 58*, 299–303.

Holmes, P. (2005). Imagination in practice: A study of the integrated roles of interpretation, imagery and technique in the learning and memorisation processes of two experienced solo performers. *British Journal of Music Education, 22*(3), 217–235.

Hunter, D., & Russ, M. (1996). Peer assessment in performance studies. *British Journal of Music Education, 13*, 67–78.

Jorgenson, H. (2000). Student learning in higher instrumental education: Who is responsible? *British Journal of Music Education, 17*(1), 67–77.

Kamin, S., Richards, H., & Collins, D. (2007). Influences on talent development process of non-classical musicians: Psychological, social and environmental influences. *Music Education Research, 9*(3), 449–468.

Karpov, Y. (2003). Vygotsky's doctrine of scientific concepts. Its role for contemporary education. In A. Kozulin, B. Gindis, V.S. Ageyev, & S.M. Miller (Eds.), *Vygotsky's educational theory in cultural context* (pp. 65–82). Cambridge, UK: Cambridge University Press.

Kelly, A. (2003). Research as design. *Educational Researcher, 32*(1), 3–5.

Latukefu, L. (2007). The constructed voice: A sociocultural model of learning for undergraduate singers. *Australian Voice, 13*, 8–16.

Latukefu, L. (2009). Peer learning and reflection: Strategies developed by vocal students in transforming tertiary setting. *International Journal of Music Education, 27*(2), 128–142.

Latukefu, L. (2010). Peer assessment in tertiary level singing: Changing and shaping culture through social interaction. *Research Studies in Music Education, 32*(2), 1–13.

Liu, C., & Mathews, R. (2005). Vygotsky's philosophy: Constructivism and its criticisms examined. *International Education Journal, 6*(3), 386–399.

McKenny, S., Nieveen, N., & van den Akker, J. (2006). Design research from a curriculum perspective. In J. van den Akker, K. Gravemeijer, S. McKenney & N. Nieveen (Eds.), *Educational design research* (pp. 67–90). London: Routledge.

McWilliam, E., Carey, G., Draper, P., & Lebler, D. (2006). Learning and unlearning: New challenges for teaching in conservatoires. *Australian Journal of Music Education, 1*(1), 25–31.

Montalvo, F., & Torres, M. (2004). Self-regulated learning: Current and future directions. *Electronic Journal of Research in Educational Psychology, 2*(1), 1–34.

Nerland, M. (2007). One-to-one teaching as cultural practice: Two case studies from an academy of music. *Music Education Research, 9*(3), 399–416.

Nielsen, S. (2004). Strategies and self-efficacy beliefs in instrumental and vocal individual practice: A study of students in higher music education. *Psychology of Music, 32*(4), 418–431.

Parncutt, R. (2007). Can researchers help artists? Music performance research for music students. *Music Performance Research, 1*(1), 1–25.

Reeves, T.C. (2000). *Enhancing the worth of instructional technology research through "design experiments" and other development research strategies.* Paper presented at the International Perspectives on Instructional Technology Research for the 21st Century, New Orleans.

Reid, A. (2001). Variation in the ways that instrumental and vocal students experience learning music. *Music Education Research, 3*(1), 26–40.

Riggs, K. (2006). Foundations for flow: A philosophical model for studio instruction. *Philosophy of Music Education Review, 14*(2), 175–191.

Sandoval, W., & Bell, P. (2004). Design-based research methods for studying learning in context: Introduction. *Educational Psychologist, 39*(4), 199–201.

Sansom, M.J. (2005, April). *Understanding musical meaning: Interpretative phenomenological analysis and improvisations.* Paper presented at the British Forum for Ethnomusicology, 2005 Annual Conference — Music and Dance Performance: Cross-Cultural Approaches, SOAS, London.

Searby, M., & Ewers, T. (1997). An evaluation of the use of peer assessment in higher education: A case study in the school of music, Kingston University. *Assessment & Evaluation in Higher Education, 22*(4), 371–383.

Trounson, A. (2009, August 26). Money woes hit a sour note at music school. *The Australian*, p. 29.

van der Veer, R., & Valsiner, J. (Eds.). (1994). *The Vygotsky reader*. Oxford, UK: Blackwell Publishers.

Vialle, W., Lysaght, P., & Verenikina, I. (2005). *Psychology for educators*. Melbourne, Australia: Thomson Social Science Press.

Vogel, D.E. (1976). An empirical look at combined group and private voice studio teaching. *The NATS Bulletin, 33*, 20–21.

Vygotsky, L. (1978). *Mind in society the development of higher psychological processes*. Cambridge, UK: Harvard University Press.

Vygotsky, L. (1986). *Thought and language*. Cambridge, UK: The MIT press.

Vygotsky, L. (1987). *The collected works of L.S. Vygotsky: Vol 1. Problems of general psychology*. New York: Plenum.

Wang, F., & Hannafin, M.J. (2005). Design-based research and technology-enhanced learning environments. *Educational Technology Research and Development, 53*(4), 5–23.

Wertsch, J. (1991). *Voices of the mind: A sociocultural approach to mediated action*. Cambridge, UK: Harvard University Press.

Willig, C. (2001). *Introducing qualitative research in psychology: Adventures in theory and method*. Buckingham, UK: Open University Press.

Chapter 14

One Size Doesn't Fit All: Tailored Training for Contemporary Commercial Singers

Irene Bartlett

Singers of non-classical styles have urgent need for a pedagogy that fits their genre, one that recognises that produced vocal tone, registration and sound qualities inherent in their commercial singing differ greatly from accepted, western classical-music standards. As vocal longevity is reliant on the singer finding a vocal balance in whatever genre or style they sing, the prevailing "one size fits all" philosophy is fraught with danger. By effectively ignoring genre and style, the philosophy leaves the singer with a single option for vocal training that runs with a rigid adherence to western classical tradition alone. Research of healthy vocal technique in classical singing has provided bountiful information for that significant genre. However, its unabridged application to contemporary commercial styles may lead singers to avoid training that they consider irrelevant, or worse, to develop a vocal technique that is inappropriate and deleterious to their vocal health. Diverse and less than optimum performance environments, specific characteristics of vocal production, style-driven vocal effects and embellishments, are a reality for contemporary commercial singers and must be recognised, addressed and managed through a training system that is engaging and genre relevant. The purpose of this chapter is to bridge the classical and non-classical divide by contrasting the individual elements of technique and style-driven vocal production of the two genres. I propose that with some modification to accepted thinking and practice, it is possible for voice teachers to develop an effective pedagogy that recognises the realities of contemporary commercial performance.

A large body of literature exists concerning the singing voice in relation to production and vocal health issues. However, this literature has focused heavily on classical singing styles and the practice of classical singers (e.g., Miller & Verdolini, 1995; Thalen & Sunberg, 2001; Timmermans, De Bodt, Wuyts, Boudewijins, Clement, Peeters, & Van de Heynig, 2002). Whilst this literature is useful where foundational aspects of singing voice production are common regardless of style, the research bias towards classical singers continues a tradition of neglect for the ever-increasing population of singers who perform non-classical styles (Sataloff, 1997; Thalen & Sundberg, 2001; LoVetri, 2008; McCoy, 2004).

In progressing the proposition that the western classical tradition offers the only legitimate and healthy vocal technique for singers, singing voice pedagogues have failed to recognise the inherent style differences of classical and non-classical vocal music. This is problematic for singers of the non-classical genre who need to develop reliable technique, but who have difficulty in finding significance in traditional classical singing methods (Bartlett, 2010; Sullivan, 1989). Reports in the literature suggest that teachers of singing have been reluctant to move away from their traditional ideas of registration, tone and voice quality, and have either excluded non-classical students from their studios or given them a technique that is inefficient when applied to non-classical styles (Edwin, 2000). On the other side of this divide, it would appear that many singers of non-classical styles have rejected any voice training that might make them sound "trained" (i.e., to sing with developed vibrato, legato line and consistent tone). Typically, they perceive traditional classical techniques as irrelevant to their contemporary commercial performance styles as they strive for individuality in tone and voice quality.

Jeanette LoVetri, a United States based singing teacher and researcher, has written widely on the need for a developed pedagogy for singers of "non-classical" styles, one that recognises that the produced vocal tone, registration and sound qualities of non-classical styles differ greatly from accepted, western classical music standards. To focus this need and to delineate the two genres, she proposed "contemporary commercial music" (LoVetri, 2002) as a generic term to describe the range of non-classical music styles. In a later article, she gave this definition:

> Contemporary Commercial Music (CCM) is the new term for what we used to call non-classical music. This is a generic term created to cover everything including music theatre, pop, rock, gospel, R&B, soul, hip hop, rap, country, folk, experimental music, and all other styles that are not considered classical. (LoVetri, 2002, p. 260)

For the purposes of this chapter, I have used LoVetri's terminology directly while adapting it to describe those singers who choose to perform in the range of CCM styles, namely contemporary commercial singers (CCS).

My intention in writing this chapter is to construct a bridge over the classical/non-classical divide by offering an insight into the realities of CCM singing performance, while contrasting the individual elements of technique and style-driven vocal production of each genre (classical and non-classical). I propose that with some modification to accepted thinking and practice, it is possible for voice teachers to build a healthy vocal technique for all singers, regardless of style. This will necessitate adaptations to current pedagogical practice and these adaptations must be based on recognition of the performance realities and specific style demands of CCM.

An Insider's View

The lack of relevant research from within the field of contemporary commercial singing and the aesthetic bias of classically-oriented writers towards contemporary commercial music (CCM) caused me to ponder my own performance experience of 42 years in the CCM industry and on my 28 years of teaching non-classical styles.

Throughout this lengthy career, I have met and continue to meet other professional contemporary "gig" singers of both genders, who enjoy enduring careers singing the range of styles consistently reported as inevitably damaging to vocal health (Bartlett, 2010). This is an insider's view evolved from my current and past CCM gig performances as a freelance vocalist and lead band singer for concert, corporate and private events, singing across a wide range of CCM repertoire from music hall to jazz through to music theatre, and the rock, pop, country, dance/funk and R&B styles of today. Throughout my extensive singing and teaching careers, I have maintained a healthy and robust speaking and singing voice, whilst also experiencing a significant increase in vocal range and stamina. For example, before the age of 40, I sang in contralto and contemporary alto (C3-B4) ranges exclusively. Since this time, I have been able to develop an additional upper register octave, which has enabled me to perform "legit" styles (modified classical technique with a speech quality), in addition to my established belt/mix and belt repertoire (mostly straight tone, speech dominant singing voice production). I attribute my vocal strength and longevity, and the gains in useable vocal range, to a continuing education in anatomy and physiology of the voice and to the constant engagement and conditioning of the laryngeal and exhalation support muscles established through my teaching and performance practice. My continuing vocal health and reliable vocal production "flies in the face" of the accepted view that CCM styles cannot be sustained throughout a performance career, and that voices necessarily deteriorate with age, particularly if non-classical singing styles are employed. Interestingly, this view is not supported by grounded research, but stems from small-sample, laboratory-based research, from studies of treatment-seeking singers (e.g., Batza, 1971), or from opinion-based anecdotal reports from observers outside of the CCM field.

The Dangers of a "One Size Fits All" Policy

Today's CCM industry is dominated by "star" singers, whose vocal individuality and style innovation is basic to the establishment of their career success and longevity. Similarly, aspiring CCS are reliant on their ability to bring their individual voice to their style-based performances. As vocal longevity is reliant on singers finding a vocal balance in *whatever* genre or style they sing, the prevailing "one size fits all" philosophy (i.e., that classical training is best for singers of any repertoire) is fraught with danger. By effectively ignoring the specific genre and style elements of a given repertoire, the philosophy leaves singers with a single option for vocal training that runs with a rigid adherence to western classical tradition alone, regardless of specific genre and style demands of the music or a singer's individual training needs.

Training and Style Relevance

The literature of voice science describes style as a method of voice production that has actual defining acoustic, physiological and perceptual features (Burns, 1986; Osborne, 1979; Schutte & Miller, 1993; Titze, 1994). In a comparative study of classical and non-classical singing styles, voice scientists Schutte and Miller identified three distinguishing characteristics of non-classical singing style that would be considered faults and deemed unacceptable in the western classical tradition. These are:

- text dominance — "... it is essential that they [the texts] be understandable, even on first hearing";
- naturalness of sound — "... often even at the expense of beauty"; and
- vocal individuality — "... it is not unusual to adapt the song to the strengths and weaknesses of the singer" (Miller, 1993, p. 144).

These observations challenge the traditional aesthetic of "good" singing when applied to the CCM genre. For CCS, the expectation of beautiful tone or flowing vocal line must be viewed in terms of relevance to, and authentic production of, idiosyncratic elements of each style and the individual vocal characteristics of a singer (e.g., rhythmic emphasis, mood of the music, vocal tone and vocal embellishments). Surely then, the effectiveness of any "one size fits all" vocal training policy must be viewed with suspicion.

Most importantly, teachers should be mindful that CCM audiences expect CCS to incorporate recognisable style elements and strong personae in their performances rather than beautiful tone and line. LoVetri (2008) highlighted these issues as significant for CCS, as she commented that CCM standards of vocal production are set by individual "star" performers and driven by commercial realities, such as audience expectation, rather than any traditional model:

> The standards of a style and the vocal characteristics it [contemporary commercial singing] requires are established and maintained by those who have a successful professional career in that style, and by their audiences. They are neither set by stars who venture into a style from another unrelated one nor by academics. (p. 261)

LoVetri's observations and those of the voice scientists are important, as they continue to highlight the field of contemporary commercial singing as undertheorised. For example, the extensive range of substyles evolving from within the mainstream style group are rarely discussed (see Table 14.1). Yet, each substyle has identifying characteristics of vocal production, including specific vocal effects and embellishments. CCM audiences are readily able to identify these characteristics as unique markers for each style and substyle. Therefore, if CCS are to establish a successful career, they must meet their audiences' expectations of style authenticity by incorporating these characteristics in their style-based performances. The diversity of styles, the level of audience expectations and the technical demands that each style places on the vocal production of CCS may surprise those who are not practitioners in the field.

Singers may incorporate original compositions in their performances where they promote their individual vocal tone and idiosyncratic voice qualities. However, the majority of CCS want to sing in the style of their favourite recording artist. This reproduction will involve all aspects of the "star's" performance, including vocal quality, style embellishments and dance movements (Ng, 2006). Professional "covers" singers must meet their audiences' expectations by reproducing exactly the recording star's rendition of the song, which commonly includes demanding style elements such as belt.

TABLE 14.1
Mainstream Styles and Some Associated Substyles

Style	Substyles
Pop	House, dance, rap, disco, hip hop
Rock	Heavy metal, grunge, soft/hard rock, rock and roll
Country	Bluegrass, modern country, country and western.
R&B	Funk, gospel/pop, Motown, doo-wop
Jazz	Swing, Latin, blues, ballad, be-bop
Music theatre	Broadway, rock opera, modern operetta, juke-box

Belt Singing

Belt singing is used to some degree in all CCM styles including Broadway music theatre, pop, rock, country and jazz styles; therefore any developed pedagogy for CCS must include targeted training of belt technique. This speech-based, forward, bright singing voice quality encompasses all the elements that typify CCM styles. It is very different to the vocal production of female classical singers in terms of coordination of the laryngeal musculature, acoustic set up, breath management and, most importantly, registration (keys are set in the lower female octave over a range of F3–C5 up to Eb5). Additionally, a neutral to higher larynx position, narrowed pharynx, high back of tongue position and personalised speech oriented phrasing (consonant driven, with little or no vibrato), is accompanied by speech-like articulation (voicing of diphthongs as in speech, rather than pure vowels), and a specific acoustic set up (presence of the raised 2nd formant, the absence of the singer's formant). These differences in technique have been considered to be vocally damaging and therefore regarded as flawed by classically-backgrounded teachers and pedagogues (Spivey, 2008). Consequently, the vocal production of CCS was viewed as aesthetically-inferior by classically-oriented commentators in the past (Edwin, 2002). Given the extent of recent research afforded to belt singing, it is surprising that this view remains prevalent today, prompting even classically-oriented voice pedagogues and researchers to comment on the aesthetic divide. For example:

> Classically oriented voice teachers often misunderstand this form of vocal production [belting] and have little aesthetic appreciation for either the sound or the literature [of singing] for which it is required. Objectively [from a voice science perspective] there are many similarities between female belt voice and the male operatic head voice. (McCoy, 2006, p. 75)

Similarly, in a paper concerning choral singers and World Music compositions, Wells (2007) reflected on the historical opposition to belt singing:

> Belt technique has been perhaps the most controversial subject in the field of voice research and pedagogy in the past half century. Outright condemnation of the technique as a valid mode of phonation has been expressed by many in the classical singing community, which has resulted in a pariah-like status for the style in the field of voice training. Only in the past two decades has a chorus of advocacy from voice scientists, physicians, practitioners, and pedagogues begun to sound through the din of opposition and prejudice. (p. 2)

A Day in the Life of a Professional Contemporary Commercial Singer

Singers are often described as "vocal athletes". For professional and semiprofessional CCS, "long distance" vocal athletes is a more accurate descriptor as they are regularly engaged in a range of physical activities other than those involved with actual singing and speaking-voice production (Bartlett, 2010). In addition to the frequency and duration of their performances (the physicality of actual singing for three to five hours), these singers are required to dance to, or at least move in time with, the rhythm of the repertoire, while simultaneously employing a range of stylistic vocal effects to deliver an authentic performance in each style (Bartlett, 2010; Radionoff, 2006). As gig protocol demands, these singers are required also to set up musical instruments and sound gear both prior to and after each performance. These pre and postperformance activities serve to extend the actual performance call time of four to five hours, often to at least six hours of physical involvement for each gig.

These are very different performance challenges to those experienced by classical singers. From my "insider" perspective as a CCM performer and through my extensive pedagogical involvement with all of its styles, I can report that CCS are engaged in a complex array of orchestrated relationships in each and every performance. For example, the lead singer "fronts" the band acting as a conduit between the instrumentalists and the audience while managing a range of complex music activities. Music theatre performers have to manage elements of choreography, memorisation of script and acting in addition to singing. Jazz singers are expected to engage their audience while simultaneously improvising rhythm and phrasing using the chord progression rather than the melody line to interpret a piece (Wilson, 2003). Singers in "covers" bands face similar, but different, challenges as they satisfy their audiences with a carbon copy of the visual and sound production of original recording artists. In addition to a lead singing role, many CCS are called on to double as back-up singers and/or to play an instrument as they interact with other members of the band (Bartlett, 2010).

The frequency and duration of their performances, the onstage multitasking, the audience expectations, the artistic and physical demands of both the singing and the set-up and pull-down of instruments and sound equipment, can negatively impact the vocal production and vocal health of CCS, regardless of their singing styles. Yet, as with the lack of any focused studies of CCS technique, research into the physical and mental stress of CCS' onstage and off-stage professional and social interactions is non-existent.

The Impact of Style on Vocal Health

Style in itself does not cause damage to the vocal instrument; poor technique does. However, it is apparent that some style elements do have potential to be harmful to the vocal instrument if employed inefficiently. For example, vocal fry and glottal attack increase the collision-shearing-abrasion forces on the vocal folds, while breathy onset increases vocal fold tension; all induce habitual muscle effort in the larynx (Thurman, Klitzeke, & Hogikyan, 2000). If used as vocal effects only, these elements can be managed within a healthy, balanced vocal production. More importantly, for both classical singers and CCS alike, the individual's use of style elements, their speech habits and performance environments, are more likely to contribute to vocal damage (nodules etc.) or alterations in laryngeal function (muscle tension dysphonias, fatigue, hoarseness and so on).

As discussed earlier in this chapter, the production of specific style elements is essential to a successful performance career for CCS and, therefore, should be addressed within any training program for this group of singers. While voice qualities such as speech, twang, sob and belt (Estill, 1997) are basic to all contemporary commercial singing styles, some style elements are specific. For example, grit, growl, glottal onsets, and scream used particularly for rock singing; soft onset, yell and vocal fry, particularly for pop singing; yodeling, crying and riding an American "r", particularly for Country singing; breathy onset, glottal stroke and scat (imitating instrumental sounds on random vowels over an improvised harmonic line), particularly for jazz singing; and character voice, belt, legit (modified classical), and pop/rock elements, particularly for music theatre singing. When considering that any or all of these elements or vocal effects may crossover style boundaries and be employed by a CCS in a single performance, the relevance of classical technique (legato line, developed vibrato and even tone) and the "one size fits all" philosophy becomes highly questionable. Similarly, a teacher's well-meaning advice to CCS students to not sing "damaging" styles, or to avoid singing "risky" style elements will be of little use to CCS trying to "break in" to the highly competitive CCM industry, and impossible to implement for those professional CCS with established careers.

The Relationship of Technology and Vocal Health

The development of specific music-based technology, for example, microphones, amplification, analogue and digital effects, and computer generated music programs, has had a major impact on singers' voice production and vocal performance. The introduction of live sound reinforcement systems in the 1930s dramatically changed the nature of singing, as amplification made it possible for singers to be heard while using a conversationally expressive, low intensity speech quality production against a background of loud and large instrumental backings. This colloquial vocal sound quickly became the preferred choice of audiences for both female and male singers. Electrification and amplification raised the intensity of instrumental accompaniments to levels that physically overwhelmed the singer's proprioception of the level of their own vocal intensity, further establishing a necessity for both amateur and professional CCM singers to rely heavily on amplification in order to hear their own voice and to be heard by their audiences in less than optimum acoustic environments.

The management of acoustically poor performance venues is a major challenge for CCS. Their performance environments are most usually pubs, clubs, restaurants and hotel function rooms where low ceilings, carpeted floors, windowless, acoustic material lined walls or open air performances are the norm (Bartlett, 2010; Wilson, 2003). These acoustically deficient spaces can only be managed with the assistance of "live sound reinforcement" (i.e., amplifiers, mixers, front of house speakers, monitor or foldback speakers and microphones). LoVetri (2008) confirmed this insider view:

> All CCM [contemporary commercial music] styles evolved from colloquial speech, and all of them are electronically amplified. Therefore, CCM vocal production cannot be divorced from amplification. The microphones, speakers, monitors, soundboard, and sound engineer impact what the singer hears, and consequently, what the singer does. This means that the singer's auditory function and perception must be examined in direct relationship to vocal production. (p. 261)

The last sentence of LoVetri's statement is particularly relevant, as vocal damage is most likely to occur when the singer has difficulty monitoring their vocal output. Therefore, familiarity with amplification equipment should be considered essential in any training program for CCS.

For stylistic authenticity, CCS must maintain speech quality and speech phrasing across their vocal range, while achieving the necessary vocal volume to be heard over amplified instruments in poor acoustic venues. The development of a microphone voice technique (maintaining core tone while minimising subglottal pressure) and an ability to set-up, run and adjust PA equipment to establish an optimum acoustic environment for the voice is crucial to vocal longevity for CCS. This is especially true for professional CCS, whose performance conditions have to be managed against a 3- to 5-hour performance "call" broken into 45- to 50-minute "sets" with 15- to 20-minute "breaks" (Bartlett, 2010). For this group, all singing is produced over amplified instruments in a background of continuous white noise (i.e., general conversation and communication between patrons and staff in addition to noise created in food and drink preparation) and poor acoustic spaces (e.g., hotel function rooms, pubs, clubs, alfresco restaurants and other open air venues). Amateur CCS face similar challenges in noisy entertainment venues, such as Karaoke bars and dance parties, where they need to raise their singing and speaking voice levels to be heard over the continuous background noise (Yiu & Chan, 2003).

To protect and maintain their vocal health in these unfavourable environments, CCS must use P.A. equipment effectively through adjustments to the volume controls, the frequency band equalisation (E.Q.) and, if available, digital effects to create and balance the room acoustics. If these skills are not mastered, then CCS will increase their vocal volume through over production of muscle fatiguing and unsustainable subglottal pressure levels.

A Comparative View of Technique and Style-Driven Vocal Elements

The following is a brief set of comparisons to illustrate similarities and differences for the contemporary and classical genres in relation to vocal elements ranging from vocal training to general performance. The definitions have been mostly formulated from my own experiences; however, some of the classical definitions have been informed or reconstructed from the work of Chapman (2006) and Estill (1998). They are presented here to assist voice teachers to recognise and manage the realities of vocal production and performance demands for singers of contemporary commercial styles.

1. Training

Contemporary

Within the bounds of good technique and vocal health, the aim of contemporary singing is:

- to condition the instrument to be flexible across the necessary vocal range, employing a variety of onsets, resonances and stylistic elements to achieve the desired style-driven aesthetic; and
- to enhance the singer's vocal production while nurturing individuality both in tone and presentation.

Classical

The aesthetic, technical and stylistic demands of classical singing require a consistency of vocal production. The aim is, for example:

- to condition the vocal instrument to be extensive in range;
- to be able to create and maintain consistent acoustic resonance across the vocal range; and
- to create a tone which is consistent, beautiful and emotionally-expressive.

2. Alignment

Contemporary

Alignment and balance must be achieved within the context of motion, as the singer moves, dances, holds an instrument, such as a guitar, or sits/stands at a piano. Regardless of style, it is vital to develop correct spinal alignment, paying special attention to the alignment of the head.

Classical

In the classical context the singer often stands still, with a notable exception being opera performances. Alignment and balance must be established within a singer's stance.

3. Breathing

Contemporary

The breath point is not governed by the written music notation or phrasing. As in speech, phrasing and emotion dictate where the breath is taken. Generally, this is where any punctuation mark is possible. Breath should not usually be taken within a word, or where it might break a spoken phrase.

Classical

Generally, the breathing points are set within the music arrangement, with no improvisation permitted. Legato phrasing demands that breath be taken at the end of the grammatical phrase with the occasional breath at the half-way or comma point.

4. Vibrato

Contemporary

Generally, style authenticity demands mostly straight tone (i.e., speech), but vibrato is permissible at the ends of phrases or long held notes, except in rock styles where straight tone is applied exclusively. A contemporary singer may choose not to use vibrato or may choose to allow vibrato to occur naturally as a by-product of balanced breath flow and vocal fold action.

Classical

Vibrato is considered an essential element of beautiful singing and is allowed to occur naturally, as a by-product of balanced breath flow and vocal fold action. The degree of vibrato is dictated by the period of the composition (e.g., bel canto, Baroque).

5. Resonance

Contemporary

Resonance options constantly change, depending on the stylistic qualities and effects inherent in the composition. The first formant (F1) has marked strength and a high second (F2) formant is desirable. The singer's formant (F3) is not as necessary as all contemporary styles are performed with the assistance of live sound reinforcement. As CCM is mostly presented in less than ideal performance environments (e.g., poor acoustic venues, background noise, electrified instruments), longevity and vocal health are dependent on the quality of live sound reinforcement (P.A., microphone).

Classical

Resonance remains fairly constant, no matter what type of classical repertoire is sung. Classical singers need to develop the singers formant (a clustering of the third, fourth and fifth formants) in order to produce volume without injury to the vocal instrument, yet be able to be heard above an orchestra while singing acoustically.

6. Tone

Contemporary

As in classical singing, a strong core tone is desirable. If this is present the singer's natural voice, enhanced by a skilful use of breath support and clear diction, produces an authentic contemporary tone. Individuality is paramount, therefore style elements, such as breathiness, glottal stroke and attack, can be utilised as effects. Uniformity of tone colour is not important and may be considered style-restrictive. Larynx position will change according to range, emotional expression (driven by the lyrics) and the stylistic demands of the song.

Classical

The larynx is usually low and relaxed for uniformity of tone. Tone is extremely focused with no breathy or harsh tones. All volume gradations and tonal colourings are produced by a sustained, regular breath flow and a stabilised larynx position.

7. Registration

Contemporary

Female contemporary singers have to develop a tessitura at an octave below their classical counterparts. In pop styles and jazz/ blues, female singers must be able to stay in speech quality (a thyroarytenoid [TA] dominant mechanism) with lower register production taken past the second passaggio to Bb4. This is a critical area of registration for the female contemporary singer. If the singer is employing a loud, bright, straight tone, this is referred to as *belting.* Belting should not be considered as chest voice in the traditional sense of low larynx/wide pharynx. Female singers of Broadway music theatre are often called on to maintain shortener dominance to D5 or Eb5

— this is referred to as *Broadway belt*, This style demands a higher larynx position, a significant engagement of the aryepiglottic sphincter and a narrower vocal tract than would be desirable in classical styles. If speech quality is maintained over a lighter tone, with some release to vibrato at the end of long held notes, a *belt/mix* will be produced. At this register transition, a smooth coordination to upper register (cricothyroid dominance [CT]) is desirable, unless the singer chooses to use the register transition as a stylistic effect (yodel, flip, breathy tone etc.). In this case, the TA/CT shift is purposefully audible. Speech quality must be maintained across and through all registration shifts.

Classical

Beauty of tone is paramount. A unified vocal quality must be maintained across pitches and vowels. There should be no perceptual change of timbre from one register to another. Lowered larynx and open throat (pharynx) must be maintained across a singer's range to achieve this consistent tone production. Female singers maintain CT dominance across their range with reference to Fach.

8. Vowels

Contemporary

Speech vowels and vowel mixes (diphthongs) are necessary to produce and maintain speech quality (AH, A, EE, I, O, OO). Style authenticity may require vowel distortions. Pure vowels are used to focus pitch, but are modified to enable speech quality and accents.

Classical

Classical style demands consistency of timbre across the vowel spectrum (best achieved through the practice of Italian vowels). Vowel mixes are used when appropriate to the language of the song (e.g., Italian, German, French etc). Full bodied, rich timbre carried through the vowels conveys beauty and evenness of tone.

9. Diction

Contemporary

Clearly articulated consonants are essential to maintain speech quality and to assist rhythmic phrasing. However, to assist optimum microphone technique, consonants may be modified; for example, to maintain a relaxed speech quality "p" is produced as "b" at the beginning of words, and, "t" is modified to "d" especially at ends of words. Speech vowels (often produced as diphthongs, e.g., my life = mah-ee lah-if) are necessary to sustain a contemporary sound. However, the front or open vowel of the diphthong is emphasised, unless dialect or characterisation is involved (e.g., Australian accent in bush and country songs, Cockney dialect as in *Oliver* or *My Fair Lady* and American country and western styles). As with classical singing, vowels become modified in upper register singing.

Classical

The tessitura of the repertoire impacts lyric intelligibility (diction). Consonants are less articulated and vowels less distinct as they become modified in high register singing. Clarity of diction is dependent on registration and the inter-relation of fundamental frequency (Fo) and the first formant (F1). Vowels become less distinct as Fo rises beyond the normal range of F1 (e.g., coloratura).

All styles

Good singing is grounded in the communication of meaning. As well as inflection, tone colour and dynamics, diction plays a vital part in conveying the meaning. Singers talk to an audience every time they perform. Stories, characters, emotion, mood and dialogue are presented through song.

10. Interpretation and Vocal Freedom

Contemporary

Singers have complete freedom to express and develop their own style. In many cases, the song is allowed to find its own flow, texture and aesthetic meaning by an individual singer's interpretation and articulation of general outlines rather than specific directions for melody, pitches, rhythm, tempo and dynamics. For example, improvisatory elements, such as ad lib sections or syncopation of the voice with other instruments, are especially important for singers of jazz styles with the sung line being chordal in emphasis rather than melody based, while R&B singers may use the "rave" (sequences of connected notes within the scale of the chord) and melissmatic runs. Many of these specific style elements have been used by singers to create style fusion compositions (e.g., pop with R&B elements, country with pop elements, pop with jazz influences, etc).

Classical

Strict, score-bound music representation is the tradition. Singers are tied to Fach, the composer's intentions and the musical style of the period.

11. General Performance

Contemporary

- Movement/dancing is expected in contemporary style performance.
- Persona often overlays a singer's entire output, and a song is delivered from the context of the persona.

Classical

- Little or no body movement except in opera performances.
- The composition determines both persona and context for the classical singer.

Summary

This snapshot of voice production and performance realities for CCS highlights the need for pedagogy to fit the genre, one that recognises that produced vocal tone, registration and sound qualities inherent in commercial singing styles differ greatly from accepted, western classical-music standards. The possibility of enduring vocal health for CCS requires a thorough investigation of all aspects of their performance lives rather than a convenient attribution of voice damage to singing style. The diverse and less than optimum performance environments, specific characteristics of vocal production, style-driven vocal effects and embellishments, physical and social relationships for singer/band and singer/audience interaction, are a reality for CCS and must be recognised, addressed and managed through a training system that is engaging and genre relevant. Research of vocal technique in classical singing has provided bountiful information for that significant genre. However, its unabridged application to contemporary commercial styles may lead singer exponents of those styles to avoid training that they consider irrelevant, or worse, to develop a vocal technique that is inappropriate and deleterious to their vocal health.

Modification to accepted thinking and practice does not mean a surrendering of the basic principles of healthy vocal production. Basic goals pursued by the classical vocal field over the past 300 years (i.e., the development of technique and theory to improve practice and maintain the beauty of the sound) have been and continue to be a noble enterprise. However, for many teachers the general shift of audiences away from western classical music to popular, commercial music styles challenges the integrity of traditional techniques when applied to training for CCS. Indications are that this audience shift will continue, simultaneously driving student demand for a relevant pedagogy where vocal individuality (i.e., a singer's "own" sound) is applauded, and style driven techniques are developed in keeping with the ever-changing audience aesthetic in a commercially-driven marketplace.

References

Bartlett, I. (2010). *Sing out loud, sing out long* (Unpublished DMA thesis). Griffith University, Brisbane, Australia.

Batza, E. (1971). Vocal abuse in rock and roll singers: Report of five representative cases. *Cleveland Clinic Quarterly*, *38*, 35–38.

Burns, P. (1986). Acoustical analysis of the underlying voice differences between two groups of professional singers: Opera and Country and Western. *Laryngoscope, 96,* 549–554.

Chapman, J.L. (2006). *Singing and teaching singing: A holistic approach to classical voice.* Abingdon, UK: Plural Publishing.

Edwin, R. (2000). Apples and oranges: Belting revisited. *Journal of Singing, 57*(2), 43–44.

Edwin, R. (2002). Belting: bel canto or brutto canto? *Journal of Singing, 59*(1), 67–68.

Estill, J. (1980). *Compulsory figures for voice: A user's guide to voice quality, level two, six basic voice qualities.* Santa Rosa, CA: Estill Voice Training Systems.

Estill, J. (1997). *Compulsory figures for voice — level two, six basic voice qualities.* Santa Rosa, CA: Estill Voice Training Systems.

Estill, J. (1998). Belting and classic voice quality: Some psychological differences. *Medical Problems of Performing Arts, 3*(1), 37.

LoVetri, J. (2008). Contemporary commercial music. *Journal of Voice, 22*(3), 260–262.

LoVetri, J. (2002). Contemporary commercial music: More than one way to use the vocal tract. *Journal of Singing, 58*(3), 249–252.

McCoy, S. (2004). *Your voice: An inside view.* Princeton, NJ: Inside View Press.

Miller, M.K., & Verdolini, K. (1995). Frequency and risk factors for voice problems in teachers of singing and control subjects. *Journal of Voice, 9*(4), 348–362.

Ng, S.S. (2006) *Filipino bands performing hotels, clubs, and restaurants in Asia: Purveyors of transnational culture in a global arena* (Doctoral dissertation). University of Michigan, Ann Arbor, MI.

Osborne, C. (1979). The Broadway voice: Part 1, Just singin' in the pain. *High Fidelity, 28,* 57–65.

Osborne, C.L. (1979). The Broadway voice: Part 2, Just singin' in the pain. *High Fidelity, 29,* 53–65.

Radionoff, S.L. (2006). Artistic vocal styles and techniques. In M. Benninger & T. Murry (Eds.). *The performer's voice* (pp. 51–59). San Diego, CA: Plural Publishing.

Sataloff, R.T. (1997). *Professional voice: The science and art of clinical care.* San Diego, CA: Singular Publishing Group.

Shutte, H.K., & Miller, D.G. (1993). Belting and pop, nonclassical approaches to the female middle voice: some preliminary considerations. *Journal of Voice, 7,* 142–150.

Spivey, N. (2008). Music theatre singing … let's talk. Part 2: Examining the debate on belting. *Journal of Singing, 64*(5), 607–611.

Sullivan, J. (1989). *The phenomena of the belt/pop voice.* Denver, CO: Logos Ltd.

Thalen, M., & Sundberg, J. (2001). Describing different styles of singing: A comparison of female singe's voice source in "classical", "pop", "jazz" and "blues". *Logopedics Phoniatrics Vocology, 26,* 82–93.

Thurman, L., Klitzeke, C., & Hogikyan, N. (2000). Cornerstones of Voice protection. In L. Thurman, & G. Welch (Eds.): *Bodymind & voice: Foundations of voice education* (pp. 646–656). Collegeville, MN: The VoiceCare Network.

Timmermans, B., De Bodt, M., Wuyts, F., Boudewijins, G., Peeters, A, & Van de Heynig, P. (2002). Poor voice quality in future elite vocal performers and professional voice users. *Journal of Voice, 16*(3), 372–382.

Titze, I.R. (1994). *Principles of voice production.* Engelwood Cliffs, NJ: Prentice-Hall.

Wells, B. (2007). On the voice — belt technique: Research, acoustics, and possible World Music applications. *Choral Journal, 46*(9), 65–77.

Wilson, P. (2003). Sinful modern music: Science and the Contemporary Commercial Singer. *Australian Voice, 9*, 12–16.

Yiu, E., & Chan, R. (2003). Effect of hydration and vocal rest on the vocal fatigue in amateur karaoke singers. *Journal of Voice, 17*(2), 216–227.

■ ■ ■ ■ ■ ■ ■ ■ ■ ■

Chapter 15

Developing Vocal Artistry in Popular Culture Musics

Diane Hughes

For effective singing of popular culture musics (PCM), the development of vocal artistry is essential. Based on reflective practice, observations and research, this chapter discusses accumulated pedagogical understandings, considerations and strategies to facilitate the development of vocal artistry. In the context of PCM, embodiment and the physicality of contemporary vocal performance are discussed. This includes appropriate vocal technique, microphone technique, stance, movement, gesturing and stage presence. Pedagogical strategies for facilitating embodied performance are proposed, together with the development of expressive musicality and stylistic integrity. The relevance of originality and vocal creativity is outlined. An active listening process is fundamental to vocal expressivity and creativity in PCM where the singing voice is rarely heard without the application of a form of technology. In a live performance, the singing voice is typically heard through the use of sound reinforcement. In recorded formats, the singing voice is often framed in a complex series of compilations and manipulations. In these contexts, the singer's voice is converted from acoustically formed wavelengths into a series of electrical signals. The resultant sound is no longer singularly representative of the embodied instrument. The singer's ability to "own" and understand vocal sound, or at least having been afforded the skills to mediate vocal sound with influencers, is considered in the context of vocal proprietary. This chapter details pedagogy to facilitate the development of vocal artistry and, in doing so, provides the foundation for the teaching of singing in PCM in the 21st century.

Encompassing both mainstream and alternative styles, popular culture musics (PCM) is a term that is inclusive of all musical styles in popular culture. It is introduced in this discussion, and is viewed as an embracing term. It eliminates potential confusion stemming from the use of the term "contemporary", broadens the narrowness of the term "pop" and lessens the connotation of music as "commodity", as not all musical styles or performances are "commercial" in their primary intent. In doing so, it acknowledges the diversity of musical styles in popular culture. Within the overarching PCM context, each musical style contains its own characteristics and integrity. Some styles emerge from existing styles; others are a fusion of two or more styles. Incorporating reflective practice, observations and research, this chapter presents accumulated pedagogical understandings, considerations and strategies relevant to the development of vocal artistry in PCM. While the effective singing of any particular style requires an understanding of specific stylistic nuances, it is essential that interrelated key components are also implemented. Embodiment, originality, reflection, active listening and vocal proprietary are the key components discussed individually and progressively throughout this chapter.

Reflective Practice, Observations and Research

Reflective practice, involving both reflection and reflexivity, has been included in my teaching methodology for over two decades. Entering the teaching profession from a performance background at a time when only limited vocal pedagogy training opportunities existed, it was imperative to adopt strategies that have informed, developed and structured my teaching in PCM. When considering the ways in which reflection informs development of professional practice, there are several types of reflection (Fox, Martin, & Green, 2007; Schön, 1987) and levels of interpretation in reflection (Alvesson & Sköldberg, 2000; Larrivee, 2008) that are relevant to my teaching. Schön (1987) distinguished reflection as being reflection "*on* action [emphasis in text]" (p. 26) when previous action is attentively considered and "reflection-*in*-action" (p. 26) when questioning or critically thinking within an action. Reflexivity or "the phenomenon of self-reference" (Rooney, 1999, p. 738) may originate through actively engaging in reflection-in-action. Examples of these types of reflection used in my own practice include analysis of a past performance (reflection-on-action), consideration of the way I am currently singing a phrase (reflection-in-action) and incorporating my reflective thoughts into singing that phrase differently (reflexivity).

Early in my performance career, the singing training I received from classical pedagogues facilitated an understanding of vocal technique. Using elements of reflexivity, where my "identity and lived reality" (Fox et al., 2007, p. 186) mirrored each other, I developed technical elements specifically suited to singing in PCM. My own practice of consistently engaging in active listening and reflexivity facilitates understanding of the musical and stylistic nuances evident in PCM. The contribution of reflective practice to the development of the pedagogical understandings, considerations and strategies presented in this chapter is supported by extensive study, observation and specific research projects. It is this combination that largely engendered the development of my own vocal artistry and provides the foundation for my teaching of singing in PCM in the 21st century.

Components of Vocal Artistry

The term artistry encompasses "the creative ability and skill of an artist, or the expression of this" (Rooney, 1999, p. 98). Given the evolutionary nature of PCM, vocal artistry characteristically involves individuality as evidenced through artistic inventiveness or vocal creativity. Inventiveness is clearly seen in varying stage persona and in image branding. Vocal creativity may be heard in the delivery of original phrasing, unusual vocal arrangements, vocal improvisation and ornamentation, variance in vocal tone and dynamic versatility. Aided by technical fluency, artistic expression may also be seen in performance prowess.

Vocal artistry includes qualities that are sometimes less tangible than audible or physical components. For example, stage presence is an elusive quality that is "hard to define" (Lydon, 2009, p. 28). It is a quality that may differentiate the technical performer from the artist. Stage presence, being more than charisma or being present in a performance moment, involves a number of factors, including performer confidence in both identity and ability. Howard (2008) notes that "presence is an authentic sense of self, and projection is an outward manifestation of it" (p. 97). The key components of vocal artistry discussed in this chapter as authentic representations of self are shown in Figure 15.1. While the existence of self-identity is acknowledged through reflection and active listening, embodiment and embodied performance entails individual presence. Expressivity is evident in both originality and vocal creativity. The ability to identify and convey one's own sound, that is, vocal proprietary, underpins vocal artistry in PCM.

Used as a noun, proprietary relates to individual possession, ownership or "the right of ownership, or something exclusively owned" (Rooney, 1999, p. 1509). Introduced in this discussion, vocal proprietary relates to the singer's ability to "own" vocal sound. In PCM, the application of technology to the singer's voice can modify the natural singing characteristics. Control of the resultant sound has the potential then to move beyond that of the

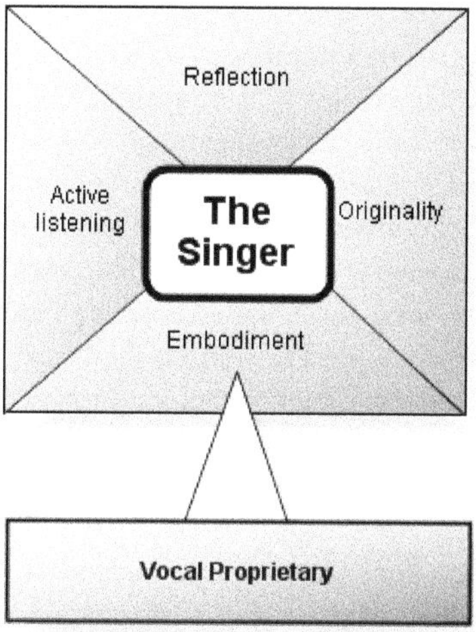

FIGURE 15.1

Key components of vocal artistry in popular culture musics.

singer. Vocal proprietary therefore includes a singer's understanding of vocal sound and of the different types of technology that may be applied to the voice in live and recorded formats. It also includes the capability of mediating a resultant sound with others. Without this, the transformed sound becomes the sole responsibility of other influencers — primarily sound technicians, recording engineers, producers and, at times, artist managers. While acknowledging that there are other factors that may compromise resultant sound, including substandard or malfunctioning equipment, facilitating understanding in vocal proprietary affords the singer greater control in most circumstances.

Facilitating Embodiment

In a broad context, embodiment requires collective expression within a "comprehensive whole" (Treffry, 1998, p. 505). On a deeper level, embodiment in singing involves a physical presence that is our whole being or our "neuropsychobiological selves" (Thurman & Welch, 2000, p. xxiii). Embodiment is therefore a connectedness that compliments expressivity and requires an assimilation of "the knowledge of the past in order to learn technique and discipline" (Mock & Way, 2005, p. 202). In essence, our voices are linked to our cultural and social identity, to our history and to our lived experiences (Thurman & Welch, 2000, p. xxiii). For novice and developing singers, embodied learning evolves through the acquisition of skills that foster ability, confidence and connectedness.

As the singing voice is a unique, embodied musical instrument, it requires the coordination of a number of anatomical, physiological and psychological elements. The acquisition of appropriate technical skills to aid this coordination is typically achieved through a combination of vocal exercises and repertoire. Exercises should be appropriate to the developmental stage and needs of each individual singer, and incorporate exercises for vocal warm-ups, those to address specific technical issues and cool-downs. To progressively prepare the voice for singing, warm-ups are essential and subsequent technical exercises are tailored to facilitate vocal development. Ornamentation and improvisation exercises, such as melismatic runs over simple chord progressions, are included to aid in the progress of musicality and expressivity skills. Instruction in pitch replication, dynamic variation, phrasing and melodic form are also targeted through vocal exercises. A series of cool-down exercises, designed to restore the voice to speech mode, follow periods of singing in lessons, practice or performance.

Recognising the uniqueness of each singing voice, individuality in artistic development and expression is fostered by vocal programs tailored to the needs and abilities of each student. It is the responsibility of singing teachers to vary the tessitura of the repertoire in student programs, as singers must avoid constantly reinforcing the same area of the voice. For those times when changing repertoire may not be possible, programs should utilise exercises to balance voice usage. While vocal exercises aim to minimise passaggio events and stabilise transition areas within the singer's vocal range, often the vocal delivery of PCM necessitates exaggerated transitions. At times, vocal expressivity will be enhanced with variations in vocal colour. Some variations, such as adding breath to the vocal tone or including emphasis through the use of hard onsets, should be used cautiously as artistic choices and not as the typical means of vocal production.

Singing in PCM requires the use of a microphone to aid, rather than hinder, resultant sound. Pedagogical strategies facilitate the use of a microphone, either hand held or placed in a stand, during lessons and in practice. Microphone management consists of implemented techniques that reduce the effects of plosive sounds, foster effective adjustment for dynamic variance, allow for changes in position and minimise the transference of handling noise. When the singer is proficient in microphone technique, the microphone becomes an unobtrusive extension of the singing voice or it is used with purposeful exaggeration.

The physicality of singing PCM extends to stance, suitable movement and to the use of gesture. While these aspects may be mentored, evaluations of visually recorded sessions and performances provide effective student feedback. Through visual playback, students are able to clearly see physical issues that affect or inhibit their performance. Movement, expected stagecraft in PCM, needs to suit the individual student and the repertoire being sung. Similarly, the use of gesture should be a natural reflection of expressivity and not something that is specifically devised or predictable. These aspects of embodied performance, when well executed, aid the stylistic integrity of singing in PCM. For example, the intensity executed in rock singing styles requires powerful movement and gesture. In comparison, indie folk singing often requires fluidity and naturalness.

Perceived presence in embodied performance may correlate to levels of confidence. However, connectedness in the presence of self, self-identity, is required for absolute presence in performance. Performance presence may be "intuitively" recognised (Dayme, 2005, p. 162), but what constitutes performance presence as an "objectively real quality" (Goodall, 2008, p. 3) is not so easily defined (Lydon, 2009, p. 28). In some personality types, performance presence may be inherent or partially inherent. For others, reflective practice has shown that confidence may be developed through physical, mental (visualisation) and performance practice. Presence also develops when there is a strong connection with repertoire that allows for honesty to be conveyed in performance.

Originality

The expressivity and evolutionary nature of PCM often requires singers to incorporate originality in learned ornamentation or spontaneously improvised words, sounds and phrases. Creativity may be expressed through unique vocal phrasing and accented words, as well as in the vocal tone and dynamics. Transposition and variation in instrumentation may also be heard in original interpretations. Creativity is evidenced in songwriting that characteristically stems from personal reflection and/or a confidence in self-expression. With a focus on chords and melody, creative songwriting skills may develop without traditional musicological training. However, such skills can be taught, and reflective practice and observation has shown that these skills may also be mentored through co-writing.

Reflection

The act of reflection is giving considered and detailed thought to events or processes. Reflective thought may be expressed in written or verbal form, in places of learning (lessons and practice) or in performance, or through active listening. Reflective expression and analysis aids the development of vocal artistry, so it is the responsibility of the singing teacher to ensure various forms of reflection are incorporated in student learning.

In a typical singing lesson, a student sings exercises, explores repertoire and is offered feedback. Learning tasks, established collaboratively, and guidance of student practice time are usually mediated during lessons. It is in the intervening time, between lessons and potentially isolated from teacher feedback, where the realisation of student goals may be attempted, reinforced, achieved or possibly negated. For the time between lessons, comprehensive teaching strategies require the inclusion of effective monitoring of student vocal activities. While underpinning teacher directed learning, maintaining a vocal journal, in which students are encouraged to be honest in their "reflective thinking" (Moon, 1999, p. 33), is one strategy for such monitoring.

Written Reflection

Structuring a vocal journal to promote and document student understanding is a useful tool in the learning and teaching of singing. In this context, the vocal journal becomes more than a vocal practice record. It documents an individual student program and student learning; it may also provide insight into student aspirations and achievements. For the beginning vocalist, the vocal journal records vocal practices in their frequency, duration and structure. It aids in establishing student vocal programs and, if student entries are diligent, the journal provides an accurate record of student progress. A vocal journal may also serve to monitor aspects of student vocal care and vocal health, and to potentially highlight issues requiring attention.

Preliminary research into developing a model for the vocal journal suggests that there is the capacity to stream the format of the vocal journal for varying levels of study that is suited to both pedagogical requirements and student learning. Kuit, Reay, and Freeman (2001) notes that it is beneficial to "formally identify categories of what to observe" (p. 136) in relation to journal content. Utilising an emergent process to develop the structure and implementation of the vocal journal relevant to levels of tertiary vocal studies, research findings reveal that maintaining a vocal journal may also facilitate student reflexive learning. Qualitative data was collected from tertiary students in the form of questionnaire responses to the purposes, benefits and format of maintaining a vocal journal (see Table 15.1). The sample was of 81 tertiary students (57% [annual cohort]) who voluntarily and anonymously participated in the preliminary study at an introductory level (n = 48), an intermediate level (n = 21) and an advanced level (n = 12).

At an introductory level, the vocal journal was structured to include the length and content of practice sessions, together with information on vocal progress. This structure was expanded for intermediate level students and included the documentation of a typical practice session or vocal program, individual development and weekly reflection statements. At an advanced level of study, students focused on reflection of their artistic development. While the majority of students (n = 52; 64.2%) reported that the vocal journal recorded and/or tracked their vocal progress, advanced vocal students (n = 5; 41.7% [advanced participants]) indicated that the process of reflection created and/or clarified singing intent, goals and artistry. The vocal journal was seen to facilitate engagement in reflexivity (n = 20; 24.7%), to focus areas requiring further development (n = 24; 29.6%) and to change perspectives (n = 16; 19.8%).

Verbal Reflection

In addition to written types of reflection, the inclusion of verbal reflection during lesson time may also aid artistic development. Reflective practice indicates that periodically prompting student reflective comment is a valuable

Table 15.1
Examples of Tertiary Student Responses to Maintaining a Vocal Journal

	Introductory	Intermediate	Advanced
Purposes	To maintain a log of practices, to show improvements in your voice, to show a teacher what you may be doing wrong or what you need to work on.	Keeping up regular practice and being responsible for your own learning.	To get into the habit of understanding our voices as more than just a voice; as a tool that we need to take care of and regularly analyse [our voices].
Benefits	Inspired me to practice; showed how I progressed.	It helps to jot down the progression of vocal development and also helps formulate sustained methods of assisting with things that need work. Focused.	Helps keep track of vocal health. In the beginning [the journal] helps you structure your practice and figure out where you are and where you want to be. Weekly reflection is the best as it sums up and helps you gain an understanding of yourself as a singer.
Format	I chose to handwrite mine, so I enjoyed the honesty of writing it.	I preferred the vocal program and weekly entries over each practice entries we did in the first session [introductory]. Second [intermediate] session's format gave better reflection and thought.	Goal [setting] beginning of semester/week and reflection following.

pedagogical strategy. Additionally, collaboratively (student and teacher) reflecting on performance adds depth to the student learning.

Active Listening

A singer's vocal identity is shaped primarily by one's anatomy, physiology and vocal technique. It is also shaped by how singers hear and perceive themselves. For all types of singing, the internally perceived vocal sound is different to the externally heard vocal sound. It is therefore beneficial for singers to understand and identify their external sound through auditory perception. This is typically achieved through actively engaging in listening to recorded or monitored vocal sound. In this context, active listening is a reflective process and involves a multifaceted approach to listening that incorporates vocal identity and perception, expressivity, creativity and proprietary. Active listening is a continual process for vocal artists in PCM.

Active listening is particularly relevant when any form of technology is applied to the voice or when sound engineering occurs. Sound engineering involves designing a resultant sound. In a live performance, the voice is usually heard through the use of sound reinforcement (amplification). In recorded formats, the singing voice is framed in a series of technical alterations and compilations. In these formats, acoustically formed wavelengths are converted into a series of electrical signals. The resultant vocal sound is therefore no longer singularly representative of the embodied vocal instrument. It is the singer's vocal identity and the reflective listening process that potentially enables continued "ownership" or management of a resultant vocal sound. Active listening in the learning process facilitates greater vocal proprietary and is fundamental to vocal artistry in PCM.

Vocal Proprietary

Singers of PCM need to be aware that the capturing of their voice in amplified and recorded contexts may result in their vocal sound being either inadvertently or intentionally altered. The resultant sound is dependent on production technology used to alter such things as dynamic variance (e.g., through the use of compression), duration (e.g., through the application of reverb or delay), pitch (e.g., auto tune) and frequencies (e.g., graphic equalisation). When applying graphic equalisation, engineered through boosting or reducing partial frequencies (low, mid and high), the singer's resultant sound may be very different from the natural vocal sound. Even different microphones may affect the resultant sound; not every microphone will suit every sound or situation (Crich, 2005, pp. 25–26). It is therefore advisable that a microphone is suited to the singer's natural sound (White, 1998) and the situation in which it is used.

The Use of Sound Reinforcement

Vocal pedagogy in PCM includes the use of sound reinforcement in ways to ensure that singers become familiar with its use. When sound reinforcement is used, the singer's voice is transferred to an amplifier as electrical energy. This energy is converted to the acoustic output heard through speakers. As Figure 15.2 shows, the front of house speaker output is usually directed towards the audience; the stage monitor output is orientated towards the stage. As the singer typically stands behind the front of house speakers, it is impossible for the singer to clearly hear the output directed towards the audience. Without monitors, the singer may hear, at most, reflected output that is possibly slightly delayed. Compound this with the level of on stage instrumental accompaniment and the singer will then have difficulty hearing their own voice. If a singer's auditory perception is compromised through inadequate monitor level, then the resultant sound is immediately affected. Most singers in this situation will sing too loudly, vocally tire and will often display pitch inaccuracies.

On stage monitors (foldback), or direct "in-ear" monitoring, allow the singer to hear their own voice. The monitor output may be set independently to the front of house output. This allows the singer to hear accompanying

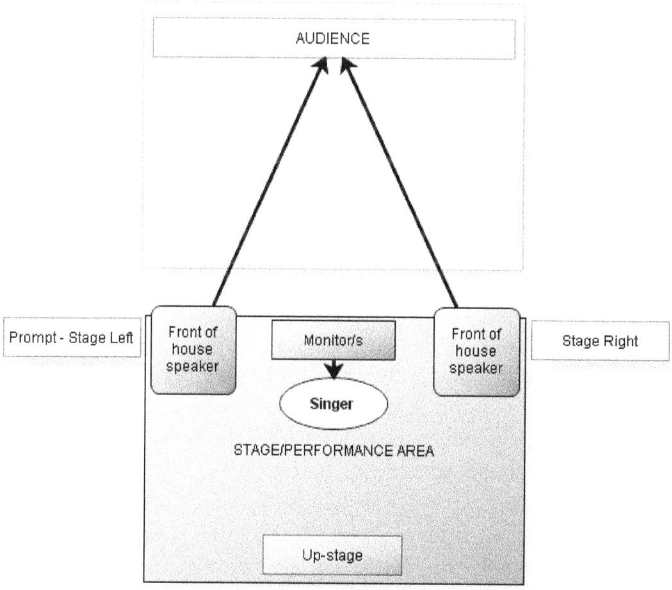

FIGURE 15.2

Output orientation in sound reinforcement.

instrumentation and their voice at differing levels suited to their performance requirements. As the resultant monitor mix of sounds (instruments and voice) may be different to the front of house sound, singers should also be encouraged to discuss the vocal sound heard in the front of house mix. Understanding sound reinforcement and its use aids vocal proprietary and fosters vocal artistry in a performance context. This understanding is exemplified in a soundcheck process.

A pre-performance soundcheck offers a level of control of resultant sound, but only if singers are familiar with how their voice sounds through their own auditory perception. In situations where the sound reinforcement equipment is operated by sound technicians, a soundcheck provides singers with an opportunity to request, if necessary, that levels and effects be adjusted so that optimum results may be achieved. It is ideal that this process occurs prior to the venue opening; although at times the process occurs in venues already open to an audience. Irrespective of the soundcheck context, singers are advised to sing through repertoire sections that display dynamic range. If the monitor feed is different to the front of house mix, then singers should try, at some point in the soundcheck process, to focus on reflected front of house sound.

Pedagogical Strategies

Singers need to develop strategies for different conditions (systems and venues) that facilitate optimum resultant sound. While much can be observed through watching and listening to other singers, a singer's understanding of sound reinforcement usually develops through its actual use. Pedagogical strategies must therefore include those to prepare and support the singer. Lessons may be structured to include a proportion of time spent on microphone work and the use of sound reinforcement. A good introduction for novice singers is to instruct on how to appropriately hold a microphone whilst singing, without the microphone being connected to an amplifier. Over time, holding and using a microphone must become ingrained for its effective use.

Singers should also become familiar with hearing the voice through sound reinforcement and monitors. Devising and structuring "soundcheck" workshops are particularly useful for developing singers. This type of learning situation is ideal as a cooperative event between the singing teacher, sound technician and students. It enables students to hear the application of graphic equalisation and various types of reverb on the voice. It also fosters an understanding of appropriate terminology that enables mediation with technicians to achieve the optimum resultant sound. With this type of training, and repeated experience, the soundcheck process becomes second nature.

In some performance settings, the responsibility for the set-up and operation of sound reinforcement lies with the singer and/or the accompanying musicians. Pre-performance practice in the set-up and use of sound equipment in various locations with different room acoustics is ideal. The active listening developed in this type of practice teaches singers how to optimise their resultant sound in a variety of conditions.

The Recording Context

Singers of PCM are increasingly more likely to record now than in previous decades, due to the proliferation of accessible recording options, including purpose built studios and "home" locations. With appropriate training, singers are able to maximise recording opportunities and much can be done in the pre-production phase to prepare the singer for recording. If a singer has an understanding of the recording process and the terminology typically used during recording, then the easier and more constructive the production phase is likely to be.

An understanding of the recording phases of pre-production, production and post-production aids vocal proprietary. Pre-production clarification in repertoire selection, instrumentation, form and stylistic nuances can reduce expensive recording time in the production phase. An understanding of recording discourse may alleviate potential miscommunication and add to the professional standard of the production (Porcello, 2004) and post-production recording phases. While recorded vocals should typically reflect honesty and embodied emotion, in contrast, and as Middleton (2006) describes, it is in recorded vocals that the singing voice "is separated from the [singer's] body" (p. 95). In this context, the recorded voice functions with independence and implies to the listener notions of gender, mood and intention. Therefore, vocal autonomy originates in the production phase. In post-production, it is possible for the singing voice to be interpreted by others who are unfamiliar with the singer. In this scenario, the resultant sound may be further removed from the singer. While there is the potential for this to occur, the deliberate application of technology on the recorded voice also allows scope for highly creative artistic choices. Creative intention may be planned in the pre-production phase. This may be developed during the recording phases and particularly during the mixing process.

Contemporary vocal pedagogy must therefore afford the singer the terminology required to effectively discuss and even negotiate the vocal sound throughout the phases of the recording process. Singers, although not typically present during mixing and mastering, should also have an understanding of the mixing process, tonal balance and placement of a voice in the final mix. Horning (2004), in relation to listening to engineered mixes, emphasises that the listening required involves "the ability to detect sounds embedded within a dense matrix" (p. 714). Reflective practice has shown that mediated mixing between engineer/producer and artist facilitates a higher level of artistic integrity and vocal proprietary, particularly in the early stages of artistic development. It also affords a deeper level of understanding. Fostering understanding in a singer's development enables subsequent insight. When professional, singers may aspire to work with specific producers to complement vocal artistry.

In a recording studio, constraints on time for both recording and mixing are typical. Instrumental tracks are often recorded and layered prior to the final vocal track. The recording studio, the physical space usually devoid of natural light, can present as being unfamiliar, dark and isolated. In this unfamiliar environment, a guide vocal is sometimes the singer's first introduction to the recorded sound. The function of a guide vocal track is typically to enable subsequent layering of instrumental tracks. As a vocal track, a guide vocal is sometimes a less than an ideal take, and for inexperienced singers, it can be confronting to hear the voice in playback. Subsequent vocal tracks may feature prominently in the playback "mix". Momentary "flaws" (White, 1998) that would possibly escape attention in a live performance may be clearly evident in playback. Striving for perfection or for the ideal vocal take may result in vocal fatigue and frustration. For these reasons alone, facilitating understanding aimed at achieving optimum recording results is imperative to vocal artistry.

Concluding Comments

Fundamental to the understandings and considerations presented in this chapter is the premise that singing ability develops over time (Welch, 2000). While all singers possess innate abilities, the development of vocal artistry in PCM is typically achieved through a program that combines exercises, repertoire, performance and recording. Formal and informal feedback, reflection and reflexivity, are essential to artistic development. The process of active listening, engaging in the use of sound reinforcement and understanding the recording process is paramount in achieving optimum resultant vocal sound. The key components and pedagogical strategies discussed in this chapter are the result of professional practice that includes performance, recording, composing, directing, teaching and research. As such, the pedagogical understandings are relevant in a variety of contexts and address the complexity of developing vocal artistry in PCM in the 21st century.

References

Alvesson, M., & Sköldberg, K. (2000). *Reflexive methodology: New vistas for qualitative research*. London, UK: SAGE Publications Inc.

Crich, T. (2005). *Recording tips for engineers: For cleaner, brighter tracks*. Oxford, UK: Elsevier Focal Press.

Dayme, M.B. (2005). *The performer's voice: Realizing your vocal potential*. New York, NY; London, UK: W.W. Norton.

Fox, M., Martin, P., & Green, G. (2007). *Doing practitioner research*. London: Sage Publications.

Goodall, J. (2008). *Stage presence*. London: Routledge.

Horning, S.S. (2004). Engineering the performance: Recording engineers. *Social Studies of Science [Special issue on sound studies: New technologies and music*], *34*(5), 703–731.

Howard, T.J. (2008). Improving stage presence. *Dance Magazine, 82*(12), 96–98.

Kuit, J.A., Reay, G., & Freeman, R. (2001). Experiences of reflective teaching. *Active Learning in Higher Education, 2*(2), 128–142.

Larrivee, B. (2008). Development of a tool to assess teachers' level of reflective practice. *Reflective Practice, 9*(3), 341–360.

Lydon, K. (2009). The "it factor". *Dance Spirit, 13*(8), 28–28.

Middleton, R. (2006). *Voicing the popular: On the subjects of popular music*. London: Routledge.

Mock, R., & Way, R. (2005). Pedagogies of theatre (arts) and performance (studies). *Studies in Theatre and Performance, 25*(3), 201–213.

Moon, J. (1999). *Learning journals: A handbook for academics, students and professional development*. London: Kogan Page Limited

Porcello, T. (2004). Speaking of sound: Language and the professionalization of sound-recording engineers. *Social Studies of Science [Special issue on sound studies: New technologies and music], 34*(5), 733–758.

Rooney, K. (Ed.). (1999). *Encarta world English dictionary*. Sydney, Australia: Macmillan.

Schön, D. A. (1987). *Educating the reflective practitioner*. San Francisco, CA: Jossey-Bass Inc.

Thurman, L., & Welch, G.F. (Eds.). (2000). Foreword: Sunsets, elephants, vocal self-expression, and lifelong learning. In *Bodymind & voice: Foundations of voice education* (Rev. ed., Vol. 1, Book 1, pp. xi–xxiv). Collegeville, MA: The VoiceCare Network, the National Center for Voice and Speech, Fairview Voice Center, Centre for Advanced Studies in Music Education.

Treffry, D. (Ed.). (1998). *Collins English dictionary*. Glasgow, UK: HarperCollins Publishers.

Welch, G. (2000). The developing voice. In L. Thurman, & G. Welch (Eds.), *Bodymind & voice: Foundations of voice education* (Rev. ed., Vol. 3, Book IV, pp. 704–717). Collegeville, MA: The VoiceCare Network, the National Center for Voice and Speech, Fairview Voice Center, Centre for Advanced Studies in Music Education.

White, P. (1998). 20 tips on recording vocals. *Sound on sound* . Retrieved October 16, 2009, from http://www.soundonsound.com/sos/oct98/articles/20tips.html

▪ ▪ ▪ ▪ ▪ ▪ ▪ ▪ ▪

Chapter 16

Jazz Improvisation: The Voice Teacher's Challenge

Wendy Hargreaves

This chapter discusses the difficulties singing teachers face in addressing one of the most cognitively complex musical skills. It presents six key learning areas for vocalists that were uncovered during the author's journey as a student, teacher and researcher of improvisation. This personal experience is combined with a discussion of recent literature and current data gathered from a landmark survey of Australian jazz performers. By addressing fear, engaging referents, fostering an ideas bank, developing a scat syllable vocabulary, redefining the vocalist's role and simply practising improvising, a framework is established for a well-rounded and effective curriculum. The key learning areas blend tried and tested methods of teaching instrumentalists with insight into the unique characteristics of singers. Examples of teaching strategies given in this chapter provide more detailed direction for those choosing this path. In all, a balanced examination of curriculum and strategies provides valuable tools and structure for voice teachers to boldly address the challenge of jazz improvisation.

Hearing the word "improvisation" conjures up one of the most excruciating memories of my life. Years ago I sang in a vocal jazz ensemble called "Scat". You would think with such a name its members would be competent in the art of vocal improvisation. Surprisingly, despite complex jazz arrangements and many scripted "shoo bee doo"s, we never actually improvised anything. Even our signature four bar scat solos were perfectly rehearsed and identical each time to the point where we could perform each other's.

One day at rehearsal, I foolishly confessed to our director that I didn't have a clue how to scat. To my horror, he asked us to stand around the piano and improvise over a blues progression. Everyone cheerfully obliged in turn until it came to me. Like a deer in the headlights, I stood there stunned and silent, completely unable to squawk out anything. "Never mind," he said patiently, and moved to the next singer. Around the circle it continued and each time it returned to me I stood motionless for four bars of hell. The director gave up after the ninth unsuccessful circuit and I died the death of a thousand voiceless screams.

Several years after that disastrous first attempt, I admitted I had some unfinished business with the art of vocal jazz improvisation. I began actively exploring the craft, first as a student, then teacher and later as a researcher. The progressive roles gave me insight into the craft from three different perspectives.

The purpose of this chapter is to present six key learning areas for the student of vocal improvisation, which I have uncovered through my journey. Personal experience will be combined with a discussion of recent literature and data, gathered from a study of Australian jazz performers, to explore how the key areas can be addressed by voice teachers. In particular, I will examine the unique needs of singers that are frequently overlooked in jazz education. Armed with these key areas and teaching strategies, voice educators can venture into the challenging world of jazz improvisation.

Defining Jazz Improvisation

A logical place to begin this discussion is with succinct definitions of jazz and improvisation. Unfortunately, this proves very difficult because like most constructs in the social sciences, the concepts are subjective and intangible. Those who attempt to define jazz commonly range in approaches from describing characteristics of rhythm and orchestrations, to eras and repertoire. Potter (2000) aptly summed up his frustration with the task by remarking, "just as you think you have stumbled on an author who has finally got it right, you realize that there are so many exceptions that the exercise is futile" (p. 53).

Likewise, those attempting to define improvisation encounter difficulties with the broad spectrum of opinions. Some argue every performance is an act of improvisation, including the strictest adherence to a detailed prescribed score (e.g., Gould & Keaton, 2000). Conversely, others deem that without significant deviance from the composer's written work during performance, improvisation has not occurred.

The heated debate over both terms seems to make hopeless any attempt at a definition combining them. There is however one reprieve. If the task is approached by examining the functional application of the words by those in society using them regularly, a definition can be derived which adequately meets the needs for this discussion.

Berliner's (1994) interviews with 52 American jazz musicians provides insight into their functional application of the terms. In this snapshot of the jazz community, the term *improvisation* is favoured in discussions of solos, which commonly occur after the first full presentation of the composer's tune (referred to as the chorus or head). In contrast, the term *interpretation* is applied when discussing how a performer alters the first rendition of the chorus. Interpretation is traditionally seen as an important tribute to the composer, where performers make artistic changes to the rhythm, melody, harmony or arrangement while keeping the melody's identity recognisable to an audience. The Australian perception of these constructs appears consistent with that of the American counterparts detailed in Berliner's work. In a survey of Australian jazz performers, 83% distinguished the terms the same way (Hargreaves, 2010).

It is unsurprising to find the adoption of these popular definitions is not favoured by vocalists. Improvisation is frequently cited as a characteristic of jazz (e.g., Coker, 1990, p. 4; Cooke, 1998, p. 12). If the vocal chorus is deemed to be interpretation, it removes singers from the status of "jazz musician". Granted, interpretation incorporates improvisatory skills, but I shall adopt the popular functional definition as it delineates the activity under discussion. Hence, improvisation throughout this chapter refers to the solos that commonly occur after the chorus, thus requiring vocalists to employ scat syllables to occupy the notes.

The Challenge of Teaching Improvisation

Before proceeding to the central discussion, it is also important to address the debate over whether it is possible to teach improvisation at all. Hickey (2009) argues that improvisation springs from a pre-existing natural disposition of freedom, creativity and intuition that can only be enabled and nurtured, not taught. I am of the pragmatic perspective that anything that can be learnt can ultimately be taught. By definition, learning occurs within learners. No one can go through this process for them, regardless of the subject matter. The role of the teacher is therefore to facilitate, broaden and/or hasten this process. From my experience, it is possible for a teacher to provide stimulus and guidance in improvisation, which achieves these goals.

Perhaps the argument on whether improvisation can be taught is a diversion from the real difficulty. How do you teach something that occurs almost entirely subconsciously? The speed of the act of improvising necessitates direction by the subconscious to produce fluidity (Johnson-Laird,

2002). This chapter will address this inbuilt conflict that arises time and time again throughout the examination of the six key areas.

Key Area 1: Addressing Fear

The first of the six key learning areas for the student of vocal improvisation identified in this chapter is addressing fear. The freedom permitted in improvisation allows the opportunity for some magical moments in performance. Conversely, the removal of the safety net of a prescribed composition also allows for some hideous disasters bordering on aesthetic torture. Like beginners in all artistic fields, early attempts are frequently clumsy and unskilful. Fear of failure is a natural anxiety to arise from what Campbell (1991, p. 23) identifies as one of the most cognitively complex musical skills to develop. The public nature of improvisation also means most failures are witnessed, which can compound performance anxiety.

Fear is unfortunately capable of seriously derailing improvisation. Noted vocal jazz educators, Stoloff (Wadsworth, 2005, p. 12) and Madura (1999, p. 5), both cite fear as the major blockage of attempts. Respected vocal improviser Mark Murphy (Pellegrinelli, 2001) demands in his workshop participants "get rid of your four letter word called 'fear'. You come to me, we're going to work on that first 'cause you can't open the doors until the fear is gone" (p. 408).

Addressing fear is an area in which teachers can offer significant guidance. No matter how closely singers observe another performer, they will not know the thinking processes that were adopted to overcome fear. Teachers, by contrast, can equip learners with cognitive strategies for meeting the challenge. Their guidance can unlock the gates of self-consciousness and encourage the flow of ideas that fear obstructs. Here are five strategies educators have adopted.

Strategy 1: Separating Self Esteem

Research by Dews and Williams (1989, p. 45) found the musician's self-esteem is frequently connected to achievement in performance. Students can, therefore, be advised to make a conscious effort to separate the two. Jazz pianist Werner (1996), recommends musicians have a "sense of self that is stable, durable and not attached to your last solo" (p. 42). Likewise, Evans (2003, p. 59) encourages the creation of a "constant self" to defend against the vulnerabilities to which performers are prone. Bonnetti (1997) and Rigby (2001) suggest protecting self-esteem with positive affirmations, constructive imagery, contingency planning, relaxation, meditation or prayer.

Strategy 2: Adjusting Personal Expectations

Berliner (1994) describes mature artistry in improvisation as "the artful handling of dissonance" (p. 252). Unfortunately, to reach this summit, one must first travel through the valley of artless mishandling. For myself, sounding awful was a difficult learning phase to revisit as an adult student. Combating this problem was as simple as adjusting my expectations and granting myself permission to sound dreadful. I found it a surprisingly empowering act. It recognises the process of learning to improvise is long and it is unrealistic to expect to sound good at the beginning. Just as Evans (2003, p. 57) suggests, realistic self-expectations of performance can result in maximum peace.

Strategy 3: Discouraging Judgement

The suggestion of lowering expectations can be complemented with another adjustment to thinking. Both Nachmanovitch (1990, p. 171) and Lebler (2006, p. 43) recommend a reduction of focus on reflection or judgement during performance, as it blocks flow. Their conjecture has been recently supported by Limb and Braun's (2008) study of how the brain operates during improvisation. Functional neuroimaging (involving a magnetic resonance imaging brain scan) was undertaken on six professional jazz pianists performing improvised and non-improvised music. Results showed that during improvisation, there is a general deactivation of the portions of the brain responsible for self-monitoring and inhibition.

Strategy 4: Connecting With the Fun

Engaging in music is not usually an unpleasant activity (with the possible exception of bagpipe recitals). Somewhere along the road to achievement, improvisation students may have disconnected from the fun of play. Nachmanovitch (1990, p. 42) deems play to be the "starting place of creativity". Connecting with the delight of exploration can be key to making experiments a positive experience. Diana Krall (Enstice & Stockhouse, 2004), noted jazz pianist and vocalist, recounted being advised, "Every time you sit down to play you should have the excitement of the red sparkle drum set" (p. 187). The delight of play can alone overcome fear.

Strategy 5: Do it

Perhaps the most obvious approach for accelerating confidence in improvising is to engage in the act itself. A succession of positive experiences (or at least harmless ones) can boost confidence and motivation. In the words of phenomenal vocal improviser, Bobby McFerrin (n.d.), "just do it". McFerrin revealed that during his own development, the "only thing I had to practice was getting over the fear of doing it". Voice teachers can be proactive in encouraging this process by ensuring time is set aside each lesson for just doing it.

It may be helpful for students "doing it" to have some sort of gradation in performance risk, beginning with becoming comfortable with accepting their unacceptable sounds in the privacy of their homes. This can progress to improvising in front of the teacher, then a group of students, a group of instrumentalists, a supportive public audience then finally a paying public or critical audience.

Another successful strategy I have utilised in group situations is to ask students to find their own space in a large room and improvise simultaneously to a single accompaniment. Everyone is too engaged in their own efforts to hear anyone else's voice. There is no perceived risk in the task and students are in the company of others who are participating.

Fear of improvising is not a problem unique to vocalists. The body's physiological responses can have negative consequences for all musicians. Excessive muscular tension, quivering hands and perspiration, for example, can create interference ranging from mild distraction to disabling behaviours. The problem for the singer is the vocal instrument is highly vulnerable to any physiological change. Strong fear reactions have a higher probability of impacting on the performance of the vocalist's apparatus than that of the instrumentalist. For example, a dry mouth may be uncomfortable for pianists, but creates a lubrication problem for singers. A player's hands may shake on the saxophone, but the metal instrument remains unaffected by tremor, unlike the organic composition of the larynx. While fear is an issue helpful for teachers to address with all improvising musicians, it seems particularly important to discuss it with singers because of the greater vulnerability of their instrument.

Not only do the physical manifestations of fear have deeper implications for singers than instrumentalists, but the sense of personal risk may be greater too. Improvisation is often described as a form of self-expression, thus exposing all musicians to a degree of personal criticism. It is worth pondering if there is a perception of even greater self-revelation for vocalists whose very instrument is housed within the body. As famous American jazz vocalist, Jackie Cain (Grime, 1983), observes, "An instrument is an extension of you. Whereas a voice is part of you, part of your being" (p. 123). Welch (2005) expounds, "Voice is an essential aspect of our human identity: of who we are, how we feel, how we communicate, and how other people experience us" (p. 245).

As part of postgraduate research, I explored this possible perception by surveying 209 Australian jazz performers regarding which musician they consider takes greater personal risk by improvising. The response showed 51% believed vocalists take greater risk, compared with 20% who nominated instrumentalists, 21% selected neither, and 8% indicated they didn't know

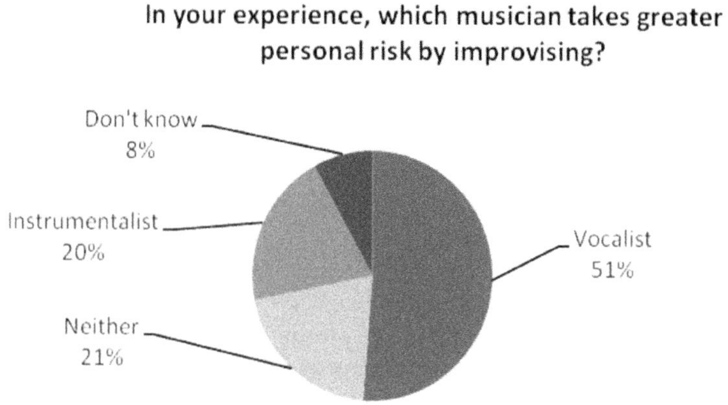

FIGURE 16.1.

The participants' response to a question on personal risk in Hargreaves' (2010) study of Australian jazz performers.

(Hargreaves, 2010; see Figure 16.1). The data suggests vocalists are perceived to be risking more.

This study and the previously mentioned collateral evidence found in literature shows fear is clearly worthy of being addressed in the curriculum of vocal improvisation. The potential for it to disrupt creativity, physiologically alter the vocal apparatus and impact on the psyche means it should not pass without discussion.

Key Area 2: Referents

The second and third key learning areas for vocal improvisers arise from the nature of how improvisation is generated. Improvisation is composition in real time, created in a linear fashion and performed at conception. The improviser's lack of opportunity for forethought and revision afforded to conventional composers can mislead us to think there is an absence of preparation in the craft. To the contrary, professional jazz musicians invest a great deal of time and effort in familiarising themselves with the musical tools of the jazz trade in the form of referents and an ideas bank. It is the understanding and incorporation of these two factors that provide the major distinguishing features between a professional's and a beginner's jazz solo. The next two key areas to be examined are therefore referents and the ideas bank, respectively.

Referents are parameters within the art form with which the performer creates a relationship. The harmonic progression of a song, for example, acts as a referent for melodic choices made during an improvised solo. Other elements, such as time signature, tempo and style, also specify variables to which the experienced musician responds. The nature of the relationship an improviser has with the referents is pivotal. How the performer chooses to move within these boundaries, or travel outside them, creates the excitement and interest of the performance. Nachmanovitch (1990) explained it in allegory: "Everything in nature arises from the power of free play sloshing against the power of limits" (p. 33).

The role of referents in improvisation is substantial, as outlined by Pressing (1998). They greatly reduce cognitive congestion by specifying parameters, from an infinite array of possibilities, for the musician to explore. An additional benefit Pressing notes is the provision of common boundaries which unifies a band of musicians.

A knowledge of referents is integral to the superiority of an improvised solo. Its usefulness alone justifies its inclusion as a key criterion in the teaching curriculum. For the novice, referents provide the much needed plan and tools with which they can begin to improvise.

As previously discussed, most of the cognitive processing that occurs during improvisation happens at a subconscious level, thus making the acquisition of referents challenging to teach. There are ways, however, the teacher can facilitate this learning by drawing conscious attention to the value, role and nature of referents. Some popular approaches take the form of lessons in jazz cultural history, repertoire extension, transcription, analysis and directed listening. Another common approach is teaching music theory. Theory can hasten and deepen familiarity with referents, make connections and provide a language for analysis and discussion. Studies have shown that those who have a better understanding of music theory are better improvisers (e.g., Madura, 1992). Unfortunately, vocalists may begin adult jazz education with a deficit in this knowledge. A study of Australian jazz performers indicated 88% of respondents observed from their experience that instrumentalists use music theory more frequently than vocalists when learning music (Hargreaves, 2010).

Aside from intentional focus, the learning of referents can also occur effectively through subconscious absorption. Ella Fitzgerald's total immersion in music as the vocalist for Chick Webb's band is commonly credited with equipping her with the skills she needed to manoeuvre through complex harmonic changes. As a young man, Jon Hendricks stood in front of a public jukebox, learnt and then sang all the songs in exchange for the nickel customers intended for the box (Reid, 2002, p. 103). It appears here that the learning of improvisation by these two celebrated jazz singers did not occur through the contribution of a teacher elaborating on referents. A reasonable argument could be made for ignoring teachers in place of an intense, self directed, immersion method occurring entirely by listening and imitating. If this was, however, the only way to acquire vocal improvisation skills, then the world may not have seen the arrival of other successful singers without the backgrounds of Fitzgerald and Hendricks.

On reflection, it would seem both methods, the conscious teaching and the subconscious absorption of referents, are complementary. The conscious approach can quicken the overall learning process of the craft, whereas the slower, subconscious internalisation is ultimately from where the improviser draws most material.

The role of educators in the conscious teaching of referents seems straightforward; to explain, elaborate, demonstrate and analyse the item under examination. For the subconscious absorption, the role is subtle. Teachers can illuminate the contribution the subconscious plays in improvisation and how important it is to feed it. This can be followed by the incorporation of strategies to ensure listening and imitation do occur in class and home time.

Key Area 3: The Ideas Bank

Closely related to the study of referents is the development of an ideas bank, which constitutes the third key area of learning. Within the boundaries of referents are infinite possibilities for musical movement. Referents can be used and reused in many different combinations and progressions, making them familiar yet unique. Essentially, the ideas bank is a repertoire of specific musical ideas that serve as possibilities for successfully navigating referents.

The ideas bank is discussed frequently in jazz literature under many different guises. It has been called the repertory storehouse (Berliner, 1994, p. 102) and incorporates terms commonly used in jazz literature, such as patterns, licks and clichés. Historical jazz recordings capture a myriad of pathways musicians have trodden while negotiating the variables (referents). Beginner improvisers start to accumulate their own personal collection of pathways ready for future use in improvisation. These musical cells, introduced consciously or subconsciously, can be germinated on their own or adopted and adapted from external sources. Stored together in the subconscious, they form the musician's personal ideas bank.

The ideas bank performs a very important function in improvisation. Like referents, it reduces conscious cognitive processing time and provides options, boundaries and stimulation for ideas. Teachers can present materials for developing the bank, but ultimately have no control over which ideas are absorbed by students. This is another instance where the unconscious nature of improvisation presents an educational challenge. As with referents, the teacher's role in this key area is to create an awareness of the bank, explain its function and elaborate on how ideas can be acquired for it. Teachers can acquaint students with numerous appropriate sources of ideas and then facilitate plentiful opportunities for subconscious absorption to take place.

There are many common methods jazz musicians engage to develop a bank. The imitation of a pre-recorded solo has been a staple used by generations (Berliner, 1994, pp. 95–97). Other approaches include studying pattern books, learning scales, and extensive listening to recordings and live performances. Investing time in each of these strategies assists students to develop their own personal bank, which is key to the success of improvisation.

Key Area 4: Scat Syllables

The fourth key area for the student of vocal improvisation is scat syllables. This discussion refers specifically to the acquisition, selection and performance of the phonemes vocalists use while improvising. Unlike instrumentalists, every vocal sound uttered by singers must be encased in vowels and/or consonants. It earns its place as a key learning area because of the integral relationship it has with a solo and the unique challenge it presents vocalists.

Aitken and Aebersold (1983, p. 8) complain that a poor choice of syllables alone can destroy an improvisation, yet the subject of scat syllables has not yet attracted much attention in jazz education. Many texts that address the topic offer a concise lexicon of popular syllables, and a suggestion to listen to other vocal and instrumental improvisers (e.g., Di Blasio, 1996, p. 6; Weir, 2001, p. 81). In contrast, Binek (2007, p. 130) made a substantial contribution by providing a detailed analysis of the language used in scat solos by six renowned vocalists. He concludes that syllabic choice is driven by the use of the initial consonants [b] and [d].

Another enlightening contribution to the topic of syllable selection is offered by Niemack (2004, pp. 35–39). Her informative summary traces the historical conventions. Niemack's discussion recognises that contrary to the vague advice "just sing anything", there are in fact some syllables that are more fashionable than others.

Niemack also discussed the difficulties her non-English speakers have in deciphering various spellings of scat syllables. In discussing this problem, Niemack indirectly reveals a convention of the preferred use of the English phoneme set in jazz, probably due to the origin of the craft in an English speaking country. It would explain the challenge non-English speakers face to sound authentic. For example, the phonetic palette of Japanese speakers, does not include [l] and thus reduces a staple from their range that Binek identified (2007, p. 130) as commonly used in the articulation of triplets.

In attempting to teach this key area, the conflict between the conscious and subconscious arises yet again. The enormity of decisions made during improvising necessitates that most occur subconsciously. The syllables flow much too quickly for each to be individually, consciously selected, particularly considering there are over 200 possible syllables in the English palette from which to select.

As with the ideas bank, the teacher's role can be to make students aware of existing conventions and to make conscious the possible syllabic options. Opportunities can then be provided for the subconscious absorption and development of a personal vocabulary through repeated listening to vocal and instrumental solos, imitation and personal exploration in practice time. A teacher's intervention can increase the breadth of knowledge of the key area and the speed of acquisition of skill compared with leaving students to fend for themselves.

A common method of teaching syllables is to provide a list with a few options for vocalists to adopt. There are criticisms of this method on the grounds it may induce an artificial quality to the solo, thus degrading the aesthetics. It is a fair comment to say teaching a set of common scat syllables may cause students to think the syllables will always be successful when superimposed on musical ideas. It fails to consider the natural acoustic qualities of a phoneme may be in conflict with the musical intention. For example, [n] will naturally sound more muted than the unobstructed syllable [di]. If you place these two articulations in this order on succeeding swing quavers, it will sound as if the second quaver is accented, highlighting the syncopation. The musical idea, however, may at times be better expressed with a ghosting effect, achieved when the first quaver is accented and the second muted. Hence, providing prescribed syllables is not the easy answer it appears to be.

Nonetheless, failure to give any syllable options can be alarming for students, particularly those unfamiliar with jazz. I attended one vocal jazz improvisation workshop where a participant pleaded forlornly, "Is there some sort of scat dictionary?" Niemack (2004, p. 37) and London (2007) also reported students asking for guidance on which syllables to sing.

Conscious teaching of syllables can expose students to a wide range of options and increase awareness of their impact. Perhaps the best teaching strategy is to present some common syllables as a starting place for beginners, but also explain what it is about the acoustic properties that make them preferable. This will help students to understand that the success of syllables is linked to their application. For example, the use of plosives [p], [b], [t], [d], [k] and [g] as the initial consonant in a syllable is desirable because of their clear, detached start. Niemack (2004, p. 36) likens the use of [b] and [d] to the tonguing action used by saxophonists and trumpeters.

Voiced fricative continuants, [v], [ð], [z] and [ʒ], provide an exciting blend of note and noise, whereas the unvoiced equivalents [f], [θ], [ʃ], [s] and [h], offer percussive textures. In contrast, the slow delivery of liquid approximants [j] and [w] allow gradual change in resonance, as the lips or tongue glide from one phoneme to the other. A lateral approximate articulated with the tongue has the ability to move quickly to slice up the components of a triplet as well as adding a soft muting effect without interrupting phonation. This is why [l] is an effective choice for the middle syllable. All vowels are suitable for carrying sustained tone, but knowledge that other voiced continuants, [m], [n] and [ŋ], can achieve the same purpose with a gentler quality, equips the singer with more options.

In addition to phonetic analysis, teachers can discuss the historic conventions of syllable choice. Such asides as "vo dee oh do" are reminiscent of the 1920s (Niemack, 2004, p. 35) and "shoo bee doo bee" belongs to the 1950s (Berliner, 1994, p. 254), illustrate the interesting role musical fashion plays in deciding what is acceptable. Another important lesson teachers can impart is the difference between articulating lyrics and scat syllables. Voice students may be accustomed to the importance of a clear delivery of lyrics for audience comprehension. In contrast, the jazz application of syllables does not require it and in fact instrumentalists complain overemphasised vowels and consonants distort the melodic line (Wadsworth, 2005, p. 110).

Key Area 5: Redefining the Role

The fifth key area under examination for the education of the vocal improviser is the perception of role in jazz performance. The incorporation of improvised solos in jazz has been evident since its early years. Predominantly, the role was fulfilled by instrumentalists, with few vocalists involved. The singer mostly functioned as the connection with the audience and interpreter of the lyrics during the choruses between the instrumental solos and orchestrated arrangements. The vocalist was also expected to be the visual focus of the band, and hence a great emphasis was placed on appearance, particularly for females who dominated the position (Dahl, 1984, p. 122). Interestingly, very little has changed in perceptions of the role over generations. Over 79% of Australian jazz performers who responded to a survey observed being visually appealing to an audience is still a function of jazz vocalists today (Hargreaves, 2010). Additionally, 75% deemed vocalists to have a stronger connection with audiences because they sing lyrics.

The data that are most pertinent to role, however, concern the perceptions of improvising vocalists by jazz performers today. A notable 97% of respondents believed an instrumentalist should be able to improvise a solo if requested during a performance, compared with a 67% expectation of a vocalist to do likewise. A marked difference between the groups is observed.

In a later question, respondents elaborated why they believed being a vocalist reduced the number of opportunities to improvise compared with instrumentalists (Hargreaves, 2010). Several respondents cited that average audiences are unfamiliar with scat singing, feel uncomfortable with it or simply "don't want to hear [it]". One musician wrote audiences "find scatting weird or they wonder if the singer has forgotten the lyrics". The comments of respondents on instrumentalists' reactions to scat singing were equally negative. Participants described vocalists who scat as infringing on the instrumentalist's "air time," not being "very good" and vocalists are not invited to participate, because it is assumed they can't improvise.

Unfortunately, this less cordial reception of vocalists in the role of improviser can undermine efforts to learn the craft. With instrumentalists intolerant of poor skills, audiences perplexed with unorthodox singing and vocalists struggling for acceptance, there is little reason to risk making a fool of oneself doing something instrumentalists and audiences may deem undesirable. In this key learning area, teachers can play a pivotal part in redefining the role of student vocalists to positively include improvisation. The perception of instrumentalists and audiences may be resistant to change, but by instilling scat singing as an acceptable and desirable skill, vocal students can be empowered to overcome external obstacles.

The voice teacher can demonstrate an expectation that students will improvise during lessons and that all attempts will be accepted. Listening to recordings of masters of the craft, such as Ella Fitzgerald and Mel Torme, promotes scat singing as a valid use of voice. Without this personal perception, students' efforts may be thwarted before they begin. Kurt Elling (Nemeyer, 2008, p. 158) provided a fabulous example of how a lack of knowledge of role expectations worked to his advantage when he attempted to scat. He recalled how everyone in the band was improvising solos so he simply jumped in for his turn because, while he didn't know what he was doing, he didn't want to miss out on the fun.

There is another pertinent reason why redefining the vocalist's role to include improvisation is beneficial. Eisenberg and Thompson's (2003) study of musicians found that participants who were intrinsically motivated produced more creative, complex and technically good improvisations than those who were less. With a near 100% expectation that jazz instrumentalists should be able to improvise (Hargreaves, 2010), it is reasonable to assume this necessity contributes to their motivation. By presenting vocal students with a similar necessity, teachers may strategically forge that valuable link between motivation and success.

Key Area 6: Do It

The final key learning area for vocal improvisers is a reiteration of an earlier point: Do it. The discussion has already identified how the act of improvising itself can build confidence and adjust perceptions to see it as a positive role for vocalists. There are other benefits that reinforce why engaging in the craft deserves its place as a key learning area. Researcher Johnson-Laird (1987, p. 86) argues that the best method to develop the necessary tacit skills for the unconscious generation of ideas is by the act of improvising itself. Another benefit is it develops skills for dealing successfully with mistakes. Berliner (1994, pp. 379–383) and Pressing (1984, p. 354) both cite making errors as an integral part of a craft that occurs in real time, leaving no opportunity to correct them. Learning to manipulate unintentional dissonance into consonance is a valued skill that is only mastered during the act itself.

Finally, responding to and engaging in the variables of live performance is a learning experience best afforded during improvisation. Berliner (1994) details the reactions of performers to changes in accompanying musicians, audience response, repertoire, arrangements, venue size and performance occasion. The experience of improvising a thousand times in a thousand different settings impacts positively on development.

The teacher's role in the key learning area of "doing it" is twofold. First, teachers can make students aware of the previously listed benefits and therefore the value of the act. Encouragement to "go away and improvise" is likely to have more relevance to students when coupled with a list of reasons why. The second major contribution of teachers is as facilitators of opportunities. Creating regular space in a lesson for uninterrupted, un-analysed improvisation gives students the experience of getting down to the task of doing it. It models for students the value of spending time purely engaged in improvising, without other agendas.

One strategy for elementary public performance that encourages students to improvise is to create an overlap in adjoining lesson times. Ask students to arrive 10 minutes early to sit in and listen to the last portion of the previous student's lesson, which is a live, uninterrupted improvisation. End of semester concerts are another popular approach. These can range from small, informal performances in front of friends and relatives, to an annual public concert in a larger, professional venue. Making a recording of an improvisation in "one take" is another way to encourage "doing it". It mimics the pressure of a public performance. The recording method can vary from the use of amateur equipment to a professional studio, yet achieve the same results.

Brisbane-based jazz singer and teacher Ingrid James established her own strategy. In 2001, she began the hugely successfully Jazz Singers Jam Nights to complement her studio teaching with a "professional education" (I. James, personal communication, January 15, 2010). The event is currently held at the Brisbane Jazz Club every fortnight before a paying audience. James designed it so singers would have the opportunity to network with other musicians, learn the skills of band leading and the art of performance. Ultimately, the experience serves to develop a more skilled and professional local jazz singing community.

Jazz Singers Jam Nights take a more structured format than the name suggests. Singers volunteer in the weeks prior to the event, pre-select their two performance songs and arrive on the night with charts for the hired accompanying trio. From this point, the event reflects the more spontaneous nature with the singers and instrumentalists performing the songs without prior rehearsal, and responding to the organic nature of live performance. The jam nights were not specifically created for improvising vocalists, but those who choose to incorporate it in their performance are welcomed and encouraged. It has proved to be a remarkably positive and successful venture.

Beyond each of the strategies mentioned for fostering engagement in improvisation, teachers can also encourage students to explore avenues on their own in the music industry. Pursuing gigs, talent quests, karaoke nights, joining bands, playing for friends and busking all instigate their own performance opportunities, with more chances to gain experience in the sixth key area: Do it.

Conclusion

The improvising vocalist presents a considerable challenge to voice teachers due, in many ways, to the subconscious nature of the craft. It seems the inadequate "just sing anything" approach is ready to be replaced by a considered syllabus. By addressing fear, engaging referents, fostering an ideas bank, developing a scat syllable vocabulary, redefining the vocalist's role and simply practising improvising, the vocal student will be on the way to a well-rounded, effective education in improvisation. These six key learning areas blend tried and tested methods of teaching instrumentalists with an insight into the unique challenges for singers. A detailed curriculum could not be given in the space of a single chapter, but these broad categories provide a curriculum framework, and the examples of teaching strategies give direction for those choosing this path. The contribution of motor learning and the challenges of audiation merit further investigation as possible additional key areas in the future. At this point in time, however, more research is required before their inclusion.

This chapter has sought to combine the personal experiences of students and teachers to provide insight into the teaching of vocal jazz improvisation. The survey of Australian jazz performers (Hargreaves, 2010) provided data to reflect on the current perceptions and experiences of the Australian jazz community. One particular statistic from the study, which I have withheld until now, is probably the most important of them all. A telling 85% of participants found Australian instrumentalists to be superior at improvisation to vocalists. It is too simplistic to believe addressing the six key learning areas is enough to rectify the imbalance. There are greater forces at work worthy of more research and future discussions. In the meantime, the key learning areas and teaching strategies addressed here provide the valuable armour and direction for voice teachers to boldly address the challenge of jazz improvisation.

References

Aitken, G., & Aebersold, J. (1983). Vocal jazz improvisation: An instrumental approach. *Jazz Educators Journal, 1*(1), 8–10, 73.

Berliner, P. (1994). *Thinking in jazz.* Chicago, IL: The University of Chicago Press.

Binek, J. (2007). The art and craft of scat singing and melodic alteration. In D. Spradling (Ed.), *Jazz singing: Developing artistry and authenticity* (pp. 77–131). Edmonds, WA: Sound Music Publications.

Bonetti, R. (1997). *Taking centre stage.* Sutherland, Australia: Albatross Books.

Campbell, P. (1991). Unveiling the mysteries of musical spontaneity. *Music Educators Journal, 78*(4), 21–24.

Coker, J. (1990). *How to listen to jazz.* New Albany, IN: Jamey Aebersold.

Cooke, M. (1998). *Jazz.* London: Thames and Hudson.

Dahl, L. (1984). *Stormy weather: The music and lives of a century of jazzwomen.* London: Quartet Books.

Dews, B., & Williams, M. (1989). Student musicians' personality styles, stresses and coping patterns. *Psychology of Music, 17,* 37–47.

Di Blasio, D. (1996). Scat singing: Imitating instruments. *Jazz Educators Journal, 28*(5), 33–35.

Eisenberg, J., & Thompson, W. (2003). A matter of taste: Evaluating improvised music. *Creativity Research Journal, 1*(2 & 3), 287–296.

Enstice, W., & Stockhouse, J. (2004). *Jazzwomen : Conversations with twenty-one musicians.* Bloomington, IN: Indiana University Press.

Evans, A. (2003). *Secrets of performing confidence,* London: A & C Black Publishers.

Gould, C., &w Keaton, K. (2000). The essential role of improvisation in musical performance. *The Journal of Aesthetics and Art Criticism, 58*(2), 143–148.

Grime, K. (1983). *Jazz voices.* London: Quartet Books Limited.

Hargreaves, W. (2010). *National survey of jazz instrumentalists and vocalists.* Unpublished survey, Queensland Conservatorium, Griffith University, Brisbane, Australia.

Hickey, M. (2009). Can improvisation be 'taught'?: A call for free improvisation in our schools. *International Journal of Music Education, 27*(4), 285–299.

Lebler, D. (2006). The master-less studio: An autonomous education community. *Journal of Learning Design, 1*(3), 41–50.

Limb, C., & Braun, A. (2008). Neural substrates of spontaneous musical performance: An FMRI study of jazz improvisation. *Plos One, 3*(2), 1–9.

London, A. (Speaker). (2007). *Sing along with Ella: The key to vocal improvisation.* (CD Recording No. IAJE07-062). West Palm Beach, FL: Onsite Recording.

Johnson-Laird, P.N. (1987). Reasoning, imagining and creating. *Council for Research in Music Education Bulletin, 95*, 71–87.

Johnson-Laird, P.N. (2002). How jazz musicians improvise. *Music Perception, 19*(3), 415–442.

Madura, P. (1992). Relationships among vocal jazz improvisation achievement, jazz theory knowledge, imitative ability, previous musical experience, general creativity, and gender. *Dissertation Abstracts International, 53* (12) 4245A.

Madura, P. (1999). *Getting started with vocal improvisation.* Reston, VA: MENC — The National Association for Music Education.

McFerrin, B. (n.d.). *Bobby McFerrin: Solo improvisation.* Retrieved from http://www.bobbymcferrin.com/solo_bobby.php#

Nachmanovitch, S. (1990). *Free play.* New York: Tarcher Putnam.

Nemeyer, E. (2008). Interview: Kurt Elling. *Jazz Improv, 8*(1), 156–159.

Niemack, J. (2004). *Hear it and sing it!* New York: Second Floor Music.

Pellegrinelli, L. (2001). An unsung tradition: Teaching instrumentalists to sing. *Jazz Education Guide, 2001/2002*, 44–50.

Potter, J. (Ed.). (2000). *The Cambridge companion to singing.* Cambridge, UK: Cambridge University Press.

Pressing, J. (1984). Cognitive processes in improvisation. In W.R. Crozier & A.J. Chapman (Eds.), *Cognitive processes in the perception of art* (pp. 345–363). Amsterdam: Elsevier Science Publishing Company.

Pressing, J. (1998). Psychological constraints on improvisational expertise and communication. In B. Nettl & M. Russell (Eds.), *In the course of performance: Studies in the world of musical improvisation* (pp. 47–67). Chicago: University of Chicago Press.

Reid, K.I. (2002). An exploration of the lineage of jazz vocal improvisation through the analysis of representative solos by Louis Armstrong, Ella Fitzgerald, Jon Hendricks, Mark Murphy, Kevin Mahogany and Kurt Elling. *Dissertation Abstracts International, 63*(11), 3786A.

Rigby, D. (2001). *Singing for fun and healing.* Moorooka, Australia: Merino Litho.

Wadsworth, C. (2005). Pedagogical practices in vocal jazz improvisation. *Dissertation Abstracts International, 65*(12), 4504A.

Weir, M. (2001). *Vocal improvisation.* Advance Music.

Welch, G. (2005). Singing as communication. In D. Miell, R. MacDonald, & D. Hargreaves, (Eds.), *Musical communication.* Oxford, UK: Oxford University Press.

Werner, K. (1996). *Effortless mastery.* New Albany, IN: Jamey Aebersold Jazz Inc.

Chapter 17

Teaching the Contemporary Worship Singer

Daniel K. Robinson

The singing community comprises a vast array of singers. The Contemporary Worship Singer is a relatively new member of this community. Noland (1999) surmised that 30 years ago the assumption would be that music ministry meant you sang in a choir. The church singer today plays a different role to that played by singers before 1970. Bob Kauflin in Worship Matters (2008) noted that "I don't think anyone back then had any clue how the thinking, structure, and practices of the church would come to be dominated by worship music and worship leaders" (p. 51). Little research has been conducted into this specialised field and as a result the activities and needs of this group are widely misunderstood. Furthermore, as Dawson (2005) commented, "At best the church singer has been exposed to classical [voice] pedagogy, which does not equip them for 'crossover' demands of the contemporary commercial styles most commonly practiced in their church environments" (p. 3). For the purposes of this chapter, the Contemporary Worship Singer is defined as coming from the Protestant Christian tradition and the scope of musical repertoire under consideration will cover hymns as well as the modern praise and worship chorus. Specifically, this chapter will concern itself with Australian Contemporary Worship Singers, their culture, environment and task. The intention is to provide an introductory insight into the process of training this unique singer.

Australian Worship Styles

The nature of music within the church service has been formed over centuries of transition, transformation, conflict and creativity (Webber, 1994; White, 2000; Wilson-Dickson, 1992). The history of church music is linked closely to church history itself and is strongly influenced by monastic traditions, dating from Pope Gregory the Great in the 6th century. Among others, Guido D'Arrezzo, (995–1050) Martin Luther (1483–1546), John Calvin (1509–1564) Johann Sebastian Bach (1685–1750) and John Wesley (1703–1791) made significant contributions. Internal influences of church doctrine, debate and denominational formation have played a role in shaping and defining what is witnessed in modern churches.

In Australia today, denominations can be broadly associated with particular styles, but individual churches can often select one outside of their denominational norm. As Duncan (2009) commented, "someone who visits various churches is likely to experience as many worship 'styles' ... as there are churches" (p. 99).

Five main worship styles are employed in Australian churches: Liturgical, Traditional, Contemporary, Blended and Charismatic/Pentecostal. Each of these worship styles has distinctive attributes that affect the Contemporary Worship Singer in different ways. Other worship styles (such as the Emerging Worship style) have enjoyed wide use in the United States, but the scope of this chapter is on the five styles that have wide acceptance throughout Australian churches. Of these, it is also important to recognise that American worship liturgy incorporated Charismatic/Pentecostal under the definition of Contemporary. Although this trend is developing in Australia, there are still observable distinctions between the two styles, and they will be addressed as separate entities here.

Defining Worship Styles

The Liturgical worship style is the oldest and most conservative of the five worship styles. The label 'liturgical' should not be misinterpreted as synonymous with the term liturgy. Liturgy or leitourgia, from the Greek *ergon* ("work") and *laos* ("people"), refers to the involvement of the people (Dawn, 1995). The Liturgical style follows a highly structured format that historically finds its roots in the Roman Catholic Latin Mass, and predominantly uses hymns interspersed throughout the overall service. Denominations that are often associated with the Liturgical style of worship include Lutheran and Anglican.

The Traditional style of worship is similar to the Liturgical style in its conservative nature, but does not use dedicated forms of liturgy, such as the Anglican Prayer Book for Australia. Duncan (2009) noted that "the principal concern of this approach is not with the circumstances of worship for their own sake but for the sake of the elements and substance of worship, and for the sake of the object and aim of worship" (p. 110). The Traditional style also predominantly uses hymns, but in a less structured yet reasonably predictable fashion. Denominations usually associated with the Traditional style include Presbyterian, Salvation Army and Wesleyan Methodist.

A third worship style, Contemporary, is best defined by its use of songs (hymns and choruses) interlaced with scripture and prayer to form a thematic progression that often culminates in the sermon. Horness (2004) described the use of music in Contemporary worship as using "modern instrumentation (e.g., guitars, drums, synthesisers, percussion, horns), contemporary musical styles (e.g., rock, jazz, hip hop, rap, gospel), and freshly written or arranged songs (both new choruses and fresh treatments of traditional hymns)" (p. 102). Unlike the Liturgical and Traditional styles, which intersperse hymns throughout the liturgy, the Contemporary worship style will often assemble the songs together to form a 20–30 minute set of congregational singing, but will intentionally interrupt the flow of the songs with church announcements and other activities. The Contemporary style of worship can often be experienced in Baptist, Church of Christ and Uniting churches.

A fourth worship style, Blended worship, seeks to merge both the Liturgical and Contemporary worship styles. Blended worship brings together the "content of the liturgical movement and the experience of the contemporary movement[s]" (Webber, 2004, p. 178). In so doing, the nature of the service holds to a structured form, but employs a variety of stylistic features. Lawrence and Dever (2009) explained that gatherings of this nature "would include a mix of hymns, choruses and praise songs that span the centuries" (p. 223). The Blended worship style is less likely to be aligned with particular denominations; churches whose historical affiliation lies with either the Liturgical or Contemporary styles might conduct a dedicated service that employs the ideals of the Blended worship style. Some Anglican churches, for example, may hold a Sunday night church service that will also employ the stylistic features of a Contemporary worship style, while holding to the narration of Anglican liturgy.

The final major Australian worship style is that of the Charismatic/Pentecostal movement. Perhaps best associated with the Assemblies of God denomination, the Charismatic/Pentecostal style is a blend of two distinct movements from the 20th century. Modern Pentecostalism is founded in the American Azuza Street revival of 1906, whereas the Charismatic movement "emerged in the 1960s and has made, with its openness to the Spirit, an undeniable impact on worship around the world" (Webber, 1994, p. 122). The

Charismatic/Pentecostal worship style encourages the least structured liturgy of all the worship styles, and although hymns are sometimes used, the predominant musical style used is the modern worship chorus. Segler and Bradley (2006) referred to the charismatic model as a "free-flowing praise, Old Testament worship pattern, accommodation of contemporary culture, use of popular sounding music, embrace of technology, and emotional appeal" (p. 47).

The Charismatic/Pentecostal worship style has become the stylistic choice for many of Australia's largest churches, including Hillsong, an Assemblies of God church based in Sydney, New South Wales. Due to the Hillsong Conference and its publishing arm, the Charismatic/Pentecostal worship style has also become the stylistic choice of many smaller sized churches (Evans, 2002). Referring to the influence of the Hillsong movement, Tim Hanna (2005) wrote, "Without a doubt, the greatest influence on the worship life of the Australian church in the last ten to fifteen years, especially from a musical point of view, is Hillsong" (p. 33).

Defining Worship Form

Each of the five worship styles displays a mode of delivery that can be classified as either liturgical, thematic or flow (Liesch, 1996). These three forms recognise the manner in which the order of service moves. To avoid further confusion with the use of the term liturgical, we will substitute its use with the term "modular" when describing worship forms. Thus, the three worship forms become modular, thematic and flow. Simply, a worship service displaying a modular form will move through distinct modules of worship with no one module regarded more highly than another, though the Eucharist (communion) is often seen as a climactic point. Typically, the Liturgical and Traditional worship styles will present a modular format. The thematic form moves the worshipers along a designated topic which often culminates in the sermon and this form is generally observed in the Contemporary and Blended style. Generally seen in the Charismatic/Pentecostal style, the flow form emphasises a progression of worship using mostly sung choruses and will "insist on the freedom to abandon plans and follow the Spirit" (Liesch, 1996, p. 80).

We can further categorise the five main worship styles used throughout Australia under two headings, conservative and contemporary. The Liturgical and Traditional worship styles are readily recognised as conservative in nature, whereas the Contemporary and Charismatic/Pentecostal worship styles can be classed as contemporary. These two labels, conservative and contemporary, could equally align with modern vocal pedagogy, which observes the delineation between classical (conservative) and contemporary.

The Blended worship style straddles both conservative and contemporary practice, much in the same way music theatre spans both modern classical and contemporary vocal pedagogy. Indeed, when deciding on the best vocal instruction for the Worship Singer, classical or contemporary, the informed vocal pedagogue should inquire as to the student's worship setting. Characteristically, the church singer who attends a Lutheran church service is involved in a Liturgical service with a modular form, and this singer will possibly benefit from classical voice instruction more than contemporary pedagogy. Alternatively, singers who are engaged in a Pentecostal church will almost certainly be best served by contemporary vocal instruction due to the flow form configuration of the Charismatic/Pentecostal style and the nature of the repertoire.

Being able to determine both style and form is the first step in working with the Contemporary Worship Singer. The title Contemporary Worship Singer generally denotes those singers who are involved with either the Contemporary or Charismatic/Pentecostal worship styles that make use of either the thematic or flow worship forms. This is rarely categorical and informed singing teachers should use their discretion in the tuition of Contemporary Worship Singers.

Cultural Identity

The singers themselves clearly identify with particular styles of singing and worship. A recent national survey of Australian worship singers (n = 85 participants) conducted across 16 churches from seven protestant denominations (Baptist n = 30; Assemblies of God n = 19; Churches of Christ n = 15; Christian Outreach Centre n = 11; Christian City Church n = 5; Uniting n = 4; and Salvation Army n = 1) observed that singers identified their role across a range of definitions. Survey participants were asked what role their singing took in the worship service. Figure 17.1 shows the survey participants' responses.

Responses in the 'Other' category describe their roles in the worship service as:

- Lead the congregation to focus on God 14.3% (17)
- Personal worship 5.9% (7)
- Inviting the Holy Spirit/presence of God 4.2% (5)
- All of the above 3.4% (4)
- First three: 1.7% (2)
- Other 1.7% (2)

The diversity of definition is striking, as is the importance that the survey participants placed on their activity as worship singers. Over 85% of respondents considered their role as either 'Medium' (42.9%) or 'High' (42.9%) in

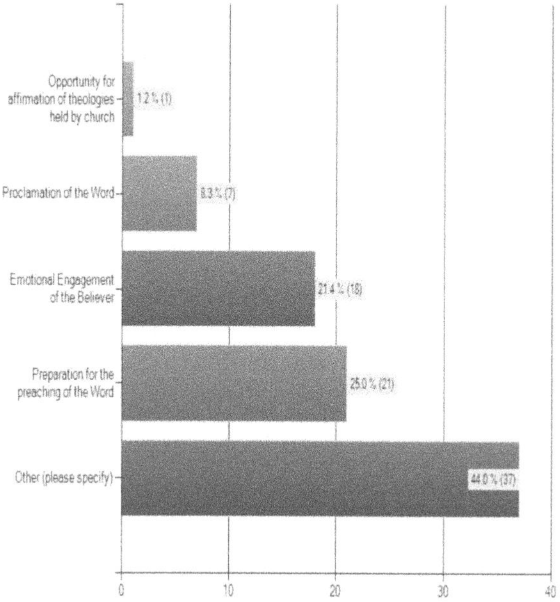

FIGURE 17.1

Range of definitions and titles.

the overall church service and 82.1% thought that the worship service (congregational singing) is of equal importance to the preaching of the Word (sermon). These findings confirm recent writings relating to the flow form of worship that acknowledge the slow decline of the significance of the sermon in relation to the rising popularity of congregational worship (Gilley, 2005; Kauflin, 2008; Kraeuter, 1996).

For centuries, music has been used as a means to conveying Christian theology (Wiersbe, 2000), but the recent rise of congregational singing as a dominant cultural factor has seen a reconstitution of singing and it's role in presenting theology. Traditionally, the belief system was enshrined in the lyrics. Recently, this has shifted and worshippers suggest that it is what is sung that determines what is believed. As Kauflin (2008) contended "Songs are de facto theology … 'We are what we sing'" (p. 92).

The recent attraction of worship, a term now synonymous with that part of the service traditionally known as congregational singing (Evans, 2002; Kimball, 2004; Parrett, 2005; Willis, 2007) has also led to a reconstitution of power within many church settings. Almost 70% of survey respondents believed that their worship team was a dominant group within the life and general activity of their church.

Of additional significance, 88.2% of survey respondents classified their singing as contemporary as opposed to pop, sacred or classical. When asked whether they would refer to themselves as a pop singer, the majority of respondents said "no" (85.9%). The Contemporary Worship Singer seems to be accepting of the term "contemporary" to designate musical style, but is quite eager to distance himself or herself from the title of pop singer.

Contemporary Worship Singers, although not ready as a group to call themselves a pop singer despite the "pop" nature of their vocal task, engage in a physically energetic vocal function that ultimately upholds, moreover, determines the theological position of their denominational affiliation; both through style and form. The weight of the responsibility carried by the Contemporary Worship Singer or the impact on their voices should not be underestimated.

Environmental Issues

Historically, church buildings were constructed to provide, among many considerations, a live acoustic that supported the unamplified instrumentation and human voice. Today's church buildings come in a variety of sizes and shapes, but most have been treated with soft surfaces, including carpet and cushioned seating. The modern worship space, with its dead acoustic environment, requires significant electronic amplification to support the presentation of both instrument and voice. This being said, "There's not usually enough funding available for such things as high-quality sound systems until it becomes apparent that there is a team capable of using such a sound system effectively" (Gibson, 2007, p. 1). In reality, the average size Australian church of 70 people (NCLS, 2002, p. 1) may never have the budget for purchasing a high-quality sound system and so many Contemporary Worship Singers are working with a low-quality sound system, and in the rare case, no sound system at all.

Marva Dawn (1995) highlighted a second impact of the modern church auditorium with its dead acoustic by noting, "... during hymns, members hear only themselves and the organ, because the sound of others singing is soaked up. Most people are embarrassed to sing alone, so they will sing with progressively less gusto until some might quit entirely" (p. 155). Dawn's observation accounts for the conservative liturgical service, which still uses the organ for instrumental accompaniment, but the sentiment is no less pertinent for the Contemporary and Charismatic/Pentecostal worship styles using instrumentation, such as keyboards, guitars and bass. A Contemporary Worship Singer's main role is to lead the congregation in singing. Any perceived retreat by the congregation can cause the Contemporary Worship Singer to engage more vocal effort in an attempt to entice participation and in turn, as Dan Lucarini (2002) observed, congregational members can be, "intimidated into silence by the great singers in the worship team 'belting it out' on the platform" (p. 114). This creates a nasty cycle of increased vocal loading, which can result in significant vocal wear and tear.

Most churches, regardless of their size or the quality of their sound system, require the Contemporary Worship Singer to use a microphone and this is reflected in the survey with 97.6% of survey participants using a microphone in their worship setting. William Gibson, in his book, *The Ultimate Church Sound Operator's Handbook* (2007), highlighted the simple mistakes church singers can make simply by holding the microphone incorrectly. All survey respondents indicated that they hold the microphones exclusively (54.2%) or in combination with microphone stands (45.8%). Gibson stresses the need for instruction of Contemporary Worship Singers in the area of microphone technique. Additionally, all Contemporary Worship Singers would benefit from purchasing their own microphone, as most singers in most churches use commonly shared microphones. This would enable the singer to regularly work on a microphone that best enhances the individual voice and avoid potential transfer of illness through shared equipment. A further technical skill that most Contemporary Worship Singers need to develop is the ability to work with a foldback system, as proposed by Gibson (2007)

> The monitor system, sometimes referred to as a foldback system, is designed to provide adequate musical mix for the musicians on stage. They need to hear what the rest of the singers and instrumentalists are doing so that they can accurately perform their portion of the whole performance. (p. 275)

The majority of survey participants indicated they have foldback of some kind, including monitors on the floor (74.7%), in-ear monitors (8.4%) or both (8.4%). Respondents are, for the most part, able to hear themselves clearly through the foldback system (see Figure 17.2).

This result might be due in part to 77.1% of survey respondent's churches having dedicated foldback sends for the singers. A dedicated foldback send allows the Contemporary Worship Singer to request an individual mix; that is, the singer might ask for more voice and less piano through a monitor placed closest to them. The degree of variability is determined by how many foldback sends the church might have. Contemporary Worship Singers should be instructed on what to ask for in their foldback mix. Roma Waterman, in her book, *The Working Singers Handbook* (2002), suggested, "A good rule to follow in most situations is to have as little instrumentation as possible in your wedge. This is so you can hear yourself more clearly" (p. 96).

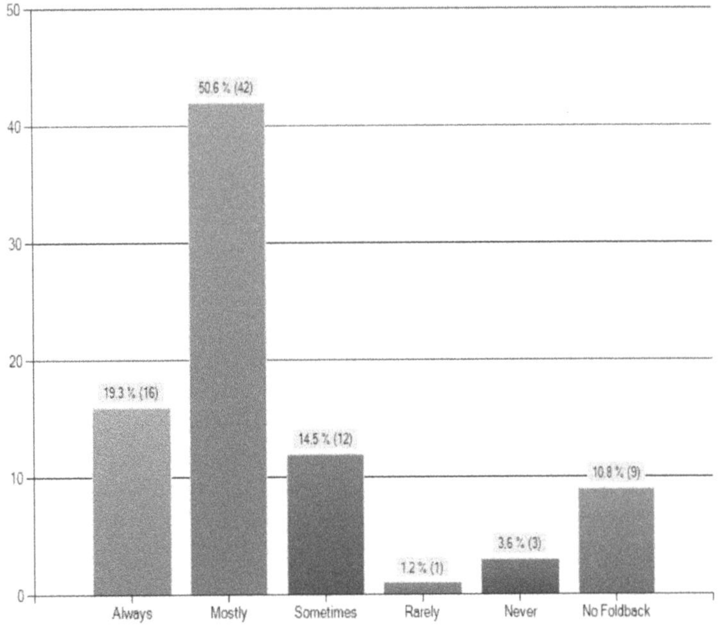

FIGURE 17.2

Clarity of foldback as perceived by the Contemporary Worship Singer.

When instructing the Contemporary Worship Singer, it is highly beneficial to have the student working on a microphone that is directed through a foldback wedge. This helps the student to develop the familiarity of their own voice through a foldback wedge, while refining their ability to request changes in the mix.

The Contemporary Worship Singer's physical stature on stage is also considered to be of some importance. Warren Wiersbe in *Real Worship* (2000) commented,

> All of the faculties of my body should be open to His blessing and available for His service. I should see to it that I am at my best on Sunday morning — and this might mean saying no to late night activities on Saturday evening. (p. 99)

A final environmental consideration is the unusual time at which most Contemporary Worship Singers use their voices and the duration of the worship set. Most churches conduct their services on a Sunday morning with some services conducted as early as 7 a.m.

Pat Wilson, in her book, *The Singing Voice: An Owners Manual* (2001) advised singers to "Get out of bed three hours before you need to use your voice ... and that goes for your speaking voice too" (p. 51). The general church service conducted at 9 am would therefore require the Contemporary Worship Singer, according to Wilson, to be up at 6 am on a Sunday morning. This is a challenge for Contemporary Worship Singers, who may find they are up late the night before.

The length of time spent singing is also significant. Dan Wilt, in his apologetic for contemporary worship in *Perspectives on Christian Worship: 5 Views* (2009) observed, "The 'worship' component of any given service in a contemporary worshipping community can vary widely, from 15 minutes to more than an hour. That segment of worship typically is set aside for singing song after song" (p. 173). This practice is distinct from that of the secular pop singer. The secular pop singer might sing up to four sets a night, with each set limited to a maximum of 50 minutes, thereby giving the singer necessary vocal and physical respite. The early morning starts and the extended worship set formats can create very real challenges to the Contemporary Worship Singer.

Teaching the Contemporary Worship Singer

Many established contemporary pedagogical ideals are suited to the Contemporary Worship Singer. As previously indicated, not all church singers require contemporary vocal tuition, but those singers who are engaged in Contemporary, Blended or Pentecostal/Charismatic worship styles with either thematic or flow forms are almost certainly best served with appropriate contemporary technique. The question then arises as to the best way to instruct the Contemporary Worship Singer in order to best prepare them for this specific vocal task.

First, Contemporary Worship Singers must be made aware of the significant vocal load that their role requires. Dawson pointed this out in his 2005 treatise, "In order for church singers to reach their full potential, it is vital that they become more aware of the vocal demands placed on them by their participation in both church worship and service to the church generally" (p. 4). Due to the amateur and voluntary nature of the Contemporary Worship Singer's role, singers often don't place necessary importance on matters such as lessons or warm-ups. "Pop singers may be particularly resistant to the suggestion of voice lessons, yet they are in great need of training" (Sataloff, 2006a, p. 12). While Contemporary Worship Singers do not regard themselves as pop singers and would not label themselves as such, they nonetheless sing pop idioms that are very much in keeping with their pop vocal colleagues. Lucarini (2002) recognised this when he reflects on his days as a Contemporary Worship Singer, "When I opened my mouth to sing, years of CCM-style [Contemporary Christian Music] vocals left me sounding too much like the rock musicians I once worked hard to imitate" (p. 36). In keeping with this observation, Contemporary Worship Singers are not dissimilar to other contemporary singers who require professional voice instruction.

Such comments could also be applied to the Contemporary Worship Singer, despite them not identifying as pop singers.

Only 57.7% of survey respondents indicated that they had received singing lessons with just 42.2% of those lessons taken over a period longer than two years. Chapman (2006) contended that "Some singers argue that after a certain point singing lessons are no longer necessary. In my opinion this is a foolhardy concept — unsupervised singers very rarely maintain their level of technical prowess" (p. 9). When considering Chapman's judgment, ongoing singing lessons for the Contemporary Worship Singer should be the optimal norm. The term "optimal" is used to qualify the ideal, because singing lessons are not always possible; personal circumstances or financial restrictions may place limitations on some, and accessibility is an issue for regional and remote areas of Australia. One survey respondent commented,

> Being out in the bush it is really hard to find adequate training, it is also from a coordinators perspective difficult to find singers who are eager to go beyond the training they get at rehearsals ... we are in the process of having separate training for singers at the rehearsal and encouraging them to warm up before they get to the service run through. We are in desperate need to resource to help the music directors to help there own singers [sic].

The respondent's comment leads us to a second consideration when training the Contemporary Worship Singer — vocal warm-ups. The pedagogue should not presume that vocal warm-ups or cool-downs are the standard practice of the Contemporary Worship Singer. Survey participants were asked how disciplined they were in the regularity of their vocal warm-ups (Figure 17.3).

Figure 17.3 suggests that irregularity is the norm for vocal warm-ups. Whilst the significance of warm-ups is still relatively under-researched (Sundberg, 1987), the process and benefits are widely acclaimed by recent literature (Dawson, 2005; Peckham, 2000; Robinson, 2002; Sataloff, 2006b; Sundberg, 1987; Waterman, 2002). Dawson (2005) specifically noted the unsatisfactory approach to vocal warm-ups by many church singers:

> Some singers considered [the] rehearsal as their vocal warm-up for the day while others stated that by rehearsing the least demanding songs first they were gradually warming the voice ... Such flippant approach to warm-up is insufficient to prepare the muscle system required for singing. (p. 60)

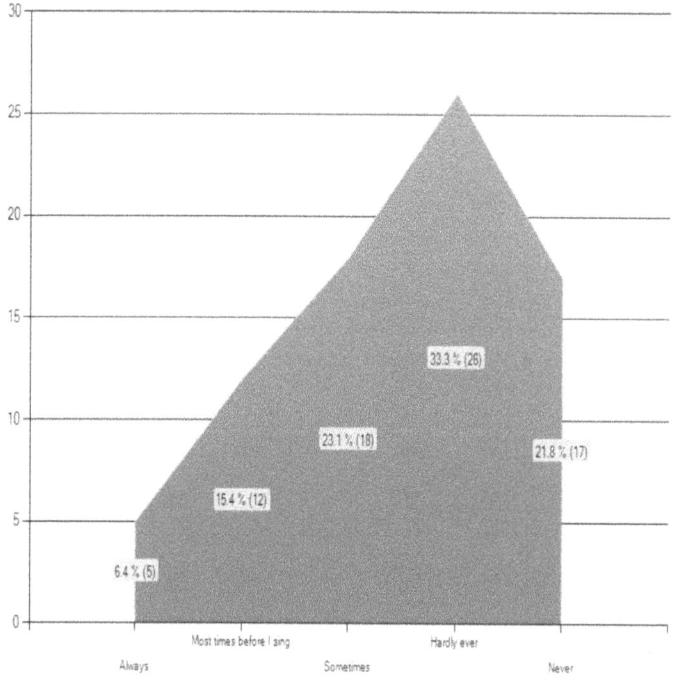

FIGURE 17.3

Regularity of vocal warm-ups..

In describing the content of their warm-ups (Figure 17.4) only 12.8% of respondents described their warm-ups as a rehearsed procedure. Dawson (2005) stressed the necessity of warm-ups for the Contemporary Worship Singer by stating, "An understanding and regular use of vocal warm-up would be one practice that could make a difference to the singers of worship teams in the charismatic evangelical church movement" (p. 64). It falls to the singing teacher to instruct the student in the discipline of warm-ups and cool-downs.

One positive result that will come from dedicated regular warm-ups and cool-downs is increased vocal stamina. As previously recognised, many Contemporary Worship Singers do not view their role with the necessary concern in such matters as lessons, warm-ups or vocal stamina.

> ... many performers of popular music are evanescent because they begin at an early age, some are poorly trained; they tend to work in emotionally over-charged atmospheres for long hours and they may "burn out" before they develop their full potential. (Dayme, 2009, p. 33)

Dayme's comments are pertinent when considering the longevity of Contemporary Worship Singers who should be encouraged to consider their

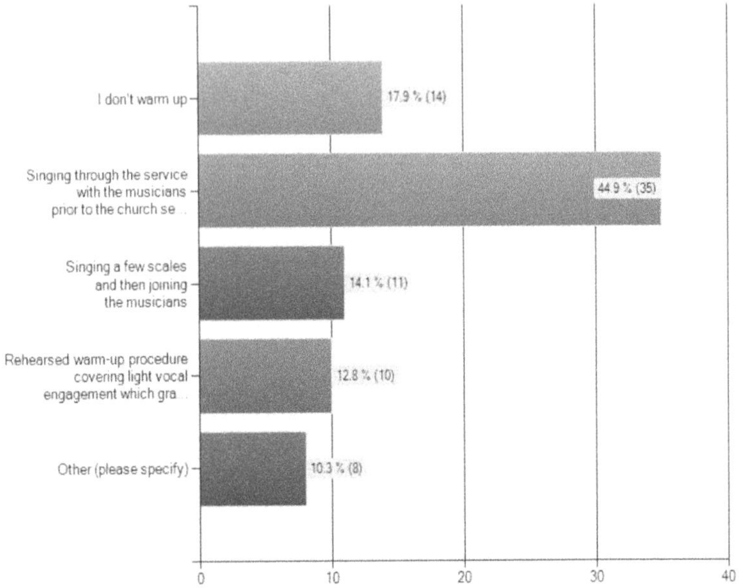

FIGURE 17.4

Content of the vocal warm-ups.

vocal condition beyond the next church service. This will interact with continued voice instruction, general vocal hygiene and the discipline of warm-ups and cool-downs.

While specific vocal exercises for training of the Contemporary Worship Singer are not included here, much of the technical work that is typical of teaching the modern pop singer is appropriate to the learning of healthy vocal skill for modern church singing. However, special attention should be paid to matters such as body alignment, the development of twang and belt, and general breath management principles described below.

When addressing alignment issues, both teacher and student should be mindful of the worship posture. "Many of the singers strain the front of the external laryngeal muscles by 'goose-necking'. This can be attributed to the 'worship posture" (Dawson, 2005, p. 7). Lifting the head and raising the chin maintain the worship posture. This poor postural positioning has been brought about by the use of data-projection of lyrics onto screens that sit above level eye sight, as opposed to the use of printed lyrics in hymnals (Basden, 1999). Twang and belt are both technical skills that should be developed by the Contemporary Worship Singer.

> Good ('true') belting is shared vocal fold activity between the thyroarytenoid (TA) and cricothyroid (CT) muscles. Bad belting is the overly thick vocal fold posture that most classical as well as most good CCM voice pedagogues try to change through systematic technical exercises. (Edwin, 2007, p. 326)

While not used exclusively, both twang and belt will help to reduce vocal fatigue while maintaining good resonance with strong volume levels, which are necessary for good microphone technique.

> Timid and inexperienced singers tend to shy away from the microphone, which makes the sound operator turn up the mic so that the vocalist can be heard, which increases the chance of feedback … A good singer with great mic technique will do most of the mixing for the sound operator. (Gibson, 2007, p. 279)

Contingent on the use of twang and belt is a measured system of breath management. Chapman (2006) stated, "There is always an ongoing monitoring of breathing, support, and postural alignment thereafter" (p. 55). Further discussion of appropriate methodologies when instructing the Contemporary Worship Singer in breath management fall outside the scope of this chapter, but as with most popular forms of contemporary singing, a supported and even flow of air is recommended.

The Contemporary Worship Singer will also benefit greatly if his or her singing teacher can teach the skill of singing harmonies. Whilst 71% of survey respondents indicated that the worship choruses/hymns sit comfortably within their vocal range, many survey participants indicated that they have stopped singing because a song was uncomfortable (34.6%). One solution engaged by Contemporary Worship Singers who have to sing material outside their comfort zone is the employment of harmonies. One survey respondent wrote,

> Many of the songs sung are in male dominant keys. So they can be either really high or really low. I will mime some notes that are too uncomfortable to sing if I cannot find a suitable harmony to compensate.

Generally, harmonies are sung within a block chord configuration with a simple soprano (melody), alto and tenor (SAT) construction. These harmonies are generally not transcribed and so the Contemporary Worship Singer must be able to sing the block harmony by ear. Singers who cannot sing harmonies by ear will generally sing the melody.

Finally, singing teachers who regularly teach the Contemporary Worship Singer should take the time to visit a variety of Christian churches in their local area. Even singing teachers who regularly attend their own local church will profit from visiting, viewing and experiencing the broad range of worship styles (Liturgical, Traditional, Contemporary, Blended, Pentecostal/

Charismatic) and forms (modular, thematic, flow) found in Australia. Some readers may hesitate at this suggestion, citing personal bias regarding religion; however, one cannot underestimate the value of triangulating informed reading, student perception and personal experience.

Conclusion

The Contemporary Worship Singer is an active member of the Australian singing community. Until recently, the unique role of this singer has been under-researched and poorly understood. The wide variety of Australian worship styles fuelled by two millennia of Christian worship history creates a diversity of vocal form not often seen within one subculture (White, 2000). As the 21st century unfolds, the Australian Contemporary Worship Singer will continue to evolve. So too will our understanding and refinement of method when training these singers and equipping them to best outwork their function within their unique culture and environment.

References

Basden, P. (1999). *The worship maze: Finding a style to fit your church.* Downers Grove, IL: InterVarsity Press.

Chapman, J.L. (2006). *Singing and teaching singing: A holistic approach to classical voice.* San Diego, CA: Plural Publishing.

Dawn, M.J. (1995). *Reaching out without dumbing down: A theology for worship for this urgent time.* Grand Rapids, MI: William B. Eerdmans Publishing Company.

Dawson, A. (2005). *Voice training and church singers: The state of vocal health of church singers of contemporary commercial styles in charismatic evangelical churches* (Unpublished dissertation). Queensland Conservatorium, Griffith University Brisbane, Australia.

Dayme, M.B. (2009). *Dynamics of the singing voice* (5th ed.). Vienna, Austria: SpringerWienNewYork.

Duncan, J.L. (2009). Traditional evangelical worship. In J.M. Pinson (Ed.), *Perspectives on christian worship: 5 views* (pp. 99–123). Nashville, TN: Broadman and Holman Publishers.

Edwin, R. (2007). What Richard Miller hath wrought. *Journal of Singing, 63*(3), 325–327.

Evans, M. (2002). *Secularising the sacred: The impact of Geoff Bullock and Hillsong church on contemporary congregational song in Sydney, 1990–1999* (Unpublished thesis). Macquarie University, Sydney, Australia.

Gibson, W.A. (2007). *The ultimate church sound operator's handbook.* New York: Hal Leonard Corporation.

Gilley, G. (2005). *This little church went to market: Is the modern church reaching out or selling out?* (2nd ed.). Webster, NY: Evangelical Press.

Hanna, T. (2005). *A strategy for evaluating and revitalising the corporate worship life of gateway church* (Unpublished Ministry Focus Paper). Pasadena, CA: Fuller Theological Seminary.

Horness, J. (2004). Contemporary music-driven worship. In P.A. Basden (Ed.), *Exploring the worship spectrum: 6 views* (pp. 97–116). Grand Rapids, MI: Zondervan.

Kauflin, B. (2008). *Worship matters: Leading others to encounter the greatness of God.* Wheaton, IL: Crossway Books.

Kimball, D. (2004). *Emerging worship: Creating worship gatherings for new generations.* Grand Rapids, MI: Zondervan.

Kraeuter, T. (1996). *Worship is...what?!: Rethinking our ideas about worship*. Lynnwood, WA: Emerald Books.

Lawrence, M., & Dever, M. (2009). Blended worship. In J.M. Pinson (Ed.), *Perspectives on Christian worship: 5 views* (pp. 218–268). Nashville, TN: Broadman and Holman Publishers.

Liesch, B. (1996). *The new worship: Straight talk on music and the church*. Grand Rapids, MI: Baker Books.

Lucarini, D. (2002). *Why I left the contemporary Christian music movement: Confessions of a former worship leader*. Webster, NY: Evangelical Press.

NCLS (2002). *What difference does congregational size make?* Retrieved from http://www.ncls.org.au/default.aspx?sitemapid=2278

Noland, R. (1999). *The heart of the artist: A character-building guide for you and your ministry team.* Grand Rapids, MI: Zonderan Publishing.

Parrett, G.A. (2005). 9.5 Theses on worship. *Christianity Today*, *49*, 38–42.

Peckham, A. (2000). *The contemporary singer: Elements of vocal technique*. Boston, MA: Berklee Press.

Robinson, D. (2002). *Contemporary worship leaders and their environments* (Unpublished dissertation). Queensland Conservatorium, Griffith University Brisbane, Australia.

Sataloff, R.T. (2006a). Common medical diagnoses and treatments in patients with voice disorders: Introduction and overview. In R.T. Sataloff (Ed.), *Vocal health and pedagogy: Advanced assessment and treatment* (2nd ed., pp. 1–16). San Diego, CA: Plural Publishing.

Sataloff, R.T. (Ed.). (2006b). *Vocal health and pedagogy: Advanced assessment and treatment* (2nd ed. Vol. 2). San Diego, CA: Plural Publishing.

Segler, F.M., & Bradley, R. (2006). *Christian worship: Its theology and practice* (3rd ed.). Nashville, TN: B&H Publishing Group.

Sundberg, J. (1987). *The science of the singing voice*. Dekald, IL: Northern Illinois University Press.

Waterman, R. (2002). *The working singer's handbook*. Kerrimuir, Australia: Roma Waterman.

Webber, R. (2004). Blended worship. In P.A. Basden (Ed.), *Exploring the worship spectrum: 6 views* (pp. 173–191). Grand Rapids, MI: Zondervan.

Webber, R.E. (1994). *Worship: Old & new* (Rev. and expanded ed.). Grand Rapids, MI: Zondervan.

White, J.F. (2000). *Introduction to Christian worship* (3rd ed.). Nashville, TN: Abingdon Press.

Wiersbe, W.W. (2000). *Real worship: Playground, battle ground, or holy ground?* (2nd ed.). Grand Rapids, MI: Baker Books.

Willis, K. (2007). A larger view of worship. *Interact, 18*, 1–2.

Wilson-Dickson, A. (1992). *The story of Christian music: From gregorian chant to black gospel; an illustrated guide to all the major traditions of music in worship.* Oxford, UK: Lion Publishing.

Wilson, P. (2001). *The singing voice: An owners manual* (2nd ed.). Strawberry Hills, Australia: Currency Press.

Wilt, D. (2009). Contemporary worship. In J.M. Pinson (Ed.), *Perspectives on Christian worship: 5 views* (pp. 143–217). Nashville, TN: Broadman and Holman Publishers.

Chapter
18

Showtime! — Teaching Music Theatre and Cabaret Singing

Pat H. Wilson

Singing teachers need to be familiar with current international criteria in order to prepare their students for the demands of professional music theatre and cabaret, because these fields have become worldwide industries, with broadly accepted standards, aesthetic requirements, audition protocols and employment conditions. Modern music theatre covers so broad a range of genres that it is now impossible to say that a singer has a "music theatre sound". Appropriate singing pedagogy is no longer all about "legit" versus "belt" — much more needs to be taken into consideration. Music theatre performance requires acting, singing and dance skills of equally high order (frequently simultaneously); appoggio often becomes an issue. Repertoire for music theatre is largely sung in English. Music theatre shows have long runs and often tour. Music theatre is now performed with sound reinforcement. Curiously, auditions for music theatre are rarely done with sound reinforcement. Cabaret is an art form for self-starters; in cabaret, the artist becomes auteur. The cabaret performer must have a strong entrepreneurial streak and a clear vision of what they wish to say in their show. Chamber music aspects of cabaret put a strong focus on the individual. There's no hiding in the back row of a one-man show. An advantage of cabaret is that it is so stripped-back that performers can frequently produce a show themselves, at minimal cost. The way teachers approach cabaret and music theatre genres should be informed by viewing a wide range of professional performances of music theatre and cabaret, both nationally and internationally. This gives singers and teachers alike benchmarks of excellence and inspiration to excel in these two rewarding music genres.

A faithful pedagogue (παιδαγωγέω), loyal to Greek tradition, will labour to lead each student entrusted to their care towards whatever learning experiences they think that student needs. A pedagogue is, after all, a leader. Thus, in music theatre and cabaret, the singing teacher needs a practical and up-to-date working knowledge of current industry requirements; how else may they confidently lead their students towards working either nationally or internationally in these very commercial genres?

Pamela Wurgler (1997), in her overview article on singing pedagogy, proposed that the educational tasks of the singing teacher fall into three main areas: the cognitive domain (factual knowledge), the psychomotor domain (skills development) and the affective domain (development of attitudes and values). This threefold framework forms a useful way of viewing the range of pedagogical tasks which fall to any singing teacher working in contemporary commercial music (CCM) (LoVetri, 2002), more specifically, the genres of music theatre and cabaret. The major portion of this chapter relates to the specifics of music theatre singing pedagogy; because of its distinctive demands on both performer and teacher, cabaret is considered in a separate section at the end of this chapter.

Cognitive Domain — Factual Knowledge

Facts — How We Sing

It is true of all singing teachers that one of their main tasks is to give their students factual information about the structure and function of the singing voice. This forms the basis for much of the instruction within the psychomotor (skills acquisition) domain. The basic facts of vocal anatomy, acoustics and effective phonation remain the same across genres. Additional facts needed by the students of music theatre repertoire include a clear and confident understanding of belt technique, ready access to male or female falsetto, identification of "pop-belt mix," and knowing when to use these effects appropriately. Bartlett (1999) pointed out that contemporary style, found in much modern music theatre, "… often demands the use of glottal attack, soft onset, flattened vibrato and glottal fry. These stylistic elements should not be written off by the voice teacher as poor technique, but should be recognized and managed" (p. 47). A further vital fact relating to vocal technique is the requirement for singing in English. Lovely Italian vowels are no longer enough; in addition, both teacher and student must grapple with the barrage of English diphthongs and triphthongs. In energetically dismissing vowel modification in music theatre singing, Mary Saunders-Barton said, "Acting is everything. In musical theatre you have to act, sing, and dance, in that order of priority … but the singing and dancing skills are at the service of the dramatic imperative" (Melton, 2007, p. 63). Intelligibility is paramount.

Facts — How We Audition

Effective singing teachers need to be familiar with facts relating to the music theatre trade worldwide in order to prepare their students for work within an industry that has specific demands relating to auditioning, performing, recording and touring. Music theatre is an international multimillion-dollar business, with all the inflexibilities inherent within a global industry. Singing teachers need to prepare their auditioning students by explaining the protocols surrounding professional music theatre auditions. The objective of the first-round audition is simply to get a callback. The usual requirement for a first-round audition is two contrasting music theatre songs, often one up-tempo and one ballad. However, equally effective paired contrasts could be a rock song and a folk song, or a song that shows belt and belt-mix capability, and a song in legit quality. It all depends on the show for which the audition is being held. It is generally preferable that one of the songs is written by the composer of the show for which the student is auditioning. Australian panels generally frown on the performance of a song directly from the show for which auditions are being conducted. There are a number of up-to-date books dealing with the practicalities of professional music theatre auditions; Gillyanne Kayes' and Jeremy Fisher's *Successful Singing Auditions* (2002) is excellent, although slanted towards United Kingdom practice.

Practical details vary, but it is becoming a rarity for any auditionee to complete a whole song in their first-round audition. Current practice in New York music theatre auditions for performers at entry level of the industry is for 16 bars only to be performed. Teachers can prepare their students by helping them identify the most vocally and dramatically effective 16 bars in each of their audition songs, marking the scores appropriately, and giving the students opportunity to practice performing the truncated version. No matter how thoroughly a student has prepared, an unanticipated request in the audition room for "Just 16 bars, please" can be enough to tip the most confident auditionee off-balance.

There is a paradox relating to auditioning for music theatre: sound reinforcement is never used in audition, whereas no major professional music theatre show is performed without sound reinforcement — generally head-worn (i.e., a lavalier microphone on a wire) or headset microphones. A practical grasp of the questions raised by sound reinforcement in professional music theatre is more than useful for the pedagogue; informed consideration of this topic, such as that of Wendy LeBorgne, as reported by Melton (2007, p. 16), is invaluable.

Facts — How We Work

Singing teachers need to be aware of the facts of the industry; in this way they can best prepare their students for a successful working life in the music theatre industry. Teachers training students to audition should include, in that process, factual information about what those students are letting themselves in for, should they be successful.

However a company elects to order their working week, eight shows a week is an industry norm. Performers are athletes, from whom their director and producer demand high-energy, meticulously accurate, consistent and emotionally honest performances eight times a week. The harsh economic argument is, "If today's seats cost as much as yesterday's, then today's audience deserve as good a performance as yesterday's received".

Once the show is up and running, lucky young performers who have been awarded understudy roles will also have to attend understudy calls weekly in order to rehearse their role in case they are needed to go on for an injured or sick principal performer.

Unlike most operas and theatre, music theatre shows may run for many months at a time, frequently touring. This is the way producers attempt to recoup the very high costs of mounting this art form. Long runs and tours add their own particular stresses for the neophyte music theatre performer. The well-informed music theatre teacher will be able to give students practical tips for maintaining vocal health, emotional energy and freshness of interpretation throughout long runs and whilst touring.

Psychomotor Domain — Skills Development

Singing is the end result of the orchestration of a number of neuromuscular tasks — breathing, phonation, articulation and resonation (Miller, 1996, p. 48). All of these tasks together form the physical foundation of the act of singing in any genre. It can be said, with some justification, that good pedagogic practice is much the same for all genres — a larynx is a larynx, and, barring pathologies, universal rules govern efficient phonation. The source-filter model holds true (Sundberg, 1987, p. 58). While acknowledging the essential truth of this viewpoint, three considerations modify it for singing teachers working in the field of music theatre — breath, belt and speech-into-song.

Breath

Psychomotor Domain

Much like religion, protocols surrounding the training of effective breath support and management for singing differ widely, are debated passionately by researchers and practitioners, and are described in many different, frequently confusing ways. Sometimes two techniques, held to be utterly different, and seemingly so from the language used to describe them, are effectively the same. Miller's discussion of the technique of appoggio is pertinent here, "Appoggio cannot narrowly be defined as 'breath support', as is sometimes thought, because appoggio includes resonance factors as well as breath management" (Miller, 1996, p. 23). It is precisely this global, somatic approach to the support and management of breath that music theatre pedagogues need. As Jean Callaghan put it, "... the body is the voice ..." (cited in Melton, 2007, p. 149).

For at least the past 17 years, pedagogues have known that the subglottic pressure and airflow for CCM singers are different than for classical singers (Sundberg, Gramming, & LoVetri, 1993). Many music theatre triple-threat performers began their performance training with dance classes at an early age. They will have been taught the "pull-up," in which the abdominal and associated muscle groups are energetically recruited to reinforce the lumbar and sacral spine areas. Dancers will tell you that the purpose of the "pull-up" is to maintain the integrity of the spinal column, unload body joints, provide a basis for good alignment and help build the axis for pirouettes. It is plain that singing pedagogues need to be aware of the "pull-up," and its consequences. The singing teacher that advises a singer/dancer/actor to "Just release all those tight belly muscles" in order to facilitate breath support, is inviting disaster of one kind or another. Students who obey will sustain injuries, because their core strength has been compromised. Disobedient students will find the inflexibility of the abdominal musculature in the "pull-up" prohibits them from reliable access to sufficient breath, from the nuances of breath management that enables legato tone and smooth volume variations, and (worst of all) from free and intuitive access to truthful emotion in their acting and singing. This is one of the major pedagogic questions to be addressed in the teaching of "triple-threat" performers. Once the singing teacher understands the biomechanical imperatives associated with acting, singing and dancing simultaneously, they can realistically assist their students to sing with breath and muscle management tailored to the needs of each individual performer. Janice Chapman's practical approach to reconciling these questions includes use of Accent Method work (Chapman, 2008).

Research very pertinent to this is currently being set up in Queensland, using real-time ultrasound to give a clearer picture of muscle activation patterns in both the abdomen and chest walls of elite vocal performers across genres. This research pursues directions outlined in a pilot study undertaken in London by Joan Melton, in association with physiotherapists Ed Blake and Jane Grey (Melton, 2009). All music theatre performers and their singing teachers stand to benefit from the findings of this investigation.

Belt

This is an area that has occasioned much attention in the past 20 years amongst singing pedagogy circles. Sometimes, more heat than light has been generated by collegial discussions about belt quality at conferences worldwide. Leon Thurman, Graham Welch, Axel Theimer, Patricia Feit and Elizabeth Grefsheim have co-authored a balanced chapter titled "Singing various musical genres with stylistic authenticity: Vocal efficiency, vocal conditioning and voice qualities;" it is published in Thurman and Welch's foundational three-volume pedagogic work, *Bodymind and Voice* (Thurman & Welch, 2000). In this chapter, the authors observed that this style of singing is "a staple of musical theatre in Western civilization. But for thousands of years, children, adolescents and adults of nearly all the world's cultures have sung their folk and popular musics in a strong belted way" (Thurman & Welch, 2000, p. 520). The authors, while conceding that belt quality occasions strenuous laryngeal muscle use, as well as high collision and shearing forces on the vocal folds, assert that lifetime vocal health is possible when:

- voices are coordinated with physical and acoustic efficiency;
- the laryngeal muscles and vocal fold tissues are well conditioned; and
- singers know how to protect their voices (Thurman & Welch, 2000, p. 521)

These succinct guidelines point to those specific areas of singing pedagogy in which singing teachers working in the music theatre genre ought be best informed and most capable.

Speech-Into-Song

Unless the musical is through-sung, that is, all text is sung, not spoken, the singer is faced with the task of transitioning smoothly and convincingly from spoken voice to sung voice and back again, whilst losing neither emotional intensity nor quality of tone. Examples of through-sung musicals include *Les Misérables* (Boublil/Schönberg), *The Phantom of the Opera* (Lloyd Webber), *Rent* (Larson), *Seussical* (Flaherty/Ahrens), *Tommy* (Townshend/McAnuff) and *Next To Normal* (Kitt/Yorkey). These musicals are exceptions in the canon; most musicals demand both speaking and singing, and today's direction styles and production values insist on emotionally honest and convincing musical drama. Pedagogues with spoken-voice training and experience are at an advantage here, because they can readily build a practical bridge between an actor's spoken-voice techniques and singing-voice techniques in order to integrate the end product — the triple-threat performance. Singing teachers who have worked with actors in tertiary training institutions are all too aware of the vocal discontinuities that can ensue from performers approaching their singing voice with a different set of technical tools from those they have learned to employ with their singing voice. In Melton and Tom's book, *One Voice*, they said "Maintaining the same basic technique for singing and speaking, and integrating that technique with requirements for dance and movement, is essential for the musical theatre actor" (Melton & Tom, 2003, p. 136). Thurman and Welch stated, "We have one voice, not two ... Speaking and singing are two ways we coordinate our one voice to express ourselves. There is more similarity in the two coordinations than there are differences" (Thurman & Welch, 2000, p. xx).

Taking Contemporary Commercial Music Voices Seriously

There has been a perceptible shift internationally in the literature of singing pedagogy towards more scientific research, more educational focus and more in-service practitioner training for singing teachers and their students working in contemporary commercial music, including music theatre and cabaret. Having reviewed the paucity of research literature directly relevant to music theatre practitioners seven years ago (Wilson, 2003), it is encouraging to see much more work placing the physical, emotional and intellectual demands of music theatre performers at centre stage. If there was a need for justifying greater scientific interest in music theatre performers, then the work of Koufman et al. (1996) provides incentive. Investigating laryngeal biomechanics by using transnasal fibreoptic laryngoscopy on a sample of 100 healthy, proficient singers drawn from a wide range of genres, Koufman et al. reported that levels of laryngeal muscle tension were lower in classical singers than in non-classical singers, with "the highest being seen in those singing jazz/pop (65%), musical theater (74%), bluegrass/country and western (86%) and rock/gospel (94%)". Australian researchers, Phyland, Oates and Greenwood (1999), in surveying professional singers in opera, musical theatre and contemporary (excluding rock) styles, reported that, "The MT [music theatre] singers performed the most hours a month (46.5 hours) ..." (p. 606). These researchers further noted "a trend toward a higher number of reported incidents of vocal edema in the MT singers than in the other groups" (Phyland et al., 1999, p. 609). These findings should encourage vocal pedagogues to do everything practical that they can to enhance the biomechanical processes involved in phonation for singers working in music theatre.

Music theatre pedagogues should be servicing the skills acquisition requirements of their student singers just as carefully and as thoroughly as classical voice pedagogues serve their students. It is heartening to see pedagogues such as Anne Peckham, who has devised vocalises specifically for developing appropriate tonal qualities and intervallic agility in contemporary singers. She observed, "As the music theater genre has expanded to include many ... different influences, it has become important for working singers to be capable of performing with appropriate style and embellishment in a variety of idioms" (Peckham, 2003, p. 216).

A regular contributor to the *Journal of Singing*, (official publication of the National Association of Teachers of Singing, United States) is Robert

Edwin, whose articles have consistently advocated the importance of CCM music and the necessity for pedagogues to take the challenges of these musics seriously. In a typical article, Edwin (2005) encouraged voice pedagogy to catch up with the times:

> In spite of the theater world's obvious and overwhelming shift to pop, rock, and R & B-based music, the majority of college and university music theater voice departments continue to be heavily populated with current and former classical opera singers who know little if anything about nonclassical voice pedagogy and repertoire. Their mantra is, "If you can learn to sing classically, you can sing anything," which is equivalent to a tennis instructor saying "If you learn to play tennis, you can play any sport". (p. 292)

Practical repertoire resource articles, such as Alt and Greene (1996), help teachers find their way through the massive body of music theatre repertoire, enabling song choices that are not only appropriate to the singer, but also offering precise pedagogical challenges.

The existence of Jeanette LoVetri's Contemporary Commercial Music Vocal Pedagogy Institute at Shenandoah University (Virginia, United States), albeit as a regular summer program only, is an encouraging sign that thoughtful pedagogues are at last being enabled to address the specific vocal needs of CCM performers, including music theatre and cabaret singers.

Affective Domain — Development of Attitudes and Values

Music theatre and cabaret vocal pedagogy is not frequently considered in the literature, yet is at the core of all successful performances. Helping students to forge their own benchmarks of excellence, their aesthetic sensibilities, and their individual outlook on the profession in general and their place within it, is a task for a passionate, industry-aware teacher. "Attitudes are caught, not taught. The exemplary teachers of singing have not forgotten the wonder of music and the joy of making music ... Teachers must inspire their students to see music as an art, worthy of value" (Wurgler, 1997, p. 7). Here, Wurgler reinforces the role of pedagogue as leader; what the teacher models is what the student will — consciously or unconsciously — emulate and imbibe.

With this in mind, teachers of music theatre should keep up-to-date with the industry and always work with attitudes that reflect international best practice, while understanding how to build benchmark standards of excellence in their students' aesthetic perceptions. The inspirational music theatre pedagogue will know what's playing on Broadway and the West End now, who's starring, who are the newest composers in the field and have an exemplary library of CDs and DVDs of recent musicals as well as from the canon of music theatre. A passion for music theatre is best caught from a singing teacher who is passionate about music theatre.

The pedagogue who helps a student develop a work ethic that accords with the way music theatre is rehearsed, performed and toured, gives that student an invaluable life-long professional tool. As Wurgler (1997) suggested, these attitudes are "caught, not taught"; it's what the teacher *does* that conveys these values.

Cabaret — Its Distinctive Challenges

"Cabaret," said Eric Bronner in his review article, "is the unique and titillating genre in which artistic experimentation and expression meet social commentary, political criticism, and popular culture" (Bronner, 2004, p. 453). It should be noted that, in some countries, "cabaret" is not a common term, although the genre persists; performances billed as "one-person shows," usually performed in small theatres or intimate alternative venues, can be cabaret in all but name. The pedagogue who works across the range of music theatre repertoire need have no qualms in approaching work with a cabaret performer, much the same conditions apply. It is, however, in the generation of new work; conditions of employment and performance convention that the singing teacher may need some extra information. In cabaret, unlike CCM genres, performers are on their own. It is an art form best suited to the most creatively robust and emotionally stable performer. Here, the artist is auteur. The children's folk tale of *The Little Red Hen* (Golden Press, 1992) is an apposite fable for all would-be cabaret performers.

Cabaret is the most accessible performance format for the entrepreneurial artist. Establishment costs are minimal, unlike music theatre. Mounting the most modest musical costs a great deal in both time and effort; traditionally, cabaret merely requires one artist (although sometimes there are just a few more), an accompanist, a venue and a program of theatrically coherent material. Many music theatre performers devise a one-person show for themselves, with the help of a director and musical director, so that they have the chance to work between engagements, not only raising a modest income, but also performing in a professional arena where their skills can be seen publicly by producers, directors, musical directors and agents. A well-crafted cabaret thus acts as an effective business card, maintains and hones performance skills between jobs, and keeps the unemployed triple-threat out of the call centre or the coffee shop.

To create an effective cabaret, it is necessary to have something specific to say — a viewpoint, an opinion or a theme. The origins of cabaret belong among the dissidents, experimental artists, political satirists and bohemians of a culture. Good cabaret is always risky and sometimes even risqué. Theatrical content is what distinguishes a cabaret from a concert.

Peter J. Casey (2006) proposed five different subgenres of cabaret:

1. You Know Me Already, And Here's How I Got Up Here [This is for when you're famous, and tell a bit of your life story].
2. You Don't Know Me But Should, And Here's How I Got Up Here [This is for when you're not at all famous, but tell a bit of your life story].
3. An Evening of Songs by [insert Composer or Team].
4. An Evening of Songs About [Insert theme].
5. Original material [very rare]. (Casey, 2006, p. 1)

This practical template should be helpful for both cabaret performers and their singing teachers. It is at this stage of planning a cabaret that the singing teacher's function may unexpectedly morph into musical director, repetiteur and/or director. Students will often seek their teacher's advice, asking for suggestions for suitable themes and repertoire that fit the structure and theme, and showcase the performer's acting and singing to best advantage. Advice about confecting medleys of songs (a musical director's domain) or planning the sequence of songs (a directorial task) may also be sought. Few young cabaret performers can afford to pay a professional director and a musical director; in the first instance, it is to their trusted singing teacher that performers frequently turn for a range of practical professional advice.

Pedagogues should be aware of the importance of patter; that is, the spoken material between each sung item. Patter (sometimes also called "glue," in that it sticks the disparate songs together into a theatrically cohesive whole) must be scripted. No matter how casual and "ad lib" it appears in performance, every good cabaret artist's chat between songs is crafted to maintain the emotional momentum of the whole. Casey advised, "script it to within an inch of its life and then present it as if you just thought of it" (2006, p. 2).

Teachers assisting their students with the selection, development and presentation of cabaret material should understand the genre's performance conventions. In cabaret, there is no "fourth wall," that imaginary, transparent wall at the front of the stage through with an audience views a conventional stage performance. Some theatre and music theatre productions break this convention — often to good dramatic effect — but they are the exception. Cabaret allows a performer to notice, interact with and respond to his or her audience. The reverse is also true. This fact delights many performers; it terrifies others, who find safety in performing on a brilliantly-lit stage, with a big black orchestra pit between them and a darkened auditorium of audience members. Cabaret artists can see their audience seeing them. This needs to be factored into not only the repertoire chosen, but also the way in which it is performed. The gung-ho mezzo-soprano who nightly bellows "Everything's coming up roses" (from Styne's *Gypsy*), accompanied by a 20-piece pit orchestra, in a 2500-seat auditorium, cannot successfully replicate her performance in a 100-seat cabaret venue, with some audience members an arm's length away from her.

The chamber-music format of cabaret is very revealing — it is one of the charms of the genre. It also displays an artist's ability to work in close collaboration with their accompanist. Good cabaret should work in the same way as a lieder recital. Both singer and accompanist collaborate with sensitivity in order to produce an artistically and theatrically satisfying end product. It should also be noted that piano is not the only likely accompaniment for a cabaret artist.

Deer and Dal Vera offered a slightly jaundiced view of performers creating and presenting their own cabaret shows: "Guaranteed to pay virtually nothing and to cost you a fair amount in self-promotion" (2008, p. 390). Nevertheless, they give a good summary of the place of cabaret in a music theatre performer's professional life and development: "Cabarets offer performers a chance to develop distinctive performing identities and establish direct audience rapport in ways that traditional theatre doesn't allow" (p. 390).

Conclusion

Practitioners of vocal pedagogy for music theatre and cabaret styles need reliable, practical, industry-based, scientifically moderated information relevant to their work. If Sondheim is seen as important as Schubert, if Bach and Bacharach are alike respected, if the works of Brown (Jason Robert) and of Beethoven (Ludwig van) are taken equally seriously, then it is clear that the training of singing pedagogues in music theatre and cabaret styles should be far more than a few extra lectures from a CCM practitioner inserted into a 3-year course rooted in European art musics from Baroque to Contemporary.

Irene Bartlett surveyed "voice teachers who identified themselves as teaching contemporary music styles ... to determine their beliefs and practices in relation to classical voice techniques, specific contemporary voice techniques and unusual demands of contemporary styles" (Bartlett, 1999, p. 45). Her investigation results caused her to observe,

> A major area of concern was a perceived shortfall in what voice teachers know about contemporary singing generally and about how to teach it specifically. Voice teachers and tertiary educators in the survey shared a perception that acquiring both types of knowledge may be problematic. (Bartlett, 1999, p. 45)

LoVetri and Weekly (2003) undertook a survey of CCM singing teachers, both American and international, in the period January–April 2002. The researchers sought to define the teachers' training, education and experience, as well as examining the ways in which they taught CCM genres, especially music theatre. "Only 56 (45%) of the 124 respondents who teach MT had any training to teach music theater" (LoVetri & Weekly, 2003, p. 210).

Dedicated undergraduate and postgraduate courses designed to train singing teachers in the specifics of music theatre and cabaret are desperately necessary, both in Australia and overseas. While classical-voice singing teachers continue to offer young students such legit vocal quality songs as "I Could Have Danced All Night" (from *My Fair Lady*) or "Younger Than Springtime" (from *South Pacific)* as a nice change from the *Twenty-four Italian Songs and Arias* repertoire, without contextualising the music theatre repertoire or addressing its stylistic demands, music theatre repertoire will continue to be seen as a soft option for budding singers, blessedly free of Italian language problems, and not too hard on a developing voice. It is this approach that eviscerates the integrity of both the song and its art form. What sense a 17-year-old girl could hope to make of either text or subtext in "Memory" (from *Cats*) or "Send in the Clowns" (from *A Little Night Music*) is hard to discern. I have heard both of these songs sung by a 17-year-old girl. Respecting the genre and training pedagogues fit for 21st century music theatre and cabaret will reduce the incidence of debacles such as these.

In summary, 21st century pedagogues in the fields of music theatre and cabaret would benefit greatly from a more practical awareness of worldwide industry standards, dedicated training of music theatre and cabaret specialist teachers, and research that investigates realistic conditions for professional performers in these areas and assists both singers and their pedagogues to develop and maintain vocal, emotional and spiritual health. Harking back to Robert Edwin's (2005) amusing analogy about tennis, it makes sense to employ golf pros (not tennis coaches) to train elite-level golfers in their sport. It makes just as much good sense to use singing teachers trained in the specific pedagogic requirements of music theatre and cabaret, and supported by researchers investigating the voice science behind contemporary vocal styles, to train music theatre and cabaret performers.

References

Alt, D., & Greene, N. (1996). Teaching music theatre songs: A graded list. *Journal of Singing, 52*(3), 25–32.

Bartlett, I. (1999). Unique problems and challenges of contemporary voice — What do teachers think? *Australian Voice, 5*,45–49.

Bronner, E. (2004). Cabaret for the classical singer: A history of the genre and a survey of its vocal music. *Journal of Singing, 60*(5), 453–465.

Casey, P.J. (2006, October). *Cabaret is not a dirty word.* Paper presented at ANATS conference, Canberra, Australia.

Chapman, J. (2008). Speaking out — Janice Chapman replies ... *Communicating Voice, 8*(3), 9.

Deer, J., & Dal Vera, R. (2008). *Acting in musical theatre: A comprehensive course.* London: Routledge.

Edwin, R. (2005). Contemporary music theater: Louder than words. *Journal of Singing, 61*(3), 291–292.

Golden Press: 50 years of Little Golden Books, 1942–1992. (1992). *The little red hen* (Illustrated by Rudolf). Racine, WI: Western Publishing.

Kayes, G., & Fisher. J. (2002). *Successful singing auditions.* London: A. & C. Black.

Koufman, J.A., Radomski, T.A., Johanji, G.M., Russell, G.B., & Pillsbury, D.C. (1996). Laryngeal biomechanics of the singing voice. *Otolaryngology — Head and Neck Surgery, 115*(6), 527–537.

LoVetri, J.L. (2002). Contemporary commercial music: More than one way to use the vocal tract. *Journal of Singing, 58,* 249–252.

LoVetri, J.L., & Weekly, E.M. (2003). Contemporary commercial music (CCM) survey: Who's teaching what in nonclassical music. *Journal of Voice, 17*(2), 207–215.

Melton, J. (2007). *Singing in musical theatre: The training of singers and actors.* New York: Allworth Press.

Melton, J. (2009). Ab prints and the triple threat. *Voiceprints: Journal of the New York Singing Teachers' Association, January–February,* 6–7.

Melton, J. & Tom, K. (2003). *One voice: Integrating singing technique and theatre voice training.* Portsmouth, NH: Heinemann.

Miller, R. (1996). *The structure of singing: System and art in vocal technique.* New York: Schirmer Books.

Peckham, A. (2003). Vocalise patterns for the contemporary singer. *Journal of Singing, 59*(3), 215–220.

Phyland, D.J., Oates, J., & Greenwood, K.M. (1999). Self-reported voice problems among three groups of professional singers. *Journal of Voice, 13*(4), 602–611.

Sundberg, J. (1987). *The science of the singing voice.* DeKalb, IL: Northern Illinois University Press.

Sundberg, J., Gramming, P., & LoVetri, J. (1993). Comparisons of pharynx, source, formant, and pressure characteristics in operatic and musical theater singing. *Journal of Voice, 4,* 301–310.

Thurman, L., & Welch, G. (Eds.) (2000). *Bodymind and Voice: Foundations of Voice Education* (Rev. ed., Vols. 1–3). Collegeville, MN: The VoiceCare Network, National Center for Voice and Speech, Fairview Voice Center.

Wilson, P. (2003). Sinful modern music: Science and the contemporary commercial singer. *Australian Voice, 9,* 12–16.

Wurgler, P.S. (1997). Voice pedagogy: The process of teaching the art of singing. *Journal of Singing, 53*(5), 3–8.

Chapter 19

Advocating for Change: Interdisciplinary Voice Studies in Australian School Education

Diane Hughes and Jean Callaghan

This chapter outlines the context and motivation behind national advocacy for the introduction of interdisciplinary voice studies in Australian school education. The benefits of singing in schools have been documented since colonial times. At times synonymous with music education, singing is an activity in which all students will participate at some stage during their school life. Associated with school singing and music education have been recurring issues relating to appropriate teacher training and expertise. Contemporaneously, advances in voice science have afforded greater understandings of the vocal mechanism than ever before. Educational policies and curriculum content have not, as yet, incorporated these understandings. Voice studies, progressively implemented in cross-curriculum areas, have the potential to provide the foundation for voice usage, vocal care and vocal health. Interdisciplinary studies may aid communication skills and underpin the development of musicality associated with the singing voice.

This chapter concerns both singing in Australian schools and the need for interdisciplinary voice studies. We discuss the context of school singing in Australia. In doing so, we outline recurrent themes evident in school singing and music education research. Scientific understandings of the voice are highlighted, and together with the considerations arising from historical perspectives and school music education research, the foundation for interdisciplinary voice studies in school education is discussed.

Singing in Australian School Education

Singing has traditionally been an integral part of school life in Australia. Having its origins in the procurement of social and personal benefits (Hughes, 2007, pp. 27–31), singing was viewed as a method for the simultaneous development of musical expression and civil temperament (New South Wales [NSW] Legislative Assembly, 1856). By 1870, singing lessons were scheduled "on the time-table of every school" in the Sydney District (Johnson & Bradley, 1871, p. 130). School inspectors reported on the proficiency of school singing within the categories of "good", "fair", "tolerable" and "indifferent" (Johnson & Bradley, 1871, pp. 133–134). Other inspectors noted that singing had a "beneficial effect on the general spirit of a school" (McCredie, 1871, p. 59) and that at times singing acted "as a safety valve to children of excitable temperament" (Allpas, 1871, p.118). In addition to singing being valued for its socialising benefits, music education during this time was synonymous with singing or vocal music (Stevens, 1978, p. 2).

In the early 1900s, support documents for teachers in NSW schools included articles on singing, singing technique, the artistry of singing and the teaching of singing to school children (Hughes, 2007, pp. 32–33). In-service opportunities for the teaching of singing were provided through the Sydney Training College. Lectures included instruction in the use of the singing voice, breathing, enunciation and rhythm exercises (Kenny, 1908). Suitable repertoire lists were provided and the essential characteristics of good class singing were clearly defined (Kenny, 1908, p. 252). The first of the essential characteristics (see Table 19.1) related to "the general tone of the class" (Kenny, 1908, p. 252), characteristics 2–5 were connected to singing technique, and characteristics 6 and 7 encompassed musicality skills. The last characteristic related to song interpretation and the inclusion of "intelligence" implied that implemented learning should be evident in relation to the musical score (Kenny, 1908, p. 254). In addition to these characteristics, the unifying benefit of group singing was identified as being "of great value to discipline" (Kenny, 1908, p. 252).

TABLE 19.1
Essential Characteristics of Good Class Singing (Kenny, 1908)

Essential characteristics
1. Brightness and cheerfulness
2. Sweetness and purity of tone
3. Clearness of enunciation and articulation
4. Beauty of phrasing
5. Precision in attack and release
6. Blend and balance of voices
7. Beauty of rhythmic flow
8. Intelligence in the rendition of song

Teaching Expertise

The potential benefits and outcomes of school singing were detailed in official documents (Hughes, 2007, pp. 27–31). However, reports by inspectors, particularly in relation to rural districts, noted a lack of adequate teacher training and expertise:

> Except in a few instances I cannot speak highly of the singing. It has made little progress during the year ... Considering its importance as a means of aesthetic, moral, and intellectual culture, it is to be regretted that all teachers are not compelled to qualify them selves for teaching it. (Jones, 1871, p. 41)

> It is to be hoped the Council [of Education] may be enabled to extend the period for the training of teachers, in order that some arrangements may be made for giving the candidates a complete course of instruction in this very important branch of elementary education [singing]. (McIntyre, 1871, p. 99)

Gender-related issues were also evident. One inspector noted that school singing was more effectively taught by female teachers:

> Occasionally lessons are given on what is called "theory", but no singing is practised, the explanation being that pupils cannot sing. Strange to say those schools are all under male teachers. In schools under the direction of women, singing is rarely neglected. (Cotterill, 1909, p. 115)

The issue of adequate teacher training and expertise in relation to school singing (Hughes, 2007, pp. 32–38) and music recurred throughout the 20th century (Stevens, 1978, pp. 414–431). An example of this is the 1963 revision of the music component of the Curriculum for Primary Schools (NSW Department of Education, 1952, pp. 441–523). In 1952, music was a school subject for students in NSW primary schools. Curriculum content included sequential programming in the areas of singing, pitch, rhythm and notation. The curriculum recommended that sol-fa names with corresponding hand signs be introduced in infants' classes. Strategies and exercises for securing student pitch and for developing student vocal tone were also offered. Breathing, quality of tone and interpretive elements, such as dynamics and tempo, were suggested for introduction in first-grade singing activities. Vocal repertoire and suitable children's ranges were also described, with teaching strategies outlined for teachers who may have had difficulty singing in children's vocal ranges.

The teaching expertise necessary for the effective delivery of this curriculum was clearly outlined. Teachers were required to model the voice, having "the ability to hold a tune accurately, good production and breath control, clear diction, sufficient flexibility to cope with pitch and general expression of the song being taught, a knowledge of phrasing, and an appreciation of rhythm and time" (NSW Department of Education, 1952, p. 443). However, modifications in relation to required teaching expertise were made in a subsequent revision of the curriculum (NSW Department of Education, 1963), where instruments were noted as being an "excellent substitute for an uncertain singing voice" and broadcasts were recommended "for the teacher lacking confidence" (p. 13).

A research study published by the Australian Council for Educational Research in 1968 included music education related singing practices in Australian primary and secondary schools (Bartle, 1968, pp. 125–130). Survey findings identified common criteria used in vocal music selection. These included "songs with popular appeal", "a wide variety" of songs and "songs of suitable difficulty" (p. 125). Less common criteria included songs to "tie in with courses in music reading and aural training" and songs that had rhythmic appeal (p. 125). The study found that there were fewer attempts to include vocal exercises for vocal training purposes (p. 125). The report on singing concluded that an "alarming situation" (p. 129) existed, where a large proportion of students were given only lyrics to learn songs. The study also identified the emergence of a song approach to the teaching of singing and music that was possibly, in part, related to teaching expertise.

Subsequent research studies have also identified inadequate teaching expertise in relation to the delivery of music and/or music-related singing activities in schools (Russell-Bowie, 1993, 1997; Jeanneret, 1996; Paterson, 1995; Vaughan, 2000; Hughes, 2007). Acknowledging that the voice is both accessible and a useful learning tool, the National Review of School Music Education (Australian Government, 2005) also included implications arising from teachers' fear of inadequacy in singing and called for specific pre-service and in-service teacher education to "raise the standards of vocal music in schools" (p. 128). One respondent called for resources in teacher training to "be directed towards the provision of a trained music specialist in every primary school," stating that "at present this situation exists only in Queensland" (p. 60). Queensland initiatives in music education, in relation to both instrumental music and primary specialist music, provide examples of implemented specialist teaching programs (Queensland Department of Education and Training, 2008).

Scientific Understandings

For over 30 years or so, developments in voice science, technology and research have presented understandings of the detailed anatomy and physiology of voice, vocal acoustics, and vocal health (e.g., Sundberg, 1987; Sataloff, 2006; Dayme, 2009). The stages of vocal development (Cooksey & Welch, 1998; Cooksey, 2000a, 2000b; Gackle, 2000a, 2000b) have been researched and documented. Holistic, systematic, research-based approaches to the teaching of singing have been published (Phillips, 1996; Callaghan, 2000; Chapman, 2006). However, these understandings have not been incorporated into school curricula in Australia.

Singing competency is the example par excellence of auditory-oral musical intelligence. Gardner (1993) defined this intelligence as the ability to discern meaning and importance in sets of pitches rhythmically arranged and also to produce such metrically arranged pitch sequences as a means of communicating with others. The process of hearing, perceiving and remembering sound forms a loop with the production of sound. In speaking and singing, the sounds being produced by the vocal mechanism are constantly being fed through this loop — the phonological loop — dictating what is produced by the vocal apparatus (Callaghan, Hughes, & Power, 2009).

Use of the voice in speech and singing involves both the physiological process of motor coordination, and the neurological and psychological processes related to pitch and rhythm perception and memory (Callaghan et al., 2009). Neurobiological research suggests that children's learning of both music and language is achieved by the establishment of mental representations that are reflected by cortical activation patterns (Deacon, 1997; Gruhn, 1997). Thus, for children, learning to sing involves their physical and psychological development, as well as training in particular skills. Understanding the transition stages in vocal development, together with skills to guide voices through these changes, may help to reduce a gender bias identified in school singing activities (Hughes, 2007; Harrison, 2001, 2004) and the effects on singing participation due to boys' changing voices (Stupple, 2007).

Recent research has demonstrated a hierarchy in children's developing singing competencies (Welch, 2000; 2003). Because songs combine words and music, and accurate reproduction of words begins much earlier than accurate reproduction of melody, putting the two together in songs is difficult. For a large majority of children in our culture, linguistic competence appears much earlier than the ability to learn the melodic contour and musical intervals of songs (Welch, 2005, pp. 240–241). Approaches to teaching singing should therefore be grounded in understandings of developmental stages and strategies to underpin learning.

Knowing how to care for the voice is also necessary. For students, whose physical, intellectual and emotional development is constantly changing throughout their school education, knowledge of healthy voice use and vocal health is important. Studies on vocal health have produced prescriptions relating to maintaining hydration; managing general health, fitness and lifestyle; avoiding vocal strain and fatigue; and using good technique to achieve efficient voice use (Callaghan, 2000, pp. 97–108). Vocal health means eliminating risk factors, so that optimum function is maintained; vocal care implies efficient vocal use, in order to avoid vocal damage (Hughes, 2008, p. 133). Affording students the skills to incorporate vocal care into their daily lives will aid in maintaining their vocal health and longevity.

Interdisciplinary Units of Work

An accumulation of research in voice science, cognition and music education makes it plain that the voice is an integral part of learning and growth in language, music and personal development (Callaghan et al., 2009). Interdisciplinary voice studies in school education should account for these accumulated understandings, so now is the time to put them on the Australian national curriculum agenda. The incorporation of school singing in interdisciplinary activities means that school singing activities would support student learning in both musical and non-musical areas.

Advocacy for interdisciplinary voice studies (Hughes, Callaghan, & Power, 2009) includes the development of focused units of work in Music (the singing voice), Science (anatomy and physiology), English (vocal expression), Drama (voice projection), and Personal Health and Development (vocal health and care; vocal development). Incorporating units of work for primary and secondary students, the proposed interdisciplinary curriculum would provide a comprehensive, sequential continuum of voice studies. This may be realised through specifically designed curricula in which learning underpins discipline specific requirements, while at the same time fostering appropriate voice usage suited to the developmental stage of students. For example, a unit of work for Year 6 students may target vocal care strategies by incorporating safe methods of vocal projection in relation to vocal expression in English and/or drama exercises. An interdisciplinary curriculum would undoubtedly also support the connection between the singing voice and music. The implementation of interdisciplinary voice studies requires changes to policy and curriculum, and has implications for the pre-service and in-service training of teachers.

Appropriate teacher expertise, a recurrent theme in relation to the teaching of singing and music in Australian education, may indeed be aided by an interdisciplinary approach that applies understandings of voice science, voice technology and vocal pedagogy that have developed over the past 50 years or so. The progress of voice science and technology in the latter part of the 20th century "now means that voice knowledge is no longer based on conjecture or on the unseen" (Hughes, 2008, p. 138). Development of specifically targeted resources, and equitable access to existing resources, would support the implementation of interdisciplinary voice studies.

It is imperative that the new national curriculum currently being developed for Australian schools includes voice education: voice knowledge, voice health, voice care, voice use and vocal expression (Callaghan et al., 2009). If the school curriculum is in reality to "contribute to creating a modern Australia, with a workforce that will benefit from being educated by a world-class national curriculum" (Gillard, 2008), then interdisciplinary voice studies are an essential component of that curriculum (Hughes, 2008).

The implementation of a world-class national curriculum would undoubtedly require professional development in relation to pre-service and in-service teacher education and would provide the opportunity for this to include vocal studies.

Advocacy in the Early 21st Century

In 2009, VOICE (Vocal Ownership In Cross-curriculum Education), a national advocacy group championing the introduction of cross-curricula voice studies in school education (Hughes et al., 2009) presented a submission to the Australian Curriculum, Assessment and Reporting Authority (ACARA) and to the Federal Minister for Education. The submission included expressions of support from singing teachers, professional singers, professional voice users, vocal health practitioners, lecturers in music education and associated professional organisations. With various phases of national curriculum development currently underway, it is vital that we continue to lobby, collectively and individually, for change. Educational directives need to address the recurrent themes outlined in this chapter, incorporate the understandings discussed and facilitate voice studies so that they are equitable. Access to skill development should be unbiased and all school students should have opportunities to learn an embodied approach to the voice and to singing (Hughes, 2008). The beautiful and perceptive drawing (see Figure 19.1) illustrates a level of under-

FIGURE 19.1

Drawing By Mareta Crowdy, 5 years.

standing that connects the singing voice with music. It is envisaged that such understanding may result from the implementation of interdisciplinary voice studies in school education.

References

Allpas, J.W. (1871). *Newcastle District — General Report for the Year 1870* (Inspector's Reports). Votes & proceedings New South Wales Legislative Assembly, Appendix II, 116–127.

Australian Government, Federal Department of Education, Science and Training (2005). *National review of music education.* Canberra, Australia: Australian Government Department of Education, Science and Training.

Bartle, G. (1968). *Music in Australian schools.* Melbourne, Australia: Australian Council for Educational Research.

Callaghan, J. (2000). *Singing and voice science.* San Diego, CA: Singular Publishing.

Callaghan, J., Hughes, D., & Power, A. (2009). Towards an interdisciplinary school curriculum in voice studies. In A. Power (Ed.), *Proceedings of the Joint Conference of XXXIst ANZARME Annual Conference and the 1st Conference of the Music Educators Research Centre, Akaroa, New Zealand* (pp. 41–48). Melbourne, Australia: ANZARME and MERC.

Chapman, J. (2006). *Singing and teaching singing. A holistic approach to classical voice.* San Diego, CA: Plural Publishing.

Cooksey, J. (2000a). Male adolescent transforming voices: Voice classification, voice skill development, and music literature selection. In L. Thurman & G. Welch (Eds.), *Bodymind & voice: Foundations of voice education* (Rev. ed., Vol. 3, Book V, pp. 821–841). Collegeville, MN: The VoiceCare Network, National Center for Voice and Speech, Fairview Voice Center.

Cooksey, J. (2000b). Vocal transformation in male adolescents. In L. Thurman & G. Welch (Eds.), *Bodymind & voice: Foundations of voice education* (Rev. ed., Vol. 3, Book IV, pp. 718–738). Collegeville, MA: The VoiceCare Network, the National Center for Voice and Speech, Fairview Voice Center.

Cooksey, J.M., & Welch, G. (1998). Adolescence, singing development and national curriculum design. *British Journal of Music Education, 15*(1), 99–119.

Cotterill. (1909). Report by Mr Inspector Cotterill (Kempsey District). *The Public Instruction Gazette.* Published under the authority of the Minister of Public Instruction, New South Wales, III(5), 115.

Dayme, Meribeth (2009). *Dynamics of the singing voice.* Vienna, Austria: Springer Verlag.

Deacon, T.W. (1997). *The symbolic species: Language and the evolution of the human brain.* Harmondsworth, UK: Penguin.

Gackle, L. (2000a). Female adolescent transforming voices: Voice classification, voice skill development, and music literature selection. In L. Thurman & G. Welch (Eds.), *Bodymind & voice: Foundations of voice education* (Rev. Ed., Vol. 3, Book V, pp. 814–820). Collegeville, MN: The VoiceCare Network, National Center for Voice and Speech, Fairview Voice Center.

Gackle, L. (2000b). Understanding voice transformation in female adolescents. In L. Thurman & G. Welch (Eds.), *Bodymind & voice: Foundations of voice education* (Rev. ed., Vol. 3, Book IV, pp. 739–744). Collegeville, MN: The VoiceCare Network, National Center for Voice and Speech, Fairview Voice Center.

Gardener, H. (1993). *Frames of mind. The theory of multiple intelligences* (2nd ed.). London: Fontana Press.

Gillard, J. (Minister for Education. Minister for Employment and Workplace Relations. Minister for Social Inclusion. Deputy Prime Minister). (2008). *Delivering Australia's first national curriculum* (media release). Media Centre, Department of Education, Employment and Workplace Relations. Canberra, Australia: Department of Education, Employment and Workplace Relations. Retrieved from http://mediacentre.dewr.gov.au/mediacentre/ gillard/releases/deliveringaustraliasfirstationalcurriculum.htm

Gruhn, W. (1997). Music learning — Neurobiological foundations and educational implications. *Research Studies in Music Education, 9*, 36–47.

Harrison, S.D. (2001). Real men don't sing — or do they? *Australian Voice, 7*, 31–36.

Harrison, S.D. (2004). *Musical participation by boys: The role of gender in the choice of musical activities by males in Australian schools* (Doctoral dissertation, Queensland Conservatorium, Griffith University, Brisbane, Australia). Retrieved from http://www4.gu.edu.au:8080/adt-root/public/adt-QGU20040528.142148/ index.html

Hughes, D., Callaghan, J., & Power, A. (2009). Vocal ownership in cross-curriculum education (VOICE Advocacy Statement). Retrieved from http://www.dcms.mq.edu.au/staff/dianehughes/VOICE.html

Hughes, D. (2008). Considerations for school singing activities: An innovative pedagogical model. In J. Southcott (Ed.), *Proceedings of the XXXth Annual Conference Innovation and Tradition: Music Education Research* (pp. 132–140). Melbourne, Australia: Australian and New Zealand Association for Research in Music Education.

Hughes, D. (2007). *Teaching singing in Sydney government schools.* Doctoral thesis, University of Western Sydney, Sydney, Australia. Retrieved from http://handle.uws.edu.au:8081/1959.7/36654

Jeanneret, N. (1996). Competencies for generalist teachers: What do they need to teach music in the primary setting? *Australian Journal of Music Education, 1*, 1–8.

Johnson, E., & Bradley, J. D. (1871). *Sydney District – General Report for the Year 1870* (Inspector's Reports). Votes & proceedings New South Wales Legislative Assembly, Appendix II, 127–139.

Jones, J.S. (1871). *Armidale District — General Report for the Year 1870* (Inspector's Reports). Votes & proceedings New South Wales Legislative Assembly, Appendix II, 34–53.

Kenny (1908). The teaching of music and singing in schools. Abstract of lectures delivered by S.A. Kenny. *The Public Instruction Gazette.* Published under the authority of the Minister of Public Instruction, New South Wales, *II*(10), 251–255.

McCredie, J. (1871). *Bathurst District General Report for the Year 1870* (Inspector's Reports). Votes & proceedings New South Wales Legislative Assembly, Appendix II, 53–73.

McIntyre, W. (1871). *Inspector General's Report Upon Public, Provisional, Half-time Schools for 1870.* Votes & proceedings New South Wales Legislative Assembly, Appendix II, 94–105.

NSW Department of Education (1952). *Curriculum for primary schools.* Sydney, Australia: NSW Department of Education.

NSW Department of Education (1963). *Curriculum for primary schools*: Music. Sydney, Australia: NSW Department of Education.

NSW Legislative Assembly. (1856). *Final Report from School Commissioners* (Report No. 22). Votes & proceedings New South Wales Legislative Assembly, 1856–1857, II, 1–32.

Paterson, D. (1995). Teacher attitudes: Their effects on curriculum implementation and implications for the professional development of music educators. In N. Jeanneret & N. Temmerman (Eds.), *The Professional Development of Music Educators: Association of Music Education Lecturers 17th Annual Conference* (pp. 52–55). Wollongong, Australia: University of Wollongong.

Phillips, K.H. (1996). *Teaching kids to sing.* New York: Schirmer Books.

Queensland Department of Education and Training (2008). *Education Queensland arts education programs and initiatives.* Retrieved from http://education.qld.gov.au/curriculum/area/arts/curriculum-programs.html

Russell-Bowie, D. (1993). Where is music education in our primary schools? *Research Studies in Music Education, 1,* 52–58.

Russell-Bowie, D. (1997). Excellence and equity in primary music education? *Australian Music Teacher, 5*(6), 358–360.

Sataloff, R.T. (2006). Common medical diagnosis and treatments on patients with voice disorders: Introduction and overview. In R.T. Sataloff (Ed.), *Vocal health and pedagogy* (Vol. 2, pp. 1–17). San Diego, CA: Plural Publishing.

Stevens, R.S. (1978). *Music in State-supported education in NSW & Victoria 1848–1920* (Unpublished doctoral dissertation). University of Melbourne, Melbourne, Australia.

Stupple, C.M. (2007). The male changing voice: The student's experience. *Teaching Music, 15*(1), 36–41.

Sundberg, J. (1987). *The science of the singing voice.* Dekalb, IL: Northern Illinois University Press.

Vaughan, L. (2000). The missing males: Low participation of adolescent boys singing in secondary school. *Sing Out: Journal of the Australian National Choral Association, 17*(2), 6–8.

Welch, G. (2000). The developing voice. In L. Thurman & G. Welch (Eds.), *Bodymind & voice: Foundations of voice education* (Rev. Ed., Vol. 3, Book IV, pp. 704–717). Collegeville, MA: The VoiceCare Network, the National Center for Voice and Speech, Fairview Voice Center.

Welch, G. (2003). The importance of singing. In A. Paterson, & E. Bentley (Eds.), *Bluebirds and crows: Developing a singing culture in and out of school* (pp. 2–5). Matlock, UK: National Association of Music Educators.

Welch, G. (2005). Singing as communication. In D. Miell, R. MacDonald, & D.J. Hargreaves (Eds.), *Musical communications* (pp. 239–259). Oxford, UK: Oxford University Press.

About the Authors

Cathy Aggett is a soprano, pianist and choral conductor. Current doctoral studies at the University of Western Sydney revolve around practice-based research and pedagogical issues of Australian art song. Following a long career teaching in many of Sydney's leading schools, Cathy now teaches music privately at Northern Beaches Music Studio. Performance highlights have included soprano solos in Sculthorpe's *Child of Australia*, Bach's *St John Passion*, Beethoven's Mass in C and Handel's *Messiah*, as well as performing Australian art songs — her greatest passion. Cathy is a co-author of *Songs from Australia* (Publications by Wirripang, 2005).

Noel Ancell is Artistic Director of the Australian Boys Choral Institute, conducting the Australian Boys Choir, the Kelly Gang (teenagers) and The Vocal Consort (adults). He conducts a women's choir (the Majellan Singers), composes, and his voice studio has produced a number of successful professional singers. Formerly President of the Australian National Choral Association, he has guest conducted NYCA (the National Youth Choir of Australia) and at international festivals, including World Alliance Festivals of Singing in the United States and Prague. He was awarded the Medal of the Order of Australia in 2009 for service to choral music.

Irene Bartlett has an enduring career as a professional vocalist and is in demand for both corporate, private and concert performances. She lectures and develops coursework in Jazz/Contemporary Voice and Vocal Pedagogy to undergraduate and postgraduate students at the Queensland Conservatorium, is the Coordinator of the Young Conservatorium, Contemporary Voice Program and a visiting lecturer to the postgraduate Vocal Pedagogy at the Sydney Conservatorium. Irene's students have been the recipients of prestigious awards and many work professionally in the popular music industry and in nationally touring music theatre productions. As a doctoral candidate, she continues to study the working lives of professional contemporary gig singers in Australia.

Tracy Bourne is a singer, actor, singing teacher and writer with a special interest in new music theatre works. For the past 10 years, she has been the Lecturer in Singing at the University of Ballarat Arts Academy, where she has been responsible for the vocal training of students in the Bachelor of Arts (Music Theatre) course. She is currently undertaking a PhD on music theatre vocal qualities at the University of Sydney, under the supervision of Professor Dianna Kenny and Dr Maëva Garnier.

Jean Callaghan is a freelance teacher, researcher, and consultant in vocal performance and pedagogy. She has worked as a professional singer in Australia, Singapore, England and Germany, and has taught singing privately and in various tertiary institutions. For the University of Western Sydney, she designed and delivered Australia's first full postgraduate qualification in singing pedagogy. Her book, *Singing and Voice Science*, explores modern voice science findings in the context of the musical concerns of the singer. She was part of the research team that developed Sing&See software and author, with Pat Wilson, of the extensive teachers' manual *How to Sing and See*.

Sally Collyer is a private singing teacher in Melbourne, Australia, specialising in classical, music theatre and cabaret. Doctoral and postdoctoral studies on singing acoustics and breathing have been presented internationally in journals, such as the *Journal of the Acoustical Society of America* and at conferences, such as the *International Symposium of Performance Science*. Sally is also in demand as an adjudicator and as a presenter of advanced workshops for singing teachers. As a playwright, 2010 will see *My Friend, the Vet* and the return season of *The Price of Genius*. Sally is a committed member of ANATS, NATS and the AVA.

Soprano **Rowena Cowley** has sung extensively nationwide, performing with many of Australia's major musical organisations. She holds a Doctor of Music Arts degree from the Manhattan School of Music, New York, and is now a Senior Lecturer in voice and pedagogy at the Sydney Conservatorium of Music. Her students include many professionals in opera and music theatre in Australia and internationally, and finalists and winners in a number of major competitions. Her pedagogy students have taken positions as teachers at regional conservatoria and in university voice departments. She gives master classes nationally, and was recently a guest lecturer for RNCM, Manchester, United Kingdom. She is the current National President of ANATS.

Maëva Garnier is a voice researcher in the music acoustics group of UNSW in Sydney. Originally from an engineering background, she was awarded a PhD in Phonetic Acoustics from the University of Paris 6 in 2007. Her research focuses on the notion of vocal straining. In that line, she works on speech communication in noisy environments and on expert techniques of phonation at loud intensity (projected voice of actors, high range of classical sopranos, belting technique of music theatre singers.

Wendy Hargreaves is currently a PhD candidate at the Queensland Conservatorium Griffith University. She is researching how Australian jazz education addresses the unique needs of improvising vocalists. Wendy studied popular music at QUT and obtained a Bachelor of Arts (Music), a Graduate Diploma in Education and a Master of Music in between regularly singing with several Brisbane bands, none of which qualified her to change the nappies of her four children!

Scott Harrison is a senior lecturer in music and music education and coordinates research higher degrees at Queensland Conservatorium, Griffith University. A graduate of Queensland Conservatorium and the University of Queensland, Dr Harrison has experience in teaching singing and music in primary, secondary and tertiary environments. Performance interests and experience include opera and music theatre as both singer and musical director. His teaching areas focus on teacher education, research design and gender. His major research areas are music and wellbeing, vocal education, music teacher education, and masculinities and music. In 2009, he published *Masculinities and Music;* and *Male Voices: Stories of Boys Learning through Making Music*. In 2010, Scott will co-edit (with Graham Welch) *International Perspectives on Males and Singing* for Springer International. Scott is the immediate past President of ANATS.

Diane Hughes is a Lecturer in Vocal Studies in the Department of Media, Music, Communication and Cultural Studies, Macquarie University. She has an extensive background in singing pedagogy, and has been an invited speaker at conferences and seminars on a range of issues relating to the singing of popular culture musics. Her work within the industry has involved artist development and recording. Research interests include singing popular culture musics, vocal pedagogy, vocal assessments, vocal performance and singing in schools; current research projects include singing assessment, improvisation and creative practices, vocal artistry and the vocal journal.

Dianna Kenny is Professor of Music and Professor of Psychology at the University of Sydney. In 2003, she became the foundation Director of the Australian Centre for Applied Research in Music Performance, where, together with a group of dedicated higher degree research students, she established a centre of excellence for the empirical study of the singing voice, focusing on acoustic, perceptual, physiological and pedagogical issues related to classical, contemporary and world music styles. Dianna has published widely on a range of issues related to both vocal and instrumental performance. She specialises in the study of music performance anxiety.

Lotte Latukefu is Lecturer in Voice in the School of Music and Drama at the University of Wollongong. She has performed at the Lincoln Centre in New York, Opera Australia and State Opera of South Australia, as well as appearing with the Western Australian Symphony Orchestra and in numerous Australian music festivals. Lotte regularly premieres and records new works by Australian composers. Her research interests include application of sociocultural theory to vocal pedagogy and the study of musical performance as creative practice. She is a research associate named in an ARC discovery grant investigating performance of songs that use microtonal tuning.

Tenor **Paul McMahon** is active as a performer, teacher and music researcher. He is a graduate of the University of Southern Queensland, the Queensland Conservatorium Griffith University and he holds a Master of Music (Performance) degree from the Sydney Conservatorium of Music. A Churchill Fellowship awarded in 2002 enabled Paul to undertake an intensive period of study in baroque repertoire at the Royal Conservatoire, The Hague. Paul makes regular appearances as a soloist with major orchestras, choirs and chamber music groups throughout Australia, New Zealand and Asia. He is highly acclaimed for his interpretation of baroque music, particularly the Evangelist roles in the Passions of Johann Sebastian Bach. Paul's research interests include the role of *affect* and expression within 18th century vocal music and baroque performance practice pedagogy.

Adele Nisbet is currently Head of Vocal Studies and Lecturer in Voice and Vocal Pedagogy at the Queensland Conservatorium Griffith University. She was a soprano in the vocal sextet Jones & Co, performing both nationally and internationally. Adele coordinates the undergraduate and postgraduate Vocal Pedagogy courses at the Queensland Conservatorium. She regularly presents at national and international conferences, was founding editor of the ANATS journal, *Australian Voice*, current Deputy Chair of the Australian Voice Association and a committee member of the ANATS Queensland Chapter. Her doctoral work is through the School of Education and Professional Studies, Griffith University.

Jessica O'Bryan is undertaking a PhD in classical vocal pedagogy at the University of Queensland. Currently employed as a casual lecturer and researcher at Griffith University, she has presented papers on vocal pedagogy at a number of national and international conferences. She is current Vice

President of ANATS Queensland Chapter and Editor of the ANATS national newsletter *Voice of ANATS*. Previously President of AMUSE, she was Head of Voice at Wesley College, Victoria, from 2002–2007. She has sung in jazz and rock bands, and appeared as principal artist with Victorian Opera and Opera Queensland. Her last CD release in 2007 was *Irish Songs of Pride*, appearing with Roy Best and Damien Leith.

Daniel K. Robinson is a freelance artist and educator. Having obtained his MMusStudies in 2002, Daniel is currently completing his doctoral research (DMA) into the Australian Contemporary Worship Singer at Queensland Conservatorium Griffith University. He serves as National Vice President and National Secretary for the Australian National Association of Teachers of Singing (2006–). Daniel is the principal voice coach for Djarts and presents workshops and seminars to church singers across Australia and abroad. He and his wife Jodie have three children and live in Brisbane, Queensland.

Margaret Schindler is a Senior Lecturer in Voice at the Queensland Conservatorium of Music, Griffith University, where she has been a member of academic staff since 1995. Her vibrant professional profile comprises a large teaching practice, a busy performance schedule as concert artist and member of renowned chamber ensemble, Southern Cross Soloists, and a research focus as a student of the Griffith University professional doctoral program, which she commenced in 2005. Margaret's pedagogical style has been shaped by over 25 years of performance experience at a national and international level, as well as knowledge continually acquired through an interdisciplinary approach to voice and voice teaching. Margaret is passionate about the practical teaching of singers, the need to equip them with a sound understanding of their instrument and themselves, and the role of voice teachers as inspired working models of the music profession.

Beth Willis: As student, teacher, performer or arts administrator, Beth's life has been governed by music and singing. In an administrative and/or teaching capacity, she has worked for The Australian Opera, the Australia Council and the University of Sydney in both the Conservatorium and Music Department. As a performer, she has sung in opera, and has toured in Australia and overseas. In addition to her work as Voice Adviser for AMEB — NSW, Beth has been involved with many groups promoting community involvement in music — among these, the Australian National Choral Association, the World Symposium on Choral Music (Sydney, 1996), the City of Sydney Cultural Council and the United States-based VoiceCare Network. Beth's private singing-teaching practice encompasses students of all ages, one-to-one, in small groups and in choirs. She regularly presents workshops and papers at conferences both in Australia and overseas, with major presentations of her PhD research into adolescent voice at the ISME conference (Norway, 2002) and at the Conference on Interdisciplinary Musicology (Estonia, 2007).

Pat Wilson is a singing teacher specialising in music theatre. Initially trained in classical singing and piano, she also works as a performer, composer, musical director and voice researcher. Currently teaching at the Australian International Conservatorium of Music and Springboards Performing Arts, as well as in her own studio. Books: *The Singing Voice: An Owner's Manual* and *How to Sing and See: Singing Pedagogy in the Digital Era*, co-authored with Dr Jean Callaghan.

Lightning Source UK Ltd.
Milton Keynes UK
UKHW022016130220
358684UK00013B/218

9 781921 513732